Y0-AQM-917

SOMETHING ABOUT THE AUTHOR®

Something about
the Author *was named
an "**Outstanding
Reference Source,**"
the highest honor given
by the American
Library Association
Reference and Adult
Services Division.*

ISSN 0276-816X

SOMETHING ABOUT THE AUTHOR®

**Facts and Pictures about Authors
and Illustrators of Books for Young People**

volume 153

THOMSON
GALE

Detroit • New York • San Francisco • San Diego • New Haven, Conn. • Waterville, Maine • London • Munich

Something About the Author, Volume 153

Project Editor
Maikue Vang

Editorial
Katy Balcer, Sara Constantakis, Michelle Kazensky, Julie Keppen, Joshua Kondek, Mary Ruby, Lemma Shomali, Susan Strickland, Tracey Watson

Permissions
Edna Hedblad, Mari Masalin-Cooper, Shalice Shah-Caldwell

Imaging and Multimedia
Leitha Etheridge-Simms, Lezlie Light, Dan Newell

Composition and Electronic Capture
Carolyn Roney

Manufacturing
Drew Kalasky

Product Manager
Chris Nasso

LIBRARY OF CONGRESS CATALOG CARD NUMBER 62-52046

ISBN 0-7876-6999-7
ISSN 0276-816X

Printed in the United States of America
10 9 8 7 6 5 4 3 2 1

Contents

Authors in Forthcoming Volumes

Below are some of the authors and illustrators that will be featured in upcoming volumes of *SATA*. These include new entries on the swiftly rising stars of the field, as well as completely revised and updated entries (indicated with *) on some of the most notable and best-loved creators of books for children.

*Frank Asch ▮ Frank Asch, a versatile writer and illustrator, is the creator of the popular children's series Bear Books, all of which feature a naive but lovable bear. Asch is also the author of award–winning titles such as *Turtle Tale* and *Here Comes the Cat!,* and the Pearl books (*Pearl's Promise* and *Pearl's Pirates*). Many of Asch's picture books feature simple, humorous texts and illustrations, ranging in themes from that of self–discovery to fear, love, peace, imagination, and nature.

Billy Crystal ▮ Emmy Award winning Billy Crystal, a famous actor, comedian, and director, added another facet to his career. While Crystal's writing credits are extensive, especially in television and film, this is his first attempt at writing children's literature. Using his own experience of becoming a grandfather, he penned a book titled *I Already Know I Love You* that he dedicated to his grand-daughter, Ella Ryan. Crystal's book is full of all the emotions an expectant grandfather goes through while eagerly awaiting his grandchild's arrival.

Tony DiTerlizzi ▮ Artist Tony DiTerlizzi is an illustrator of children's books, role–playing materials, and fantasy books. His work is populated by fantastic creatures of the imagination, from danger-ous beasts in fantasy and science fiction worlds to gentle, whimsical characters from children's wildly creative adventures. DiTer-lizzi has also illustrated children's books that he wrote himself, like *The Spiderwick Chronicles* series, the critically acclaimed *The Spider and the Fly,* and *Jimmy Zangwow's Out–Of–This–World Moon–Pie Adventure.*

*Richard Egielski ▮ Working mainly in watercolor, American illustra-tor Richard Egielski has been recognized for his vibrant and inti-mately detailed illustrations. Noted as an illustrator who closely weaves his art work with its corresponding text, Egielski has col-laborated with many well–known children's authors, such as Arthur Yorinks, Pam Conrad, and Bill Martin, Jr. Besides contributing il-lustrations, Egielski has also self–illustrated several of his own children's books, including titles such as *Buz, The Gingerbread Boy,* and *Jazper.*

Cornelia Funke ▮ Cornelia Funke is the author of books for chil-dren, and in her native Germany, she is the most popular chil-dren's book writer after J. K. Rowling and R. L. Stine. When her first English translation, *The Thief Lord,* was introduced in En-gland, it sold out in ten days. In the United States, it reached number two on the *New York Times* children's bestseller list.

Funke's more recent releases in English, *Dragon Rider* and *The Princess Knight,* are both international successes.

Jay Leno ▮ Most popularly known as the host of *The Tonight Show,* Jay Leno uses his comedic skills to tell a story for children in *If Roast Beef Could Fly.* Leno's story is based on his real life expe-rience as a child with a large and culturally diverse family that loves food. Few would quarrel with the assertion that Leno is one of the hardest–working entertainers in Hollywood. His continued attempts to entertain all audiences, now including children, helps to prove that.

Yuyi Morales ▮ Mexican artist Yuyi Morales is well known for her colorful illustrations in children's books, including *Sand Sister* and *Harvesting Hope: The Story of Cesar Chavez.* In *Just a Minute: A Trickster Tale and Counting Book,* Morales uses a clever method of story telling that not only entertains but also teaches counting in English and Spanish. Morales' story telling skills, in addition to her illustrations, has made *Just a Minute* a best seller.

*Laurence Pringle ▮ Formerly a wildlife biologist, Laurence Pringle took his previous experiences with the natural sciences and the environment and opened up a world to children and young adults. With over eighty books to his credit, Pringle has authored books ranging on topics from rivers, forests, oceans and deserts to that of man–made hazards such as nuclear energy, nuclear war, and global warming. In each of Pringle's works, he provides to his readers a lucid and common sense perspective on topics that could otherwise be fairly complex—thus allowing the scope of his young readers' minds to expand.

*Louis Sachar ▮ Though he graduated from law school, passed the bar exam, and practiced law part–time for a number of years, Louis Sachar is best known as the author of poignant, humorous stories for children and young adults. Sachar began his writing career with the zany *Sideways Stories from Wayside School* and continued with many other comical tales like *There's a Boy in the Girls' Bathroom.* In addition to his popularity and critical success, Sachar has won multiple awards for his writing, including the Newberry Medal and the Mark Twain Award for *Holes.* In 2003, *Holes* was released as a film by Disney starring Sigourney Weaver and Shia LeBeouf.

*Paul O. Zelinsky ▮ Noted for the magnificence and the experimen-tal nature of his work, Caldecott Medal winner Paul O. Zelinsky has enriched the domain of children's literature with his diverse and captivating illustrations. Author and illustrator of the famous children's title, *The Wheels on the Bus,* Zelinsky has an appeal that not only attracts readers, but critics as well. Several of Zelin-sky's children's books have garnered Caldecott Honors, including *Hansel and Gretel, Rumpelstiltskin,* and *Swamp Angel.*

Introduction

Something about the Author (*SATA*) is an ongoing reference series that examines the lives and works of authors and illustrators of books for children. *SATA* includes not only well-known writers and artists but also less prominent individuals whose works are just coming to be recognized. This series is often the only readily available information source on emerging authors and illustrators. You'll find *SATA* informative and entertaining, whether you are a student, a librarian, an English teacher, a parent, or simply an adult who enjoys children's literature.

What's Inside *SATA*

SATA provides detailed information about authors and illustrators who span the full time range of children's literature, from early figures like John Newbery and L. Frank Baum to contemporary figures like Judy Blume and Richard Peck. Authors in the series represent primarily English-speaking countries, particularly the United States, Canada, and the United Kingdom. Also included, however, are authors from around the world whose works are available in English translation. The writings represented in *SATA* include those created intentionally for children and young adults as well as those written for a general audience and known to interest younger readers. These writings cover the entire spectrum of children's literature, including picture books, humor, folk and fairy tales, animal stories, mystery and adventure, science fiction and fantasy, historical fiction, poetry and nonsense verse, drama, biography, and nonfiction. Obituaries are also included in *SATA* and are intended not only as death notices but also as concise overviews of people's lives and work. Additionally, each edition features newly revised and updated entries for a selection of *SATA* listees who remain of interest to today's readers and who have been active enough to require extensive revisions of their earlier biographies.

Autobiography Feature

Beginning with Volume 103, *SATA* features two or more specially commissioned autobiographical essays in each volume. These unique essays, averaging about ten thousand words in length and illustrated with an abundance of personal photos, present an entertaining and informative first-person perspective on the lives and careers of prominent authors and illustrators profiled in *SATA*.

Two Convenient Indexes

In response to suggestions from librarians, *SATA* indexes no longer appear in every volume but are included in alternate (odd-numbered) volumes of the series, beginning with Volume 57.

SATA continues to include two indexes that cumulate with each alternate volume: the Illustrations Index, arranged by the name of the illustrator, gives the number of the volume and page where the illustrator's work appears in the current volume as well as all preceding volumes in the series; the Author Index gives the number of the volume in which a person's biographical sketch, autobiographical essay, or obituary appears in the current volume as well as all preceding volumes in the series.

These indexes also include references to authors and illustrators who appear in *Gale's Yesterday's Authors of Books for Children, Children's Literature Review,* and *Something about the Author Autobiography Series.*

Easy-to-Use Entry Format

Whether you're already familiar with the *SATA* series or just getting acquainted, you will want to be aware of the kind of information that an entry provides. In every *SATA* entry the editors attempt to give as complete a picture of the person's life and work as possible. A typical entry in *SATA* includes the following clearly labeled information sections:

PERSONAL: date and place of birth and death, parents' names and occupations, name of spouse, date of marriage, names of children, educational institutions attended, degrees received, religious and political affiliations, hobbies and other interests.

ADDRESSES: complete home, office, electronic mail, and agent addresses, whenever available.

CAREER: name of employer, position, and dates for each career post; art exhibitions; military service; memberships and offices held in professional and civic organizations.

MEMBER: professional, civic, and other association memberships and any official posts held.

AWARDS, HONORS: literary and professional awards received.

WRITINGS: title-by-title chronological bibliography of books written and/or illustrated, listed by genre when known; lists of other notable publications, such as plays, screenplays, and periodical contributions.

ADAPTATIONS: a list of films, television programs, plays, CD-ROMs, recordings, and other media presentations that have been adapted from the author's work.

WORK IN PROGRESS: description of projects in progress.

SIDELIGHTS: a biographical portrait of the author or illustrator's development, either directly from the biographee—and often written specifically for the SATA entry—or gathered from diaries, letters, interviews, or other published sources.

BIOGRAPHICAL AND CRITICAL SOURCES: cites sources quoted in "Sidelights" along with references for further reading.

EXTENSIVE ILLUSTRATIONS: photographs, movie stills, book illustrations, and other interesting visual materials supplement the text.

How a SATA Entry Is Compiled

A SATA entry progresses through a series of steps. If the biographee is living, the SATA editors try to secure information directly from him or her through a questionnaire. From the information that the biographee supplies, the editors prepare an entry, filling in any essential missing details with research and/or telephone interviews. If possible, the author or illustrator is sent a copy of the entry to check for accuracy and completeness.

If the biographee is deceased or cannot be reached by questionnaire, the SATA editors examine a wide variety of published sources to gather information for an entry. Biographical and bibliographic sources are consulted, as are book reviews, feature articles, published interviews, and material sometimes obtained from the biographee's family, publishers, agent, or other associates.

Entries that have not been verified by the biographees or their representatives are marked with an asterisk (*).

Contact the Editor

We encourage our readers to examine the entire SATA series. Please write and tell us if we can make SATA even more helpful to you. Give your comments and suggestions to the editor:

Editor
Something about the Author
Thomson Gale
27500 Drake Rd.
Farmington Hills MI 48331-3535

Toll-free: 800-877-GALE
Fax: 248-699-8054

Something about the Author Product Advisory Board

The editors of *Something about the Author* are dedicated to maintaining a high standard of excellence by publishing comprehensive, accurate, and highly readable entries on a wide array of writers for children and young adults. In addition to the quality of the content, the editors take pride in the graphic design of the series, which is intended to be orderly yet inviting, allowing readers to utilize the pages of *SATA* easily and with efficiency. Despite the longevity of the *SATA* print series, and the success of its format, we are mindful that the vitality of a literary reference product is dependent on its ability to serve its users over time. As literature, and attitudes about literature, constantly evolve, so do the reference needs of students, teachers, scholars, journalists, researchers, and book club members. To be certain that we continue to keep pace with the expectations of our customers, the editors of *SATA* listen carefully to their comments regarding the value, utility, and quality of the series. Librarians, who have firsthand knowledge of the needs of library users, are a valuable resource for us. The *Something about the Author* Product Advisory Board, made up of school, public, and academic librarians, is a forum to promote focused feedback about *SATA* on a regular basis. The nine-member advisory board includes the following individuals, whom the editors wish to thank for sharing their expertise:

Acknowledgments

Grateful acknowledgment is made to the following publishers, authors, and artists whose works appear in this volume.

ACKROYD, PETER ∎ Ackroyd, Peter. From a jacket of his *Escape from Earth: Voyages Through Time*. DK Publishing, Ltd., 2003. Reproduced by permission./ Ackroyd, Peter. From a jacket of his *The Beginning: Voyages Through Time*. DK Publishing, Ltd., 2003. Reproduced by permission./ Ackroyd, Peter, photograph. Archive Photos, Inc. Reproduced by permission.

ASQUITH, ROS ∎ Williams, Sam, illustrator. From an illustration in *Babies*, by Ros Asquith. Simon & Schuster Books for Young Readers, 2002. Illustrations copyright © 2002 by Sam Williams. All rights reserved. Reproduced by permission of Simon & Schuster Macmillan./ Young, Selina, illustrator. From an illustration in *Mrs. Pig's Night Out*, by Ros Asquith. Hodder's Children's Books, 2003. Illustrations copyright © Selina Young 2003. Reproduced by permission.

BENNETT, JAMES (W.) ∎ All photographs reproduced by permission of James Bennett.

BLOS, JOAN W(INSOR) ∎ All photographs reproduced by permission of Joan W. Blos.

BOURGEOIS, PAULETTE ∎ Clark, Brenda, illustrator. From an illustration in *Franklin's Class Trip*, by Paulette Bourgeois. Scholastic Inc., 1999. Illustrations copyright © 1999 by Brenda Clark Illustrator, Inc. Reproduced by permission./ Jorisch, Stephane, illustrator. From an illustration in *Oma's Quilt*, by Paulette Bourgeois. Kids Can Press, 2001. Illustrations © 2001 Stephane Jorisch. All rights reserved. Used by permission of Kids Can Press Ltd., Toronto.

BOYER, ALLEN B. ∎ Photograph reproduced by permission of Allen B. Boyer.

BROWN, ELIZABETH FERGUSON ∎ Stevenson, Harvey, illustrator. From an illustration in *Coal Country Christmas*, by Elizabeth Ferguson Brown. Boyds Mills Press, 2003. Illustrations copyright © 2003 by Harvey Stevenson. All rights reserved. Reproduced by permission.

CARPENTER, ANGELICA SHIRLEY ∎ Tenniel, John, illustrator. From an illustration in *Lewis Carroll: Through the Looking Glass*, by Angelica Shirley Carpenter. Lerner Publications Company, 2003. Reproduced by permission of Mary Evans Picture Library./ Carpenter, Angelica Shirley, photograph by Richard Carpenter. Reproduced by permission of Angelica Shirley Carpenter.

CHARLES, NORMA ∎ Melnychuk, Monika, illustrator. From a cover of *All the Way to Mexico*, by Norma Charles. Raincoast Books, 2003. Cover illustration © Monika Melnychuk. Reproduced by permission./ Wilson, Janet, illustrator. From a cover of *The Accomplice*, by Norma Charles. Raincoast Books, 2001. Reproduced by permission.

CHRIST–EVANS, CRAIG ∎ Christensen, Bonnie, illustrator. From a photograph in *Moon Over Tennessee: A Boy's Civil War Journal*, by Craig Crist–Evans. Houghton Mifflin Company, 1999. Illustrations copyright © 1999 by Bonnie Christensen. All right reserved. Reproduced by permission of Houghton Mifflin Company./ Crist–Evans, Craig. From a jacket of his *Amaryllis*. Candlewick Press, 2003. Jacket photograph copyright © 2003 by Steve Casimiro/ Allsport/Getty Images (surfers). Jacket photograph copyright © 2003 by London Daily Express 03RLDE Archive Holdings Getty Images/The Image Bank (aircraft and soldiers). Text copyright © 2003 Craig Crist–Evans. Reproduced by permission of the publisher, Candlewick Press, Inc., Cambridge, MA./ Crist–Evans, Craig, photograph. Reproduced by permission of Craig Crist–Evans.

CRUTCHER, CHRIS(TOPHER C.) ∎ Photograph by Tony Omer. Reproduced by permission of Chris Crutcher.

DAVIS, (A.) AUBREY ∎ Daniel, Alan and Lea, illustrators. From an illustration in *Sody Salleratus*, by Aubrey Davis. Kids Can Press, 1996. Illustrations © Alan and Lea Daniel. All rights reserved. Used by permission of Kids Can Press Ltd., Toronto./ Petricic, Dusan, illustrator. From an illustration in *Bone Button Borscht*, by Aubrey Davis. Kids Can Press, 1995. Illustrations copyright © 1995 by Dusan Petricic. All rights reserved. Used by permission of Kids Can Press Ltd., Toronto./ Petricic, Dusan, illustrator. From an illustration in *The Enormous Potato*, by Aubrey Davis. Kids Can Press, 1997. Illustrations and hand lettering © 1997 Dusan Petricic. All rights reserved. Used by permission of Kids Can Press Ltd., Toronto.

EDWARDS, JULIE ANDREWS ∎ Brown, Judith Gwyn, illustrator. From an illustration in *Mandy*, by Julie Andrews Edwards. HarperTrophy, 1971. Illustration copyright © 1971 by Judith Gwyn Brown. Reproduced by permission of the illustrator./ Spirin, Gennady, illustrator. From an illustration in *Simeon's Gift*, by Julie Andrews Edwards. HarperCollins Publishers, 2003. Illustrations copyright © 2003 by Gennady Spirin. All rights reserved. Reproduced by permission of HarperCollins Children's Books, a division of HarperCollins Publishers./ Walton, Tony, illustrator. From an illustration in *Dumpy the Dump Truck*, by Julie Andrews Edwards and Emma Walton Hamilton. Hyperion Books for Children, 2000. Illustration copyright © 2000 by Tony Walton. All rights reserved. Reproduced by permission of Hyperion Books For Children.

FEARNLEY, JAN ∎ Fearnley, Jan, illustrator. From an illustration in her *Just Like You*. Candlewick Press, 2000. Reproduced by permission of David Higham Associates Ltd./ Fearnley, Jan, illustrator. From an illustration in her *Mr. Wolf's Pancakes*. Tiger Tales, 2001. Text and illustrations © Jan Fearnley 1999. Reproduced by permission./ Fearnley, Jan, photograph. Reproduced by permission.

RODDIE, SHEN ▌ Photograph reproduced by permission of Shen Roddie.

SALE, TIM ▌ Sale, Tim. Illustrator. From *Superman for All Seasons* #1 © DC Comics. All Rights Reserved. Used with Permission.

SANDIN, JOAN ▌ Sandin, Joan, illustrator. From an illustration in *A Bear for Miguel*, by Elaine Marie Alphin. HarperCollins Publishers, 1996. Illustrations copyright © 1996 by Joan Sandin. Reproduced by permission of HarperCollins Children's Books, a division of HarperCollins Publishers./ Sandin, Joan, illustrator. From an illustration in her *The Long Way to a New Land*. HarperCollins, 1981. Reproduced by permission of HarperCollins Children's Books, a division of HarperCollins Publishers.

STRASSER, TODD ▌ Strasser, Todd. From a cover of his *Help! I'm Trapped in My Teacher's Body*. Scholastic, 1993. Jacket illustration copyright © 2003 by Scholastic Inc. Reprinted by permission of Scholastic Inc./ Strasser, Todd, touring Germany as Morton Rhue in Friedrich–Shafon, photograph. Reproduced by permission of Tod Strasser

SUPEENE, SHELAGH LYNNE ▌ Photograph reproduced by permission of Lynne Supeene.

UEGAKI, CHIERI ▌ Jorisch, Stephane, illustrator. From an illustration in *Suki's Kimono*, by Chieri Uegaki. Kids Can Press, 2003. Illustrations © 2003 Stephane Jorisch. All rights reserved. Used by permission of Kids Can Press Ltd., Toronto.

WALLACE, PAULA S. ▌ Wallace, Paula S. From an illustration in her *The World of Food*. Gareth Stevens Publishing, 2003. Reproduced by permission of Getty Images./ Wallace, Paula S., photograph. Reproduced by permission of Paula S. Wallace.

WILSON, JACQUELINE ▌ Martin, Brad, photographer. From a jacket of *Girls in Love*, by Jacqueline Wilson. Delacorte Press, 2002. Reproduced by permission of Random House Children's Books, a division of Random House, Inc./ Sharratt, Nick, illustrator. From a jacket cover of *The Story of Tracy Beaker*, by Jacqueline Wilson. Corgi Yearling Books, 1992. Illustrations copyright © 1991 by Nick Sharratt. Reproduced by permission of Random House Children's Books, a division of Random House, Inc.

WINTERS, KAY ▌ Carpenter, Nancy, illustrator. From an illustration in *Abe Lincoln: The Boy Who Loved Books*, by Kay Winters. Simon & Schuster Books for Young Readers, 2003. Illustrations copyright © 2003 by Kay Winters. Reproduced by permission of Simon & Schuster./ Moser, Barry, illustrator. From an illustration in *Voices of Ancient Egypt*, by Kay Winters. National Geographical Society, 2003. Illustrations copyright © 2003 Barry Moser. Reproduced by permission./ Munsinger, Lynn, illustrator. From an illustration in *The Teeny Tiny Ghost*, by Kay Winters. HarperCollins Publishers, 1997. Illustrations copyright © 1997 by Lynn Munsinger. Reproduced by permission of HarperCollins Children's Books, a division of HarperCollins Publishers./ Regan, Laura, illustrator. From an illustration in *Tiger Trail*, by Kay Winters. Simon & Schuster Books for Young Readers, 2000. Illustrations copyright © 2000 by Laura Regan. Reproduced by permission of Simon & Schuster Macmillan./ Winters, Katharine, photograph. Reproduced by permission of Kay Winters.

YUMOTO, KAZUMI ▌ Kazuhiko Sano, illustrator. From a jacket cover of *The Friends*, by Kazumi Yumoto, translated by Cathy Hirano. Yearling Books, 1998. English translation copyright © 1996 by Farrar, Straus & Giroux. Reproduced by permission of Random House Children's Books, a division of Random House, Inc./ Yumoto, Kazumi. From a jacket cover of her *The Letters*. Laurel–Leaf Books, 2003. Reproduced by permission of Random House Children's Books, a division of Random House, Inc./ Yumoto, Kazumi. From a jacket cover of her *The Spring Tone*. Laurel–Leaf Books, 1995. Reproduced by permission of Random House Children's Books, a division of Random House, Inc.

ZEMAN, LUDMILA ▌ Zeman, Ludmila, illustrator. From an illustration in her *Sindbad's Secret*. Tundra Book, 2003. Reproduced by permission./ Zeman, Ludmila, photograph by Linda Spaleny. Reproduced by permission of Ludmila Zeman.

something ABOUT THe AUThOR

ACKROYD, Peter 1949-

Personal

Born October 5, 1949, in London, England; son of Graham and Audrey (Whiteside) Ackroyd. *Education:* Clare College, Cambridge, M.A., 1971; attended Yale University, 1971-73.

Addresses

Home—London, England. *Agent*—Anthony Sheil Associates Ltd., 43 Doughty St., London WC1N 2LF, England.

Career

Writer. *Spectator,* London, England, literary editor, 1973-77, managing editor, 1977-81; *Times* (London, England), television critic, 1977-81, chief book reviewer, 1986—. Commentator for radio in England.

Member

Royal Society of Literature (fellow).

Awards, Honors

Whitbread Award for biography, and Heinemann Award for nonfiction, both 1984, both for *T. S. Eliot: A Life;* Somerset Maugham Award, 1984, for *The Last Testament of Oscar Wilde;* Whitbread Award for fiction, and

Peter Ackroyd

fiction prize from *Guardian,* both 1985, for *Hawksmoor;* James Tait Black Memorial Prize for best biography, University of Edinburgh, 1998, for *The Life of Thomas*

More; South Bank Show Annual Award for Literature, 2000, for *London: The Biography;* named Commander of the British Empire, 2003.

Writings

FOR CHILDREN; "VOYAGES THROUGH TIME" SERIES

The Beginning, Dorling Kindersley (London, England), 2003.

Escape from Earth, Dorling Kindersley (London, England), 2003.

Ancient Egypt, Dorling Kindersley (London, England), 2004.

POETRY

Ouch, Curiously Strong Press (London, England), 1971.

London Lickpenny (also see below), Ferry Press (London, England), 1973.

Country Life (also see below), Ferry Press (London, England), 1978.

The Diversions of Purley, and Other Poems (contains poems from *London Lickpenny* and *Country Life*), Hamish Hamilton (London, England), 1987.

ADULT FICTION

The Great Fire of London, Hamish Hamilton (London, England), 1982.

The Last Testament of Oscar Wilde, Harper & Row (New York, NY), 1983.

Hawksmoor, Hamish Hamilton (London, England), 1985, Harper & Row (New York, NY), 1986.

Chatterton, Grove Press (New York, NY), 1988.

First Light, Viking Penguin (New York, NY), 1989.

English Music, Alfred A. Knopf (New York, NY), 1992.

The House of Doctor Dee, Hamish Hamilton (London, England), 1993, Penguin (New York, NY), 1994.

Dan Leno and the Limehouse Golem, Sinclair-Stevenson (London, England), 1994, published as *The Trial of Elizabeth Cree: A Novel of the Limehouse Murders,* Nan A. Talese (New York, NY), 1997.

Milton in America, Nan A. Talese (New York, NY), 1997.

The Plato Papers: A Prophecy, Nan A. Talese (New York, NY), 2000.

The Clerkenwell Tales, Chatto & Windus (New York, NY), 2003, Nan A. Talese (New York, NY), 2004.

ADULT NONFICTION

Notes for a New Culture: An Essay on Modernism, Barnes & Noble (New York, NY), 1976.

Dressing Up: Transvestism and Drag: The History of an Obsession, Simon & Schuster (New York, NY), 1979.

Ezra Pound and His World, Charles Scribner (New York, NY), 1981.

T. S. Eliot: A Life, Simon & Schuster (New York, NY), 1984.

(Editor) *PEN New Fiction,* Quartet Books (London, England), 1984.

Dickens, Sinclair-Stevenson (London, England), 1990, HarperPerennial (New York, NY), 1992.

Introduction to Dickens, Sinclair-Stevenson (London, England), 1991, Ballantine (New York, NY), 1992.

Blake, Sinclair-Stevenson (London, England), 1995.

(Editor) Oscar Wilde, *The Picture of Dorian Gray,* G. K. Hall (Thorndike, ME), 1995.

The Life of Thomas More, Chatto & Windus (London, England), 1998.

London: The Biography, Chatto & Windus (London, England), 2000.

The Collection, Chatto & Windus (London, England), 2001.

Albion: The Origins of the English Imagination, Nan A. Talese/Doubleday (New York, NY), 2003.

Illustrated London, Chatto & Windus (London, England), 2003.

Chaucer, Chatto & Windus (London, England), 2004.

PLAYS

The Mystery of Charles Dickens, first produced in London, England, 2000, produced at Belasco Theater, New York, NY, 2002.

Dickens: Public Life and Private Passion (audio cassette), British Broadcasting Corporation (London, England), 2002.

OTHER

Contributor of short story, "The Inheritance," to the anthology *London Tales,* edited by Julian Evans, Hamish Hamilton (London, England), 1983. Author of introduction, *Dickens' London: An Imaginative Vision,* Headline (London, England), 1987, and Frank Auerbach, *Recent Works,* Marlborough (New York, NY), 1994. Contributor of numerous book reviews to periodicals, including *New York Times Book Review.*

Work in Progress

More volumes in the "Voyages through Time" series; a biography of William Shakespeare for adults.

Sidelights

Sir Peter Ackroyd is a British man of letters best known for his penetrating biographies and stylized intellectual fiction for adults. Since 1986 Ackroyd has been the chief book reviewer for the London *Times* while turning out award-winning volumes of his own at a remarkable pace. His novel for adults, *Hawksmoor,* won the prestigious Whitbread award for fiction, one of many formal accolades he has received over the years. In 2003 Ackroyd was named a Commander of the British Empire, the modern-day equivalent of knighthood. An essayist for the *British Council of Contemporary Writers* Web site identified the author as "one of Britain's leading literary biographers . . . a prolific reviewer, poet and critical theorist." The same essayist went on to note that the abundance of Ackroyd's published work "speaks in itself of the varied nature of his achievements."

Only recently has Ackroyd begun writing for children. In a career spanning more than thirty years, he never published a children's book until 2003. During that year, the London firm Dorling Kindersley announced that Ackroyd would write not one, but a whole series of books for young adults on the profound subject of the history of the world. With ten titles planned, the "Voyages through Time" series promises to introduce Ackroyd to generations of readers who are perhaps not yet ready for his adult body of work. In an online feature for *The Independent,* Dina Rabinovitch maintained that the writer is "not previously best known for breaking up his dense, allusive texts with pictures and brightly coloured diagrams. . . . And yet here is Ackroyd taking on a limitless brief: the story of the world. It runs counter to everything one knows of him as a writer."

Ackroyd learned to read at the age of two, and by the time he became an undergraduate at Cambridge University, he was already writing poetry and essays. While still in his twenties he became a published poet and critic. His adult books, if it is fair to generalize, exercise his consuming interest in English literature and its important practitioners, including Charles Dickens, Oscar Wilde, T. S. Eliot, William Blake, St. Thomas More, John Milton, and Thomas Chatterton. His first novel, *The Great Fire of London,* revolves around a fictitious film production of Dickens's work *Little Dorritt. The Last Testament of Oscar Wilde* is a novel by Ackroyd written as if it were an autobiography of the flamboyant Victorian-era playwright. *Chatterton* likewise involves a fictitious autobiographical document suggesting that Chatterton, a seventeenth-century poet, did not end his own life in 1770. The Whitbread Award-winning *Hawksmoor* is a murder mystery set in eighteenth century London and featuring actual historical characters such as Nicholas Dyer and Christopher Wren. *Newsweek* contributor Peter S. Prescott called *Hawksmoor* "a fascinating hybrid, a tale of terrors that does double duty as a novel of ideas."

The publication of a new biography by Ackroyd has become something of an event in England. His second biography, *T. S. Eliot: A Life,* won a Whitbread biography award and was particularly praised because Ackroyd was forbidden by the late poet's estate to quote from Eliot's correspondence and unpublished verse. *Blake* gives a reasoned assessment of an often misunderstood English poet who claimed to converse with angels and demons, and *Dickens* explores the famous Victorian novelist by way of an imaginative reconstruction of his milieu. Ackroyd has also written a biography of Thomas More, an author and statesman who was beheaded for his opposition to the second marriage of King Henry

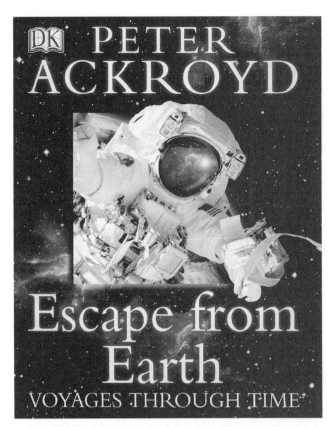

The details of space exploration, begun just sixty years after the first flight, and biographical portraits of notable astronauts and scientists are presented by Ackroyd in a title from his "Voyages through Time" series.

VIII. A *Kirkus Reviews* critic called *The Life of Thomas More* a "limpidly written and superbly wrought portrait of a complex hero."

An editor at Dorling Kindersley approached Ackroyd about taking on the "Voyages through Time" series. The scope of the project might be daunting to the most seasoned children's nonfiction writer: a history of the earth from its creation as a planet to its present-day complexity, both in biodiversity and technology. The first two volumes, *The Beginning* and *Escape from Earth* are in some respects the alpha and omega of the series. *The Beginning* charts earth history from the Big Bang to the first emergence of our species, *Homo sapiens. Escape from Earth* examines air and space travel and the modern means of studying the universe with space telescopes, unmanned spaceships, and satellites. Courtney Lewis in *School Library Journal* noted that Ackroyd's text in *The Beginning* does not talk down to youngsters, and the book is "simply and beautifully laid out." *Booklist* reviewer Jennifer Mattson praised *The Beginning* for providing "a broader view . . . than is normally transmitted." Mattson also called the work "an indispensable resource" for those students with an interest in prehistory. Carolyn Phelan in *Booklist* commended *Escape from Earth* for its "fine balance of technology and humanity."

In his interview with *The Independent,* Ackroyd estimated that he writes about 1,500 words per day. He

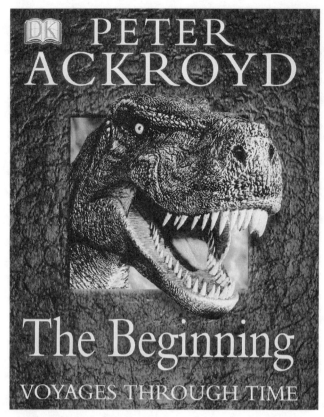

PETER ACKROYD

The Beginning

VOYAGES THROUGH TIME

Commencing with the first age of the world, the Hadean, Ackroyd's informational book explores the extraordinary development of the Earth's wildlife and the advent of human life.

usually has several projects running simultaneously, and he noted that for his "Voyages through Time" series he has read dozens of books for each volume he has produced. He said that he agreed to do the series as a contribution to children's education. "I have a sense of the importance of history in the minds of the young," he observed. "The little I can do, is the best I can do. It's just a book, but if you can help just one child learn, or be interested in reading, then it's worth it."

Biographical and Critical Sources

BOOKS

Contemporary Literary Criticism, Gale (Detroit, MI), Volume 34, 1985, Volume 52, 1989, Volume 140, 1996.

Dictionary of Literary Biography, Gale (Detroit, MI), Volume 155: *Twentieth-Century Literary Biographers,* 1995, Volume 231: *British Novelists since 1960,* 2001.

PERIODICALS

Booklist, December 15, 2003, Jennifer Mattson, review of *The Beginning,* p. 749; May 1, 2004, Carolyn Phelan, review of *Escape from Earth,* p. 1554.

English Review, April, 2003, Victoria Kingston, "Face to Face: Victoria Kingston Interviews Acclaimed Novelist and Biographer, Peter Ackroyd," p. 21.

Kirkus Reviews, September 15, 1998, review of *The Life of Thomas More;* December 1, 1999, review of *The Plato Papers,* p. 1824.

Newsweek, November 26, 1984; February 24, 1986, Peter S. Prescott, review of *Hawksmoor.*

New York Times, November 9, 1992, Christopher Lehmann-Haupt, "An Entertainment for the Library"; August 21, 1995, Richard Bernstein, "The Limehouse Killings and Much, Much More."

New York Times Book Review, December 16, 1984; January 19, 1986; January 17, 1988; January 13, 1991, pp. 1, 24; October 11, 1992, Alison Lurie, "Hanging out with Hogarth," p. 7; April 16, 1995, p. 7; April 14, 1996, Penelope Fitzgerald, "Innocence and Experience," p. 44; October 25, 1998, Andrew Sullivan, "Public Man, Public Faith"; February 6, 2000, John Sutherland, "After Mouldwarp," p. 7.

New York Times Magazine, December 22, 1991, pp. 27-36.

Publishers Weekly, October 27, 2003, review of *The Beginning,* p. 71; March 8, 2004, "For Aspiring Scientists," p. 77.

School Library Journal, January, 2004, Courtney Lewis, review of *The Beginning,* p. 138.

Sunday Times (London), September 28, 2003, "Children's Book of the Week," p. 54.

ONLINE

British Council of Contemporary Writers, http://www.contemporarywriters.com/ (June 2, 2004), "Peter Ackroyd."

Dorling Kindersley, http://cn.dk.com/ (June 2, 2004), information on "Voyages through Time."

Edutaining Kids, http://www.edutainingkids.com/ (June 2, 2004), review of *The Beginning.*

Independent Online, http://enjoyment.independent.co.uk/books/ (June 2, 2004), Dina Rabinovitch, "Peter Ackroyd: Captain of the Time Machine."*

*   *   *

ALAN, David
See HORSFIELD, Alan

*   *   *

ANDREWS, Julie 1935-
(Julie Edwards, Julie Andrews Edwards)

Personal

Original name, Julia Elizabeth Wells; born October 1, 1935, in Walton-on-Thames, Surrey, England; daughter of Edward C. Wells (a teacher) and Barbara (a pianist; maiden name, Ward) Wells Andrews; stepdaughter of Edward "Ted" Andrews (a music hall singer); married

Tony Walton (a costume and production designer), May 10, 1959 (divorced May 7, 1968); married Blake Edwards (a film producer, director, and screenwriter), November 12, 1969; children: (first marriage) Emma Kate Walton Hamilton; (second marriage) Amy Leigh Edwards, Joanna Lynne Edwards; (stepchildren) Jennifer Edwards, Geoffrey Edwards. *Education:* Educated privately by tutors; studied voice with Madame Stiles-Allen.

Addresses

Agent—William Morris Agency, 151 El Camino Dr., Beverly Hills, CA 90212.

Career

Actress, singer, and author. Actress in stage productions, including *Wynkin, Blynken, and Nod,* c. 1938; (as singer) *Starlight Roof* (revue), Hippodrome Theatre, London, England, 1947; (as title role) *Humpty Dumpty* (pantomime), Casino Theatre, London, 1948; (as title role) *Red Riding Hood* (pantomime), Nottingham Theatre Royal, Nottingham, England, 1950; (as Princess Balroulbadour) *Aladdin,* Casino Theatre, 1951; *Jack and the Beanstalk* (pantomime), Coventry Hippodrome, Coventry, England, 1952; (as title role) *Cinderella* (pantomime), Palladium Theatre, London, 1953; (as member of the ensemble) *Caps and Belles* (revue), Empire Theatre, Nottingham, 1953; (as Becky Dunbar) *Mountain of Fire,* Royal Court Theatre, Liverpool, England, 1954; (as Polly Browne) *The Boy Friend,* Royale Theatre, New York, NY, 1954; (as Eliza Doolittle) *My Fair Lady,* Shubert Theatre, New Haven, CT, then Mark Hellinger Theatre, New York, 1956, Drury Lane Theatre, London, 1958-1959; (as Guinevere) *Camelot,* Majestic Theatre, New York, 1960-1961; *Putting It Together* (revue), Manhattan Theatre Club, New York, 1993; (as Victoria Grant) *Victor/Victoria,* Marquis Theatre, New York, 1995-1997; (as host) *Hey, Mr. Producer,* Lyceum Theatre, London, 1998; (as host) *My Favorite Broadway: The Leading Ladies,* Theatre at Carnegie Hall, New York, 1998; (as host) *My Favorite Broadway: The Love Songs,* City Center Theatre, New York, 2000; also appeared in a Royal Command Performance, Palladium Theatre, 1948.

Actress in films, including (as voice of Princess Zeila) *The Singing Princess* (animated; also known as *The Rose of Bagdad*), Trans-National, 1952 (English-language version of *La rosa di Bagdad,* Ima, 1949); (as title role) *Mary Poppins,* Buena Vista, 1964; (as Emily Barham) *The Americanization of Emily* (also known as *Emily*), Metro-Goldwyn-Mayer, 1964; (as herself) *Action on the Beach,* 1964; (as Maria) *The Sound of Music* (also known as *Sing-a-long Sound of Music*), Twentieth Century-Fox, 1965; (as Jerusha Bromley Hale) *Hawaii,* United Artists, 1966; (as Dr. Sarah Louise Sherman) *Torn Curtain,* Universal, 1966; (as Millie Dillmount) *Thoroughly Modern Millie,* Metro-Goldwyn-

Mayer, 1967; (as Gertrude Lawrence) *Star!* (also known as *Loves of a Star* and *Those Were the Happy Times*), Twentieth Century-Fox, 1968; (as Lili Smith) *Darling Lili,* Paramount, 1970; (as herself) *The Moviemakers,* 1971; (as Judith Farrow) *The Tamarind Seed,* Avco-Embassy, 1974; (as Samantha "Sam" Taylor) *10,* Warner Bros., 1979; (as Amanda) *Little Miss Marker,* Universal, 1980; (as Sally Miles) *S.O.B.,* Paramount, 1981; (as Victoria Grant/Count Victor Grezhinski [title roles]) *Victor/Victoria,* Metro-Goldwyn-Mayer/United Artists, 1982; (as Marianna) *The Man Who Loved Women,* Columbia, 1983; (as Stephanie Anderson) *Duet for One,* Cannon, 1986; (as Gillian Fairchild) *That's Life!* (also known as *Blake Edwards' That's Life!*), Columbia, 1986; (as Pamela Picquet) *A Fine Romance* (also known as *A Touch of Adultery* and *Cin Cin*), Castle Hill, 1992; (as song performer) "The Lonely Goatherd" and "The Sound of Music," *Welcome to Woop Woop,* Goldwyn Films/Metro-Goldwyn-Mayer, 1997; (as Queen Clarisse Renaldi) *The Princess Diaries* (also known as *The Princess of Tribeca*), Buena Vista/Walt Disney Pictures, 2001; (as voice of Queen Lillian) *Shrek 2,* DreamWorks, 2004; and (as Queen Clarisse Renaldi) *The Princess Diaries 2: Royal Engagement,* Buena Vista/Walt Disney Pictures, 2004; also appeared in *After the Laughter* and *The Laundromat.*

Appeared in videos, including *Mary Poppins, The Walt Disney Comedy and Magic Revue,* 1985; *Mary Poppins, Disney Sing-Along-Songs: Heigh-Ho,* 1992; *Mary Poppins, Disney Sing-Along-Songs: Supercalifragilisticexpialidocious,* 1993; *Mary Poppins, Disney Sing-Along-Songs: You Can Fly,* 1993; *Mary Poppins, Disney Sing-Along-Songs: Be Our Guest,* 1994; and *A New Princess* (also known as *Making of 'The Princess Diaries'*), 2001.

Appeared in television series, including (as host) *The Julie Andrews Show,* National Broadcasting Company (NBC), 1965; (as host) *The Julie Andrews Hour,* American Broadcasting Companies (ABC), 1972-1973; and (as Julie Carlyle-McGuire) *Julie,* ABC, 1992. Actress in television movies, including (as Audrey Grant) *Our Sons* (also known as *Too Little, Too Late*), ABC, 1991; (as Catherine) *One Special Night,* Columbia Broadcasting System (CBS), 1999; (as Felicity) *Relative Values,* Starz!, 2000; (as Ethel Thayer) *On Golden Pond,* CBS, 2001; (as Nanny) *Eloise at the Plaza,* 2003; and (as Nanny) *Eloise at Christmastime,* 2003.

Appeared in television specials, including (as Lise) "High Tor," *Ford Star Jubilee,* CBS, 1956; (as title role) *Cinderella,* CBS, 1957; *The Jack Benny Hour,* CBS, 1959; *The Fabulous Fifties,* CBS, 1960; *Julie and Carol at Carnegie Hall,* CBS, 1962; (as host) *The Julie Andrews Special,* ABC, 1968; (as host) *An Evening with Julie Andrews and Harry Belafonte,* NBC, 1969; *A World of Love,* CBS, 1970; *Disney World—A Gala Opening: Disneyland East* (also known as *The Grand Opening of Walt Disney World*), NBC, 1971; *Julie and Carol at Lincoln Center,* CBS, 1971; (as host) *Julie!*

(documentary), ABC, 1972; (as host) *Julie on Sesame Street,* ABC, 1973; *Walt Disney: A Golden Anniversary Salute,* 1973; (as host) *Julie and Dick in Covent Garden,* ABC, 1974; *Julie and Jackie: How Sweet It Is,* 1974; (as host) *Julie—My Favorite Things,* ABC, 1975; (as host) *Puzzle Children,* Public Broadcasting Service (PBS), 1976; (as song performer) "Peter Pan," *Hallmark Hall of Fame,* NBC, 1976; *Julie and Perry and the Muppets,* 1976; *America Salutes the Queen,* NBC, 1977; (as host) *Julie Andrews: One Step into Spring,* CBS, 1978; *ABC's Silver Anniversary Special,* 1978; (as host) *Merry Christmas . . . With Love, Julie,* syndicated, 1979; "Julie Andrews' Invitation to the Dance with Rudolf Nureyev," *The CBS Festival of Lively Arts for Young People,* CBS, 1980; *Bob Hope Special: Bob Hope's Pink Panther Thanksgiving Gala,* NBC, 1982; *Disneyland's Thirtieth Anniversary Celebration,* NBC, 1985; (as host) *Julie Andrews: The Sound of Christmas,* ABC, 1987; *Mancini and Friends,* 1987; (as host) *The Sixteenth Annual American Film Institute Life Achievement Award: A Salute to Jack Lemmon,* CBS, 1988; *Lerner and Loewe: Broadway's Last Romantics,* 1988; *An Evening with Alan Jay Lerner,* 1989; "Julie and Carol: Together Again," *AT&T Presents,* ABC, 1989; "Julie Andrews in Concert" (also known as "An Evening with Julie Andrews"), *Great Performances,* PBS, 1990; *Carnegie Hall at One Hundred: A Place of Dreams* (documentary), PBS, 1991; (as host) *Christmas in Washington,* NBC, 1992; *The King and I: Recording a Hollywood Dream* (documentary), PBS, 1993; *The Sound of Julie Andrews,* The Disney Channel, 1994; *The Making of My Fair Lady: More Loverly than Ever,* The Disney Channel, 1995; "Some Enchanted Evening: Celebrating Oscar Hammerstein II," *Great Performances,* PBS, 1995; *Rodgers & Hammerstein: The Sound of Movies,* Arts and Entertainment (A&E), 1996; (as host) *The American Film Institute Salute to Robert Wise,* NBC, 1998; (as host) *Hey, Mr. Producer* (also known as *Hey, Mr. Producer! The Musical World of Cameron Mackintosh*), PBS, 1998; (as host) "My Favorite Broadway: The Leading Ladies," *Great Performances,* PBS, 1999; (in archive footage) *A&E Biography: The Von Trapp Family—Harmony and Discord,* A&E, 2000; (as host) "My Favorite Broadway: The Love Songs," *Great Performances,* PBS, 2001; (in archive footage) *Walt: The Man behind the Myth,* 2001; (as herself) *I Love Muppets,* 2002; (as herself) *Unconditional Love,* 2002; (as herself) *Liza Minnelli: The E! True Hollywood Story,* E!, 2002; (in archive footage) *The One Hundred Greatest Musicals,* 2002; and *Broadway's Lost Treasures,* PBS, 2003.

Appeared at televised awards presentations, including *The Thirty-Eighth Annual Tony Awards,* 1984; *The Second Annual American Comedy Awards,* 1988; (as host) *The Forty-Fifth Annual Tony Awards,* CBS, 1991; *The Seventeenth Annual People's Choice Awards,* CBS, 1991; *The Fifty-Third Annual Tony Awards,* 1999; *The Seventy-Third Annual Academy Awards,* 2001; *The Kennedy Center Honors,* CBS, 2001; and (as presenter) *The Seventy-Fifth Annual Academy Awards,* 2003. Guest

star in episodes of television series, including "Crescendo," *DuPont Show of the Month,* CBS, 1957; (as herself) *The Andy Williams Show,* NBC, 1964; (as herself) *The Muppet Show,* syndicated, 1977; *Entertainment Tonight,* syndicated, 1989; *Reflections on the Silver Screen with Professor Richard Brown,* American Movie Classics, 1990; (as herself) *Clive Anderson Talks Back,* 1994; (as herself) "Caroline and Victor/Victoria," *Caroline in the City,* NBC, 1996; also appeared in numerous episodes of talk shows.

Appeared in the British Broadcasting Company (BBC) radio series *Educating Archie,* 1950. Featured on recordings, including *My Fair Lady* (original Broadway cast recording), Columbia Special Projects, 1956; *Camelot* (original cast recording), Columbia, 1960; *My Fair Lady* (original London cast recording), Columbia, 1960; *Mary Poppins* (original soundtrack recording), Buena Vista, 1964; *The Sound of Music* (original soundtrack recording), RCA, 1965; *Thoroughly Modern Millie* (original soundtrack recording), 1967; *Star!* (original soundtrack recording), Twentieth Century-Fox, 1968; *Victor/Victoria* (original soundtrack recording), Metro-Goldwyn-Mayer, 1982; *Love, Julie,* Metro-Goldwyn-Mayer, 1987; *The King and I* (studio cast recording), Philips, 1992; *Putting It Together* (original cast album), RCA, 1993; *Broadway—The Music of Richard Rodgers,* Philips, 1994; *The Best of Julie Andrews: Thoroughly Modern Julie,* Rhino, 1995; *Victor/Victoria* (original Broadway cast album), Philips, 1995; *Here I'll Stay: The Words of Alan Jay Lerner,* Philips, 1996; also recorded *Christmas with Julie Andrews,* Columbia, *Broadway's Fair Julie, Lion's Cage,* and *Tell It Again;* with Carol Burnett, recorded *Julie Andrews and Carol Burnett at Carnegie Hall.*

Member

Actor's Equity Association, Screen Actors Guild, American Federation of Television and Radio Artists.

Awards, Honors

Theatre World Award, 1955, for *The Boy Friend;* Tony Award nomination for best actress in a musical, New York Drama Critics Circle, 1957, for *My Fair Lady,* 1961, for *Camelot,* and 1996, for *Victor/Victoria* (refused); British Academy of Film and Television Arts Award for most promising newcomer to leading film roles, 1965, for *Mary Poppins;* Woman of the Year award, *Los Angeles Times,* 1965; Oscar Award for best actress in a leading role, Academy of Motion Picture Arts and Sciences, 1965, for *Mary Poppins,* and nominations, 1966, for *The Sound of Music,* and 1983, for *Victor/Victoria;* Golden Globe Award for best motion picture actress in a musical or comedy, Hollywood Foreign Press Association, 1965, for *Mary Poppins,* 1966, for *The Sound of Music,* and 1983, for *Victor/Victoria;* Golden Laurel for musical performance (female), *Motion Picture Exhibitor* magazine, 1965, for *Mary Poppins,* and 1966, for *The Sound of Music;* Golden Laurel for comedy performance (female), 1967, for *Thoroughly Modern Millie;* Golden Globe Award for world film favorite (female), 1967, 1968; Star of the Year award, Theatre Owners of America, 1967; honorary D.F.A., University of Maryland, 1970; Emmy Award for outstanding variety musical series, Academy of Television Arts and Sciences, and Silver Rose Montreaux award, both 1973, for *The Julie Andrews Hour;* David di Donatello Award for best foreign actress, 1983, for *Victor/ Victoria;* Woman of the Year award, Hasty Pudding Theatricals, 1983; Crystal Award, Women in Film, 1993; Donostia Lifetime Achievement Award, San Sebastián International Film Festival, 2001; Honor Award, John F. Kennedy Center for the Performing Arts, 2001.

Writings

CHILDREN'S BOOKS

(As Julie Edwards) *Mandy,* illustrated by Judith Gwyn Brown, Harper & Row (New York, NY), 1971, HarperTrophy (New York, NY), 2001.

(As Julie Edwards) *The Last of the Really Great Whangdoodles,* Harper & Row (New York, NY), 1974.

(As Julie Andrews Edwards) *Little Bo: The Story of Bonnie Boadicea,* illustrated by Henry Cole, Hyperion (New York, NY), 1999.

(As Julie Andrews Edwards) *Little Bo in France: The Further Adventures of Bonnie Boadicea,* illustrated by Henry Cole, Hyperion (New York, NY), 2002.

"DUMPY" BOOKS; WITH DAUGHTER EMMA WALTON HAMILTON; AS JULIE ANDREWS EDWARDS

Dumpy the Dumptruck, illustrated by Tony Walton, Hyperion (New York, NY), 2000.

Dumpy at School, illustrated by Tony Walton, Hyperion (New York, NY), 2000.

Dumpy and His Pals, illustrated by Tony Walton, Hyperion (New York, NY), 2001.

Dumpy's Friends on the Farm, illustrated by Tony Walton, Hyperion (New York, NY), 2001.

Dumpy Saves Christmas, illustrated by Tony Walton, Hyperion (New York, NY), 2001.

Dumpy and the Big Storm, illustrated by Tony Walton, Hyperion (New York, NY), 2002.

Dumpy and the Firefighters, illustrated by Tony Walton, HarperCollins (New York, NY), 2003.

Dumpy to the Rescue!, illustrated by Tony Walton and Cassandra Boyd, HarperCollins (New York, NY), 2004.

Dumpy's Happy Holiday, illustrated by Tony Walton and Cassandra Boyd, HarperCollins (New York, NY), 2004.

Dumpy's Apple Shop, illustrated by Tony Walton and Cassandra Boyd, HarperCollins (New York, NY), 2004.

WITH EMMA WALTON HAMILTON; AS JULIE ANDREWS EDWARDS

Simeon's Gift, illustrated by Gennady Spirin, HarperCollins (New York, NY), 2003.

Dragon: Hound of Honor, HarperCollins (New York, NY), 2004.

Work in Progress

Two more books in the "Little Bo" series; an autobiography for Hyperion (New York, NY).

Sidelights

Although she is best known as a singer and actress, star of such musical films as *Mary Poppins* and *The Sound of Music,* in recent years Julie Andrews has become a prolific children's book writer under the name Julie Andrews Edwards. Andrews began her career in show business as a child, performing in her mother and stepfather's vaudeville shows. She soon graduated to performing on her own in pantomimes, performances of fairy tales and other classic stories for children that were popular in Britain at that time. Her tremendous, four-octave vocal range was recognized early, and by the time she was a teenager Andrews was much sought-after as a stage entertainer. At the age of eighteen, she signed on to perform in her first Broadway musical, *The Boy Friend,* which opened September 30, 1954, one day before her nineteenth birthday.

Andrews made several other successful turns on stage in the following years. She played the lead role of Eliza

Ten-year-old parentless Mandy sneaks out of the orphanage and refurbishes a small cottage in the woods to be her new, secret home. (From Mandy, *written by Julie Edwards and illustrated by Judith Gwyn Brown.)*

in *My Fair Lady* for over three years, first on Broadway and then in London, and then starred as Guinevere in *Camelot.* After being passed over for the role of Eliza in the film version of *My Fair Lady* (the role went to Audrey Hepburn), Andrews starred in another film, as the cheerful, magical governess Mary Poppins. She won a best actress Oscar and Golden Globe for the film. The next year, Andrews starred in another award-winning film, *The Sound of Music,* which garnered her a second Golden Globe and became one of the highest-grossing films of all time.

Throughout the 1960s, Andrews appeared in one more highly-acclaimed film, *Thoroughly Modern Millie,* and several less-successful works. In 1969, she married her second husband, director Blake Edwards. With children from her and her new husband's prior marriages, as well as two girls adopted from Vietnam in 1975, Andrews began to spend more time at home with them and less time singing and acting. During this period, Andrews wrote her first two children's books, *Mandy* and *The Last of the Really Great Whangdoodles,* under the name Julie Edwards. She wrote the first story after losing a bet with her stepdaughter, who demanded that Andrews write her a story in payment. The latter book was inspired by a trip to the dictionary. "I was looking up a word, and suddenly I saw 'Whangdoodle,'" Andrews once commented. "I thought to myself, that's a sensational word, and the title of my book occurred to me immediately. Once I started writing, I enjoyed myself so much I couldn't wait to get back to Whangdoodleland every day. My own children became as involved as I was, and naturally there is a lot of them in Lindy, Tom, and Ben."

A boy and his grandfather lovingly transform an old rusted dump truck in Edwards's book from her cheery series about the anthropomorphized machines of Merryhill Farm. (From Dumpy the Dumptruck, *illustrated by Tony Walton.)*

Andrews also received much acclaim for her work in *Victor/Victoria,* a film directed by Edwards, about an opera singer who pretends to be a male transvestite when she is having trouble landing roles as a woman. In the late 1990s, Andrews played Victor/Victoria on Broadway, a role which earned her a third Tony Award nomination. (Andrews refused the nomination to protest the fact that no one else involved with the musical was nominated.) Andrews' return to Broadway came to an abrupt end in 1997, when surgery to remove a benign polyp from her vocal cords went wrong. Although her voice has been much diminished, Andrews has continued to act in films in roles that do not require her to sing or otherwise strain her voice, including a popular performance as Queen Clarisse Renaldi in the 2001 *The Princess Diaries* and its 2004 sequel, *The Princess Diaries 2: Royal Engagement.*

In the late 1990s Andrews returned to the world of children's literature, writing the first two books in a series about Bonnie Boadicea, a kitten nicknamed "Little Bo." Bo's father names her, the smallest of the litter, after an ancient British warrior queen who fought the Roman invasion two thousand years ago. Although Bo and her littermates are due to be drowned, they escape, and Bo finds a home on a ship with a sailor named Billy. In *Little Bo: The Story of Bonnie Boadicea* and its sequel, *Little Bo in France: The Further Adventures of Bonnie Boadicea,* Bo and Billy share a series of adventures. "The atmosphere is agreeable throughout," Michael Cart wrote of *Little Bo* in *Booklist,* and a *Publishers Weekly* reviewer concluded about the same work that "children will come away with the moral that, like Bo, their size may be small, but they can accomplish big things."

Andrews has also partnered with her daughter from her first marriage, Emma Walton Hamilton, in several other works. Together the two have penned a series of books about Dumpy, a child-like, anthropomorphic dump truck. In the first book in the series, *Dumpy the Dumptruck,* a young boy named Charlie convinces his grandfather not to junk a run-down old truck. Instead, the two fix him up and return him to service. In the second volume, *Dumpy at School,* Charlie and the truck bond over their anxiety about their first day at school, Charlie as a student, Dumpy as a member of the crew building the new playground. *School Library Journal* critic Martha Link thought that the books' stories were "slight," but praised their "colorful onomatopoeia" in a review of *Dumpy the Dump Truck* and *Dumpy at School.* To a *Publishers Weekly* contributor, one notable feature of *Dumpy the Dump Truck* was its "retro look and feel, [which] harks back to times when townspeople knew one another's names and things were not so disposable." The books are illustrated by Tony Walton, Andrews' first husband, an acclaimed Broadway set designer.

In 2003, HarperCollins announced the formation of its first ever celebrity imprint, "The Julie Andrews Collec-

Set in the Medieval era, Edwards's picture book, cowritten with Emma Walton Hamilton, depicts a young musician who must overcome his insecurity to develop his talents fully. (From Simeon's Gift, *illustrated by Gennady Spirin.)*

tion." All of the books published under the imprint will be personally approved by Andrews, and some, including its first title, will be written by her. Coauthored by Hamilton, *Simeon's Gift,* the first book published by the imprint, is about a poor young musician during the Renaissance. In love with a noblewoman named Sorrel, Simeon sets out to compose the perfect song for her. In search of inspiration, he goes traveling, and as he wanders, he hears music in the noises around him: the marching of soldiers, the chanting of monks, the sounds of the city and the country. Overwhelmed by all of the new things he hears, Simeon wants nothing more than to go home. He sells his lute to buy a boat and turns toward Sorrel, rescuing a fish, bird, and fawn along the way. Inspired by his interactions with these creatures, he fashions himself a flute out of a reed and plays Sorrel a beautiful song that he has composed, winning her heart.

Biographical and Critical Sources

BOOKS

Arntz, James, and Thomas S. Wilson, *Julie Andrews,* foreword by Carol Burnett, Contemporary Books (Chicago, IL), 1996.
Contemporary Musicians, Volume 33, Gale (Detroit, MI), 2002.
Cottrell, John, *Julie Andrews: The Story of a Star,* Mayflower (London, England), 1968.
Hopkins, Lee Bennett, *More Books by More People: Interviews with Sixty-five Authors of Books for Children,* Citation Press (New York, NY), 1974.
International Directory of Films and Filmmakers, Volume 3: *Actors and Actresses,* St. James Press (Detroit, MI), 1996.
Newsmakers, Issue 1, Gale (Detroit, MI), 1996.

Windeler, Robert, *Julie Andrews,* 1970, revised edition published as *Julie Andrews: A Biography,* St. Martin's Press (New York, NY), 1982.

Windeler, Robert, *Julie Andrews: A Life on Stage and Screen,* Thorndike Press (Thorndike, ME), 1997.

PERIODICALS

Back Stage, September 14, 2001, Mike Salinas, "Kennedy Center Awards Go to Andrews, Nicholson," p. 6.

Booklist, February 15, 2000, Michael Cart, review of *Little Bo: The Story of Bonnie Boadicea,* p. 1112; December 1, 2002, Kathy Broderick, review of *Dumpy and the Big Storm,* p. 673.

Christian Science Monitor, November 11, 1971.

Family Circle, July 10, 2001, Glen Plaskin, interview with Andrews, pp. 28-29.

Kirkus Reviews, November 1, 2003, review of *Simeon's Gift,* p. 1310.

M2 Best Books, November 3, 2003, "Julie Andrews Launches New Imprint with HarperCollins."

People, May 27, 1996, "Victor Victorious," p. 88; December 13, 1999, "Missing Melodies: Julie Andrews, Her Singing Voice Stilled, Keeps on Trouping as an Actress," p. 175.

Publishers Weekly, November 1, 1999, review of *Little Bo,* p. 84; September 11, 2000, Jennifer M. Brown, "Julie Andrews Edwards," p. 32; September 25, 2000, review of *Dumpy the Dump Truck,* p. 115; August 27, 2001, John F. Baker, "Julie Andrews Edwards," p. 13; April 8, 2002, review of *Little Bo in France: The Further Adventures of Bonnie Boadicea,* pp. 229-230; October 27, 2003, review of *Simeon's Gift,* p. 68; November 3, 2003, Steve Anable, "Busy Brit," p. 23.

Saturday Evening Post, May-June, 1996, Earl L. Conn, interview with Andrews, pp. 36-40.

School Library Journal, December, 1999, Lee Bock, review of *Little Bo,* p. 94; April, 2001, Martha Link, review of *Dumpy the Dump Truck* and *Dumpy at School,* p. 106; October, 2002, Linda M. Kenton, review of *Little Bo in France,* p. 103; November, 2003, Rosalyn Pierini, review of *Simeon's Gift,* p. 91.

Time, May 20, 1996, Belinda Luscombe, "You Can Take This Nomination and . . .," p. 81; October 16, 2000, Evan Levy, review of *Dumpy the Dump Truck,* p. F20.

Time for Kids, October 24, 2003, Carson Satterfield, interview with Andrews, p. 8.

Variety, September 24, 2001, Richard Natale, "Julie Andrews Resonates in Seventh Showbiz Decade," p. 60.

ONLINE

Internet Broadway Database, http://www.ibdb.com/ (April 12, 2004), "Julie Andrews."

Internet Movie Database, http://www.imdb.com/ (April 12, 2004), "Julie Andrews."*

ASQUITH, Ros

Personal

Born in Sussex, England; married John Fordham; children: two sons. *Education:* Camberwell Art School, B.A. (with honors).

Addresses

Office—The Guardian, 119 Farringdon Rd., London EC1R 3ER, England. *Agent*—Rosemary Canter, Peter Fraser Dunlop, Inc., 34-43 Russell St., London WG2B 5HA, England. *E-mail*—rosasquith@aol.com.

Career

Graphic designer and mural painter, 1973-77; *City Limits,* theatre editor, 1981-90; *Time Out* and *Observer,* theatre critic, 1976-90; *The Guardian,* London, England, cartoonist, 1982—.

Member

Society of Authors, British Cartoonists Association, Cartoon Art Trust, Critics Circle.

Writings

SELF-ILLUSTRATED

Baby!, Macdonald Optima (London, England), 1988.

Toddler!, Pandora Press (London, England), 1989.

I Was a Teenage Worrier, Piccadilly Press (London, England), 1989.

Babies!, Pandora Press (London, England), 1990.

Green!, Pandora Press (London, England), 1991.

I Was a Teenage Worrier: Dilemma Handbook, Piccadilly Press (London, England), 1992.

The Teenage Worrier's Friend: All-in-One Diary, Address Book, and Survival Kit, Piccadilly Press (London, England), 1993.

The Teenage Worrier's Guide to Lurve, Piccadilly Press (London, England), 1996.

The Teenage Worrier's Christmas Survival Guide, Piccadilly Press (London, England), 1996.

The Teenage Worrier's Guide to Life, Corgi (London, England), 1997.

The Teenage Worrier's Pocket Guide to Romance, Corgi (London, England), 1998.

The Teenage Worrier's Pocket Guide to Families, Corgi (London, England), 1998.

The Teenage Worrier's Pocket Guide to Mind & Body, Corgi (London, England), 1998.

The Teenage Worrier's Pocket Guide to Success, Corgi (London, England), 1998.

The Teenage Worrier's Worry Files, Corgi (London, England), 1999.

The Teenage Worrier's Panick Diary, Corgi (London, England), 2000.

JUVENILE FICTION

Nora Normal and the Great Shark Rescue, Hodder Children's Books (London, England), 1996.

Nora Normal and the Great Ghost Adventure, Hodder Children's Books (London, England), 1997.

Bad Hair Days, Orchard Books (London, England), 1997.

Keep Fat Class, Orchard Books (London, England), 1997.

Unbridled Passion, Orchard Books (London, England), 1998.

Make It Me, Orchard Books (London, England), 1998.

Ball!, illustrated by Sam Williams, Dorling Kindersley (New York, NY), 1998.

My Do It!, illustrated by Sam Williams, Dorling Kindersley (New York, NY), 2000.

Trixie Tempest and the Amazing Talking Dog, Collins (London, England), 2003.

Trixie Tempest and the Ghost of St. Aubergine's, Collins (London, England), 2003.

Boo!, illustrated by Andi Good, HarperCollins (London, England), 2003.

Babies, illustrated by Sam Williams, Simon & Schuster (New York, NY), 2003.

Drama Queen, Orchard Books (London, England), 2003.

The Love Bug, Orchard Books (London, England), 2003.

All for One, Orchard Books (London, England), 2003.

Frock Shock, Orchard Books (London, England), 2003.

Three's a Crowd, Orchard Books (London, England), 2003.

Mrs. Pig's Night Out, illustrated by Selina Young, Hodder & Stoughton (London, England), 2003.

Trixie Tempest's ABZ of Life, Collins (London, England), 2004.

Also author of *Pass the Parcel,* Collins (London, England), and *Trixie Tempest and the Witches' Academy,* Collins (London, England).

ILLUSTRATOR

(Contributor of photographs) Elizabeth Leyh, *Concrete Sculpture in the Community,* Institute for Social Enterprise (Boston, MA), 1980.

Angela Phillips, *Your Body, Your Baby, Your Life,* Pandora Press (London, England), 1983.

Diana Coles, *The Clever Princess,* Sheba Feminist (London, England), 1983.

Yvonne Coppard Quirk, *Not Dressed Like That, You Don't!,* Piccadilly Press (London, England), 1991.

Yvonne Coppard Quirk, *Everybody Else Does! Why Can't I?: More Diaries of a Teenager,* Piccadilly Press (London, England), 1992.

Amanda Cuthbert and Angela Holford, *The Briefcase and the Baby: A Nanny and Mother's Handbook,* Mandarin (London, England), 1992.

Nick Fisher, *Inside Men's Minds,* Piccadilly Press (London, England), 1992.

Dick King-Smith, *Dirty Gertie Mackintosh,* Corgi (London, England), 1996.

The adorable qualities of infants are depicted in a charming picture book with rhyming text by Ros Asquith, culminating with a mirror page for infant readers to enter the story. (From Babies, *illustrated by Sam Williams.)*

Francesca Simon, *Helping Hercules,* Dolphin (London, England), 1999.

Anne Fine, *Charm School,* Doubleday (London, England), 1999.

Rosie Rushton, *All Change,* Barrington Stoke (Edinburgh, Scotland), 2001.

Yvonne Coppard and Emily Huws *Mega Miliwn* (title means, "To Be a Millionaire"), Gwasg Gomer (Llandysul, Wales), 2001.

Also illustrator, Patricia Hewitt, *Your Second Baby,* and Angela Phillips, *Until They Are Five.* Illustrator of numerous nonfiction titles for young readers in the United Kingdom, including *Answers to Acne, Herpes, Law Book, Pay Less to Keep Warm, Gareth Parry's DIY Book, Sic Transit, Judging Women, Genital Herpes and What to Do about It, HIV AIDS and What to Do about It, Thrush and What to Do about It,* and *Out on a Limb.*

Work in Progress

Baby's Shoe, for Random House; *Wizard's Walk,* for Little Tiger; *Mrs. Pig II,* for Hodder & Stoughton; *THING!,* for Oxford University Press; and *The Life and Loves of Amy Chicken,* for Transworld.

Sidelights

Ros Asquith contributes a regular cartoon feature, *Doris,* to England's *Guardian.* Many young readers in Great Britain know her better, however, for her lively "Teenage Worrier" books that realistically explore the many anxious moments facing teens, and how to solve them with humor and self-reliance. Asquith covers some of the same ground in her fiction, particularly the "Trixie Tempest" books aimed at the "tween" market of readers between the ages of nine and twelve. Although Asquith is better known in the United Kingdom, where her "Teenage Worrier" series includes some bestsellers, she is becoming more visible in the United States as the author of read-aloud books for the very youngest audience: babies and toddlers. These dual interests in simple picture books and humorous commentary for teens have been a part of the author's publishing profile since early in her career.

An honors graduate of Camberwell Art School, Asquith worked in graphic design and mural painting before moving into cartooning in the 1980s. She has also served as a theatre critic for several English periodicals. By 1990 she was well established as a cartoonist, author, and illustrator, with many projects running simultaneously. The "Teenage Worrier" series, for instance, has run into a dozen volumes, many of which were published in the same years that she wrote other fiction or picture book titles. Additionally, the artist/author herself told *SATA* that she has lost count of the number of covers she has designed for books by other writers.

Among Asquith's popular titles in America are *My Do It!, Babies,* and *Mrs. Pig's Night Out.* All three of these books aim at a preschool audience and reflect actions

Mr. Pig and his young ones let things get out of hand when Mrs. Pig is absent for the evening in Asquith's fun-loving picture book. (From Mrs. Pig's Night Out, *illustrated by Selina Young.)*

and adventures common to all young children. In *My Do It!,* a toddler insists on accomplishing tasks that his mother wants to do for him. Readers are invited to lift a flap to help the enterprising toddler along. Olga R. Barnes in *School Library Journal* found *My Do It!* "enjoyable," particularly for Sam Williams's "simple, uncluttered illustrations."

Babies, also illustrated by Williams, celebrates the many facets of babyhood and the wide variety of baby appearance and behavior. The final double-page spread, a Mylar mirror, invites a youngster to see himself or herself as part of the book. "Young children and their parents will find this short, simple picture book irresistible," predicted Carolyn Phelan in *Booklist.* In *School Library Journal,* Blair Christolon praised *Babies* for its "cozy rhyming text" and "colorful illustrations."

A cluster of piglet siblings run amok in *Mrs. Pig's Night Out.* As Mrs. Pig prepares to go out without her children, they weep and wail for her—until she leaves. Then the youngsters manipulate their weary father, despite his protests that it's time for bed. Pillow fights and extra television-watching ensue, and eventually it's Father Pig who goes to sleep. A mad scramble for bed at Mrs. Pig's return does not fool the wise mother: She notes that the piglets are in bed in their daytime clothes. Nevertheless, she is good-natured about it, praising her husband for a job well done. A *Publishers Weekly* critic noted of the title: "The premise may be an oldie, but this team turns it into a goodie." Be Astengo in *School Library Journal* felt that both parents and children "will recognize and laugh at the ruses of the clever piglets over their domestically incompetent father."

Biographical and Critical Sources

PERIODICALS

Booklist, February 1, 2003, Carolyn Phelan, review of *Babies,* p. 999; May 15, 2003, Ilene Cooper, review of *Mrs. Pig's Night Out,* p. 1668.

Publishers Weekly, December 16, 2002, p. 65; May 12, 2003, review of *Mrs. Pig's Night Out,* p. 65.

School Library Journal, October, 2000, Olga R. Barnes, review of *My Do It!,* p. 110; March, 2003, Blair Christolon, review of *Babies,* p. 176; August, 2003, Be Astengo, review of *Mrs. Pig's Night Out,* p. 122.

B

BARRINGER, William 1940-1996

Personal

Born April 17, 1940, in Toronto, Ontario, Canada; died, 1996; son of William (an actor) and Joyce Barringer; married second wife, Judi Saltman (a professor); children: Jeff, Brandy, Anne. *Education:* Attended Ball State University. *Hobbies and other interests:* Folk music, singing.

Career

Actor in television and film, Los Angeles, CA, 1961-63; *The Journal Herald,* Dayton, OH, columnist, 1968-69; *Detroit Free Press,* Detroit, MI, columnist, 1969-70; *Monday Magazine,* Victoria, BC, Canada, founding editor and contributor, 1975-77; *Vancouver Sun,* Vancouver, BC, Canada, editor and contributor, 1980-84; *The Province,* Vancouver, BC, Canada, editor and contributor, 1984-85; writer. *Military service:* U.S. Army, 1963-65.

Writings

Gregory and Alexander, Orca Book Publishers (Custer, WA), 2003.

Sidelights

William Barringer worked as a journalist and editor in Canada and the United States. His only picture book, *Gregory and Alexander,* was published seven years after his death. *Gregory and Alexander* is the story of a mouse, Gregory, and his caterpillar friend, Alexander. When Gregory saves Alexander from an insect collector, the two become fast friends. One day, as they watch a kite in the park where they live, Gregory wishes he could fly one himself. Alexander cautions patience, spins a cocoon, and eventually emerges as a butterfly. A helpful spider provides the string, and Gregory finally has his kite. Susan Mille in *Resource Links* liked the way the story offers readers "an opportunity to talk about the 'cycle of life' and friendship."

Biographical and Critical Sources

PERIODICALS

Resource Links, June 1, 2003, Susan Mille, review of *Gregory and Alexander.*
School Library Journal, September, 2003, Grace Oliff, review of *Gregory and Alexander,* p. 168.

*   *   *

BARTLETT, Alison

Personal

Female.

Addresses

Home—Bristol, England. *Agent*—c/o Author Mail, Candlewick Press, 2067 Massachusetts Ave., Cambridge, MA 02140.

Career

Author and illustrator of children's books.

Writings

Cat among the Cabbages, Levinson (London, England), 1996, Dutton (New York, NY), 1997.
Eric the Reindeer, Hodder (London, England), 1997.

ILLUSTRATOR

Malorie Blackman, Alexander McCall Smith, and Sally-Ann Lever, *Crazy Crocs,*, Longman (Harlow, England), 1994.

Vivian French, *Oliver's Vegetables,* Orchard Books (New York, NY), 1995.

Vivian French, *Bob the Dog,* Hodder (London, England), 1996.

Meredith Hooper, *A Cow, a Bee, a Cookie, and Me,* Kingfisher (New York, NY), 1997.

Rory S. Lerman, *Charlie's Checklist,* Orchard Books (New York, NY), 1997.

Meredith Hooper, *Honey Biscuits,* Kingfisher (London, England), 1997.

Cally Poplak, *Only Molly,* Mammoth (London, England), 1998.

Vivian French, *Oliver's Fruit Salad,* Orchard Books (New York, NY), 1998.

Judy Hindley, reteller, *Ten Bright Eyes,* Peachtree (Atlanta, GA), 1998.

Berlie Doherty, *Paddiwak and Cosy,* Orchard Books (New York, NY), 1999.

Cally Poplak, *No More Pets!,* Mammoth (London, England), 1999.

Anna Wilson, *Over in the Grasslands,* Macmillan (London, England), 1999, Little, Brown (Boston, MA), 2000.

Vivian French, *Growing Frogs,* Candlewick Press (Cambridge, MA), 2000.

Michael Lawrence, *The Caterpillar That Roared,* Dorling Kindersley (New York, NY), 2000.

Abby Irvine, *Dougie Duck Can't Swim,* Tango (London, England), 2000.

Vivian French, reteller, *The Tiger and the Jackal,* Walker (New York, NY), 2001.

Vivian French, *Oliver's Milk Shake,* Orchard Books (New York, NY), 2001.

Juliet Dallas-Conté, *Cock-A-Moo-Moo,* Macmillan (London, England), 2001.

Simon Puttock, *A Story for Hippo: A Book about Loss,* Scholastic Press (New York, NY), 2001.

Sally Grindley, *Outside Bears,* Oxford University Press (Oxford, England), 2002.

Simon Puttock, *Pig's Digger,* Egmont (London, England), 2002.

Giles Andreae, *Welcome to the World,* Macmillan (London, England), 2002.

Marjorie Blackmand, *Jessica Strange,* Hodder (London, England), 2002.

Penelope Lively, *A Martian in the Supermarket* (previously published as *Judy and the Martian*), Hodder (London, England), 2002.

Janet Thomas, *Can I Play?,* Egmont (London, England), 2003.

Vivian French, *T. Rex,* Candlewick Press (Cambridge, MA), 2004.

Sidelights

Alison Bartlett's career as a children's book author and illustrator started in the early 1990s and met with immediate success. Bartlett has adorned the pages of numerous children's books, including *Growing Frogs,* the popular "Oliver" series by author Vivian French, and *Over in the Grasslands* by Anna Wilson, just to name a few. Bartlett's use of bright colors and her simplistic drawing style promise picture-book afficionados plenty of excitement peppered with an air of mystery.

Bartlett has collaborated most frequently with children's author Vivian French. Part of French's "Oliver" series, *Oliver's Fruit Salad* follows picky protagonist Oliver, as he expands his pallet beyond his staple diet of French fries. Prompted by fond memories of helping his grandfather tend to his fruit garden, Oliver now admits an interest in helping his mother to make a fruit salad. While Oliver may not initially want to actually eat fruit, he enjoys helping his mom with shopping and salad-making. When the time comes to taste the fruits of his labor, Oliver realizes fruit salad is not half bad. Praising "Bartlett's sturdy, unbordered double-page-spread paintings"—colored with "srawberry red, lemon yellow, lime green, and more"—*Booklist* contributor Stephanie Zvirin described the illustrator's style as "so unaffected that it resembles children's own artwork."

Bartlett once again captures readers with her vibrant illustrations for French's *Growing Frogs.* In this quirkily titled book, a young girl studies the development and growth cycle of frogs with her mother. Collecting eggs from a nearby pond, the two monitor the metamorphosis from tadpole to frog, as it takes place before their eyes. Readers share in watching the change take place with the help of Bartlett's detailed illustrations, as intense hues of greens and purples help communicate the amphibian transformation. Jody McCoy, writing in *School Library Journal,* called *Growing Frogs* a "hopping-good collaboration," and commented that the illustrations "are just right for a first encounter with tadpole mysteries." A reviewer for *Horn Book* complimented Bartlett's use of color: vibrant hues are used in depicting the discovery period, while more subdued colors are utilized when developmental changes slow. Bartlett's "use of multiple frames showing tadpole and frog development paces the action well while allowing enough detail for readers to see small, but important, changes," added the *Horn Book* contributor.

Biographical and Critical Sources

PERIODICALS

Booklist, February 1, 1997, Carolyn Phelan, review of *Cat among the Cabbages,* p. 994; June 1, 1997, Ilene Cooper, review of *A Cow, a Bee, a Cookie, and Me,* p. 171; June 1, 1997, Julie Corsaro, review of *Charlie's Checklist,* p. 1719; October 15, 1998, Stephanie Zvirin, review of *Oliver's Fruit Salad,* p. 426; August, 1999, Shelley Townsend-Hudson, review of *Paddiwak and Cozy,* p. 2063; August, 2001, Shelley Townsend-Hudson, review of *Oliver's Milk Shake,* p. 2129.

Horn Book, May, 2000, review of *Growing Frogs,* p. 332.

Kirkus Reviews, August 1, 2001, review of *A Story for Hippo: A Book about Loss,* p. 1130.

Publishers Weekly, March 24, 1997, review of *Charlie's Checklist,* p. 83; July 24, 2000, review of *Over in the Grasslands,* p. 247.

School Library Journal, September, 2000, Bina Williams, review of *The Caterpillar That Roared,* p. 203; May, 2000, Jody McCoy, review of *Growing Frogs,* p. 161; November, 2000, Gay Lynn Van Vleck, review of *Over in the Grasslands,* p. 138; June, 2001, DeAnn Tabuchi, review of *Oliver's Milk Shake,* p. 114; November, 2001, Kathy M. Newby, review of *A Story for Hippo,* p. 133; May, 2002, Shawn Brommer, review of *Cock-a-Moo-Moo,* p. 111.*

* * *

BENNETT, James (W.) 1942-

Personal

Born in 1942; son of William (a pastor) and Margaret (a homemaker) Bennett; married Judith Vensel (a nurse), 1967; children: Jason. *Education:* Illinois Wesleyan University, B.A., 1964; Illinois State University, M.A., 1966. *Hobbies and other interests:* Mythology, photography.

Addresses

Agent—c/o Author Mail, Holiday House, 425 Madison Avenue, New York, NY, 10017.

Career

Writer. Worked as a teacher of creative writing at a community college until 1976; aide to high school-aged, mentally handicapped students, Bloomington, IL, 1983-95. Writer-in-residence for Illinois secondary schools.

Awards, Honors

1995's Finest YA Novel designation, *Voice of Youth Advocates,* 1996, for *The Squared Circle.*

Writings

FOR YOUNG ADULTS

I Can Hear the Mourning Dove, Houghton (Boston, MA), 1990.
Dakota Dream, Scholastic (New York, NY), 1994.
The Squared Circle, Scholastic (New York, NY), 1995.
Blue Star Rapture, Simon & Schuster (New York, NY), 1998.
Plunking Reggie Jackson, Simon & Schuster (New York, NY), 2001.
Faith Wish, Holiday House (New York, NY), 2003.

OTHER

A Quiet Desperation, Nelson (Nashville, TN), 1983.
The Flex of the Thumb, Pin Oak Press (Springfield, IL), 1996.

James Bennett, 2004

(With Donald Raycraft) *Old Hoss,* McFarland, 2002.
Harvey Porter Does Dallas, PublishAmerica, 2004.
(With Charles Merrill Smith) *How the Bible Was Built* Eerdman's (Grand Rapids, MI), 2004.

Work in Progress

Fresh Killed and *Grounded Out,* novels for young adults.

Sidelights

Writer James Bennett draws heavily on personal experience in his novels for young adult readers. His high school-aged protagonists are often emotionally or intellectually confused individuals unable to summon the emotional strength to deal with the circumstances that confront them in school, at home, and in other social situations. Only the caring, compassionate support of others can provide Bennett's characters with a resilient lifeline to adulthood. Many of Bennett's novels have the theme of the individual set against the institution; Bennett theorizes that everyone has feelings of rebellion against institutional wounds. "I think any book that I have written would take any reader on a trip to answer these questions: 'Who am I within this framework? How do I define myself? How do I establish integrity but know the difference between just rebelling for its own sake and rebelling based on some imperative?', " Bennett explained to Jon Saari in an interview with *Authors and Artists for Young Adults (AAYA)*. Some of Bennett's books also deal with mental illness. "I would like my readers to recognize that the handicapped are not throw-away people," Bennett told *Publishers Weekly* interviewer Lynda Brill Comerford. "Within them lies enormous courage and a strong nourishing drive."

Bennett enjoyed journalism since he was fourteen and created his own newspaper, but it was not until his junior year at college that he had his first thoughts of becoming a writer. Subsequent graduate studies in English at Illinois State University led Bennett to a career teaching creative writing to community college students. In 1974, however, Bennett suffered an emotional breakdown; during his recovery in a psychiatric hospital, he began to view writing as a way of expressing his feelings and promoting an increased awareness of the plight of many who are challenged by mental and emotional disorders.

During the period of his own hospitalization in the late 1970s, Bennett was particularly troubled by the acquaintance of a young woman, a fellow patient who was notably emotionally withdrawn. *I Can Hear the Mourning Dove,* his first novel for young adults, is based on his impressions of that young woman. "I knew nothing about the girl's background or diagnosis," Bennett explained to Comerford. "She was difficult to approach, but I realized that it was worth the effort to get through her shy exterior and discover the human being inside." In addition to recreating the young patient's speech and mannerisms—both on and off medication—in his novel, Bennett had to do some extensive research into the world of female adolescents to realistically portray his young heroine. Three years of effort culminated in Bennett's first highly praised work for young adults. Published in 1990, *I Can Hear the Mourning Dove* is the story of Grace Braun, a "crazy wild" sixteen-year-old attempting to return to the outside world after spending several weeks in the supportive environment of a hospital psychiatric unit following her most recent unsuccessful attempt at suicide. This was not Grace's first stay in a psychiatric ward: she had suffered from periods of depression for many years. The recent death of her father and the stressful transition to a new school add to the young woman's difficulties in readjusting to "normal" teen life after her release; unfortunately, it takes only the hateful actions of a group of rowdy, uncaring teens to send her back to the hospital in a highly depressed, manic state. Fortunately, Grace's condition improves with the help of her psychiatrist, her mother, and Luke Wolf, a brash and angry teen hospitalized in police custody after he knowingly killed a paralyzed friend. "Few novels written for teenagers have dared to probe as deeply into mental illness" as *I Can Hear the Mourning Dove,* according to

Stephanie Zvirin, who praised Bennett's novel in *Booklist.* "With tenderness and remarkable insight, Bennett identifies the causes and effects of Grace's suffering," noted a *Publishers Weekly* reviewer.

In Bennett's second young adult novel *Dakota Dream,* teen protagonist Floyd Rayfield has replaced his early childhood memories of his natural mother and father with those of a long sequence of foster families and group homes. With a desperate need to belong somewhere, fifteen-year-old Floyd creates an internal sense of being a part of something by convincing himself that he is really a misplaced Dakota Indian; his main goal now becomes escaping the foster care system and joining "his people." Stealing a motorcycle, the young man makes an eight-hundred-mile journey to the Dakota tribe's Pine Ridge Reservation, where a vision quest taken with Chief Bear-in-cave and the active intervention of a naive but compassionate social worker help him to understand the real reasons for his fight against inflexible teachers and insensitive social workers. A *Kirkus Reviews* critic praised *Dakota Dream,* writing that the "dynamics between a thoughtful boy struggling to keep his unique spark alive and the oblivious public employees doing their best to quench it are poignantly realized." Deborah Stevenson of the *Bulletin of the Center for Children's Books* maintained that "this is a measured, serious story and Floyd, not your stereotypical problem kid, is admirable in his devotion and application." *Voice of Youth Advocates* contributor Shirley Carmony added: "Floyd is finely drawn and comes painfully alive for the reader."

Like Bennett's other novels, 1995's *The Squared Circle* features a teen struggling to deal with a series of emotional problems. This time, though, Sonny Youngblood must also try to cope with his mother's mental breakdown as she spirals toward hospitalization. Basketball provides the eighteen-year-old high school senior with an escape, and when his obsession with the game helps him to earn a sports scholarship to a university, it appears that he is on the verge of burying his troubles for good. Sonny's presence has an immediate impact on the team's success, as it moves up in the national rankings while Sonny himself emerges as a media celebrity. But not all is right with this picture; Sonny learns that there are strings attached to big-time college sports. He has already realized that campus fraternity life makes some unpleasant social demands through its ingrained hazing and racism, and his game has been affected by lethargy. In a dramatic scene that shows Sonny's emerging understanding of previously invisible forces, he challenges his uncle about the under-the-table payoffs. Then, in what appears to be a deliberate act, Sonny cuts the fingers off his right hand while chopping wood for an art class. "Interwoven around gritty, occasionally brutish, guys-only scenes of fraternity hazing, basketball team practice and tension-filled games is an acutely perceptive account of a young man's emotional and intellectual awakening," asserted a *Publishers Weekly* reviewer.

Calling the novel "a sobering read," Tom S. Hurlburt recommended in a *School Library Journal* review that *The Squared Circle* "should be thrust into the hands of any high school students who are contemplating playing revenue-producing sports" at large colleges or universities. "It is difficult to adequately describe the power of this book," exclaimed Dorothy M. Broderick in *Voice of Youth Advocates*. "It is a masterpiece." *The Squared Circle* was named "America's finest YA novel" for 1995 in *Voice of Youth Advocates*.

Blue Star Rapture, Bennett's second book on the corruption of college sports, takes place at a basketball camp, where Tyrone, a six-foot, nine-inch high schooler, is attracting the attention of the college scouts. The novel's narrator, T. J., is Tyrone's best friend, and the street agents (men who receive illegal payments for influencing high school players to sign with college teams) reason one way to Tyrone is through T. J. Meanwhile T. J. has befriended a girl at a nearby Bible camp who commits suicide, a plot development that permits Bennett to draw a parallel between religious fanaticism and college recruiting methods, as both use undue pressure tactics.

In *Faith Wish,* Bennett's main character is Anne-Marie, a popular teenage girl who is struggling to pass her classes her senior year. When she encounters the charasmatic evangelist, Brother Jackson, she is swept up in her new-found faith and her interest in the spiritual leader himself. The first time they are alone, Brother Jackson takes advantage of her and seduces her. At the same time that Anne-Marie discovers she has failed her senior year and will not be allowed to graduate, she also finds out that she is pregnant with Brother Jackson's baby. Instead of attending summer school in order to finish high school, she allows Brother Jackson to take her to an isolated girls' camp, where Anne-Marie tries to find God and herself. "This tale raises provocative questions about religious conviction and religious cults, blind faith and obsessive infatuation," wrote a reviewer for *Publishers Weekly.* Joel Shoemaker in *School Library Journal* also noted, "The book clearly communicates that religion can serve as a haven for evildoers and that vulnerable people can be harmed by religious people who take advantage."

The Flex of the Thumb, a baseball novel for adults, allowed Bennett to collaborate with his son, Jason, although not on the writing process. Jason, at the time twenty-three, published the book himself, setting the type and printing 10,000 copies. Jason marketed the book to libraries and bookstores on his own as well. "It helps me that dad has a good reputation as a writer," Jason told James Keeran of the *Pantagraph. The Flex of the Thumb* is an adult novel and the story of high school pitcher Vano Lucas who gets hit with a baseball bat between the eyes. The event changes his whole career, and when he goes to college, his focus is no longer on competetive sports; instead, he focuses on more contemplative arts. Bennett told Keeran that he'd written the novel five times over a span of twenty-five years. "It was the manuscript that was always lying around," he explained. "When I wasn't embroiled in something else, I went back to it." Bennett's other adult novels include 1983 title *A Quiet Desperation* and his satiric comedy *Harvey Porter Does Dallas,* a novel about a young man searching for his past.

Today, Bennett visits secondary schools to talk about writing and help students along the path to be writers. "I like to tell the students I was an underachiever. There are always kids who need to hear that," Bennett told Saari in *AAYA,* continuing, "I do like to be up front with them with the fact that I was not an outstanding student when I was young. I did not achieve a lot as a teenager. I did not mature until later. Teachers like to hear that too. I like to work with basic kids as well as honors kids."

Biographical and Critical Sources

BOOKS

Authors and Artists for Young Adults, vol. 26, Gale (Detroit, MI), 1999.

PERIODICALS

Booklist, January 15, 1991, Stephanie Zvirin, review of *I Can Hear the Mourning Dove,* p. 1052; January 15, 1994, Jeanne Triner, review of *Dakota Dream,* p. 918; December 15, 1995, Susan Dove Lempke, review of *The Squared Circle,* p. 697.
Bulletin of the Center for Children's Books, February, 1994, Deborah Stevenson, review of *Dakota Dream,* p. 182.
Kirkus Reviews, February 1, 1994, p. 138; November 1, 1995.
Kliatt, July, 2002, Barbara Jo McKee, review of *The Squared Circle,* p. 15.
Pantagraph, August 28, 1983, Barb Kueny, "Quiet Desperation," p. D2; August 13, 1996, James Keeran, "Author's Son Takes to the 'Road' to Sell Dad's Book," p. D1.
Publishers Weekly, July 13, 1990, Diane Robuck, review of *I Can Hear the Mourning Dove,* p. 57; December 21, 1990, Lynda Brill Comerford, interview with Bennett, p. 15; December 20, 1993, review of *Dakota Dream,* p. 73; November 20, 1995, p. 79; July 21, 2002, review of *The Squared Circle,* p. 92; June 2, 2003, review of *Faith Wish,* p. 53.
School Library Journal, December, 1995, Tom S. Hurlburt, review of *The Squared Circle,* p. 128; July, 2003, Joel Shoemaker, review of *Faith Wish,* p. 123.
Voice of Youth Advocates, October 1990, pp. 213-14; April, 1994, Shirley Carmony, review of *Dakota Dream,* pp. 22-23; February, 1996, Dorothy M. Broderick, review of *The Squared Circle,* p. 379.

Autobiography Feature

James Bennett

James Bennett contributed the following autobiographical essay to *SATA:*

In order to write an autobiographical essay, I will need to share candidly with readers my more than thirty year struggle with mental illness. For the struggle not only defines the person I've been most of my adult life, but substantially accounts for what I've accomplished—or been unable to accomplish—as an author.

But the "puzzle house" is not the place to begin.

I recall my childhood years as mostly carefree, happy, and secure. Some of that recollection may be by choice, as a means of escape from adult stress and disorientation, but not much, I think.

As a fiction writer, I was a late bloomer. I didn't publish my first book, *A Quiet Desperation,* until I was nearly forty-one. But as a journalist, I was like one of the early crocus breaking through the snow.

When I was about fourteen, in the small town of Canton, Illinois, I wrote, edited, and published my first newspaper. It was a weekly called the *Spectator.* I also handled the deliveries. I wrote the copy in longhand, essentially just outlining my take on the news items of the week which appeared in daily papers. This was in the middle fifties, so you could say I was a "Butch Wax" talking head, doing much the same thing as the news analysts do nowadays on cable channels such as Fox News or CNN.

At least half of the *Spectator* was about sports. For instance, I might analyze and break down Stan "The Man" Musial's weekly production as a batter (he and another Hall of Famer, Ted Williams, were the Barry Bonds and Sammy Sosa of their era.)

My mother typed the paper for me because I didn't know how. She used an old-fashioned Royal upright to cut a stencil. The use of stencils for such purposes nowadays is about as frequent as the use of horse-drawn plows.

As a youngster (and as an adult) I was very close to my mother. She was a stay-at-home mom of course; remember, this was the '50s of the *Ed Sullivan Show* and *Mickey Mouse Club.* Like most boys my age, Mousketeer Annette (Funicello) activated my developing hormones, even as Elvis Presley was doing likewise for the girls.

Author's parents, Rev. William and Margaret Morris Bennett, 1938.

In any case, I produced my newspaper during the summer months when school was out. We didn't have air conditioning in our house, but then neither did most other people. I can remember vividly the sweat rolling down my mother's face and frizzing her hair as she typed away at our dining room table, cutting the weekly stencil.

Bennett with sister Nancy, 1948.

When it was ready, I took it across the street to the Methodist Church, where my father was the pastor. He had no objection to my using the church's mimeograph machine (another dinosaur) to run my copies. Then it was time to collate and staple and make deliveries. I charged ten cents a copy. Most of the people who "subscribed" to the paper were friends of our family or downtown merchants who thought such creative efforts by a boy so young ought to be rewarded. I have no idea who actually read the thing.

*

But it was in the even smaller town of Monticello, Illinois, that I was first bitten by the newspaper bug. Monticello, which I still consider my "home" town, is located about 20 miles from Champaign-Urbana, home to the University of Illinois.

By the time I was ten or twelve, I was fascinated with newspapers. I had a morning paper route, delivering the Champaign-Urbana *Courier.* My mother rolled me out of bed at 5:30 each morning so I could be at the "warehouse" before six. The warehouse wasn't a warehouse at all, but that's what all the paperboys called it

(there were no girls delivering newspapers back then). It was actually an abandoned factory building but none of us knew what might have been manufactured there in the past.

The lights in the warehouse were harsh and glaring. One hundred-watt bulbs with no shades hung from the ceiling. All of us folded our papers in a tight tuck on a long counter. We were very good at this. We had to be, because we delivered the papers while riding our bicycles, throwing them on porches as we rode by. If they weren't tightly tucked they would fly open, forcing us to stop and gather up their scattered sections. Why we weren't smart enough to use rubber bands mystifies me even to this day.

I was usually the last one to leave the warehouse. My problem was that I tried to read the newspapers as I folded. I read the sports section to get scores and results. I read the comics. I skimmed the national news headlines and the letters to the editor. I even read obituaries sometimes. I was often a little late with my deliveries, but I can't remember getting into any trouble over it.

Reading newspapers rapidly improved my reading skills, although that certainly wasn't my goal. In any case, I was an advanced reader during my elementary school days and my newspaper interest was no doubt a factor.

WASHINGTON
SCHOOL DAYS 54-55

Sixth grade school picture, 1954-55; Bennett already had a paper route.

Monticello was a wonderful place to grow up—even for a "preacher's kid." It was, and is, a prosperous community with a Norman Rockwell courthouse square, church suppers, and Little League baseball. Churches and schools were the town's nerve centers. The locals were enthusiastic supporters of the high school athletic teams, as well as those of the University of Illinois. Monticello High School athletic teams carry the nickname "Sages." I've never heard of another school with the same nickname.

All of this rubbed off on me. At a very young age I was a bona fide sports "nut," trying to decide which professional sport I would star in when I grew up. My earliest heroes were high-profile athletes at Monticello High or the University. High school track phenom Larry LeCrone seemed larger than life as he often won six or seven events in the same meet. I can still recall his flashing white socks as he zoomed around the curve of the 220.

"Fightin' Illini" All-Americans like Johnny "Red" Kerr were often speakers at our Little League banquets. Kerr went on to play many years in the National Basketball Association (NBA) and was later the first head coach of the Chicago Bulls.

Except for math, I was a straight-*A* student in elementary grades, primarily because school came easy

for me. I certainly never worked at it much. But math gave me fits. I suppose I had some classic "mental block" in this area.

Monticello is also home to the sublime Allerton Park, the State of Illinois' best-kept tourist secret. Its several hundred acres of timber and nature trails along the Sangamon River include an immense Georgian mansion (now a conference center), reflecting pools, acres of formal European gardens and outdoor galleries of Old World statuary. Our church often had Sunday picnics there as well as softball games and nature walks. My first love, about the seventh or eighth grade, was Bonnie Schroth, whose father, Buck, was resident director of the park. The Buck Schroth Nature Trail is still a signature location in Allerton. And Bonnie is still a dear friend of mine these forty years later.

*

My trouble with math brought me into conflict with our fifth grade teacher, the fearsome take-no-prisoners Mrs. Fisler. Mrs. Fisler clumped as she walked due to a heavy leg wrap she wore as a phlebitis treatment; you could always hear her coming down the hall. Many years later, at a class reunion, a close friend of mine named Lou Burgess admitted that he was scared of her, too, even though "I never even had her for a teacher." Her reputation was that menacing. Lou never had her because he attended Monticello's other elementary school.

Mrs. Fisler held me inside most days during recess so that I could try and catch up on my math workbook, which was always behind and usually full of errors. She gave the boys regular whippings with a long wooden paddle. I was on the painful end of several of these paddlings, although not nearly so often as some of the other boys in class, especially the luckless Chad Hubbard. She never paddled the girls.

I can remember the sharp pain along the back of my legs as well as the overwhelming smell of Mrs. Fisler's leg wrap medication which she tried to mask with generous latherings of perfume.

Although Monticello was a small town, the Methodist Church was large. It had more than a thousand members. The church had active choirs, Bible study groups, youth fellowship groups, Sunday school for all ages, and many other groups and activities. Potluck suppers were a weekly occurrence; I always liked them because of the array of homemade pies, cakes, cobblers, and cookies.

We even had occasional "revival meetings," usually in the summer, which I didn't like at all. I did everything possible to avoid them, usually with no luck. I was a normal youngster, so dressing up in scratchy suits and tight formal collars to listen to evangelical preachers rave on about fire and brimstone didn't cut it for me.

My father was a devoutly religious, often stern man, who gave countless hours each week to the needs of parishioners and church activities. Because of his devotion he was beloved by the town and the congregation. But he spent so much time attending to professional duties there was little time left over for me or my two younger sisters, Nancy and Martha Jean. (When I write e-mails to her even today, I call her "MJ" to tease her into a sort of Michael Jordan connection.)

Even in the little spare time he had, Dad was devout. I have vivid memories of stopping halfway down the stairs when I realized he was reading Bible passages aloud to himself in the living room. The 23rd Psalm was always in his repertoire. Looking back, I assume his private Bible reading and meditating were ways of dealing with stress (or maybe even crises). My father was a driven man in his profession, and a "worried man" as the Johnny Cash song puts it. He was a worry wort who slept fitfully. I don't believe he ever had a disorder on any clinical level, but I was—and am—a product of his genetics, so it's likely some of the mental health episodes I've experienced as an adult were already seedlings in my psychological soil.

My dad came by his piety naturally. His father, my Grandpa Bennett, was a Methodist pastor himself, serving churches in several small towns in Southern Illinois. He died when I was only nine, but my memories of this gentle, playful man are firm and fond. He loved to recite poems to us kids at bedtime (mostly those of Edgar Guest, which he had committed to memory). My wheelchair-bound grandmother used to pluck chickens at the kitchen sink before she burned off the pinfeathers. The smell was repulsive; when I recall those visits, it's still strong in my nostrils.

I did have modest athletic ability in those years. I was a good Little League baseball player and, by seventh and eighth grade, a promising basketball talent. I was also by this time an avid book reader, devouring the Tom Swift books, as well as those by authors such as John R. Tunis and Jackson Scholz. Unfortunately, I didn't spend near as much time reading homework assignments so my grades began to slide.

Because preachers' families move so often, I never got to attend Monticello High. It was traumatic for me and my sisters (as it would be for any young adolescent) when we moved away after I finished eighth grade. I had to part with many of my fastest friends—the Miller Brothers, Tim and Tom—and most significantly, my closest buddy, Lynn Hays, who lived on a farm I often visited for "sleepovers." Lynn died tragically in a tractor accident at age nineteen when we were both sophomores in college; it's a sorrow that still haunts me. He was a young man of integrity and generosity of spirit rarely found in teenagers. And of course there was Bonnie, the love of my life.

I've been blessed in recent years by attending Monticello High School class of '60 reunions, reestablishing

Bennett, 1957, already writing, editing, and distributing his first newspaper.

dozens of friendships. They call me "the ringer" but they let me come anyway.

We lived in Canton only two years. In 1958, we moved to Bloomington (IL), a large city (by my standards) of 40,000 residents. Its twin city, Normal, is home to Illinois State University. I completed my junior and senior years at Bloomington High.

*

At first I was lonely and lost in Bloomington. The move was another difficult adolescent adjustment. The friendship I made with Terry (Terrence) Smith helped me immensely. Terry and I were instant soul mates and established a deep friendship which lasted over many years and many places.

Terry was an aspiring writer and enjoyed early success with his first novel, *The Thief Who Came to Dinner,* which was published by Doubleday in 1969. Later, the book became a major motion picture. He published several other books of lesser success, and he loved "whodunits" so much that he wrote a series of detective novels under the pen name Phillips Lore. Unfortunately, Terry died in an automobile accident in December of 1988.

I need to mention too that his father, the Reverend Charles Merrill Smith, was highly significant in my life too. He was an author of religious satire, and his *New York Times* bestseller, *How to Become a Bishop without Being Religious,* is still a wickedly funny piece of work. Charles was such a mentor to me over the years that he soon became like a second father.

It was at Bloomington High that I was first exposed to serious journalism. Our school newspaper was annually the recipient of awards for excellence in statewide judging contests. The paper came out every Friday, so we had to write material on a tight deadline. Writers on our staff knew they had to produce good articles. We had a very demanding sponsor, a history teacher named Mr. Hostetler. If Mr. Hostetler didn't think our work measured up, he simply blue penciled it and left it out of the paper.

It happened to me often enough, that's for sure. And it hurt. As a junior, I was writing sports articles. I can remember writing what I thought was a terrific article about a thrilling BHS football victory on a Friday night. The next Monday, Mr. Hostetler blue penciled it, then privately told me why. "That game is old news already," he said. "By this coming Friday it will be stale as rotting fruit. Nobody will care."

"What about the writing?" I asked.

"The writing is good," he was willing to admit, "but it's not appropriate for a weekly newspaper. It would be fine for a daily. You need to be writing about things which will happen in the near future."

That is the guiding principle for a weekly newspaper—to write about events or situations which are upcoming events.

It did help that we had a staff of ten or twelve students who met in journalism class every day. We had the time to produce what our sponsor demanded. Still, it always hurt our pride when he would make us revise our copy and then maybe revise it again. He used to say, "There is only one standard—excellence."

Whenever people ask me who was influential in my development as a writer, my answer is simple and immediate: "More than anyone else, it was Roy Hostetler."

By my senior year I was sports editor of the paper. Rarely did I write an article which failed to meet his standards. For the first time in my life I understood the "rush" that could come from producing good writing. Because I played on the basketball team too, I had understood for a long time the high that came from scoring on the court. But my newspaper scoring was new to me and has served me well to this day. As for basket-

ball, I never was very good at it. I gave it up after high school.

*

In college (Illinois Wesleyan University, also in Bloomington) I joined the newspaper staff as a freshman. It wasn't too long before I was promoted to the sports editor position. By the time I was a junior, I was the newspaper's editor. This success came as a result of my demanding high school journalism experience.

I was also writing part time for the local newspaper, the Bloomington *Pantagraph,* a daily with a circulation of nearly 80,000 readers. I began as a sportswriter covering high school football and basketball games, then later took assignments that allowed me to branch out. I was covering political activities such as city council meetings, zoning board sessions, concerts, art shows and school board meetings. So I was involved in a great deal of journalism during my college days. Too much, in fact; I didn't have enough time to spend on my academic work and my grades suffered.

Journalism is excellent training ground for any would-be writer, fiction or otherwise. Like any newspaper writer, I learned about people and their issues. I learned about the community I lived in and agendas which disturbed or gratified it. Through countless interviews, I began to understand where/why people found their passions, took gratification from their successes, and suffered through their failures.

I found that my journalism experiences were also factors in my own growth as a person. Young adults are usually bored when it comes to community issues such as zoning guidelines, local taxes, liquor licenses, street repair, snow removal budgets, and so on. Journalism can be a crash course in maturity. That which makes us more mature makes us better candidates for authorship. That which gives us information is even more crucial.

Even today I still have journalism in my blood. I do occasional freelance articles for newspapers and magazines. I write a weekly column for a small "community" newspaper called the *Normalite.* I recently had the great fun of writing an article about a 102-year-old ex-football and basketball coach who is his university's oldest living alum. Interviewing him taught me about geography, philosophy, sport in West Virginia, values, and even the secrets to a long-lasting marriage.

*

Throughout high school and during my first two years of college, I was (and this is being generous) a mediocre student. I wasn't mature enough to get motivated in subject areas I found difficult or boring (mostly math and science). Repeatedly, I got what Jack Buck, the late St. Louis Cardinals broadcaster, called the "God Bless America" report card: "From sea (*C*) to shining sea (*C*)."

Family photo, 1958; back row: Bennett and sister Nancy; front row: father, William, sister Martha Jean, and mother, Margaret.

As I've said, the only reason I got *A*s in elementary school is that everything came easy to me; I never had to work. If you happen to be a student working below ability level, I hope you grow up faster than I did. Still, it's good to know that underachieving students can somehow find the level of maturity needed for academic success eventually, as well as success beyond the classroom. It wasn't until my junior and senior years of college that my name started showing up on the Dean's List. By this time, as an English major, I was studying literature almost exclusively. Because my interest level was high, so were my grades.

For the first time in my life I was captivated by great writing and great writers. I liked poetry, but I became deeply engrossed in the fiction of such major novelists as John Steinbeck, William Faulkner, Ernest Hemingway, James Joyce, F. Scott Fitzgerald, Flannery O'Conner, Lawrence Durrell, Virginia Woolf, and many others. I didn't have much spare time, since I was still editing the campus newspaper and working part time for the local daily. But in the spare time I did have, I devoured the novels of Edgar Rice Burroughs (he wrote the "Tarzan" series) and plenty of the detective "potboilers" by leading authors like Dashiell Hammett and Raymond Chandler. So I was gobbling up "great litera-

ture" at the same time I was reading novels more popular with the general public.

I decided I wanted to be one of these guys. I wanted to be a novelist. It was just as cool as scoring touchdowns or hitting home runs. And anyway, my life as an athlete (such as it was) had ended after high school.

Nowadays, my reading habits are quite different, although they are not aimless. What I read—for the most part—is dictated by the books or articles I'm working on. There is always research to do. Because I don't have as much energy as I did when I was younger, I don't read much fiction for pleasure. Nearly all of the books I read now are strategy driven rather than pleasure driven. They're still fun, though.

The research factor leads me to more nonfiction books and articles. Many of them are excellent works with narrative elements very similar to those found in fiction. For instance, when I was doing research for *Dakota Dream,* I read, among others, *Black Elk Speaks* by John Niehardt, and *Lakota Woman* by Mary Crow Dog. Both of them provided me with important background information about the Dakota Nation.

Later, I satisfied my thirst for American Indian history and culture by reading the superb *Counting Coup* by Larry Colton. I also added two other excellent Native American books to my personal library. *A Season on the Reservation* by basketball hall of famer Kareem Abdul-Jabbar and *Dancing at Halftime* by Carol Spindel not only increased my knowledge of Indian tribes and customs, but also helped me sketch out a *Dakota Dream* sequel. That goal has not been achieved yet, but if (when?) the time comes, all of these varied and consequential books will have increased my readiness.

College Sports Inc.: The Athletic Department vs. the University by Indiana University Professor Murray Sperber helped me better understand the corruption and deceit of college athletics, especially in terms of misleading accounting procedures usually practiced by athletic departments. Big-time football programs like those found in Florida or Ohio State claim to make huge profits, but they really don't, if you sit down carefully and count the costs.

Sperber's book provided solid information about big-time college sport in American culture. It helped me establish credible background material for *Blue Star Rapture* as well as *The Squared Circle,* perhaps my most honored book.

I read a very good book recently by legendary novelist Stephen King titled *On Writing: A Memoir of the Craft.* Like other books of its type, it aided me in outlining, character development, and narrative strategy. You could call it self-improvement reading. But please understand that such reading is much more than mere "homework." The books I choose to read to help in my own research are sources of pleasure as well.

And I haven't abandoned fiction reading altogether, although my habits in this area might seem a little peculiar. I read the same books over and over, often for the third or fourth time. These are usually books that reinforce my own personal philosophy of lean, mean, and tight.

When people ask me to name my favorite novels or works of fiction, this is the place I start. If I read a work of fiction several times over, it must be a piece that brings me exceptional gratification. Some of this fiction is the short story work of Flannery O'Conner. I read the stories ("A Good Man is Hard to Find" or "Parker's Back") for the pleasure of reading fine fiction, but also to study her techniques of narration, character development, irony, and the presence of evil. It amounts to reading two ways at once.

Other books which never cease to give me pleasure are Steinbeck's *Of Mice and Men,* and Hemingway's *The Old Man and the Sea.* Both books are tight and economical (they turn a little into a lot). Or, perhaps, they reach their goals without seeming to work at it. It all seems so easy, which, of course, it's not. But that's what good fiction can do. Any would-be writer can learn much about the importance of setting by reading either book, while the Hemingway masterpiece shows us layer upon layer of meaning. The way he does this by weaving seemingly inconsequential details (a ship's

Bennett as a college freshman, 1961.

mast, a defiant fish, bleeding hands, and Joe Dimaggio) into the total fabric of the tale teaches us ways to transform the ordinary into the extraordinary.

I have cited quite a few titles and authors here. I hope not too many. I do so because they have helped me while giving me pleasure. I also do so because I can recommend each of them to you with enthusiasm.

*

When spring of my senior year in college rolled around, I was toying with my own vague blueprints for plotting and characterization, but not with enough focus to write any competent fiction or even a useful outline. I applied for, and received, a graduate assistantship in English at Illinois State University, Normal, Illinois. I spent the next two years earning a master's degree while grading hundreds upon hundreds of freshman essays. As a "grad ass" (graduate assistant) I was paid 140 dollars a month but able to live on it.

I boarded with a close friend of mine, Rodney Sakemiller. His mother, a wonderful woman named Ruth, put me in the heavyweight division. She'd grown up on the farm and while she didn't have much formal education, she sure knew her way around the baking

Wedding photo of Bennett and bride Judie Vensel with both sets of parents, 1967.

pan. Breakfasts were generous servings of eggs and bacon. Dinners always included homemade pies and cakes; even her noodles were made from scratch. My mouth still waters. I gained more than twenty pounds during those two years and had trouble crossing my legs.

I paid Ruth eighty dollars a month for room, board, and laundry service. I had a paid-for '54 Ford which my grandmother had given me when her failing eyesight prevented her from driving. That left sixty dollars to cover all other expenses for the month. I got by on it. You could get a lot more mileage out of sixty dollars in the middle sixties than you can today.

In the fall of '66, I took my first teaching job at Black Hawk Junior College in Moline, Illinois. I was a very green teacher dipping my toe in the shallow end of the pool. Lots of support came from my department head, Tom Batell, a kind man who had earlier been one of my professors at Illinois Wesleyan.

It was in 1967 that I met and married Judie Vensel, who has now been my wife for nearly forty years. Un-

usual circumstances brought us together. A local community theatre director talked me into taking the romantic lead in Kaufman and Hart's *You Can't Take It with You.* Judie was the other romantic lead. We were the "straight guys" in a play filled with outrageous characters. I stumbled through my part in undistinguished fashion but at least I fell in love. I had never been in a play before, nor since.

In the spring of '68, Judie and I longed to experience some of the big, bad world beyond the Midwest. I landed a job teaching at Orange County Community College in Middletown, New York, located some sixty-five miles northwest of New York City in the graceful Catskill Mountains. It was a a warm and pleasant campus where we made many friends with students and faculty. Some of my colleagues there remain close friends even today. At OCCC, I was soon promoted to associate professor and took on the role of sponsor for the student newspaper. I remembered all of Mr. Hostetler's newspaper guidelines and imposed them on the student staff, although several of these students weren't pleased or amused. The college newspaper was voted best community college newspaper in the state of New York two years running.

During this period of time, we all experienced the electric counterculture movement of life on a college campus. "Peace, Love, Dope," seemed to carry voltage all the higher since we were located so near to New York City. Neither my wife nor I had much to do with drugs, but we stood with friends, colleagues, and students in countless candlelight vigils and marches protesting the Vietnam War. We were part of protest marches in Middletown, New York City, and Washington, D.C. In those controversial times it seemed nearly impossible to get through an entire class session without at least a brief discussion of The War. After all these years, I still regard the wrongheaded presence of U.S. military might in Vietnam to be one of the most shameful periods in our nation's history.

In 1971-72, I took a year's leave of absence so we could spend that year in County Cork, Ireland. Terry Smith, his wife, and his dad Charles Merrill (along with wife Betty) joined us. This was the year I was going to write the "great American novel." That didn't happen, but I did learn more about my own writing goals, strengths, and shortcomings.

What did happen was that we circulated intimately with the charming Irish rural folks, helped build thatched roofs for homes and barns, carried milk home in cans from local farms, tried to survive with hopeless "beaters" of old English cars, and traveled extensively in Europe. That was a year we will never forget.

*

Back in New York, the greatest blessing of our lives occurred in February of '73 when our son, Jason, was born. I was a parent two months before my thirty-first birthday, and I took such joy in my new son I found my world revolving around him. When he was scarcely more than three months old I was taking him to class, picnics, shopping, parks, hiking and the like. I regretted leaving the house without him. I kept a daily journal of his development, from first words to first teeth, even to first poem. His first verbal poem was: "P.U. Sidney has cows."

*

But on a cold and snowy morning in January of 1974, I got out of bed to discover that my life would never be the same again. With no warning, I was undergoing a major mental breakdown characterized by runaway anxiety and depression. My stomach was tight as a fist, day after day, and week after week. I couldn't eat or sleep. I was constantly terrified, with no observable cause, perpetually in the "fight or flight" mechanism, as they say out in the wild.

I spent some time in the Orange County mental facility and lots more time with counselors over the next months. I still don't know how I made it through class-

Bennett, Judie, and son, Jason, 1973.

room sessions; sometimes I didn't. Lots of those I did complete I suspect were pretty ragged and unproductive. If I got two hours of sleep during the night I considered myself lucky. My failing appetite (not surprisingly) caused a severe weight loss; during the twelve months from January '74 till January '75 I went from 180 pounds to 120. I had the shakes most of the time and often lost my balance. I remember flashbulbs going off behind my eyes. I had become completely dysfunctional, but neither doctors nor counselors could figure out why. And that made it all the more hopeless and helpless; if there was no way to identify a cause, then how could I hope to find a cure?

It was in the spring of '75 that I resigned my teaching position at OCCC. I couldn't perform my teaching duties anymore and it was a terror to try. I had no idea what I would do and I feared for my family, but I felt more than anything that I needed to get back "home." So off we headed for Illinois, with a packed-to-the-gills U-Haul truck, bidding a woeful, tearful farewell to our town, our campus, and our many close friends.

I landed a part-time job as youth minister at First Methodist Church of Urbana, Illinois, a job I held for two years. The senior pastor, Reverend Bob Mulligan, was a friend of my father's. The pay was not nearly enough to support a family so I held other part-time jobs shoveling grain, mowing grass, and painting fences for the Champaign parks department. Judie also found part-time work as a secretary.

During these two years and the ones to follow, I was in ongoing therapy and psychoanalysis. We tried and tried to get to the bottom of what my disorder might be, but without much luck. I was diagnosed with acute anxiety disorder, acute depression, manic-depressive (bi-polar) disorder, and adult Attention Deficit Disorder (ADD). It seems now, so many years later, that all these diagnoses were right but only partly so. One psychiatrist I saw for several years eventually said I had "a cluster of symptoms" of all these forms of illness, but he had no way of saying what the primary one might be.

Many, many medications in various dosages and combinations didn't seem to help. Neither did the hundreds of counseling sessions. I still struggled day after day to eat, to sleep, to function. No matter how bad it all seemed to be, I never gave up or considered suicide, although some of the mental health professionals I was working with considered me a suicide risk. But I wasn't; I had my wife, and I had my son.

*

In the spring of 1977, my family and I caught a wonderful break when I was hired as manager of East Bay Camp on Lake Bloomington (IL). The camp had recently been purchased by the Methodists from the Baptists after it had gone into bankruptcy. Once again, my father's connections had come to my aid.

Moving to East Bay wasn't just a strong opportunity, it was a rich homecoming as well. I had gone to church camp here as a youngster and both of my parents had often been camp counselors. It really did feel like "home."

Our son Jason couldn't have been plopped down in a more desirable childhood setting. There was swimming on the beach in warm weather. There was sledding down snowy hills onto the ice in the winter. There were summer staff college students to overindulge him and hundreds of acres of woods and timber to play in. We lived in a comfortable, year-round residence, extremely busy during warm weather months, but able to throttle down a bit during the winter.

It was during those winter months that I began writing again, as well as I could. But afflicted with the never-ending anxiety, irritability, depression, restlessness and lack of focus, my efforts were shaky at best.

Not that I wasn't trying (to become a published author, that is). I always submitted manuscripts to publishers the proper way, sending a query letter first, so the editor I contacted could choose to read the book or not. It's a cardinal sin to send an "unsolicited" manuscript to a publisher. Such books don't get read and rarely get returned. They find their resting place in the publisher's dumpster, in most cases still unopened.

Eventually, when I got the green light from an editor, I sent in the manuscript with my fingers crossed. These manuscripts, all fiction, were usually rejected. Getting rejected is always a bitter pill to swallow, of course. Looking back, I realize now that those manuscripts deserved to be rejected. They weren't very good. But I was learning as I went by identifying weaknesses and striving not to repeat them. I understood that the only way I would find success as an author would be through trial and error, hard work, and persistence.

I couldn't know it at the time, but even all of my good novels—eventually praised by critics and organizations like the American Library Association—would face rocky roads to publication. The truth is every book I've published was rejected three or four times before it found its way into print.

My ambition to become a published author was strong, but it was becoming clear to me that I wasn't especially talented or gifted. Some people who are long-time students of fiction don't believe that there are inherently "talented" or "gifted" writers. These people believe that good writers achieve their success almost exclusively as a result of learning the craft, working hard, and being persistent. I would have to define my own successes in these terms, but I do believe there are gifted fiction writers.

The gift is not in a showcase vocabulary or the ability to write lyrical sentences; it is, rather, their vision. Such gifted authors are able to see quickly how parts fit together to form a whole. Two of the finest twentieth century fiction writers, James Joyce and Flannery O'Conner, had this "vision gift." I know this from reading their work, biographical information about them, and letters they wrote. Because of this superior vision, gifted writers can put together a good working outline more easily than most other authors.

Finally, in 1983, I published my first book, *A Quiet Desperation*.

The camp manager position turned out to be the best—and worst—of all possible jobs for me. There were more than five hundred acres and in excess of one hundred buildings, counting all the summer camper cabins. Never was there a day without screens to repair, painting to be done, grass to be mown, boats to be housed, or cleaning to be done (our temporary seasonal staff was never quite large enough to handle it by themselves). I also spent many hours in the manager's office conducting the camp's organizational affairs and paperwork, but I handed those chores over to the secretary as much as possible.

So the job allowed me to "throw" myself into hot, physical labor, often for as many as twelve to fourteen hours a day. Ever since the onset of my mental illness, this was a strategy I had used for relief whenever possible. Physical work, often the better if it led to the brink of exhaustion, seemed to absorb me; it kept the demons away, if only temporarily.

But as much as I loved the camp and its mission, I was driving myself toward another serious breakdown. In the winter of 1984, I suffered another massive meltdown, almost ten years to the day of the first one. I found myself (once again) sobbing and pacing throughout the night, shaking, unable to function. And, as always, there was no observable (at least to me) set of conditions causing the suffering.

In the spring of that year, I quit the camp manager job. When I did so, I put my family in peril once more, since I had no job to go to and no prospects either. There was plenty of tension between Judie and me. She was angry and disoriented, almost as much as I was. Jason was confused and mystified. But as upset as Judie was, she stuck by me once again; she said the sickness was always the culprit, not me. And I guess she was right. But that distinction didn't do much to alleviate my intense feelings of guilt and shame.

I need to share at this time that I've always felt truly blessed by Judie's never-wavering support and love. She could have left me many times, and I couldn't have blamed her. But she didn't. Her motto continued to be, "It's the sickness, not you." This dedication to the husband she always loved (although I rarely felt lovable) kept me going, more than anything else. When we stood at the altar in 1967 and she said "For better or for worse," she wasn't just repeating required wedding vows.

We packed up again. This time we moved twenty miles down the road to Bloomington (IL) where I had lived as a teen and graduated high school. We made ourselves a "home" of sorts in a small, shabby apartment in a tacky neighborhood. We were desperately poor. I took a job as a teacher's aide at Raymond School, a small institution for the mentally disabled. Although I'd never worked with this sort of student population before, I took to it quickly. I fell in love with the students, their needs, their determination, and their optimism. I even coached the basketball team, taking them to the state finals in the Illinois Athletic Association for "handicapped" team sports.

Once again, though, the pay was very low. I had to supplement it by making pizza deliveries, driving produce trucks, and doing office janitor work. Meanwhile, Judie pursued her lifelong dream by enrolling in a local college for nursing. We had to take out large loans to finance this venture, but after two years she received her diploma as a Registered Nurse. As a matter of fact she went one step better, securing her Bachelor of Science in Nursing. Not surprisingly, she chose mental health nursing as her specialty.

This was a humiliating, fragile time period for our family. We tried to live on five dollars a day, and had a card file. At the end of the week if there was any money left in the "back of the box," we used it for an ice cream cone or admission to a local softball game. We did have the pleasure of reuniting with Terry Smith, his family, and his parents, Charles and Betty.

Judie graduated from nursing college in 1986 and took a job at BroMenn Hospital on the mental health unit. This favorable turn of events meant we finally had a real breadwinner in the family. It also put me back at the typewriter. I still held part-time jobs like delivering pizza or cleaning office buildings, but school was out. There was time for me to start writing again. In 1990, I published my first novel for young adults, *I Can Hear the Mourning Dove*. It was well received by critics and reviewers as well as the American Library Association, but earned very little money. I was forty-eight years old at the time.

I also gave up counseling and psychoanalysis in favor of psychiatric care exclusively. I went through medications and more of them, as the shrinks were in ongoing frustration, still struggling to identify my primary diagnosis and an effective drug therapy. I was still shaky, going through the sleepless nights and indulging in "panic eating." I gobbled what food I could, when I could. I drank lots of milkshakes and ate lots of Jell-O and pudding. A side effect of this pattern was elevated cholesterol levels and triglycerides as well. I've been on medications for this disorder for years, while trying to watch my diet as much as possible.

In 1990, Raymond School was dissolved because as a "segregated school" it seemed to violate the federal government's Civil Rights guidelines. The students were moved into a wing of Bloomington High School. They were in no way "mainstreamed" with regular students but they were in the same building. I have a vivid remembrance of the BHS principal showing us (Raymond faculty and staff) where the lockers for our kids would be located. He was stopped up short when we pointed out to him that since our students couldn't read numbers, they wouldn't be able to operate combination locks.

So, lo and behold, I found myself working in my old high school. The building was the same but the students were different; they were much more racially diverse. Even though the former Raymond students were in the BHS building, they were essentially still segregated, in self-contained classrooms and programs. They ate in the school cafeteria but at isolated tables, carefully supervised and aided by special education staff personnel. The "family atmosphere" of the Raymond School environment was lost, but we were now in compliance with good ole U.S. of A. civil rights requirements.

*

To the extent I can, I try and work pretty much as other professional writers do. The first thing you have to do if you want to write is sit down. I sit down at a very large corner computer work station in an average-sized room. Its actual appearance might lead some to believe that I know a great deal about computer systems. They would be wrong. I can work the word-processing system. I can send and receive e-mail messages. That's about it.

It's the only place I do my writing. It is my office: A second-floor spare bedroom with lots of windows. So the room is cheery, with plenty of available natural light. I don't think I could work in a room without windows. When I glance outside from time to time, I see my neighbor's flower garden of lilies, purple cone flowers, lilac bushes, and black-eyed susans. I can also see his huge maple tree, which tracks the seasons of the year. Unlike some writers, I don't like to have any music playing when I write. I like it quiet.

My computer work station has a name: Gilbert. It is a massive unit of several particle board components. My wife and I needed three days to assemble it. Even the parts seemed to weigh a ton when I lugged each one up the stairs. Gilbert will never be moved. The corner spot is his for good.

I named the station Gilbert after a Green Bay Packer lineman named Gilbert Brown. Gilbert was a good lineman when he weighed about 330 pounds. When his weight went up to approximately 370, the Packers gave him his walking papers. They told him to find a "fat farm" somewhere and lose at least forty pounds. He put in his time at such a weight-loss center but emerged from the experience at about 390. (A year later, Gilbert returned to the team with his weight under control, although no one would confuse him with a beanpole. As of this writing, he is now a member of the team again.)

The work center has a large shelf unit right next to the computer. In addition to all the stamps, envelopes, and stationery is a shelf of reference books I return to time and again. An *Oxford Dictionary and Thesaurus* sits there as well as a copy of *Bartlett's Familiar Quotations*. A simple grammar book is there too. Three reference books keep them company: Joanna Cole's *Best-Loved Folktales of the World,* Edith Hamilton's *Mythology,* and Sir James Frazer's classic *The Golden Bough*. These last three reflect my interest in ancient religions as well as their legends and myths.

I also have several of Joseph Campbell's books close at hand. There is probably no better scholar on the landscape when it comes to ancient religions and their mythological connections. Many of these books contain research information I've incorporated into my stories.

My computer is an eMac. I'm used to Macintosh systems, although I have no reason to believe they're better than others. I used to write my material in longhand before moving to the word processor. I don't do that anymore; I skip the longhand step. Nowadays, I compose right at the keyboard. I like to pretend that makes me a modern man.

Like most professional writers, I work on a regular schedule. I'm a morning person so I do most of my writing early in the day when I'm most alert. Typically,

I work from about 7:00 until 9:00. When I was younger (and more focused), I worked the same schedule but with longer hours. In those days I worked until noon as a rule. I find now that I'm older I simply don't have the stamina I once did. That applies too to most of the other areas of my life. As the famous actress Bettie Davis once said, "Gettin' old ain't for sissies."

I know writers who do most of their work after lunch and I know others who are night people. They work primarily in the evening; I can't imagine it. I'm so whipped by suppertime I often fall asleep watching the evening news. One Connecticut author I know has the habit of walking with her dog along the beach in the early part of the morning, deciding what she's going to write on that particular day.

I don't set myself daily goals or quotas. My Attention Deficit Disorder, restlessness, agitation, and inability to concentrate for extended periods of times makes it impossible. But many writers do. They insist on finishing six or eight or ten pages a day, or a given number of words—say, 3,000 or more. I've never been comfortable with this approach. Some days I may write only a page or two, particularly if I'm writing something that's especially sensitive or challenging. Other days I may spend my morning working on revising material that's still in "first draft" condition. Sometimes sharpening one part of a writing project makes it easier to move ahead faster. At least that's the case for me.

Naturally, I've often wondered how much more good work I might have produced over the years if I were "normal." But it's not a useful or productive thing to dwell on.

The one thing professional writers have in common is working on a regular schedule. We don't wait for "inspiration" or wait to wrap our work habits around it, even when such inspiration may seem to occur. I've been asked many times, "How can you write every day at the same time, even if you're not inspired?" The answer is that my inspiration is an ongoing inner dialogue which may connect with a writing project, or projects that are in various stages of development. Sometimes I'm writing actual text for a novel I'm working on; sometimes I'm working on an outline, trying to reshape it, improve its focus, or make it more complete. Or, I might be at work on a newspaper column or a freelance article. Another device which helps me work consistently on my regular writing schedule is an old Hemingway trick. He liked to stop "in the middle of" whatever he was working on. That way, he never had to get up the next day and wonder, "What should I be writing today?" I try and use this strategy whenever possible.

Again, this "One step forward, two steps back" explains primarily why I'm such a slow worker. As I've said on many occasions, it's not unusual for me to take an average of two years to write a book if we include all steps in the process: brainstorming, outlining, revising the outline, writing the text, and finally, revising the text.

*

The first novels I wrote were done without access to computers. They were written on legal pads in longhand, then typed out. I didn't know a word processing application from a New Zealand holiday. Nowadays, as I've mentioned, I not only use a computer, but I actually compose on it.

Before we entered the electronic world, most of us (authors) had to go through the laborious process of writing material in longhand, then typing it on the typewriter, making changes and adjustments as we went. When we were "cutting and pasting," we were doing so literally. That meant a lot of work with scissors and rubber cement. Revising was slow and tedious, especially for authors like myself who are inclined toward a great deal of reorganization, added development, modulation, and all other steps associated with the revision process.

Using a computer to write a novel is like a gift from heaven. It allows for easy and speedy changes. An author can bump an outline around from several angles, and if he is still not satisfied, it's easy to just put everything back in place the way it was at the outset. And of course, it's a blessing when it comes time to make minor changes in a final draft, including such small but important elements as changing a word, dropping a phrase, removing a sentence, or even just correcting a typo.

The credit for my transition from dinosaur to modern man (if I may call myself such) goes to my son, Jason. He too is a writer. He more or less took me by the ear and forced me to learn how to write using a word processing program. *The Flex of the Thumb* was the first book I wrote on a computer (it was an old Apple 2E). *A Quiet Desperation, Dakota Dream,* and *I Can Hear the Mourning Dove* were written the old-fashioned way.

*

My most recent novel for teens (I've also written adult fiction and historical fiction) is called *Fresh Killed.* The protagonist is a polio victim at the same time his older brother is serving in the military in the Korean War. The polio epidemic was devastating in our nation during the years from 1945-1955. This ten-year period is often referred to as the "Postwar Decade." A good book called *Patenting the Sun* helped me understand the nature of the polio virus, the disease's crippling effect across the country, and the development of the Salk vaccine. Dr. Johas Salk's breakthrough in the laboratory effectively ended polio as a medical menace.

James Brady's *The Coldest War* is his memoir of military service in the Korean Conflict. It is vivid and it is brutal. The war in Korea (1950-53) often goes by the

name the "forgotten war." Even though it is often called the Korean "conflict," as Shakespeare might say, "A war by any other name will carry all the same pain, suffering, loss, and sorrow."

Brady's book reads like a novel, due to its strong narrative pattern, but it is in fact a series of tales of real men, places, and events. For a writer like myself, it's another of the books that does double duty: It provides a captivating narrative while also revealing particular and actual circumstances of that desperate battle. I was alive during Korea, but too young to remember much about it.

*

In 1995, with the publication of *The Squared Circle,* it seemed as if I might be a shooting star in the heavens of young adult fiction. I have no modesty whatsoever about this book. It may be in fact the finest basketball novel ever written. Several publications chose it as the year's best YA novel.

There's an irony here. I never wrote the book for young adults. It was meant for a broader, mainstream (adult) audience but was marketed as young adult fiction nonetheless. This pigeonholing hurt the book's sales, although it has maintained a modest sales profile over the years. All of a sudden I had literary agents knocking at my door, conferences requesting speeches and presentations, and schools asking me for author visits. I made many author visits in schools during the second half of the nineties, all over the country. Such visits are often an author's most gratifying activity. The opportunity to visit with students in their classrooms, share with them in an informal setting, to discuss books and writing, is nothing short of delicious.

But, alas, my star fell as fast as it had risen. I wasn't able to establish a successful professional connection with agents, even though I liked them all well enough, while they (I believe) enjoyed me in return. But they weren't able to spot me in presentation situations or school visits. Even worse, they weren't able to place my books with publishers. Eventually I decided to cut my ties with these people. I had shown through my history with publishers that I could collect rejection slips as well as they could, if not better. My conclusion is simply this: Literary agents don't want to be bothered with manuscripts that are hard to place, and as I've pointed out earlier, mine usually are.

Agents had no luck with the movie business either. I had nibbles from production companies on *I Can Hear the Mourning Dove* as well as *Dakota Dream,* but my representatives were never actually able to get a production company on the hook. Like any author, I would love to see one of my books on the silver screen—for one thing, that's where the real money is—but it's never happened.

I might indicate here that I, like most effective fiction writers, have never made a lot of money. In schools,

Bennett and Judie on vacation in Key Largo, 2001.

students frequently ask, "Are you rich?" Or, "Are you famous?" As to the second question, my answer tends to be the same: "If you have to ask, you've really answered your own question."

With respect to the "Are you rich?" question (which usually mortifies their teachers), I always welcome it. I like students to know that most successful authors don't make a lot of money. I know I don't. I suspect for each Toni Morrison or John Grisham, there are thousands of us "out there" doing good work, but earning very modest income.

*

Now that I've advanced in age, I guess I'm supposed to be wiser. I suppose I am, in some respects. With respect to writing, I try to impart a few fundamental guidelines to aspiring writers in classroom or workshop settings. My first piece of advice is so traditional it almost seems tired: Write what you know.

I've always done this, and I think more than anything else, it's the strategy that's brought me such success as I've had. My settings, characters, and narrative strategies are always based on elements of life I know right down to the ground. My three areas of expertise

are mental health, sports, and religions. The spine of my books is always found in one of these regions and sometimes more than one is involved significantly.

We've all read novels whose material seems unlikely and therefore implausible. There is no surer way to undermine the effectiveness of a book. When readers roll their eyes or say to themselves, "Oh this could never happen," that book is in trouble. And as authors we take great risk if we underestimate the sophistication of our readers. That's another thing that often happens in the world of YA fiction, in my humble opinion. Our teen readers can smell out the phony as easily as the drug-sniffing dog bears down on the guilty suitcase.

If a writer is going to highlight material involving music, he had better understand what arrangement means, how it works, how chord changes impact compositions, and what sequences in such chord progressions are appropriate for different kinds of music (jazz, rock, country, classical, soul, etc.).

I also tell young writers to learn to keep their mouths shut and their ears open. It may be that more than anything else, curiosity is the single characteristic necessary for effective fiction writing. People with strong curiosity learn what people think, what they do, how they deceive (even themselves), what they fear, what they relish, and what they value. People with their jaws flapping all the time aren't likely to be privy to this important information.

Such curiosity, for instance, helps writers create effective dialogue. They listen carefully to the lilt and slant, the stumbling for language, slang, frustration, expression of pleasure, and so much more. When I'm in a public place surrounded by strangers, I usually eavesdrop on conversations. Maybe the strangers are talking about stocks and bonds. Maybe they repeat phrases about political conditions. Maybe they disagree about a boss or supervisor, while really trying to say the same thing. Maybe they're teenagers talking endlessly on cell phones while sitting in a restaurant booth. There's no more reliable route to staying in touch with "teen talk" and their slang.

As for mental health, I usually try to limit the discussion, as I find teens and young adults too curious. The subject can carry us away from exploring the route to effective writing. But I don't shy away from the subject either. I don't hide my own experiences in this area of life.

I long for young people to understand that a mental illness is not necessarily a "character weakness." It's not the "fault" of the victim. Most people with a serious mental disorder such as acute anxiety or depression are wired wrong; their brain chemistry is out of whack. It's no different from a sufferer of high blood pressure (hypertension) or a pancreatic cancer victim. No one would accuse a diabetic of suffering from the disease because of a "lack of character."

Our culture attaches no stigma to the person with heart disease. Although most of the medications I've tried over the years haven't been effective for me, many of them have been for other people. So people who suffer should find a way to put aside the stigma and work with mental health professionals. I know many folks with minor depressive conditions for whom Celexa, Zoloft, or Paxil have provided real relief. I have a dear friend named Dottie who is a long-time sufferer of manic-depressive (bi-polar) disorder. She has taken Lithium for years and declares it's just like "magic."

As the years have passed, the symptoms of my emotional turmoil have become less acute, although they haven't taken a vacation. Along with my doctors, I still experiment with new medications and dosages. I still have many sleepless nights, the "racing mind," inability to concentrate or prioritize, and restlessness. Somehow I write, even if in little bits and pieces, until a project eventually comes together.

Terry Smith often remarked upon my courage. I guess he was right. Somehow I've stayed the course through all the years, when giving up would have been so much easier. As a matter of fact, I'm working on a new YA book right now. Its tentative title is *Grounded Out*. I am optimistic readers can have it in their hands one day soon. There is always room for hope.

BLOS, Joan W(insor) 1928-

Personal

Surname rhymes with "close"; born December 9, 1928, in New York, NY; daughter of Max (a psychiatrist) and Charlotte (a teacher; maiden name, Biber) Winsor; married Peter Blos, Jr. (a psychoanalyst), June 7, 1953; children: Stephen (deceased), Sarah. *Education:* Vassar College, B.A., 1949; City College (now of the City University of New York), M.A., 1956. *Hobbies and other interests:* Camping, knitting, making soup, talking with people, taking long walks with her husband, and watching a good play.

Addresses

Home and office—1725 South University Ave., Ann Arbor, MI 48104. *Agent*—Curtis Brown Ltd., 10 Astor Place, New York, NY 10003.

Career

Bank Street College of Education, New York, NY, associate in publications division and member of faculty, 1958-70; University of Michigan, Ann Arbor, lecturer in juvenile literature at School of Education, 1972-80. Volunteer reviewer of children's books for Connecticut Association of Mental Health, 1954-56.

Awards, Honors

John Newbery Medal from American Library Association, American Book Award, both 1980, and Best Books of the Year designation, *School Library Journal,* and English-Speaking Union Ambassador Book designation, all for *A Gathering of Days: A New England Girl's Journal, 1830-32;* honorary doctorate from Bank Street College of Education, New York City, 2002.

Writings

CHILDREN'S BOOKS

In the City, Macmillan (New York, NY), 1964.
(With Betty Miles) *People Read,* Macmillan (New York, NY), 1964.
(With Betty Miles) *Joe Finds a Way,* L. W. Singer (Syracuse, NY), 1967.
"It's Spring," She Said, Knopf (New York, NY), 1968.
(With Betty Miles) *Just Think!,* Knopf (New York, NY), 1971.
A Gathering of Days: A New England Girl's Journal, 1830-32 (historical fiction), Scribner (New York, NY), 1979.
Martin's Hats, illustrated by Marc Simont, Morrow (New York, NY), 1984.
Brothers of the Heart: A Story of the Old Northwest, 1837-1838 (historical fiction), Scribner (New York, NY), 1985.

Joan W. Blos

Old Henry (picture book), illustrated by Stephen Gammell, Morrow (New York, NY), 1987.
The Grandpa Days, illustrated by Emily Arnold McCully, Simon & Schuster Books for Young Readers (New York, NY), 1989.
One Very Best Valentine's Day, illustrated by Emanuel Schongut, Little Simon (New York, NY), 1989.
Lottie's Circus, illustrated by Irene Trivas, Morrow (New York, NY), 1989.
The Heroine of the Titanic: A Tale Both True and Otherwise of the Life of Molly Brown, illustrated by Tennessee Dixon, Morrow (New York, NY), 1991.
A Seed, a Flower, a Minute, an Hour, illustrated by Hans Poppel, Simon & Schuster (New York, NY), 1992.
Brooklyn Doesn't Rhyme, Scribner (New York, NY), 1994.
The Hungry Little Boy, illustrated by Dena Schutzer, Simon & Schuster (New York, NY), 1995.
Nellie Bly's Monkey: His Remarkable Story in His Own Words, illustrated by Catherine Stock, Morrow (New York, NY), 1996.
Bedtime!, illustrated by Stephen Lambert, Simon & Schuster (New York, NY), 1998.
Hello, Shoes!, illustrated by Ann Boyajian, Simon & Schuster (New York, NY), 1999.

OTHER

(Adaptor) Margaret Wise Brown, *The Days before Now: An Autobiographical Note,* illustrated by Thomas B. Allen, Simon & Schuster (New York, NY), 1994.

Brothers of the Heart (play; based on novel of the same title), performed by Wild Swan Theater, 1999.

Also author of unpublished presentations, including "Historical Fiction: Why Read It? Why Write It? Why Bother?," "45 Years Later and Still in Love with Picture Books," "You Be the Mommy: The Developmental Importance of Imagined Experience," and "Charlotte Forten Grimke and the Grimke Sisters: The Converging and Nonstereotpyical Lives of Three 19th Century Women."

Contributor of articles and reviews to periodicals, including *School Library Journal, New Outlook, Child Analysis, Michigan Quarterly Review,* and *Merrill-Palmer Quarterly.* U.S. editor of *Children's Literature in Education,* 1976-81. Author of introduction to Louisa May Alcott's *Little Women,* Aladdin (New York, NY), 1999. Contributor to books, including *Ann Arbor (W)-rites: A Community Memoir,* 2004.

Work in Progress

Dear Cousin Sallie, companion historical novel to *A Gathering of Days* and *Brothers of the Heart.*

Sidelights

Joan W. Blos is best known for her novel *A Gathering of Days: A New England Girl's Journal, 1830-32,* which in 1980 won the American Library Association's Newbery Medal for the year's most distinguished contribution to American children's literature. Set in the early nineteenth century, *A Gathering of Days* is presented as a young girl's chronicle of her life on a New England farm. The story covers a pivotal year in the life of Catherine Cabot Hill; though much of the book records daily events, over the course of the year, Catherine must adapt to her father's remarriage and must face the death of her best friend. The book took Blos twelve years to complete. Fascinated by her family's summer home in New England, the author researched its past owners and based her novel on her findings. *Kirkus Reviews* called the book "carefully researched and convincingly delivered." A reviewer for the *St. Louis Post-Dispatch* noted that the "careful tuning of psychological nuances to historic elements . . . gives the story its powerful immediacy. *A Gathering of Days* not only gives the reader a close look at the early 1800s, it offers . . . a deeply moving human experience." Noting that the novel's heroine "meets both the cruel, long and dark winter days and the all-too-short sunny summer days with sturdy endurance and quiet joy," Lavinia Russ commented further in the *Washington Post Book World* that "Blos offers a valuable supplement to students of early American history."

Blos's novel *Brothers of the Heart: A Story of the Old Northwest, 1837-1838* was praised by Tim Wynne-Jones in the Toronto *Globe and Mail* as "more powerful and more stirring that its award-winning predecessor." Commenting to *SATA* about the book, Blos once stated that *Brothers of the Heart* "began with an interest in a region and an exploration of its past: what was it like back then? This time I tell the story of a boy, Shem, the fiddler's crippled son, and the story's several settings include a newly established town, the commercial center of Detroit, and the Michigan wilderness. Among its varied characters, an elderly Ottawa woman is outstanding and her presence contributes another culture's strengths to the ongoing thread of the story." Shem spends six months in the wilderness with the Ottawan woman, learning how to survive; when he returns to his family, he has learned how better to deal with his disabilities. A writer for the *St. James Guide to Children's Writers* commented that Blos's "language, with its rhythms and lilt of earlier times, is remarkably spare, not replete with full-blown descriptions, yet giving the reader a strong sense of place and characterization. Blos has accomplished the fine feat of balancing history with universal human experience, uniting the book's past with the reader's present." The novel was adapted as a play in 1999.

Blos has also written picture books for younger readers, among them *Hello, Shoes!* and *Bedtime!* In *Hello, Shoes!* a boy and his grandfather search for the boy's shoes amid the clutter in his room. Once they are found, the boy buckles them himself for the first time ever, and then he and his grandparent head off for a fun time at the park. "This sweet slip of a story should strike a chord with very small children, who will understand the seriousness of the boy's quest and appreciate the grandfather's respect for it," noted a writer for *Publishers Weekly.* Hazel Rochman of *Booklist* commented that the "Words and pictures are just right for toddlers and grandparents to share." *Bedtime!* is a "charming, quiet" story about unwilling children being sent to bed, reported Stephanie Zvirin in *Booklist.* Childish reluctance about going to bed is perfectly captured, as is an experienced adult's manner of coping with it. A *Publishers Weekly* contributor commented on the "spare, soothing tones" of Blos's narrative voice, which is "spiced with a sly sense of humor."

As well as writing picture books, Blos also adapted a short autobiography by Margaret Wise Brown, author of *Goodnight, Moon,* into picture book format. Blos provided an afterword describing Brown's life to accompany the adapted text. Mary M. Burns of *Horn Book Magazine* praised, "This book is the perfect introduction not only to Margaret Wise Brown but also to the art of autobiography." Carolyn Phelan in a *Booklist* review commented that in their adaptation, "Blos and Allen [the illustrator] have created a lyrical picture book."

Blos once told *SATA:* "Truth is something that interests me a lot. . . . When you write a story, you find that you have to deal with three kinds of truthfulness. There is the psychological truthfulness of your characters, the social truthfulness of their situation, and the literary truthfulness of the manner of telling. The story is what results."

Biographical and Critical Sources

BOOKS

Children's Literature Review, Volume 18, Gale (Detroit, MI), 1989.
St. James Guide to Children's Writers, 5th edition, St. James Press (Detroit, MI), 1999.
St. James Guide to Young-Adult Writers, 2nd edition, St. James Press (Detroit, MI), 1999.

PERIODICALS

ALAN Review, fall, 1998, Joanne Brown, "Historical Fiction or Fictionalized History?"
American Libraries, June-July, 2004, "Local Memories for Sale," p. 28.
Booklist, September 15, 1994, Hazel Rochman, review of *Brooklyn Doesn't Rhyme,* p. 135; December 15, 1994, Carolyn Phelan, review of *The Days Before Now: An Autobiographical Note,* p. 755; March 15, 1995, Barbara Baskin, review of *Brooklyn Doesn't Rhyme,* p. 1343; February 15, 1996, Stephanie Zvirin, review of *Nellie Bly's Monkey,* p. 1024; May 15, 1998, Stephanie Zvirin, review of *Bedtime!,* p. 1629; October 15, 1999, Hazel Rochman, review of *Hello, Shoes!,* p. 450.
Detroit Free Press, February 1, 1981.
Detroit News, January 26, 1980, February 3, 1980.
Globe and Mail (Toronto, Ontario, Canada), February 8, 1986.
Horn Book, August, 1980; July-August, 1994, Jo Carr, review of *A Gathering of Days* (audio recording), p. 438; September-October, 1994, review of *Brooklyn Doesn't Rhyme,* pp. 585-586; March-April, 1995, Mary M. Burns, review of *The Days Before Now,* pp. 212-213.
Kirkus Reviews, January 15, 1980.
Publishers Weekly, July 19, 1991, review of *The Heroine of the Titanic: A Tale Both True and Otherwise of the Life of Molly Brown,* p. 56; November 7, 1994, review of *The Days Before Now,* p. 78; May 1, 1995, review of *The Hungry Little Boy,* p. 56; January 15, 1996, review of *Nellie Bly's Monkey,* p. 462; May 11, 1998, review of *Bedtime!,* p. 66; May 31, 1999, review of *Hello, Shoes!,* p. 91.
St. Louis Post-Dispatch, January 27, 1980.
School Library Journal, March, 1995, p. 196; June, 1995, p. 77; April, 1996, Starr LaTronica, review of *Nellie Bly's Monkey,* p. 99; July, 1998, Rosalyn Pierini, review of *Bedtime!,* p. 64. July, 1999, Susan M. Moore, review of *Hello, Shoes!,* p. 61.
Washington Post Book World, March 9, 1980.

Autobiography Feature

Joan W. Blos

Joan W. Blos contributed the following autobiographical essay to *SATA:*

It is a wintry afternoon. The street is dark and snowy. A mother and her four-year-old daughter make their way to the library, bent against the wind. Up the shallow steps they go, pausing at the heavy wooden door, then they enter a large bright room. At the desk a librarian stamps books with her pencil. It is a special pencil with a little outrigged stamp. She uses it to mark the dates when the books must be returned. People sit at tables. They turn pages of books.

I am the child, and the mother is mine. And from that time, long years ago, I am, have been, and will always be a lover of libraries.

We go into the children's room, find *Ola,* the book we seek. From its cover a boy's round face stares out of an old-fashioned window. The window has many small panes of glass, their corners filled with snow. Ola will travel, imaginarily, into a vast and snowy world and so, in my way, will I.

In telling this story of my life I have chosen to tell of the libraries I've loved, letting their images signify its different, evolving parts.

I

First, then, the public library of which I have just spoken. It was located in Warwick, New York, a small town about seventy-five miles northwest of New York City. My parents and I were living nearby and my father, just graduated from medical school, was serving as medical director and psychiatrist at a school for delinquent boys. Newly in operation, the school represented a hopeful experiment by the New York State Department of Social Welfare in conjunction with Columbia University's medical school and its Teachers College. Instead of punishing delinquent boys in the then-traditional manner, the new program was designed to help boys who stole, or were often truant from school, to become happier individuals and better citizens. Because it was thought wise to separate them from their difficult and disruptive home environments all of the boys lived at the school. True to the thinking of the day it was called a training school and there, in addition to regular classes, these twelve-to sixteen-year-old boys were encouraged to learn new skills, such as printing and carpentry.

My parents were both idealistic believers in the power of education and the educative process. Therefore they had accepted the challenge of living on the grounds of a public institution with their only child. I was three years old when we moved there, nearly seven when we left. Interesting though it appears in retrospect, my memories do not concern the school directly. It would have been very much in character for my parents to have been deliberately vague in what they chose to tell me about why the boys were there. (Who knows what a three-year-old might have been led to imagine as the sort of badness for which you were taken away?) So, for me, the school functioned largely as a pleasant background to our family's life. I remember the nearby countryside explored with the wife and daughters of another member of the staff and my teacher mother. In the fall we searched for bittersweet vines growing on old stone fences. We picked, or purchased, colorful Indian corn. What we ever did with it, I can no longer remember. Milk was brought by a milkman and delivered in round glass bottles. On winter mornings the milk might be frozen solid and the caps on the bottles lifted off by the rising column of the freezing milk.

My mother, attempting to make a learning opportunity out of this unusual occurrence, would try to explain to me, age three, that things get bigger when they freeze and so the milk had climbed the necks of the bottles and pushed the caps right off. This remained mysterious. As I understood the process, freezing was how you got ice cubes in your refrigerator or what made it possible for the men to drive cars onto our lake and fish through holes in the ice. Frozen was *stiff,* not bigger.

Spring was the hatching of baby chicks—rows and rows and rows of them—in metal incubators. There was also the smell of manure in the fields, and unpaved roads turning slick with yellow mud as the snowdrifts melted. My mother, although city-born, had a great sense of the environment, both natural and social. It must have given her special pleasure to show these things to me, and the kindness with which I remember them tells that I sensed that pleasure. Later I became aware of how hard it had been for her, a successful and committed teacher, to interrupt her career and to live in a situation where she had so little place. But that was later.

My father, on the other hand, was much engaged in his work. From time to time distinguished consultants of one kind and another would come out to see the school. On these occasions they would review the program with my father and be entertained at lunches prepared for them by my mother. Dimly I see my four-and five-year-old self offering bowls of celery sticks and olives to the gathered guests.

We went to the library often in those years and both of my parents, as I recall, read aloud to me. I have already mentioned *Ola,* by the d'Aulaires. There was also Marjorie Flack's *Angus,* and then *Angus and the Ducks.* Not long after came *Little Pear,* about a Chinese boy, and then *Little Fox,* about an Indian boy living on Manhattan Island before the time of the Dutch. From a small, orange-covered copy of *One Hundred Best Poems for Boys and Girls* we read my favorites over and over again—some of them so often that I still know them nearly by heart. But the book that was most central to our lives was the *Here and Now Story Book.* The book, with stories by Lucy Sprague Mitchell and drawings by Hendrik Willem Van Loon, was first published in 1921, the year in which he received the first Newbery Medal ever given, for *The Story of Mankind.*

Mrs. Mitchell, a gifted innovator, had played an active role in the establishment of the experimental school at which my mother had taught. The stories collected in her book were experimental efforts too. Mrs. Mitchell firmly believed that children younger than seven are more interested in the here-and-now world that surrounds them than in anything else. She also thought that grown-up parents, teachers, and writers should give young children every possible help in learning about their world. She believed that stories for young children should be compatible with the language used by the children themselves, and in order to learn about this language she spent a great deal of time listening to the stories spontaneously told by children and writing them down. The *Here and Now,* as we called it, included simple, repetitive stories for two-year-olds and more elaborate ones for five-year-olds. At three I loved the story about the five little babies—one red, one black, one yellow, one white, and one tan—"who just came that way" and were loved by their respective mothers. (I notice that this story was omitted from a later edition of the book when people had become more thoughtful, but maybe not much wiser, about things like race and color.) At four a story called "How the Engine Learned the Knowing Song" taught something about patience as

The four cousins (JWB at far left), about 1938.

well as the requirements of locomotives and was one of my particular favorites. Mrs. Mitchell, a tireless teacher, provided her book with a lengthy introduction in which she explained to parents, teachers, amid writers her particular approach to stories for young children.

Little did I know, or care, about the theory behind them. Mrs. Mitchell had a strong, dramatic flair, a fine sense of language and of story itself. I think this is what made her writing so much livelier than the work of many of her followers and imitators—and it was not many years before I exchanged roles with my parents and began to read the stories aloud to my two young cousins.

Cousins. Eventually there were four of us: a boy, who was closest to me in age, and the girls we called "the littles." From the time I was seven until I went to college we lived in the same house or in adjacent houses in New York City's Greenwich Village. Our families were very close—my father's best friend having married my mother's older sister—and together we children played and fought and often (and loudly) protested the injustice of early bedtimes. We not only lived near each other and attended the same schools, we spent summers together as well. When, in tenth grade, I was required to write an autobiographical essay, my opening sentence stated, "I never had a brother or a sister yet I was not an only child." But this gets ahead of the story.

When we left Warwick and returned to the city to live I was not quite seven years old. My mother went back to

teaching. My father, after a year of commuting back and forth, accepted a job in the New York City schools. As a psychiatrist with the Bureau of Child Guidance he would have the opportunity, as he saw it, to work with troubled and difficult children before they became delinquent. And I, with curly blond hair tightly braided, had not only entered the City and Country School, I had found a wonderful library at the heart of that school's life.

II

Margaret Ernst was the librarian's name. She had a deep voice and small hands. She had created a library in a room that might once have been the back parlor of one of the four brick residences that were converted into school buildings when the school had moved there from its original location in the early 1920s. The library had three tall windows that looked out on the combined backyards of the four buildings—two on West Twelfth Street and the two behind them on Thirteenth—that had been substantially remodeled to meet the needs of the school. Divided by fencing and overhung with a net to protect nearby windows from high flies and wild throws, "the Yard," as it was known, gave the school outdoor play space that was both ample and contained. From the library one looked down on all of this and also the long wooden passageway that helped to partition off the yards and connected the two pairs of buildings. Wooden bookshelves completely surrounded the room, stopping only for the doors and being snugly fitted between the three tall windows. In the center of the room was a long rectangular table surrounded by high-backed chairs where we sat when using the reference collection for our research projects. Between the bookshelves and this oversized table was a row of cushioned wicker armchairs in which to sit while reading. The younger children came to the library on schedule; the older ones signed up for it. The chairs were always occupied.

How I loved that room! It seems to me that in those years I was always in the middle of one book or another and that Mrs. Ernst possessed uncanny knowledge of each child's reading interests. She led us onward easily, encouraging the slower readers and challenging the skillful. We accepted without surprise that she knew books like *Caddie Woodlawn* when our studies centered on the westward movement, and *The Cloister and the Hearth* when we got to the Middle Ages. But there was time along the way, although not necessarily in the order remembered, for *Lad, A Dog* by Albert Payson Terhune; Stephen Meader's boys' stories, which I liked as much as my cousin did; Sherlock Holmes; Noel Streatfield's "shoe books"; and Doris Gates's *Blue Willow.*

Other books came not from the school but were gifts from my parents, my father especially. I remember Cornelia Meigs's *The Covered Bridge,* Carol Ryrie

Brink's *Caddie Woodlawn,* Ruth Sawyer's *Roller Skates,* and Lavinia R. Davis's *Keys to the City.* The Winston dictionary that is still my favorite was carefully chosen as a thirteenth-birthday present because it gave the most detailed information on the derivation of words. There were books of poetry, some still on my shelves, such as *This Singing World* with poems selected by Louis Untemeyer, and *Selected Poems for Young People* by Edna St. Vincent Millay. Later came *Letters to a Young Poet* by Rainer-Maria Rilke, *The White Cliffs* by Alice Duer Miller, and *The Murder of Lidice,* again Edna St. Vincent Millay.

One summer my father had an interesting present for me. It was a copy of *Jane Eyre,* but instead of the paper jackets and hard covers I was used to, this book had covers of stiff paper that were coated with a kind of cellophane. Its shape was unusual too, a small, neat rectangle about the size of an ordinary jacket pocket. It cost twenty-five cents, which was remarkably inexpensive even in those days. I had just seen my first paperback, or Pocketbook, the copyrighted term by which such books were then known.

In the year I turned eleven Elizabeth Enright, the author, came to speak to our class. Except for Mrs. Mitchell, which was somehow different, this was my first meeting with an author, someone whose books I had read and loved. I remember exactly where she stood, and where I sat. I remember the brightness of that sunny morning. I remember her dress, pale green and made of silk, and that she was lovely, blond, and tall. The only thing I do not remember, though, is what she said to us.

The City and Country School (we called it C&C) was unusual but not unique. In New York City and elsewhere a number of experimental or progressive schools had been established in the 1920s, often by followers of the educator-philosopher John Dewey. It was a privilege to attend such a school in the 1930s and 1940s but I don't think any of us thought about it that way or felt self-conscious about it. In addition to the school's rigorous academic program there were opportunities to work with clay and paint and music and the expectation that one would do so. It was also assumed that girls would work in the carpentry shop; boys take part in cooking. An after-school program, for those who wished to join it or whose parents were working, gave us more time still. Were we naive or was it that these activities were meaningful to us? I know we never considered that there might be reasons such as our parents' convenience for extending the school day.

Another distinctive thing about the school was the way in which classes were referred to by the chronological age of their members rather than by numbers referring to grade level. The system was so logical I don't think any of us ever questioned it. For some reason, possibly to teach us about an alternative numbering system, Roman numerals were used for this purpose. Thus nine-year-olds were in the IX's, tens were in the X's.

I am sure that everyone who ever attended C&C remembers the job program. It was as central to the life of the school as it was to the philosophy of education on which the school was grounded. It unified things by giving each class, and each *member* of each class, the responsibility for participating usefully in the life of the school community and it was enormously effective. The nine-year-old IX's had the supply store, for example, selling pencils and paper and rulers and protractors as required by all the classes. Real money was used, accuracy to the penny was expected, and we learned many an arithmetical concept and process as we kept accounts, checked our stock, and determined how many pads would be needed if each of six classes ordered twelve pads. In the XI's the social studies program had to do with European history. But the XI's did more than study the importance of Gutenberg's fifteenth-century invention of movable type. The makings of a small print shop were made part of the classroom equipment, so that the XI's could learn how to set and distribute type. Then, using both manual and electric presses, they provided the school with letterhead paper, memo forms, and library cards. The culminating project of the XI's school year was the publication, from start to finish, of the school magazine, and I now suspect that the forgotten content of Miss Enright's visit had something to do with editing or the production of books in the real world. The school, which greatly valued what children did, never confused it with adult activity. This is a fine distinction which I think is often missed. In any event, the magazine had contributions representing the entire school, not just the XI's, and that is where I was first published.

Paradoxes and anachronisms seem to attach themselves to my life experience in those growing-up years. I have already mentioned the presence of cousins as modifying my sense of myself as an only child. Similarly, my school experience was so different from that of my friends and contemporaries that now, when we match reminiscences, it is almost hard to believe that we were going to school at the same time and in the same country! Others recall formal recitations with dread. I remember original plays based on topics we had studied. (One year, the X's, I was Galileo's mother; in the XIII's, just before graduation, I was the outspoken representative of the NAACP.) My friends speak of punitive teachers. We respected ours, and liked some more than others. But we certainly did not fear them and we mostly called them by nicknames—Ollie, Delly, Braddy—derived from their last names. Friends recall how they would contrive to miss a day of school. For us the worst possible punishment was to be sent home from school.

Further paradoxes. A city child, I walked to school by myself once I was old enough to cross streets independently. The neighborhood I walked through was congenial and residential. I knew the owner of the five-and-ten; in turn, Mr. Feldman knew me and my parents and my cousins and how we were related. So did the grocer and the butcher. Ten years old when World War II began, no one of my acquaintance was personally endangered by combat. Even more strange is that although our family was Jewish, and grandparents on both sides had left close relatives behind when, as young people, they immigrated to this country, the Nazi crimes against the Jews were seldom discussed in my presence and never in personal terms.

Two days before my thirteenth birthday the Japanese bombed Pearl Harbor. On my birthday, December 9, the rumor of a possible air attack drove us out of the school and into a building across the street believed to be stronger, thus safer. I found it exciting. Looking back I realize that was the only time World War II had any kind of direct reality for me or was associated with danger. For the rest, I have some memory of food stamps and gasoline rationing and a blackout drill or two. I believe that my father volunteered as an air-raid warden. An uncle was in the Army Medical Corps as a biochemist. One time he came home on leave with a very expensive new pen purchased at the post. It was not a fountain pen, did not have to be refilled with ink. Instead, as he explained it, there was a little ball-like mechanism that turned as you wrote with it. In this way a substance similar to, but thicker than, ink was continually brought down to the surface of the paper from a special cartridge, or container, lodged within the pen. It was said to be capable of writing underwater but it was too expensive a novelty for any of us to risk the experiment. Today, of course, ballpoints are everywhere and fountain pens are owned and used only by rich eccentrics.

I think it was in that same wartime summer that my cousin Dick and I were given a deck of cards on which were shown the silhouettes of enemy and friendly warplanes. The object was to learn their names and so, in the unlikely event that we should ever see them in flight, be prepared to identify them by name. For the rest, the war was newspaper headlines and newsreels seen at neighborhood movie theaters between the double features: Mrs. Miniver, and Van Johnson making the most of his thirty seconds over Tokyo. It did not make sense to me then, and I do not see now, that we might ever have been called upon to serve as airplane spotters.

III

My memories of the high-school years are the only ones that do not include a particular library loved for particular qualities in a particular way. The school did have a library, and a good one. In fact it was presided over by Anne Eaton, who was well-known in the world of children's libraries and literature. No matter. Miss Eaton was not my beloved Mrs. Ernst, and I didn't love her library either.

In high school I had a number of excellent teachers. For English there was Helen Fern Daringer, author of a number of successful books for children and also our

Summer vacation, about 1946.

grammar text, and Benjamin Stolper, writer of published stories and a wonderfully dramatic interpreter of stories, poems, and plays.

"Blood all over the carpet," he scolded, restating Lady Macbeth's response to the murder of the king. "How *could* you have been so messy?"

As for Miss Daringer, I respected her—with her precise manner, Emily Dickinson hairstyle, and neatly tailored clothes you couldn't *not* respect Miss Daringer. But despite her best efforts, and my earnest ones, I never became competent at diagramming sentences and the intricacies of grammar elude me to this day. I was good at spelling, though.

In one of the high-school summers, when gasoline was rationed and we could not use the car very much, I learned how to do touch-typing. Again this was a joint project with my cousin, and he and I shared a self-teaching manual and a devilishly frustrating shield that fit over the keyboard so that you couldn't cheat. I do not remember the exact rules by which we turned this activity into a competition between us, but we did. My cousin was faster than I and merely keeping up with him caused me to acquire some bad habits. I also recall that we got bored by the time we reached the last chapter and quit before we mastered the keyboard's top row. The manual contained innumerable practice sentences, including one which carried the reminder: Think before you write, Mr. Orville Brock.

In tenth grade, at the urging of a teacher, I submitted a short story to a competition designed to encourage writing by young people. Publication in a national magazine and a prize of $25 was the reward and I won it. The money was piously invested in a U.S. War Bond (at $18.75) and the balance, if I remember correctly, went to British War Relief. I have absolutely no recollection of what I did with the money I received for the bond when it finally came due. Difficulty in using prize money for pleasure seems to have persisted into my grown-up life. In 1980, when a book I had written topped off winning the Newbery Medal with the American Book Award, I divided the cash prize for the latter between the New York Public Library, in gratitude, and IBBY (International Association for Books for Young People), in admiration.

April 12, 1945. That afternoon a friend called to ask if I knew what had happened and when I said that I did not, she told me that Franklin D. Roosevelt, who had been president for twelve of my sixteen years, had just died.

Three weeks later my gentle, forty-six-year-old father, who took great pride in my writing and was its foremost critic, suffered a heart attack. He had just given a talk on the needs of juvenile delinquents in New York City and was leaving the hall. Although promptly taken to a hospital, he died the following day.

The next year, my last at high school, was hardly a happy one. We had sublet our apartment and were living with my mother's sister, who had her own worries to contend with, and her daughter, my young cousin. I studied in preparation for college entrance exams and watched my mother extend her professional life. At school I participated in writing the script and song lyrics for the original, all-school musical we titled "High and Wide." Its sentimental theme and mistaken-identity plot (returning soldier seeks girl he has known only through letters) was no more trite than many commercial ventures of those early postwar days. We gave ours a happy ending, and a gala block-party scene.

In September 1946, having won admission to both Vassar and Sarah Lawrence Colleges, I set off for Vassar, a radical shift of interest, and another library.

IV

A building of tan stone outside and vaulted spaces within, Vassar's library was an impressive building, traditionally academic in style, and more austere than inviting. Actually, I did not use its resources as might have been expected. Quite unexpectedly I became a science major and spent more time in the laboratory than in reading and research.

In retrospect the decision to major in physiology can be seen as a response to a number of influences. For one thing, the physiology faculty was truly outstanding. I, who had taken only required science courses in high school, became fascinated by the revelations of the introductory course. Here was an entirely new kind of esthetic! I was delighted with the elegance and grace of natural law, of regulatory biological mechanisms set into motion by the body's changing needs. I learned to resist the temptations of teleological reasoning (explanations based on outcome rather than cause) and to appreciate the importance of basing one's conclusions on presentable data. Later, I would say that I learned about writing book reviews from doing lab reports: first the premise, then the observations, then the conclusion. In lab reports there were to be no gratuitous generalizations and in book reviews, I strongly believe, there should be no comments either laudatory or critical for which an exact and appropriate referent cannot be identified.

If my newfound interest in physiology exerted a pull toward science, disappointment with courses in the English department seemed to push me away. It was hard to respect myself, the faculty, or my fellow students when I regularly received *A*s with but little preparation. On one unfortunate occasion an improvised comment based solely on what I had heard in class was praised by the instructor as "giving evidence of perceptive and sensitive reading." It came down to the fact that I was doing too well too easily in English and I didn't like knowing I was getting away with it. Besides, doesn't every doctor's daughter want, at one time or another, to be a doctor too? I never embarked on a full premedical course. But I think the connection with my father (plus the medical students I was seeing on weekends in New York) helped to support my interest.

At Vassar my closest friends were a year ahead of me. In order to graduate with them or, more accurately, not to be left behind when they graduated, I undertook an accelerated program that would allow me to finish college in three years. This meant a consistently full course load augmented by staying on at Vassar for what were called spring half-terms and then, over the summer, taking additional courses at Columbia. Although I did what I set out to do, I missed out on many aspects of the undergraduate experience that might have made it a lot more fun and much more meaningful.

Too late to allow me to even consider a change of major I took a half-term course on contemporary American theater. Our instructor had been active in the government's theater program of the 1930s. Her professionalism was apparent and when she read aloud from plays, neither set nor stage was needed. Her readings gave me some of the best moments of "theater" I have ever known. I learned an incalculable amount about the power of language to move, as well as to persuade, in that short semester. We were expected to read two full-length plays a night, and a critical analysis of each (one page, single-spaced) was required for the next day's class. At last I was brought to realize that literature had its own high standards, that nicety and precision were qualities to be valued, and that the notion of the parsimonious statement was not restricted to science.

It was during that same brief semester that I was introduced to e. e. cummings's play *him*. An off-Broadway production allowed me to see the play then, or soon thereafter, and I also had the opportunity to attend a reading given by cummings at the Ninety-second Street "Y" in New York City. Familiarity with some of the poems he chose to read made it possible for me to realize, as I listened, how his arrangement of words upon a page gave instruction to the reader as to how they ought to sound. Wonderful! And, if one simply relaxed into enjoyment, the poetry within the poems became easier to find. Fascinated by the work, intrigued by the poet, I tentatively began to try to read the play aloud. To my surprise I discovered that friends and roommates liked to listen when I did. Many years later, teaching courses on children's literature, I would find that reading aloud was still something I enjoyed doing and that it made a good demonstration to students, some of whom had not been read to before. Again, as in my experience with cummings, I learned that the important thing is to give one's energy and attention to the meaning of the material. Then emphasis and inflection seem to take care of themselves. In the last few years I have learned to apply the same principle to reading my own work aloud. Now I am doing it more and more often, and less and less self-consciously, during my visits to schools.

When I graduated from college it was as a physiology major with no intention of becoming a physiologist. It took me three years, from June 1949, when I completed my work at Vassar, until the fall of 1952, to establish a new field of interest. It was fortuitous that in the year immediately after college I found work as a classroom assistant in a special nursery school for disturbed but very young children. Attendance at staff seminars and case presentations constituted a privileged and dramatic introduction to psychoanalytic theory. Slowly I was learning that the body, our language, and now the mind itself might be examined and understood.

The next year, following the recommendation of one of the staff members at the school, I became a candidate for the master's degree in psychology at New York's City College. This was an experimental, idealistic program. Its small faculty included some of the leading figures of the day in both experimental and dynamic psychology—busy, prominent persons who were willing to teach evening classes so that students who did not belong to an academic elite could participate. That year I read a lot, worked hard, and decided that psychology, with an emphasis on child development theory, was what I wanted to study.

Leaving an uncompleted M.A. program behind me, I became a doctoral candidate at Yale and simultaneously a research assistant in its Child Study Center. Was it a good move or a poor one? Neither of the programs which took me to New Haven proved congenial settings for me. But it was there that I met Peter Blos, Jr., a first-year medical student. When I found my next favorite library it had more to do with personal reasons than with matters of scholarship.

V

One November afternoon, not long after our first meeting, we collided at the door to the library just as I was leaving. To my pleasure it turned out that he had been looking for me. It was an unusually mild day for that time of year and he had the idea that we might take our bicycles and ride out into the country.

"You're the person I've been looking for!" he said. And that's how it all began.

A broad balcony filled with library stacks circled the central reading room of Yale's Medical School library. There were long, well-polished tables between the stacks of books and we would meet there, evenings, with books spread out between us, to study and to talk. When the library closed he would walk me home. We discovered that we had grown up in the same neighborhood, gone to similar schools, knew many of the same songs and some of the same people. It was so easy to be together. Maybe it was because we had so much in common that it did not take long for us to feel that we knew each other well. Our decision to be married at the end of his freshman year, just about six months after we met, did not seem at all precipitous.

By the time we left New Haven three years later it had become clear that academic psychology and I were not a good match. But employment in the pediatric play program sponsored by Yale's School of Nursing (I worked with child patients directly and did some teaching of student nurses) brought me, in the characteristic and circuitous way of such things, to children's literature.

With husband and young guest at wedding, June 7, 1953.

Suddenly there was a place where all I had learned about child development, all my interest in language, and all my love of books could at last come together. Since 1954 I have been a teacher, a critic, a teacher who sometimes wrote, and now a writer who sometimes teaches. But I have never lost my interest in this wonderful field or wished to enter another.

Shortly before our return to New York City I reregistered as an M.A. candidate at City College and devised a study on children's responses to books and the capacity of (trained) adults to predict those responses. It was also in our final year in New Haven that our son was born. As a result of these concurrent events my one-year-old sat on a classroom table and played with chalk while I, at my final conference with my thesis advisor, discussed the statistical significance of my interview data. I was grateful to them both.

From New Haven we moved our small family to New York City, where my husband completed his medical training, began psychoanalytic training and private practice, and our daughter was born.

VI

Parenthood, and the big old-fashioned library on Ninety-sixth Street with the children's room on the second floor, reached by a wide oak stairway. The librarians no longer used those wonderful pencils of my childhood. But neither was it the age of computerized checkouts and magnetically protected books. At the Ninety-sixth Street library there were low oak tables at which the children could read and, on several occasions, we attended traditional storyreading hours, complete with ritual candles. Although we used the library fairly regularly, I do not think any of us ever came to feel terribly keenly about it. In part this was because we were then living uptown, where the library was located, but the children attended school downtown, where we had lived before. So our sense of neighborhood was very much divided and the library never had a chance to become a center. Recently, though, saved in an old leather wallet, I found my library card and my daughter's. I had clearly been reluctant to part with either one of them after we moved away.

During the years about which I have been telling, 1959 to 1970, my work with children's books and literature became more and more important. What made the difference was my connection with Bank Street College of Education, an independent institution dedicated to a progressive point of view in education and the five-faceted development of that point of view through research, demonstration, field service, education, and publication. My mother and aunt were both members of the faculty there, directing the Teacher Education and Research Divisions respectively. And Lucy Sprague Mitchell, who had written my well-loved *Here and Now Story Book,* was still active in the life of the institution she had helped to establish, although well past retirement age.

I began by working part-time in the Publications Division. "Publications" had been a special interest of Mrs. Mitchell's and the office still contained the old-fashioned sofa on which she had liked to work. At that time our daughter was still too young to attend so much as a nursery-school program and so, when other arrangements failed, I would bring her along with me. Most of the time Mrs. Mitchell's sofa was piled with papers and manuscripts but these, it turned out, could be cleared away when a small child needed a nap.

It was a wonderful work situation for me—warm, responsive, and collegial. Beyond that, it was exciting for me to be associated with people who had been Mrs. Mitchell's students. Among them were Irma Simonton Black and Claudia Lewis, who could still tell stories about "Brownie," as Margaret Wise Brown was known to them, and her famous Kerry Blue dogs. Ruth Krauss and Eve Merriam, who had also been members of the Writers' Laboratory when Mrs. Mitchell directed it, dropped in from time to time. On one well-remembered occasion a writer I judged to be about my age read aloud a story that she had just completed. I remember thinking that the story was a very good one but also that it was the kind of thing I could try to write. This is my first memory of Betty Miles. I have admired her work and valued our friendship for more than thirty years now. So it is pleasant to record that her story, when published, became the picture book *Having a Friend.*

Work in the Publications Division had three parts: writing, reviewing, and teaching. At that time our major writing project was the collaborative development of a basal reading series for grades one to three. Our emphasis was to be on content rather than phonetics, linguistics, or word recognition as the basis of reading instruction. Part of the concept was that we would provide story material more relevant to the lives and interests of inner-city children than the all-white characters and affluent settings of traditional readers. In the early 1960s this was a radical idea and it was not easy to find a publisher willing to take the risk. Then, in 1963, Macmillan took on the challenge, and the series, later transferred to the Houghton Mifflin Company, started out as the Bank Street-Macmillan Readers.

Taking the city itself as the subject, I was largely responsible for the first pre-primer. "One house. Two houses. Three houses," I wrote. "Many houses. Many, many houses." Then the same thing for streets. Then the first section concluded, "Many houses. Many streets. One city." Together Betty Miles and I did the second pre-primer, which was called *People Read.* All of us contributed stories to the volumes that followed and, following the leadership of a reading consultant, we were also made responsible for the teacher's guides.

Another activity of our small staff was reviewing children's books for the *Saturday Review of Literature.* Every month a brief (five hundred-word) essay had to be written, as well as reviews of children's books related to the topic that the essay established. We all con-

Under the George Washington Bridge, New York, with son, age seven, and daughter, age five, 1963.

tributed the reviews and took turns writing the essays. For some time thereafter, whenever I wrote nonfiction I produced five hundred words.

The teaching was of two kinds. I was given responsibility for evening courses in language arts and children's literature by the Graduate Programs (Teacher Education) Division, and I participated with other members of the Publications Division in conducting the Writers' Lab. My graduate-student's knowledge of child development theory and psychodynamic concepts found good use in both settings and I continued to learn by reading. Over the years I developed a special interest in the prereading child and in picture books, which I came to think of as *the* literary invention of the twentieth century. Adding M.A. thesis advisement to my list of activities, I continued at Bank Street on a regular but part-time basis until the summer of 1970, when we left New York City for Michigan.

Of all these activities it was the Writers' Lab that, and most appropriately, was responsible for my initiation as a published writer. The Writers' Lab met weekly and most sessions were devoted to critiquing members' writings as they were read aloud. From time to time editors, agents, publishers, and friendly authors would

be invited guests. On one such occasion, when it was my night to read, Virginie Fowler, who was children's book editor at Knopf, was the visitor. My story, "The Mean Man," told of a disagreeable fellow who arrives in town, antagonizes his neighbors, and leaves. The manuscript interested Miss Fowler, and I was invited to submit it for publication.

Despite this auspicious start the story could not be made to arrive at a workable ending and the project was set aside. Fortunately I had another, less problematic manuscript to offer. *"It's Spring," She Said,* a simple telling of the way spring comes to the city, became my first published work. Looking back on the story it is interesting to see that when I wrote it I used intersecting story lines as a device for conveying the simultaneity of events. I was to do something similar in *A Gathering of Days* when I wrote it as a journal and the technique became even more prominent in *Brothers of the Heart.*

Atha Tehon designed the book, and Julie Maas, who lived in downtown Manhattan, as I did, became its illustrator. I believe it marked a first, or early, venture for each of the three of us. It is interesting that we have all stayed on in the roles associated with that book but we have never worked on the same project again. *"It's Spring,"* *She Said* has been out of print for some time now. But every once in a while, when I visit a school, a librarian will show me a copy, very well-used, and ask if I will sign it. Apparently there are some places where reading this story aloud has become a springtime tradition.

During the mid-1960s I worked on a number of writing projects. Some were published, such as *Just Think!* and *Joe Finds a Way,* both written with Betty Miles; others were not. But I learned something from my struggles with each and every one of them and, in several cases, themes and story ideas that were not resolvable then turned up in later works. It was at this time, too, that I began to explore the history of the old New Hampshire farmhouse that my husband's parents had purchased in 1941 and used each year thereafter during summer vacations.

VII

The town of Holderness, New Hampshire, does not have a large public library. The redbrick building that houses it has wide steps made of marble at the front but there is not much space for parking between this attractive entrance and the busy two lane road on which it stands, which is also the town's Main Street. It is my recollection that ours was the only car in the parking area on the late midsummer afternoon when my husband and I decided to make a quick stop there before heading home for dinner. The morning had been his part of the day and we had climbed halfway up Mount Moosilauke and back. In the afternoon, *my* part, we had gone to Woodsville, which was the county seat. I had become curious about the history of the house and I had the idea that the thing to do was to examine the county records. In order to do this we would have to have the deed to the property and, in anticipation of our visit that summer, my father-in-law had brought the needed document along when they came up from the city.

"Dear," said the woman seated at the desks "if you knew how many summer people come in thinking they'll find something . . ."

But we were lucky. In the space of a few hours we were able to establish that the house had been built in 1827 by the youngest of five brothers who belonged to a well-known local family. He had died, leaving the property to his wife and two infant daughters, just a few years after completing the house and clearing the nearest acres. The wife had subsequently remarried and it was by her second husband's name that the farm was locally known. Over the years parcels of land had been sold and bought back again as the family's fortunes had fallen and been regained.

When you learn so much in such a short time you invariably want to learn more. We speculated that if the builder of the house had all those nearby brothers the house might share a history with other houses in the area. Would the town library have any information about the family, we wondered? And they did—a whole privately published genealogical study that included a few anecdotes and several references to names, and also locations, with which we were familiar.

Once again, libraries became important in my life as, back in New York City, I pursued my newfound interest in New Hampshire's history. Wonderful things, such as a collection of New Hampshire legends compiled in the mid-nineteenth century by Mrs. Gore and Mrs. Moody, were to be found in the American History Room of the great Forty-second Street library. Memoirs and reminiscences, biographies and autobiographies became interesting for what they told of childhood in nineteenth-century New England. Novels and magazine stories gave further hints as to the sorts of things people cared about—the sorts of details they noticed—and how they thought they talked. I became aware of the differences between life as it was lived in the larger centers, such as Boston or Salem or Portsmouth, and in rural areas not many miles away.

I had no intention of writing a book at first. I was just curious. What had life been like, I wondered, when the house had been new and a young New Hampshire family had taken pride in it? What did they eat? What did they wear? What did the children learn in school and what were their teachers like? It might have been easier to find answers to questions about presidents and politics. But this was more fun.

It is important to stress that this had become a kind of hobby for me, something I was able to pursue with an amateur's interest. After all, these were the years of teaching, child rearing, dog walking; the years of involvement in the development of the Bank Street Readers, as they were getting to be known, and work on several independent stories, some of which I read at Writers' Lab sessions. I did not work on the New Hampshire project regularly, and perhaps the very fact that I came on the idea of a New Hampshire book slowly and gradually, and then worked on it slowly and gradually, gave me useful opportunity to reflect on what was happening in the story; to create and also correct. And of course I loved the research!

I gleaned information from sources as different and disparate as John Greenleaf Whittier's poem "Snow Bound" and William Garrison's *Liberator.* The more I read, the more I wanted to know. As I wasn't working against a deadline or even aware that I was Writing a Book I went on and on, filling notebooks, visiting Sturbridge Village, looking at quilts. I made lists of first names and last names as they appeared on school rolls, gravestones, merchants' account books, and irate letters to editors of small-town newspapers. It was quite a while before I began to think that I might have a book on my hands. Then it took me several more years before I was able to settle on the journal form.

VII

In the summer of 1970 we moved from New York City to Ann Arbor, Michigan. For several years I worked (two or three days a week) at the Child Development Project under the leadership of Selma Fraiberg. Then, in 1973, I exchanged that position for one with the School of Education, where I taught children's literature until 1980. When I had time I continued my research. It is only fair to say that, as I had already begun the writing of the book, it might have been wiser to make that task my focus. But the research was much, much easier to do. Besides, I had discovered the seemingly infinite resources of the University of Michigan libraries and I was delighted with the new material I was able to find. At the Clements Library, for example, they had actual copies of Noah Webster's blue-back spellers, newspapers from New Hampshire communities relevant to my story, and a copy of a nineteenth-century book of advice to mothers. It was exciting to hold these materials in my hands and to think that people very like the characters I was developing for my story had read these very pages, had held these books in their hands. Libraries! Libraries! It is not that I have remained the voracious reader that I was as a child but rather that there is something about being in the presence of so many books that I find satisfying. One hour easily turns into many whether I have gone to find a book for vacation reading, look up a practical matter, or explore a new idea. So perhaps it is especially appropriate and meet that one of the major awards presented me for *A Gathering of Days: A New England Girl's Journal, 1830-32* came from the Children's Services Division of the American Library Association.

"How did it feel to win the Newbery?" Children ask the question when I visit schools, and grown-ups ask it when I speak at conferences. There is no way, really, to answer. I can only say that I had never thought of it as existing in any possible connection with myself and then, in the peculiar way that such things happen, after I won it I think it took quite a while before I could really comprehend the honor's implications and the difference it would make.

By that singular event I had been converted into a Recognized Author. Thereafter I would be invited to speak at conferences and meetings all across the country, would be included in various biographical dictionaries and reference works (including this one), would be asked to autograph books in bookstores and make visits to schools. Because I was a Newbery winner, what I had to say about children's literature was more interesting to more people! I resolved to take advantage of this and I have appreciated the opportunities to travel, to meet others in the field, to belong. Also, and not the least of my rewards, I was in a better position to write the kinds of books I like, including historical fiction, which tends not to be a favorite with the business side of publishing because of its bad reputation in the matter of sales.

As for the medal itself I often take it along with me when I visit schools. Teachers are usually more impressed than students, who point out correctly that the medal is a lot less shiny than the sticker on the book and, also true, that it is not made of gold. When I give them the medal to pass around the class, I can see that they like its substantial heft and size and I tell them then to look at the back of the medal as well as the front. There they will see a man holding a book, and a boy and a girl. I explain that the figure of the man represents Mr. Frederick Melcher, who, in 1921, initiated a medal honoring authors of children's literature. But, I add, I like to think of it as reminding us that grown-ups and children together take part in children's books.

While people are looking at the medal I usually take the opportunity to say two things more: that athletic activities are not the only ones that get rewarded by medals, and that the hope of receiving a medal should not be the reason for doing what one does. These ideas, although somewhat contradictory, are both important to me.

Not long after becoming a Newbery winner I attended a gathering which included a Caldecott winner. "You know," he told me, only half seeming to smile, "getting these medals hasn't turned out very luckily for a lot of people." Perhaps it was because the comment seemed so odd and out of place that I remembered it. But it is true that for me, and not having much to do with luck one way or the other, the decade ushered in by my receipt of the Newbery Medal was only in part a good one. I knew both sadness and tragedy in those years, and learned to tell the difference. But the good parts came first.

IX

The Bentley Library at the University of Michigan is the kind of place that scholars dream about. Its main room is furnished with spacious oak tables. One entire glass wall looks out on a sculpture garden so arranged that even in winter—even in winter in Michigan, which is long and bleak and bare—the space has a kind of beauty. Among my libraries the Bentley is a favorite, a wonderful place to work. What took me there was another piece of historical fiction, this one to be set in Michigan at the time it became a state.

When Clare Costello, the Scribner editor responsible for the publication of *A Gathering of Days,* had first suggested a second book to take the story further, I had thought of another New England book, one which would perhaps take up the figure of the peddler as its leading character. However I soon discovered a more relevant interest in Michigan's history. By that time we had lived in Ann Arbor for ten years but I knew only the most ordinary facts about its early days. This would be an opportunity to find out about the settlement of the Middle West, a region where many people live but whose history is pretty much ignored and about which very little is taught in most American schools.

Actually, I began my work on the Michigan book in the Ypsilanti Historical Society, in a room set aside as a library. I was dependent on others to take me there, and home, for I had broken a leg in a sidewalk fall that winter and could neither walk far nor drive. One morning I came on a map of the area drawn by Bela Hubbard, a nineteenth-century cartographer who had explored the region and made maps for the use of prospective settlers. This particular map showed the precise location of a town I had not even known about. That afternoon, I happened to look down as my friend drove us across the Huron River using a modern bridge. Bela Hubbard's map had been so good that I could recognize the site, the very place where that town had been. When it came time to write *Brothers of the Heart* I used my impression of this setting when I described the fictional Millfield as being "set on a modest plain, crooked in the river's arm."

But Ypsilanti's materials only got me started. The major part of the work was done at the Bentley. As a library it is devoted to Michigan history, and although

there are many books on the subject the most interesting part of the collection is its maps, diaries, public documents, town histories, and letters. There are not only individual letters but entire sets of family letters—letters sent and answers received as pioneer farmers and settlers reported back to their families in the East, and each side saved its share. At the Bentley I was able to read the detailed field notes kept by the same Bela Hubbard, and among his materials I discovered a box filled with small notebooks that contained handwritten entries reporting on years of weather. They must have been written all at the same time. The handwriting doesn't change, the way it does, little by little, over the years, and the color of the ink throughout the books is all the same faded brown. It looked to me as if Hubbard had gone back over all of his notebooks and other records to locate just this information—how cold it was, how warm; wind from which direction; sun, fair, clouds or rain—and I was determined to use it. When I say (page 62, *Brothers of the Heart*) that, in 1837, at Mackinac Island on the tenth of December, although the temperature had fallen to two degrees below zero the night be-

Newbery night, July, 1, 1980, with mother, son, and daughter.

fore, "the sun made the wintry day quite pleasant," that is a matter of record.

The course of this book's composition was slowed by my mother's illness and then her death in 1982. Cancer is a cruel disease. It was hard to watch the decline of this once vibrant and keenly intelligent woman and there was nothing that could be done about her worsening helplessness and incapacity. Here was someone who had continued to work professionally all through her seventies. Here was someone who, at the age of eighty, had single-handedly prepared and hosted a lavish party to show her pleasure in her daughter's Newbery Medal. And here was that very daughter, unable to do a single thing that would really help. So I visited every day.

Altogether I spent four years on *Brothers of the Heart: A Story of the Old Northwest, 1837-1838,* two on the research and two on the writing. At the same time I was engaged in preparing a new picture book for publication. It would be called *Martin's Hats* and Marc Simont had agreed to do the illustrations. Martin is a small boy with a hat collection, and as the book goes on he becomes an engineer, a chef, a farmer. He is always in charge, and always competent. The changes take place as he puts on one hat after another from his hat collection. It is clear to me now that Martin is the direct descendent of another small, fictional boy, one whose story I had attempted years ago but had not been able to finish. Similarly, there is no doubt in my mind but that the struggle between the crippled protagonist of *Brothers of the Heart* and his father is related to difficult father-son relationships that I had attempted to tell about some twenty years before in early, unpublished works.

"How long does it take you to write a book?" I find that question nearly impossible to answer. It all depends on what you mean by "write." But I am almost certain that it takes a whole lot longer than any non-writer imagines!

X

After the work on *Brothers of the Heart,* indeed before it was finished, there came a time when libraries were no use at all and their knowledge failed us. Our son, who was married and had become a photographer, was discovered to have cancer. Diagnosed at first as being treatable, it proved both untreatable and intractable. The illness ran its course in something less than a year; three seasons' worth. Although he was desperately sick at the time, he was able to be home from the hospital for his thirtieth birthday. We celebrated it with his best friends and the closest parts of the family present. Five days later he died.

It is astonishing to me to realize that four of my picture books have been published since that time and that two more are being illustrated now. I have given many lectures, visited many schools, and worked on another story. We have moved from the house where we used to live, and we have left behind us the year and then the decade in which our son was alive. We who were his family are sad for ourselves, because we miss him so, and most of all we are sad for him because of all he missed.

You do not get over such sadness, I have found, but you do get used to it. You get used to it, but slowly. *While* that is happening or *because* it is, you begin to enjoy things like friendships, sunsets, jokes that are funny (and some that are not). Good things happen and you appreciate them. You are proud when your daughter embarks on graduate work in the field of education (how her grandmother would have welcomed that!), pleased by her marriage, and follow with interest the ideas and activities of her husband. Your daughter-in-law marries again and this, too, makes you glad. Still, there are times when you have to give yourself a good strong talking to, just to keep on going. But you do.

XI

Of all my books, *Old Henry,* with illustrations by Stephen Gammell, has won the most friends for itself. It's the story of an eccentric man who moves into a dilapidated house in a traditional town. The neighbors expect him to repair the house but it doesn't even occur to him to do so. Disputes and arguments break out. He leaves. The story is told in rhyme, so several pages after his departure the neighbors realize that, "His house looks so empty, so dark in the night. / Having him gone doesn't make us more right." At the same time Henry, wherever he is, has realized that he misses his house and yes, even the neighbors. He writes a letter proposing compromise. There the book ends.

I have received many packets containing whole classrooms-full of letters to Henry. Most readers say that he should come back. Some say they will help him clean up; some tell him this is his last chance. It pleases me to think that people are liking this book and thinking about it. One of the reasons this makes me so glad is that this story is, of course, what came of that "Mean Man" story of so many years ago, the one I couldn't complete.

The idea for *The Heroine of the Titanic: A Tale Both True and Otherwise of the Life of Molly Brown* did not come from an earlier book or story but from a visit to the Molly Brown House Museum in Denver, Colorado, a number of years ago. The character of this sad but funny lady interested me, and I thought that some of the stories told about her were wonderful.

"She'd make a great book," I said to my husband as we left the well-restored house. "But not for children," I added.

Am I surprised or was it to be expected that eventually I'd get back to Molly Brown, or that she'd catch up with me? In the spring of 1987 I spent five days doing nothing but research in Denver and came back with many vivid impressions and a lot of information. This was not at all the way I had done the research for my other books, but this story was different and shorter, being almost like a ballad, something like a tale. With the addition of some made-up episodes—Molly herself was a great confabulator—the help of a wonderful editor, and illustrations by Tennessee Dixon, my "Tale Both True and Otherwise" has turned itself into a book. I had a good time working on it and I think it is true to the spirit of Molly Brown, if not all the facts.

XII

When I was a little girl my mother and her two sisters used to tell stories about growing up in Brooklyn at the turn of the century. They had an uncle who sometimes called two hansom cabs to take himself home at night. There would be one for himself, they remembered, and one for his hat. One of my aunts, a tomboy when she was young, used to hitch rides by hanging onto the back of ice wagons while wearing roller skates. There were other stories too. I don't know if I can tell about them in the right way, but I am going

to try. Meanwhile, it has been necessary to learn more about the place, Brooklyn, and the time, the early 1900s, of which I intend to write. Once again I am asking questions: what did people wear? what did they teach in school? what sorts of things made them happy? what was happening in their world? One of my aunts, now ninety-three years old, has been able to answer some of my questions, but not all. So these last two years I've been in libraries again—some in Ann Arbor, some in New York—not yet satisfied that I have got it figured out.

It's unfortunate that you can't read real newspapers anymore, just the microfilm copies rolling noisily by. So, at the Graduate Library of the University of Michigan, I have spent a lot of time lately, with my neck at an awkward angle, reading, reading, reading. When I visited the Lower East Side Tenement Museum on Orchard Street in New York City our daughter, who teaches at a high school nearby, joined me. And, at the Ann Arbor Public Library, in bound copies of *St. Nicholas* magazine for the years 1906-1909, I found several winning poems submitted by a young Edna St. Vincent Millay to its monthly competition.

Appropriately enough, my cycle of libraries concludes as it began, not in a huge repository of techno-

School visit, 1989.

Blos and husband, Peter Blos, Jr., 1997.

logical data but in a people-sized public library where people come to sit and read, look things up, check books out, find answers to their questions. As one might expect, it has computers instead of card catalogues, and there are electronic devices at the checkout desk instead of the stamps and stamp pads that I used to admire so much. Affection, interest, and habit draw me over and over again to the children's room. Today a former student attends the librarian's desk. And sure enough, as I stand there now, a four-year-old and her mother enter hand in hand. They have come to the library to find the books they love.

POSTSCRIPT

Blos contributed the following autobiographical update in 2004:

Many things have changed since 1991 when my contribution to *Something about the Author Autobiography Series,* volume 11, was published. The cell phone has become ubiquitous, three presidential elections have

taken place (and, as I write, a fourth is imminent), and the United States has endured the shock of a terrorist attack and the tragedy of war. Global warming has become an acknowledged fact, an increasing number of transactions are accomplished electronically—and many readers of this essay were born.

Closer to home, three events warranting celebration have occurred. In 1992 and 1998 our two grandsons were born, and in the year that recently ended, my husband and I observed the fiftieth anniversary of our 1953 wedding. Otherwise I would say that the past decade has neither encompassed dramatic events nor led to major changes. Nico and Lucas are as fine a pair of boys as ever delighted a grandmother's eyes. I enjoyed a particularly proud moment when I escorted Nico to the library to receive his first library card and I look forward to doing the same for Lucas. Perhaps—as I did with Nico—I will make a small ceremony of the event by reading aloud "At the Library," one of the later chapters of *Brooklyn Doesn't Rhyme,* when we get home.

Although I regard the 1990s as a rather fallow time for me as a writer of children's books, looking back—and counting!—reveals a rather different story! It appears that since 1991, I have written and published seven picture books (two of which dealt with historical figures), and researched, written, and published *Brooklyn Doesn't Rhyme,* the novel set in 1907 to which I have just referred. Talks given at professional meetings have ranged rather widely as to content. Thus "You Be the Mommy: The Developmental Importance of Imagined Experience" was addressed to psychologists and links drama, fiction, and the free play of children. Its central thesis is that "the capacity to imagine is as distinctively human as the opposable thumb and quite possibly as important." Another paper, equally but differently interested in the human experience, looks inward. "PRIVAT [sic] KEEP OUT!" appeared in the *Michigan Quarterly Review,* summer 2000, and examines the diary as a literary device. The title refers to the almost instinctive defense of the diary in real life. "45 Years Later and Still in Love with Picture Books," for early childhood educators, takes up the picture book as a literary genre and suggests that it is the literary invention of the twentieth century. "Noah Webster, Ann Arbor and Me" is a recent tribute to the public and university libraries of Ann Arbor, Michigan, which are a significant feature of the city that has been our home since the summer of 1970.

For me, as a writer, the stand-out experience of the years since 1991 occurred in 1999. That is when Wild Swan Theater, a local company known for the excellence of the plays it presents to children and young people, invited me to dramatize one of my books. I told them that I had not written a play since high school. But, I said, if they would take the chance, so would I.

Brothers of the Heart, set in pioneer Michigan, was the book chosen for dramatization. It's about a boy with a "gimpy leg" and at the center of the story is his wilderness experience with an elderly Ottawan woman. There were esthetic and dramatic reasons for our choice, and two reasons of a practical nature: the size of the cast required and the fact that Michigan students, who study Michigan history in fourth grade, would make up most of our audiences. Working with Wild Swan proved to be the most interesting, stimulating, and enjoyable collaboration I've enjoyed since the mid-1960s when Betty Miles and I teamed up to write *People Read,* the second pre-primer of the Bank Street-Macmillan Readers.

Soon after I began working on the *Brothers of the Heart* dramatization I discovered, to my delight and surprise, that plays and picture books are really very much alike in that neither permits verbal description, both depend on dialogue and action, and both proceed by scenes! These were things I knew about from writ-

Blos with husband, friend, and grandchildren, 2002.

Blos blowing out candles of her seventy-fifth birthday cake, with second grandson assisting, 2003.

ing and reviewing picture books, and teaching about them. So I had some useful skills and valuable past experience to bring to my new assignment after all!

When rehearsals began, I attended nearly all of them. This gave me new insights into what makes a play as well as a chance to do some "fine tuning" of the script. Once, when I tried to eliminate a small scene, I was over-ruled by the cast. That scene, they said, contained some of their favorite lines and it would be a big mistake to eliminate them. So the lines stayed in.

The play grew in interest and dramatic quality as costumes, sets, and music were added. And then it was opening night! I could feel the audience being drawn into the story, and when I realized that the person seated next to me, a stranger, was crying, I was persuaded that my story evoked real emotions. The cast called me to join them on stage after the final curtain, and amidst hugs from the actors and applause from the audience, I was presented with a wonderful armful of flowers. Although *Brothers of the Heart* enjoyed several revivals over the next few years, the first production was—and remains—the best!

In 2002, as an "Author, Teacher, and Advocate of Children and Literature," I received an Honorary Doctorate from Bank Street College of Education in New York City. My friend, Betty Miles, wrote a poem for me of which the first two lines were, "Congratulations as you get / this honorary doctorate." In glorious sunlight, a brief procession led from the College to the Cathedral of St. John the Divine where the ceremony was to be held. It was an unforgettable occasion, and I am proud, indeed, to be honored in that way by Bank Street. It is where I began my teaching and my writing and gained my lasting appreciation of the worth and value of children's books. Bank Street's influence pervades many of the things I do today.

So it's not just rhetoric that when people ask me where I am from, I answer that I now *live* in Ann Arbor but I am *from* New York. After thirty years or so, that East Coast identity is still important to me and I will never say New York *City* because, as a New Yorker, it's obvious that the city is what is meant. But it is also true that since 1987, when we moved from a large house in Ann Arbor's campus area to an apartment that's one block from City Hall, I've become involved in a number of activities involving the city itself. In some five or six years ago, when a deteriorated parking structure was to be demolished and replaced, I became a member of the Downtown Public Art Committee (locally known as DPAC) in thinking about the replacement structure and how art might be made part of its design. At one of our many meetings I proposed that numerals representing symbol systems other than the Arabic, beyond the Roman, and including Braille, be integrated with the structure's more conventional signage. Placed on the elevator landings of each floor of the new building they would, I argued, be something that would be visually and cognitively beautiful to all and accessible to children. This particular set of ideas was mine, to be sure. But they definitely derive from the teaching and learning of my Bank Street years.

More recently the rehabilitation of a small downtown park a few blocks from our home inspired me to suggest that it become the site of a summertime series of outdoor readings and performances for young children. Offered free of charge, these events could, and would, be a declaration of the city's commitment to its children. These events would, I predicted, demonstrate that words, music, dance, and drama bring people together. And they did! The program has been a great success and a true community effort: the mayor opens the first program of the season, the presenters contribute their services, and bookstores, with equal but different generosity, provide books so that each child who attends a program receives a brand new book. Free! A local dealer in antique rugs lends the iconic magic carpet whose unrolling signals the start of each program, and other local businesses have contributed in other ways.

But my assignment here is to say something about myself as an author. Making it difficult is that there has been a hiatus of several years and that the book on which I am presently working has been in the making for such a long time that I hesitate to say very much about it. Provisionally titled *Dear Cousin Sallie,* it is to join *A Gathering of Days* and *Brothers of the Heart* in the creation of a "geographical trilogy." Thus, mid-nineteenth century New Hampshire is the setting of the first of these books, the second book takes place in pioneer Michigan, and the California Gold Rush provides the new book with its setting. In each case characters are brought forward from one book into the next, perhaps most significantly in the case of the presently evolving story.

And what will I do when, as it must, this project comes to an end? I like to say that I will cheerfully unplug my computer because writing is difficult for me, and I don't much enjoy the process. However, it is equally true that I love being an author! I feel fortunate to have been a writer of children's books for what has become a very long time, and there are still things I would like to put into stories. So here's what I think. I think I will probably return to stories once begun and since abandoned, but possibly I will start a new one. I will get out a yellow pad and some pencils (the computer comes later for me) and I will begin to write.

BOURGEOIS, Paulette 1951-

Personal

Born July 20, 1951, in Winnipeg, Manitoba, Canada; daughter of Mathias (a chartered accountant) and Freda (a small business owner) Bourgeois; married Ian Urquhart (a journalist), May 3, 1980 (separated); children: Natalie, Gordon. *Education:* University of Western Ontario, B.Sc., 1974; attended Carleton University.

Addresses

Home—Toronto, Ontario, Canada. *Agent*—c/o Author Mail, Kids Can Press, 29 Birch Ave., Toronto, Ontario M4V 1E2, Canada.

Career

Royal Ottawa Hospital, Ottawa, Ontario, Canada, staff occupational therapist, 1975-76; Canadian Broadcasting Corp., reporter, 1977-78, 1980-81; freelance writer, 1981—.

Member

Writers Union of Canada, Canadian Society of Children's Authors, Illustrators, and Performers.

Awards, Honors

Recipient of several Canada Council grants and numerous Children's Choice Awards from the Canadian Children's Book Centre.

Writings

FOR CHILDREN

Big Sarah's Little Boots, illustrated by Brenda Clark, Kids Can Press (Toronto, Ontario, Canada), 1987.
On Your Mark, Get Set: All about the Olympic Games, Then and Now, illustrated by Tina Holdcroft, Kids Can Press (Toronto, Ontario, Canada), 1987.
The Amazing Apple Book, illustrated by Linda Hendry, Kids Can Press (Toronto, Ontario, Canada), 1987, Addison-Wesley (Reading, MA), 1990.

The Amazing Paper Book, illustrated by Linda Hendry, Kids Can Press (Toronto, Ontario, Canada), 1989, Addison-Wesley (Reading, MA), 1990.

Grandma's Secret (also see below), illustrated by Maryann Kovalski, Kids Can Press (Toronto, Ontario, Canada), 1989, Joy Street Books (Boston, MA), 1990.

The Amazing Dirt Book, illustrated by Craig Terlson, Addison-Wesley (Reading, MA), 1990.

Too Many Chickens, illustrated by Bill Slavin, Kids Can Press (Toronto, Ontario, Canada), 1990.

The Amazing Potato Book, Addison-Wesley (Reading, MA), 1991.

Canadian Fire Fighters ("My Neighborhood" series), illustrated by Kim LaFave, Kids Can Press (Toronto, Ontario, Canada), 1991, published as *Fire Fighters,* 1998.

Canadian Garbage Collectors ("My Neighborhood" series), illustrated by Kim LaFave, Kids Can Press (Toronto, Ontario, Canada), 1991, published as *Garbage Collectors,* 1998.

Canadian Police Officers ("My Neighborhood" series), illustrated by Kim LaFave, Kids Can Press (Toronto, Ontario, Canada), 1991, published as *Police Officers,* 1998.

Canadian Postal Workers ("My Neighborhood" series), illustrated by Kim LaFave, Kids Can Press (Toronto, Ontario, Canada), 1992, published as *Postal Workers,* 1998.

(With Martin Wolfish) *Changes in You and Me: A Book about Puberty, Mostly for Boys,* Andrews & McMeel (Kansas City, KS), 1994.

Changes in You and Me: A Book about Puberty, Mostly for Girls, Andrews & McMeel (Kansas City, KS), 1994.

Too Many Hats of Mr. Minches, illustrated by Kathryn Naylor, Stoddart (Toronto, Ontario, Canada), 1994.

The Sun ("Starting with Space" series), Kids Can Press (Toronto, Ontario, Canada), 1995.

The Moon ("Starting with Space" series), Kids Can Press (Toronto, Ontario, Canada), 1995.

Oma's Quilt, illustrated by Stephane Jorisch, Kids Can Press (Toronto, Ontario, Canada), 2001.

"FRANKLIN" SERIES

Franklin in the Dark (also see below; Book-of-the-Month Club selection), illustrated by Brenda Clark, Kids Can Press (Toronto, Ontario, Canada), 1986.

Hurry Up, Franklin (also see below), illustrated by Brenda Clark, Kids Can Press (Toronto, Ontario, Canada), 1989, Scholastic (New York, NY), 1990.

Franklin Fibs (also see below), illustrated by Brenda Clark, Scholastic (New York, NY), 1991.

Franklin Is Lost (also see below), illustrated by Brenda Clark, Scholastic (New York, NY), 1992.

Franklin Is Bossy (also see below), illustrated by Brenda Clark, Scholastic (New York, NY), 1993.

Franklin Is Messy, illustrated by Brenda Clark, Scholastic (New York, NY), 1994.

Franklin and Me: A Book about Me, Written and Drawn by Me (with a Little Help from Franklin), illustrated by Brenda Clark, Kids Can Press (Toronto, Ontario,

Canada), 1994, published as *Franklin and Me: My First Record of Favourite Things, Personal Facts, and Special Memories,* 1997.

Franklin Goes to School (also see below), illustrated by Brenda Clark, Scholastic (New York, NY), 1995.

Franklin Plays the Game, illustrated by Brenda Clark, Scholastic (New York, NY), 1995.

Franklin's Blanket (also see below), illustrated by Brenda Clark, Scholastic (New York, NY), 1995.

Franklin Wants a Pet (also see below), illustrated by Brenda Clark, Scholastic (New York, NY), 1995.

Franklin and the Tooth Fairy (also see below), illustrated by Brenda Clark, Kids Can Press (Toronto, Ontario, Canada), 1995, Scholastic (New York, NY), 1996.

Franklin Has a Sleepover (also see below), illustrated by Brenda Clark, Kids Can Press (Toronto, Ontario, Canada), 1995, Scholastic (New York, NY), 1996.

Franklin's Halloween (also see below), illustrated by Brenda Clark, Scholastic (New York, NY), 1996.

Franklin's School Play (also see below), illustrated by Brenda Clark, Scholastic (New York, NY), 1996.

Franklin's Bad Day (also see below), illustrated by Brenda Clark, Kids Can Press (Toronto, Ontario, Canada), 1996, Scholastic (New York, NY), 1997.

Franklin Rides a Bike, illustrated by Brenda Clark, Scholastic (New York, NY), 1997.

Franklin's New Friend (also see below), illustrated by Brenda Clark, Scholastic (New York, NY), 1997.

Franklin's Valentines (also see below), illustrated by Brenda Clark, Scholastic (New York, NY), 1998.

Finders Keepers for Franklin, illustrated by Brenda Clark, Scholastic (New York, NY), 1998.

Franklin and the Thunderstorm, illustrated by Brenda Clark, Scholastic (New York, NY), 1998.

Franklin's Christmas Gift (also see below), illustrated by Brenda Clark, Scholastic (New York, NY), 1998.

Franklin's Secret Club (also see below), illustrated by Brenda Clark, Scholastic (New York, NY), 1998.

(With Sharon Jennings) *Franklin's Class Trip* (also see below), illustrated by Brenda Clark, Scholastic (New York, NY), 1999.

Franklin's Classic Treasury (contains *Franklin in the Dark, Franklin Fibs, Franklin Is Bossy,* and *Hurry Up, Franklin*), illustrated by Brenda Clark, Scholastic (New York, NY), 1999.

Franklin's Classic Treasury, Volume II (contains *Franklin Is Lost, Franklin Wants a Pet, Franklin's Blanket,* and *Franklin and the Tooth Fairy*), illustrated by Brenda Clark, Kids Can Press (Toronto, Ontario, Canada), 2000.

Franklin's Baby Sister (also see below), illustrated by Brenda Clark, Scholastic (New York, NY), 2000.

Franklin's Friendship Treasury (contains *Franklin Has a Sleepover, Franklin's Bad Day, Franklin's New Friend,* and *Franklin's Secret Club*), illustrated by Brenda Clark, Kids Can Press (Toronto, Ontario, Canada), 2000.

Franklin and Harriet (also see below), illustrated by Brenda Clark, Scholastic (New York, NY), 2001.

Franklin's School Treasury (contains *Franklin Goes to School, Franklin's School Play, Franklin's Class Trip,* and *Franklin's Neighborhood*), illustrated by Brenda Clark, Kids Can Press (Toronto, Ontario, Canada), 2001.

Franklin Says I Love You (also see below), illustrated by Brenda Clark, Scholastic (New York, NY), 2002.

Franklin's Holiday Treasury (contains *Franklin's Halloween, Franklin's Valentines, Franklin's Christmas Gift,* and *Franklin's Thanksgiving*), illustrated by Brenda Clark, Kids Can Press (Toronto, Ontario, Canada), 2002.

Franklin's Family Treasury (contains *Franklin Goes to the Hospital, Franklin's Baby Sister, Franklin and Harriet* and *Franklin Says I Love You*), illustrated by Brenda Clark, Kids Can Press (Toronto, Ontario, Canada), 2003.

Many of Bourgeois's books have been translated into French; several have also been translated into Spanish.

Adaptations

A television series based on the "Franklin" books was created, airing on Canada's Family Channel, the Canadian Broadcasting Corporation (CBC), and Nickelodeon. An animated movie, *Franklin and the Green Knight,* was produced by Nelvana and Hong Guang Animation in 2000. Other authors have written books in the "Franklin" series which were based on Bourgeois's characters, including *Franklin's Neighborhood, Franklin Goes to the Hospital,* and *Franklin's Thanksgiving.*

Sidelights

Paulette Bourgeois is known across the United States and her native Canada as the creator of the classic, beloved children's book character Franklin. Franklin is a tiny turtle who suffers from all of the fears and trials of childhood. As he overcomes them, Franklin teaches preschool children lessons about trust, friendship, bravery, family, and many other topics, but he accomplishes this in a different way than most children's book characters do, note critics. As Valerie Hussey, co-owner of the "Franklin" series publisher Kids Can Press, explained to *Maclean's* interviewer Diane Turbide, "Very often, there's a kind of pedantry in children's books, with adults pointing out the lesson to be learned. . . . We try hard to avoid that. Franklin's parents are there to support him, but he usually resolves it himself. That's a large part of the appeal."

Around the time that her daughter, Natalie, was born, Bourgeois thought that she might like to write children's books, but she could not think of an original idea for one. She finally came up with the idea for Franklin while sitting up late one night with her infant daughter. She was watching an episode of the television series *M*A*S*H* in which the star, Hawkeye Pierce, declared that he was so claustrophobic that if he were a turtle, he would be afraid to go inside his shell. Bourgeois sat down and in less than a week wrote a story about just such a turtle. This story eventually became her first children's book, *Franklin in the Dark.*

Franklin the turtle faces some very understandable misgivings when he hears his class is planning a trip to a museum with real dinosaurs, but he finds the adventure is educational and fun when he arrives. (From Franklin's Class Trip, *written by Paulette Bourgeois and Sharon Jennings and illustrated by Brenda Clark.*)

The "Franklin" series has grown to encompass scores of books, a television series, and a movie, but the theme of facing one's fears remains common. In *Franklin and the Thunderstorm,* the little turtle wants to stay home with his mother instead of going to visit his friend Fox on a day when there might be a thunderstorm. His mother convinces him to go, and with his friends to support him, he learns that thunderstorms are not so bad after all. "Children will relate to the situation and the gentle humor of the solution," thought a *Resource Links* contributor. In *Franklin Is Lost,* Franklin and his friends have fun playing hide-and-seek. The little turtle forgets that he is not allowed to go in the woods, tries to hide there, and cannot find his way back out. "Bourgeois captures . . . well the surprise and fear that accompanies being lost," commented another *Resource Links* reviewer.

In *Franklin's Class Trip,* both Franklin and his friend Snail are afraid. Their classmate Beaver tells them that there are real dinosaurs at the museum the class is visiting. Franklin and Snail (who rides around the museum on Franklin's shell) spend the whole morning getting more and more worried about the dinosaurs, but finally, when they make it to the dinosaur room in the afternoon, the two critters realize that the dinosaurs are not alive and stop worrying.

The "Franklin" books also teach social skills like sharing, not being bossy, and cooperating. In *Franklin's Secret Club,* the turtle creates a club that excludes one of his classmates. The girl, offended, forms her own club that excludes Franklin. Franklin comes to realize that, rather than excluding others, it is better to be friends with everyone. It's another "wonderful, lesson story," from Bourgeois, a reviewer wrote in *Resource Links.*

Franklin learns another important insight about friendship in *Franklin's Valentines.* On his way to school on Valentine's Day, he accidentally drops all of his cards for his classmates in a mud puddle. Franklin is worried that his friends will be angry that he does not have valentines for them, and that they will not give him any valentines if they do not receive one in return. However, Franklin's friends are understanding and give him their cards, and the next day, Franklin brings "Friendship Day" cards for everyone.

Another holiday tale, *Franklin's Christmas Gift* finds the little turtle trying to make a very difficult decision. His class is collecting toys to give to poor children for the holidays. Franklin likes all of his toys and does not want to give any of them up. He finally discovers a broken toy that he would be willing to give away, but then his teacher, Mr. Owl, tells the class that the chil-

dren who will be receiving these toys might not get any other presents this Christmas. Franklin realizes that his broken truck is not such a good present after all and donates one of his favorite toys instead.

Although she is best known for creating the Franklin character, Bourgeois has also written other books for children. *Oma's Quilt* offers "a gentle and subtle story about how the love and support of family members can make difficult transitions in life less painful," explained *Resource Links* reviewer Zoe Johnstone Guha. The beginning of the story finds Emily's grandmother, Oma, moving from her beloved house into a retirement home. At first, Oma hates the change. She wants to be able to cook her own meals, she misses her things, and she thinks that the other residents of the nursing home are "nincompoops." When Emily and her mother go to Oma's house to sort through her things, they realize that the old woman kept many items of clothing with sentimental value over the years. Together, Emily and her mother create a quilt for Oma out of those clothes,

Emily and her mother use treasured items to fashion a quilt so Emily's grandmother, newly settled into a retirement home, can reminisce about the past in Bourgeois's warm story of familial love. (From Oma's Quilt, *illustrated by Stephane Jorisch.*)

and being able to snuggle up with the quilt makes the move easier for Oma. The story is "told in simple, appealing language," thought *Booklist*'s Gillian Engberg, and *School Library Journal* contributor Sheilah Kosco dubbed the book "reassuring."

Bourgeois once commented: "I believe that children's books can give children a key to the world as it is, and as it can be. I try to give my characters—the children—a sense of power in a world where they are so often powerless."

Biographical and Critical Sources

BOOKS

Behind the Story: The People Who Create Our Best Children's Books . . . and How They Do It!, Pembroke (Markham, Canada), 1995.

PERIODICALS

Booklist, February 1, 1995, Stephanie Zvirin, review of *Changes in You and Me: A Book about Puberty, Mostly for Boys*, p. 1000A; September 1, 1997, Carolyn Phelan, review of *The Sun*, p. 108; April 15, 1998, Lauren Peterson, review of *Fire Fighters* and *Garbage Collectors*, p. 1447; March 1, 1999, Shelley Townsend-Hudson, review of *Franklin's Class Trip*, p. 1218; July, 1999, Carolyn Phelan, review of *Postal Workers* and *Police Officers*, p. 1948; June 1, 2000, Kathy Broderick, review of *Franklin Goes to the Hospital*, p. 1904; December 15, 2001, Gillian Engberg, review of *Oma's Quilt*, p. 738.

Canadian Children's Literature, spring, 2000, review of *Franklin's Secret Club, Franklin's New Friend, Finders Keepers for Franklin*, and *Franklin's Class Trip*, pp. 32-38; spring-summer, 2002, review of *Oma's Quilt*, p. 185.

Canadian Living, May, 2001, Paulette Bourgeois, "Franklin's Two Moms," pp. 121-122.

Canadian Materials, January, 1988, review of *The Amazing Apple Book*, p. 22; March, 1988, review of *Big Sarah's Little Boots*, p. 56; May, 1988, review of *On Your Mark, Get Set: All about the Olympics Then and Now*, pp. 107-108; September, 1989, review of *Hurry Up, Franklin*, p. 216; March, 1990, review of *Grandma's Secret*, p. 62; November, 1990, review of *Too Many Chickens*, pp. 264-265; May, 1991, review of *Franklin Fibs*, p. 170; September, 1991, review of *Fire Fighters* and *Garbage Collectors*, pp. 226-227; September, 1992, review of *Franklin Is Lost*, p. 207; November, 1992, review of *Police Officers*, p. 308; January, 1993, review of *Postal Workers*, p. 20; March-April, 1994, review of *Franklin Is Bossy*, p. 56.

Horn Book, May-June, 1990, Hanna B. Zeiger, review of *Grandma's Secret*, p. 318.

Language Arts, September, 1992, Miriam Martinez and Marcia F. Nash, review of *Too Many Chickens!*, p. 372.

Maclean's, December 11, 1995, Diane Turbide, "A Million Dollar Turtle," pp. 50-51.

New York Times Book Review, March 12, 1995, Betsy Hearne, review of *Changes in You and Me: A Book about Puberty, Mostly for Girls*, p. 20.

Publishers Weekly, April 5, 1991, review of *Too Many Chickens!*, p. 144; June 5, 2000, review of *Franklin's Pet Problem*, p. 96; April 2, 2001, review of *Franklin's School Treasury*, p. 66; April 28, 2003, review of *Franklin's Family Treasury*, p. 73.

Quill and Quire, May, 1991, Peter Carver, "Paulette Bourgeois Branches Out," pp. 21, 24; June, 1991, review of *Fire Fighters* and *Garbage Collectors*, p. 24; July, 1991, review of *The Amazing Potato Book*, pp. 52-53; February, 1992, review of *Franklin Is Lost*, p. 32; August, 1992, review of *Postal Workers*, p. 28; July, 1993, review of *Franklin Is Bossy*, p. 56; December, 1994, review of *Changes in You and Me: A Book about Puberty, Mostly for Boys*, p. 34; September, 2001, review of *Oma's Quilt*, p. 52.

Resource Links, June, 1996, review of *Franklin Has a Sleepover*, p. 208; February, 1997, review of *Franklin's School Play*, p. 109; June, 1997, review of *Franklin Rides a Bike*, pp. 204-205; December, 1998, review of *Franklin's Secret Club*, p. 2; June, 1999, review of *Franklin's Class Trip*, p. 2; October, 1999, review of *Franklin Is Lost*, p. 2; February, 2000, review of *Franklin's Classic Treasury*, p. 2; April, 2000, review of *Franklin Goes to the Hospital* and *Franklin and the Thunderstorm*, p. 2; December, 2000, review of *Franklin's Baby Sister*, p. 2; April, 2001, Judy Cottrell, review of *Franklin's Pet Problem*, p. 3; December, 2001, Zoe Johnstone Guha, review of *Oma's Quilt*, pp. 4-5; April, 2002, Elaine Rospad, review of *Franklin Says I Love You*, pp. 2-3.

School Library Journal, November, 1989, Gail C. Ross, review of *Big Sarah's Little Boots*, p. 74; July, 1990, Jane Gardner Connor, review of *Grandma's Secret*, p. 56, and Barbara B. Murphy, review of *The Amazing Apple Book*, pp. 81-82; March, 1991, Susan L. Rogers, review of *The Amazing Dirt Book* and *The Amazing Paper Book*, pp. 198-199; June, 1991, Lee Bock, review of *Too Many Chickens!*, p. 72; February, 1992, Carolyn Kenks, review of *The Amazing Potato Book*, p. 92; March, 1995, Virginia E. Jeschelnig, review of *Changes in You and Me: A Book about Puberty, Mostly for Boys* and *Changes in You and Me: A Book about Puberty, Mostly for Girls*, p. 208; May, 1997, Elisabeth Palmer Abarbanel, review of *Franklin's Bad Day*, p. 93, and John Peters, review of *The Moon*, p. 200; December, 1997, Martha Topol, review of *Franklin's New Friend* and *Franklin Rides a Bike*, p. 87; June, 1998, Stephani Hutchinson, review of *Garbage Collectors* and *Firefighters*, pp. 127-128; July, 1998, Sally R. Dow, review of *Franklin and the Thunderstorm*, pp. 64-65; May, 1999, Dina Sherman, review of *Franklin's Class Trip*, p. 86; July, 1999, Paul Kelsey, review of *Postal Workers*, p. 84; November, 2001, Sheilah Kosco, review of *Oma's Quilt*, pp. 111-112.*

BOYER, Allen B. 1963-

Personal

Born July 3, 1963, in Lebanon, PA; son of Allen C. (a teacher) and Joan (a painter) Boyer; married; wife's name, Suzanne (a teacher), 1998; children: Molly. *Education:* Millersville University, B.S., 1988; Pennsylvania State University, Harrisburg, M.Ed., 1995.

Addresses

Agent—c/o Author Mail, Perfection Learning, 1000 N. Second Ave., P. O. Box 500, Logan, IA 51546-0500. *E-mail*—alboyer2@yahoo.com.

Career

St. Joan of Arc School, Hershey, PA, computer teacher and technology coordinator, 1998-2004; writer.

Writings

Roberto's Bat, Perfection Learning (Logan, IA), 2003.
Arthur Ashe and Me, Perfection Learning (Logan, IA), 2003.
Patriot School: West Point and Its Famous Graduates, Perfection Learning (Logan, IA), 2004.

Work in Progress

The Wishing Willow Club, a novel; researching the life of Supreme Court Justice Byron White.

*   *   *

BROWN, Elizabeth Ferguson 1937-

Personal

Born October 27, 1937, in Newark, NJ; daughter of Herbert (a postal supervisor) and Elizabeth (a secretary) Ferguson; married Robert F. Brown (a teacher), June 25, 1960; children: Nancy, Ellen, Carole, Jennifer. *Education:* College of New Jersey, B.S., 1959; Kean University, M.A., 1990, M.A., 1992.

Addresses

Home and office—4496 Post Rd., East Greenwich, RI 02818. *E-mail*—brownelizf@aol.com.

Career

Bridgewater-Raritan School District, Bridgewater, NJ, classroom teacher, 1959-61; Scotch Plains-Fanwood School District, Scotch Plains, NJ, classroom teacher, 1972-85, curriculum facilitator, 1985-92, member of school district staff development team, 1985-95, class-

Allen B. Boyer

room teacher, 1992-95; writer, 1995—. Workshop leader, "Writing for Children: The Art, the Craft, the Marketing," August, 2002.

Member

Society of Children's Book Writers and Illustrators, Authors Guild, International Reading Association.

Awards, Honors

Recommended reading list citation from American Coal Foundation, 2003, notable book citation, International Reading Association, 2004, and recommended Appalachian book for children and picture book for children, both 2004, both by *Appalachian Literature Website.*

Writings

Silver Burdett Science Textbook, Grade Two (teacher's edition), Silver Burdett (Morristown, NJ), 1984.
Coal Country Christmas (picture book), illustrated by Harvey Stevenson, Boyds Mills Press (Honesdale, PA), 2003.

Contributor of stories, "The Glockenspiel," to *Jack & Jill,* 1971-72, and "The Purple Sky," to *Children's Playmate,* 1974.

Work in Progress

Wildflower Spring, a middle grade novel; *Prairie Shadows* and *Plover Prints,* picture books on endangered species; research for a picture book about the first American steam engine, the Stourbridge Lion.

Sidelights

Elizabeth Ferguson Brown told *SATA:* "Born in Newark, New Jersey, the best thing about my house was that it was just a few blocks from the movies and the public library. When I wasn't reading stories, I was at the movies watching them unfold on the big screen. Vacations, my mother, father, and I drove 'up home' to visit my grandparents in a coal mining town in Pennsylvania. My father was an avid fisherman, so there was always a lake to be found and a fishing line to be baited. Afterwards, I would stretch out on the grass and listen to my father read aloud from his favorite book, *The Song of Hiawatha.* To this day, I can still hear his deep, resonant voice when I read those rhythmic verses. In high school I joined the school newspaper which published my poetry. When I graduated, no one was surprised when I decided to become a high school English and history teacher.

"Once I was off to the College of New Jersey, I began to wonder about teaching high school students. My college roommate was a senior returning from practice teaching kindergarten. Listening to her talk about her experiences, I discovered what ages I really wanted to teach—and changed my major to Kindergarten Primary. A class in children's literature assured me I had made the right decision. While I still worked on the college newspaper and wrote poetry, I was happily immersed in those books I loved as a child and still find fascinating today.

"Graduating from college, I began teaching first grade and married my college sweetheart, Bob, who was teaching music. When Bob moved from elementary music to junior high, our first daughter arrived and I left teaching. Then Bob moved into a choral music department in high school, and our second daughter was born. With just two babies at home, I began writing again, but now it was stories for children. By the time our third daughter had arrived, I had two stories and a number of poems and games published in children's magazines. But time for writing ended when our fourth daughter was born.

"When our daughters entered school, I returned to teaching. This time, I finally taught kindergarten, then first grade and then second. Fourteen years later, I became a curriculum facilitator, helping classroom teachers. I loved working with teachers almost as much as working with students. Then I became a student again myself, studying for two master's degrees. By now, students Bob had taught in high school had married and started families. Some of their children went through my elementary classes and now were showing up in my husband's music groups in the high school. While it

was wonderful to see all those generations of students pass through our classrooms, the time had come to retire! Bob left first, and I had just three years to go before I would finally have time to write again. Those last three years, I would spend teaching second grade.

"Happy to be back in the classroom, I encouraged my students to talk to grandparents and then write the stories they told them. As they shared them, I thought about my grandparents in Pennsylvania who raised eight children on a coal miner's salary. Money was scarce, but family love was strong. My grandfather died of the miner's black lung when I was eleven. For the next ten years we went up home to visit my grandmother until she died the year I got married. My own daughters and their children never knew my grandparents or their life in coal country. These were things I needed to write about.

"I began my research of anthracite mining in museums, books, and newspapers. I had always loved history, but this history was so personal. I found articles about the mine fire that burned in abandoned mine shafts in my grandparents' town for over seventeen years before it was finally extinguished. I actually remembered the fire burning when I visited my grandmother. I had seen smoke rising from the part of town where the fire burned and houses that had collapsed when mine shafts beneath them gave way. I recalled the sadness in my grandmother's voice as she talked about people dying in their sleep when coal gas seeped into their homes. It wouldn't be easy to write about these things coal country women learned to live with, but I wanted to try.

"I had heard my father's voice reading those rhythmic verses and my grandmother's voice talking about her life, now I had to find my own voice as I began to write. It was hard to find the right words to paint a picture in readers' minds when that picture wasn't pretty. I struggled to keep the writing sparse but rhythmic and flowing. Through it all, I tried to show the closeness and love of family in the face of hardship. By the time I retired at the end of those three years, I had finished writing my story. It would be a long time before it was published, but I never gave up believing that it would happen.

"After retirement, I not only found time to write, but also met others who loved writing as much as I did. I joined the Society of Children's Book Writers and Illustrators and a local critique group which helped my writing tremendously. A couple of years later, we sold our house in New Jersey and moved to Rhode Island near one of our daughters. Although that meant finding a new critique group and new writing friends, it didn't take long because there are many wonderful writers in New England.

"Now I visit elementary schools with my picture book, *Coal Country Christmas.* It's wonderful talking with students about writing their family stories and encouraging them to pursue their own dreams. I'm working with teachers again too, sharing a packet of teaching activities I've written for my book. I even find time to speak with parents about the importance of reading aloud to their children.

"Most of all, I continue to write. It's not surprising most of my stories have a bit of history in them. The middle grade novel *Wildflower Spring* is set in the 1800s. These are my new dreams, and I'll never give up on them. Never."

In *Coal Country Christmas,* a young girl named Elizabeth travels with her family to spend Christmas in Carbondale, Pennsylvania, a coal mining town drawn in great detail. The holiday is bittersweet for the coal country women, as so many husbands and fathers have died young from working in the mines. Nevertheless, on a tight budget, Elizabeth's grandmother—also named

Elizabeth—manages to bring the warmth of Christmas into her home and the hearts of those around her. In the words of a *Kirkus Reviews* critic, Brown "touches lightly upon the unfortunate circumstances of living in coal country with a hint of sadness, inevitability, and acceptance." April Gaugler in *Childhood Education* found the book "a warm and loving Christmas story," and *Booklist* contributor Hazel Rochman styled it "harsh yet upbeat . . . a moving seasonal story of a real place."

Biographical and Critical Sources

PERIODICALS

Booklist, October 15, 2003, Hazel Rochman, review of *Coal Country Christmas,* p. 416.

With her mother, a young girl arrives in an Appalachian mining town to spend Christmas with her grandmother and learn how a holiday can be enhanced by love and meaningful traditions. (From Coal Country Christmas, *written by Elizabeth Ferguson Brown and illustrated by Harvey Stevenson.)*

Childhood Education, winter, 2003, April Gaugler, review of *Coal Country Christmas,* p. 91.

Kirkus Reviews, November 1, 2003, review of *Coal Country Christmas.*

Publishers Weekly, September 22, 2003, review of *Coal Country Christmas,* p. 71.

School Library Journal, October, 2003, Virginia Walter, review of *Coal Country Christmas,* p. 61.

BURKE, Diana G.
    See GALLAGHER, Diana G.

*   *   *

BURKE, Diana Gallagher
    See GALLAGHER, Diana G.

C-D

CARPENTER, Angelica Shirley 1945-

Personal

Born March 28, 1945, in St. Louis, MO; daughter of James (a sales manager) and Jean (a writer) Shirley; married Richard Allen Carpenter (a web page designer), June 22, 1968; children: Carey. *Education:* University of Illinois at Urbana, B.A., 1967; M.Ed., 1974; M.S. (library science), 1977.

Addresses

Office—Arne Nixon Center for the Study of Children's Literature, 5200 N. Barton Ave. M/S ML34, Fresno, CA 93740-8014. *E-mail*—angelica@csufresno.edu.

Career

Palm Springs Public Library, Palm Springs, CA, director, 1982-99; Arne Nixon Center for the Study of Children's Literature, California State University, Fresno, founding curator, 1999—. Founder and manager, BookFest of the Palm Beaches, 1990-99. Chair, National Planning of Special Collections Committee, Association for Library Service to Children, American Library Association, 2003-04. Conference coordinator, Children's Literature Association, 2004.

Member

International Reading Association, International Wizard of Oz Club (president, 2004-07), Robert Louis Stevenson Club, Lewis Carroll Society of North America (board member, 2002-05), Society of Children's Book Writers and Illustrators, American Library Association, Lewis Carroll Society of Great Britain, California Library Association.

Writings

(With mother, Jean Shirley) *Frances Hodgson Burnett: Beyond the Secret Garden,* Lerner Publications (New York, NY), 1990.

Angelica Shirley Carpenter

(With Jean Shirley) *L. Frank Baum: Royal Historian of Oz,* Lerner Publications (New York, NY), 1992.

(With Jean Shirley) *Robert Louis Stevenson: Finding Treasure Island,* Lerner Publications (New York, NY), 1997.

Lewis Carroll: Through the Looking Glass, Lerner Publications (New York, NY), 2003.

Senior subject advisor, *Best Books for Academic Libraries: Language and Literature.* Contributing editor, *The Baum Bugle: Journal of the International Wizard of Oz Club.*

Work in Progress

Editing the proceedings of "Frances Hodgson Burnett: Beyond the Secret Garden," an international conference held in Fresno, CA, 2003; researching Frances Hodgson Burnett, Victorian children's authors, and children's literature collections in the United Kingdom and Europe.

Sidelights

Angelica Shirley Carpenter told *SATA:* "My mother, Jean Shirley, was my inspiration and my co-author. She moved to Florida to be near me after I took the job as Palm Springs Library director. Mother had been writing all my life, and had published several biographies for children. She and I had a great time writing together, visiting schools, and organizing events for the Society of Children's Book Writers and Illustrators (she was the first Florida regional advisor). I am writing alone now since Mother died in 1995, but she is always with me, and especially in our books. In my books I hope to explain the importance of famous children's authors, and to relate their lives to the time period in a manner that is interesting and relevant to today's young people. Since I still have a (wonderful) day job, I write in the evening and at least two hours each weekend day. Actually when I am deeply involved in a project I write much more than this; the problem is stopping, and sleeping, not writing.

"I love to travel to sites related to children's literature—children's literature takes me to the nicest places, and introduces me to the nicest people! I take lots of photographs on my travels and am beginning to have some published. I have prepared slide-illustrated lectures to go with all my books."

The three books Carpenter co-authored with her mother are *Frances Hodgson Burnett: Beyond the Secret Garden, L. Frank Baum: Royal Historian of Oz,* and *Robert Louis Stevenson: Finding Treasure Island.* All three books have been commended for their reader-friendly but accurate treatments of the authors in question. Frances Hodgson Burnett was better known in her own time for her popular romance stories for ladies's magazines, but her fame endures as the author of *The Secret Garden.* Carolyn Phelan in *Booklist* praised *Frances Hodgson Burnett* as a "highly readable biography," and Pamela K. Bomboy in *School Library Journal* went even further in her recommendation of the work, noting that Burnett's "garden continues to grow—she would have been pleased!"

L. Frank Baum was the creator of the "Wizard of Oz" series of books. Although meant for children, the books also contained veiled references to Baum's political

In her juvenile biography of Lewis Carroll, Carpenter pays tribute to the nineteenth-century writer who revolutionized previously instructional children's literature when he published his famous adventures of Alice for the sole purpose of entertaining children. (From Lewis Carroll: Through the Looking Glass; *illustration by John Tenniel.)*

worldview. He was also determined to write stories that would not frighten young children. In her *Booklist* review of *L. Frank Baum,* Sally Estes noted: "Kids who have loved the Oz series will enjoy reading about its creator."

Robert Louis Stevenson forged an unconventional life for himself that included settling in Samoa, a decision that helped provide settings for his famous adventure novel, *Treasure Island.* Carpenter and her mother provide "an involving and well-documented account of the writer's life" in their biography, according to Carolyn Phelan in *Booklist.* In *Children's Book and Play Review,* Janet O. Francis commended *Robert Louis Stevenson* as "scholarly and readable, with attention to detail."

Lewis Carroll: Through the Looking Glass presents the life of Oxford mathematician Charles Lutwidge Dodgson, who wrote the adventures of Alice and her dream world companions to entertain the children of a close personal friend. Carpenter offers a child-friendly portrait of Dodgson while not side-stepping the speculation that has surrounded the nature of his interest in Alice Liddell. Kristen Oravec in *School Library Journal* described the book as "an accessible, well-documented portrait."

Biographical and Critical Sources

PERIODICALS

Booklist, January 15, 1991, Carolyn Phelan, review of *Frances Hodgson Burnett: Beyond the Secret Garden;* July, 1992, Sally Estes, review of *L. Frank Baum: Royal Historian of Oz,* p. 1934; November 15, 1997, Carolyn Phelan, review of *Robert Louis Stevenson: Finding Treasure Island,* p. 554.
Children's Book and Play Review, May/June, 1998, Janet O. Francis, review of *Robert Louis Stevenson.*
School Library Journal, March, 1991, Pamela K. Bomboy, review of *Frances Hodgson Burnett,* p. 200; December, 1997, Cheryl Cufari, review of *Robert Louis Stevenson,* p. 134; March, 2003, Kristen Oravec, review of *Lewis Carroll: Through the Looking Glass,* p. 248.

ONLINE

Angelica Shirley Carpenter Home Page, http://www. angelicacarpenter.com/ (June 1, 2004).

*   *   *

CHARLES, Norma

Personal

Born in Ste. Boniface, Manitoba, Canada; children: two boys, two girls. *Education:* University of British Columbia, B.S. (education), 1961, teacher-librarian diploma, 1984.

Addresses

Home and office—1844 Acadia Road, Vancouver, British Columbia V6T 1R3, Canada. *E-mail*—ncharles@ axionet.com.

Career

Writer. Vancouver School Board, Vancouver, British Columbia, Canada, elementary and high school teacher for eight years; teacher-librarian for ten years.

Member

Canadian Society of Children's Authors, Illustrators, and Performers, Writers Union of Canada, Children's Writers and Illustrators of British Columbia, Canadian Children's Book Centre.

Awards, Honors

First prize, Coquitlam Pioneers, 1989, for short story "Lum King"; British Columbia Book Award, 2000, for *Sophie Sea to Sea;* Sheila Egoff Prize for Children's Literature shortlist, 2002, for *The Accomplice.*

Writings

Amanda Grows Up, Scholastic (Toronto, Ontario, Canada), 1978.
No Place for a Horse, General (Toronto, Ontario, Canada), 1988.
April Fool Heroes, Nelson (Toronto, Ontario, Canada), 1989.
Darlene's Shadow, General (Toronto, Ontario, Canada), 1991.
See You Later, Alligator, Scholastic (Toronto, Ontario, Canada), 1991.
A Bientot Croco!, Scholastic (Toronto, Ontario, Canada), 1991.

Twelve-year-old Megan and her younger sister agree to meet with their troubled, estranged father and find themselves embroiled in a dangerous situation from which Meg must courageously escape. (Cover illustration by Janet Wilson.)

Dolphin Alert!, Nelson (Toronto, Ontario, Canada), 1998.

Runaway, Coteau (Regina, Saskatchewan, Canada), 1999.

Sophie Sea to Sea, Beach Holme (Vancouver, British Columbia, Canada), 1999.

The Accomplice, Raincoast Books (Vancouver, British Columbia, Canada), 2001.

Criss Cross, Double Cross, Beach Holme (Vancouver, British Columbia, Canada), 2002.

Fuzzy Wuzzy, Hodgepog (Vancouver, British Columbia, Canada), 2002.

All the Way to Mexico, Raincoast Books (Vancouver, British Columbia, Canada), 2003.

Sophie's Friend in Need, Beach Holme (Vancouver, British Columbia, Canada), 2004.

Several of author's books have been translated into French.

Sidelights

Canadian children's author Norma Charles worked as a librarian-teacher for over ten years before finally deciding to write full time. As the mother of four children—two boys and two girls—Charles has had plenty of experience with children, and that experience has translated into the novels *The Accomplice* and *All the Way to Mexico,* as well as several picture books.

The Accomplice, which was a Canadian Children's Book Centre Choice selection, tells an endearing story about Megan and her younger sister Jen, as the two struggle to decide between their biological parents. Megan's father arranges for Megan and Jen to come visit him and his new wife at their island home, even though she has not heard from him for months. She wonders when he persuades the two girls to keep the visit a secret from everyone, including their mother, but the air of mystery adds to the excitement of the trip. Finally, when they arrive on the island, the two sisters realize that their father intends to keep them at his remote home permanently, and Megan realizes that it is now up to her to get her sister and herself back to their mother's home safely.

Charles' descriptions of her protagonists' interactions and strained relationships add depth to the already intense plot of *The Accomplice,* according to several reviewers. Joanne de Groot commented in *Resource Links* that the characters' realistic struggles, when "combined with beautiful descriptions of life on a remote island off the west coast and suspense that builds throughout the story, will keep children reading until the end."

In *All the Way to Mexico* readers are once again confronted with a blended family, as twelve-year-old Jacob Armstrong finds himself along for the ride during his mother's camping-trip honeymoon. Jacob is not alone, however; in addition to his sister Minerva—who insists on blocking everyone else out in the car by listening to her CD player—Jacob's newly acquired stepbrothers also accompany the honeymooners on their long car ride from Vancouver, Canada, to Mexico. Jacob, who

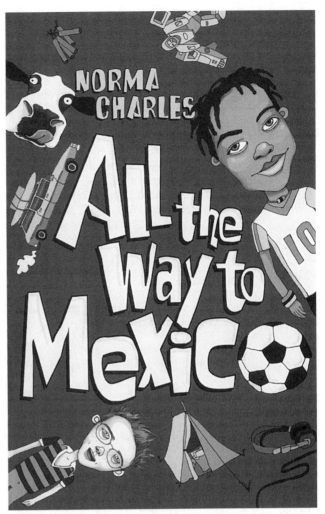

Jacob Armstrong, twelve years old, is crowded into a station wagon with his new blended family on a frustrating road trip to Mexico in Charles's humorous tale of adjusting to major, not always welcome, changes. (Cover illustration by Monika Melnychuk.)

loves soccer and dreams of one day becoming a professional soccer player, is annoyed by Barney Finkle, who keeps telling annoying cow jokes, and Sam Finkle, who sniffs constantly and can't stop playing with his action figures. In addition, Jacob's mother and her new husband are acting like stereotypical "honeymooners." The only light at the end of the tunnel for Jacob is his hope of meeting up with children in Mexico who will play soccer with him, but this light is gradually doused by problems along the way.

Praising Charles for creating a likeable protagonist in Jacob, Elaine Rosepad commented in *Resource Links* that *All the Way to Mexico* is a "humorous" tale in which "children learn to appreciate each other and deal with difficulties as they arise." Although the novel's characters experience a host of disappointments during their journey, Susan Perren maintained that readers will fare far better, noting in her *Globe & Mail* review that Charles creates an enjoyable story that contains "small miracles of accommodation."

Biographical and Critical Sources

PERIODICALS

Globe & Mail (Toronto, Ontario, Canada), September 6, 2003, Susan Perren, review of *All the Way to Mexico,* p. D14.
Quill and Quire, December, 1999, review of *Sophie Sea to Sea,* p. 38.
Resource Links, October, 1999, review of *Runaway,* pp. 24-25; December, 1999, review of *Sophie Sea to Sea,* p. 13; April, 2003, Joanne de Groot, review of *The Accomplice,* p. 9, and *Fuzzy Wuzzy,* p. 12; June, 2003, Elaine Rosepad, review of *All the Way to Mexico,* p. 10.

ONLINE

Book Rapport.com, http://www.bookrapport.com/ (February 5, 2004), "Norma Charles."

*   *   *

CRIST-EVANS, Craig 1954-

Personal

Born March 4, 1954, in Springfield, OH; son of James R. and Barbara A. Evans; married Sylvaine Montaudouin (divorced); children: Yann Crist-Evans, Kathryn Daniel. *Ethnicity:* "Caucasian Euro Mutt." *Education:* Florida Atlantic University, B.A., 1973-75; University of Colorado, Boulder, graduate studies, 1979-81; Florida Atlantic University, Boca Raton, graduate studies, 1989-90; Norwich University, Montpelier, M.F.A. (writing), 1992; Norwich University, Montpelier, postgraduate study, 1997. *Politics:* "Liberal Progressive Moderate."

Addresses

Home and office—300 East Seminar St., Mercersburg, PA 17236. *Agent*—Linda Pratt, Sheldon Fogelman Agency, 10 East 40th St., New York, NY 10016. *E-mail*—cristevans@comcast.net.

Career

Writer and poet. Poet in the Schools for Colorado, 1992-97; teacher of independent writing program in Colorado schools; Vermont College, cofounder and director of M.F.A. program in writing for children, 1990-92, director of marketing and admissions, 1998-2000; Mercersburg Academy, Mercersburg, PA, currently director of writing center and English teacher.

Awards, Honors

Florida Atlantic University faculty scholar, 1973-75; *Poetry* Mile High Arts Festival contest winner, 1987; Pushcart Prize nomination for poetry, 1995 (two), 1996,

Craig Crist-Evans

2002; New York Public Library Best Books for the Teen Age List honor, 2000, and Lamplighter Award nomination, and International Reading Association/Lee Bennett Hopkins Promising Poet Award, both 2001, all for *Moon over Tennessee: A Boy's Civil War Journal;* New York Public Library Best Books for the Teen Age List designation, 2004, for *Amaryllis.*

Writings

Moon over Tennessee: A Boy's Civil War Journal, Houghton Mifflin (Boston, MA), 1999.
Amaryllis, Candlewick Press (Cambridge, MA), 2003.
Shadow of My Father's Hand, Breakfast Serials, 2004.
North of Everything, Candlewick Press (Cambridge, MA), 2004.
No Guarantee, New Rivers Press (Minneapolis, MN), 2004.

Contributor to *Paris Review, Nebraska Review, Cimmarron Review,* and *Prague Review.* Contributing editor, *Bloomsbury Review,* 1990—.

Work in Progress

The novels *Feather in the Wind, Bull Ring,* and *Valley of the Cranes; Birds of a Feather,* a collection of poems for young readers; *If You Ever Get Lost in the Woods,* a picture-book text; *Land This Hard,* a second poetry collection; *Manthology: Poems of the Male Experience,* an anthology coedited with Roger Weingarten.

Sidelights

Craig Crist-Evans is a writer and poet who strongly believes in the power of writing and storytelling. As an educator who has been a guest speaker in many schools, Crist-Evans believes that helping children find the power of their own voices through poetry can influence the world at large. His first book for young-adult readers, *Moon over Tennessee: A Boy's Civil War Journal,* was published in 1999, and has been followed by 2003's *Amaryllis,* as well as several poetry collections. Crist-Evans continues to work on multiple projects concurrently, among them an anthology of poems titled *Manthology: Poems of the Male Experience.*

Moon over Tennessee follows a young boy who is coming of age during the U.S. Civil War. Through extended narrative free verse in the form of journal entries readers follow the boy and his father as they leave their

Written in journal entries that are poems, Crist-Evans's **Moon over Tennessee** *follows a thirteen-year-old boy who leaves his life on the family farm to fight with the Confederate forces at Gettysburg. (Illustrated by Bonnie Christensen.)*

family farm and make the long journey to join the doomed Confederate Army preparing for battle at Gettysburg. As they pass by destroyed towns, littered with burned buildings and injured or dead soldiers, the harsh reality of the war becomes apparent to the boy. He braves the imposing dread of war, the hunger, and even the death of his own father with the courage of a man, and believes he will one day go home again. Picturesque wood engravings illustrate the text, and depict the farms, soldiers, and battles discussed. "This poem, written in the form of a boy's journal, evokes the emotional power inherent in his painful experience," stated Lynne T. Burke in *Reading Today.* "With lyricism and a chilling resoluteness the boy records the real price the country paid for slavery." Randy Meyer, reviewing *Moon over Tennessee* for *Booklist,* also complimented Craig-Evans' debut, writing that it is an "evocative book, written with language so vibrant it begs to be read aloud."

The plot again focuses around war in Crist-Evans' second novel, *Amaryllis,* which describes the emotional conflict of two brothers as they struggle to assert themselves against their parents. Frank, an eighteen-year-old Florida transplant from Ohio, has decided to fight in the Vietnam war, but his motivation is a desire to flee from home and escape his personal war with his alcoholic father. Once in Vietnam, Frank realizes that he has no commitment to the cause he is risking his life for; now battling a heroin addiction, he becomes increasingly guilt-ridden over concerns for his younger brother, Jimmy. Meanwhile, Frank's father realizes that he is responsible for his son's departure; he also feels guilt at ruining his son's life. Jimmy serves as the bridge between the two men: when he suddenly stops receiving letters from Frank, he grows concerned but cannot express his worry to his troubled father. Robert Gray, writing in *School Library Journal,* noted that "Both teens are believable and likable characters with whom many young adults will identify," and went on to call *Amaryllis* "crisply written and a worthwhile addition to fiction collections." While noting that teen readers "may relate most readily to the father/son conflicts," a *Publishers Weekly* contributor added that Crist-Evans' powerful "passages about Vietnam may be what they remember longest."

Crist-Evans told *SATA:* "I live in rural south central Pennsylvania, where I enjoy mountain biking, hiking, and camping. Still, my spiritual roots are in the West, and I venture that direction every summer to spend time in the Rockies and with my son and close friends. Being the clever guy I am, I go back to Florida to visit family during the *winter* months. While I am professionally gregarious, I am also fiercely private and spend much of my time reading and working on writing projects. Of course, there is a professional side to me that loves to get up in front of any group—children or adults—to talk about writing and books. I enjoy doing

Two teenage brothers cope with their drunken father and escape their troubles by surfing, until the older boy goes to serve in the Vietnam War and his letters home reveal confusion, desperation, and struggles with drug addiction.

school visits and conference presentations and keynote speeches, while exploring the different landscapes I encounter in the process. I'm a student of culture and human dynamics, particularly in the way they impact children as they grow toward adulthood.

"An itinerant gypsy, I have lived in eight states and France, more towns and streets than I can count, and am not through traveling yet. I would like to evolve eventually to a life that is centered around my writing, allowing time for more travel, school visits and group talks, and would like to devote part of each year to working in other parts of the world, helping communities and children and their families reach upward and out of poverty, hunger, and despair. I write about war and the problematical dynamics of families because I think we need to address these difficult aspects of our human condition. A dedicated proponent of peace, I abhor any conflict that results in violence and the decimation of a people. I am a firm believer in the power of word and story, and hope that our world might learn that there is more to be gained through open, honest communication than mistrust and hatred."

Biographical and Critical Sources

PERIODICALS

Booklist, May 15, 1999, Randy Meyer, review of *Moon over Tennessee: A Boy's Civil War Journal*, p. 1695; November 1, 2003, Hazel Rochman, review of *Amaryllis*, p. 490.
Kirkus Reviews, October 15, 2003, review of *Amaryllis*, p. 1270.
Kliatt, July, 2003, Paula Rohrlick, review of *Amaryllis*, p. 8; November, 2003, Sue Budin, review of *Moon over Tennessee*, p. 29.
Publishers Weekly, May 24, 1999, review of *Moon over Tennessee*, p. 80; December 15, 2003, review of *Amaryllis*, p. 75.
Reading Today, April, 2001, Lynne T. Burke, review of *Moon over Tennessee*, p. 32.
School Library Journal, August, 1999, Herman Sutter, review of *Moon over Tennessee*, p. 155; November, 2003, Robert Gray, review of *Amaryllis*, p. 138.

ONLINE

Breakfastserials.com, http://www.breakfastserials.com/ (February 5, 2004), "Craig Crist-Evans."

*   *   *

CRUTCHER, Chris(topher C.) 1946-

Personal

Born July 17, 1946, in Cascade, ID; son of John William (a county clerk) and Jewell (Morris) Crutcher. *Education:* Eastern Washington State College (now University), B.A., 1968; received teaching certificate, 1970. *Politics:* Independent.

Addresses

Home—East 3405 Marion St., Spokane, WA 99223. *Agent*—Liz Darhansoff, 1220 Park Ave., New York, NY 10028. *E-mail*—Stotan717@aol.com.

Career

Writer, therapist, teacher, and child advocacy worker. Kennewick Dropout School, Kennewick, WA, teacher of high school dropouts, 1970-73; Lakeside School, Oakland, CA, teacher, 1973-76, director of school, 1976-80; Community Mental Health Center, Spokane, WA, child protection team specialist, 1980-82, child and family therapist, 1982-95; full-time writer and mental health specialist and counselor in private practice, 1995—.

Awards, Honors

Best Books for Young Adults selection, American Library Association (ALA), 1983, for *Running Loose*, 1986, for *Stotan!*, 1987, for *The Crazy Horse Electric*

Chris Crutcher

Game, 1989, for *Chinese Handcuffs,* 1991, for *Athletic Shorts: Six Short Stories,* 1993, for *Staying Fat for Sarah Byrnes,* 1995, for *Ironman,* and 2001, for *Whale Talk;* Best Young Adult Book of 1992, Michigan Library Association, for *Athletic Shorts;* Assembly on Literature for Adolescents Award, National Council of Teachers of English (NCTE), 1993, for Significant Contribution to Adolescent Literature; National Intellectual Freedom Award, NCTE, 1998; Margaret A. Edwards Award, ALA, for lifetime achievement in writing for teenagers, 2000; Pacific Northwest Booksellers Association and Washington State Book awards, 2002, for *Whale Talk.*

Writings

FOR YOUNG ADULTS

Running Loose, Greenwillow (New York, NY), 1983, HarperTempest (New York, NY), 2003.
Stotan!, Greenwillow (New York, NY), 1986.
The Crazy Horse Electric Game, Greenwillow (New York, NY), 1987, HarperTempest (New York, NY), 2003.

Chinese Handcuffs, Greenwillow (New York, NY), 1989.
Athletic Shorts: Six Short Stories, Greenwillow (New York, NY), 1991.
Staying Fat for Sarah Byrnes, Greenwillow (New York, NY), 1993.
Ironman, Greenwillow (New York, NY), 1995.
Whale Talk, Greenwillow (New York, NY), 2001.

Contributor to *Ultimate Sports: Short Stories by Outstanding Writers for Young Adults,* edited by Donald R. Gallo, Delacorte (New York, NY), 1995; *Dirty Laundry: Stories about Family Secrets,* edited by Lisa Rowe Fraustino, Viking (New York, NY), 1998; *Time Capsule: Short Stories about Teenagers Throughout the Twentieth Century,* edited by Donald R. Gallo, Delacorte (New York, NY), 1999; and *On the Fringe,* edited by Donald R. Gallo, Dial (New York, NY), 2001.

OTHER

The Deep End, Morrow (New York, NY), 1992.
King of the Mild Frontier: An Ill-Advised Autobiography, Greenwillow Books (New York, NY), 2003.

Contributor to *Spokane* magazine.

Adaptations

Audio versions have been made of *Athletic Shorts, Ironman, Whale Talk,* and *Staying Fat for Sarah Byrnes;* screenplay for *Staying Fat for Sarah Byrnes* in production.

Sidelights

Chris Crutcher grew up in a town so small that a local athletic competition would bring business to a standstill. Crutcher played many sports in high school, did well in college swimming, and began participating in triathlons after college. It comes as no surprise then that competitive sports figure heavily in his writing. Throughout his schooling, as he describes in his autobiography, Crutcher was a self-professed academic underachiever, his family life was challenging, and he grew up with a violent temper. Yet he eventually earned a B.A. with a major in psychology and a minor in sociology, and became a high school social studies teacher, a school administrator, and a therapist at a mental health facility. After completing his education, Crutcher taught in tough, inner-city schools and ran an alternative school for inner-city kids in Oakland, California, before becoming a child and family therapist, all of which helped prepare him to write about a wide variety of serious problems with which adolescents are confronted daily in modern day American culture.

In his works for teenagers, Crutcher surveys the struggle of young people to grow up and take charge of their own lives. "People always want us to *be* adults rather than *become* adults," he told Thomas Kozikowski in an interview in *Authors and Artists for Young Adults.* "Everybody wants the finished product, and nobody wants to look at how it's made." Louie Banks, the hero of *Running Loose,* knows better. "The thing I hate about life, so far, is that nothing's ever clear," he declares. "Every time you get things all figured out, somebody throws in another kink." Inspired by a conversation Crutcher overheard in a locker room fifteen years before in which a racist coach directed his players to eliminate an African-American player, the novel is set in Trout, Idaho—a small town much like Crutcher's hometown of Cascade. As his senior year begins, Louie thinks his life is set. He is at peace with his parents, a good-natured, insightful couple modeled on Crutcher's own mother and father; he is a starter on the school's eight-man football team, where he is surrounded by his buddies; and he has Becky, a wonderful girlfriend. But his perfect life soon begins to unravel. The trouble begins after a game with a rival school with a challenging team anchored by Washington, a talented black quarterback. In a bigoted harangue, Louie's coach orders the Trout team to sideline Washington with crippling tackles, and one of Louie's teammates complies. Louie denounces the play and storms off the field, ending his football career. His football buddies refuse to join the walkout, even if they agree with him. The coach lies his way out of the situation, and the townspeople are left to assume that Louie just lost control. Washington turns out not to be hurt very badly. Even though Louie is sure he did the right thing, he does not have the chance to feel very heroic. Becky dies in a pointless traffic accident, trying to drive around some rowdy kids on the only bridge in town. At the funeral, Louie hears Becky fondly eulogized by an out-of-town minister who never met her, and he rages again. However, a young track coach, who recognizes Louie's potential and respects the stand he took on the football play, recruits him for the team, and he wins the two-mile event. When the principal dedicates a memorial plaque to Becky—emblazoned with his own signature—Louie stays calm and takes care of it: he sneaks onto the school grounds and smashes up the memorial with a sledgehammer.

The solution to pain such as Louie's, Crutcher believes, lies in "letting go"—letting go of the search for a satisfying answer that does not exist; letting yourself admit that you are just a human being in pain. "If I keep asking why and keep not coming up with an answer," Crutcher observed, "I'm either going to get so frustrated I want to scream, or I'm just going to say 'There's no answer—hooray!' You know—'Hooray that there's no answer because I don't *have* one.'" As for sorrow, he declared, "you're not really hurt—injured—by your sadness or your grief, you're hurt by resisting it." "There's a case to be made for life being a series of losses, from the time that you lose your mother's womb, and all the times that you have to change schools, or your friends go away, or people die. If you live from zero to sixty you're going to have suffered a lot of losses. And what you can do for yourself is learn to hold yourself and grieve and allow that grief to be the

focus. Just say, 'I don't need to fight this, I don't need to do anything but just feel bad. Why? Because I *do* feel bad.'"

Writing in *Voice of Youth Advocates,* Mary K. Chelton noted of *Running Loose,* "Best of all, . . . you love [Louie] and grieve with him when Becky dies because she is presented as a really neat person." Chelton also wrote that *Running Loose* is a "good stepping stone up from Hinton and toward titles like *Vision Quest* and *Stop Time.* Good 'bridge books' are rare and first novelists this good even rarer." A *Kirkus Reviews* critic claimed that Louie tells his story with "strong feeling and no crap, as he might say," and added that as a "dramatic, head-first confrontation with mendacity, fate's punches, and learning to cope, it's a zinger." Zena Sutherland of *Bulletin of the Center for Children's Books* called *Running Loose* an "unusually fine first novel," while *School Library Journal* reviewer Trev Jones said that Louie tells his story with "sensitivity, humor, and outrage" and that the book "raises important issues for adolescents to consider."

For his second novel, *Stotan!,* Crutcher returned to the arena of high school sports. "One of the things I like about sports is that the rules are clear," he told Kozikowski. "I use sports in young adult fiction to talk about rules, usually back-to-back with information about the rules of life. Sports provides an arena for an athlete, or a character, to test himself or herself and learn about tenacity or about putting things in perspective." In *Stotan!,* the focus is on self-discipline. The story begins when four high-school swimmers—Walker, the team captain; Lion; Nortie; and Jeff—volunteer for "Stotan Week," an endurance test given by their coach, a Korean American named Max Il Song. When the boys sign up, they learn that a "Stotan" is a cross between a Stoic and a Spartan, and Max makes them live up to the billing with harsh exercises, exhausting laps in the pool, and a "Torture Lane" for swimmers who try to slack off. "I took Stotan Week out of real life," Crutcher confessed. "Actually I calmed it down to put in the book. My college coach was a madman, an absolute madman." Feats of physical courage, like falling off the diving board backward, were mandatory on Crutcher's team. "If you didn't do it you were doing push-ups until you couldn't walk. And then you'd have to run outside over the snowbank, wet, and bear-walk [hands and feet only]—we did all that. The Torture Lane was there, it was all there. It was *bizarre.*"

Amazingly, Walker and his teammates start to like Stotan Week. Sharing the challenge brings them closer together. They discover that they can endure a lot more than they thought. They realize that the less they struggle against the pain, and the more they accept and push beyond it, the easier things get. They feel energetic and confident. When the week is over, Max tosses aside his authoritarian props—bullhorn, firehose, Airborne cap—and shares some human insights, inspired by his study of Asian philosophy. "There are lessons in this week that can serve you for the rest of your lives," he says. "Remember the times when you gave up the fight [against Max and his discipline] and just went with Stotan Week—saw which way the river was flowing and went that way too. Most times the depth of your well isn't measured in how hard you fight—how tough you are—but in your ability to see what is and go with that." The team expects their toughest challenge to be the statewide swimming meet, but they must face a far greater challenge when Jeff develops a withering case of leukemia; their Stotan wisdom helps the friends through their crisis. At Jeff's urging the team goes on to the state meet without him, where they excel—for his sake—and swim an illegal three-man relay at the finals. At the end of the book, as Walker looks back over his experiences, it is clear that he has not soured on life; instead, he has come to an understanding of how precious it is. "I think my job in this life is to be an observer," he writes in his diary, and concludes, "I'll be a *Stotan* observer: look for the ways to get from one to the other of those glorious moments when all the emotional stops are pulled, when you're just so . . . glad to be breathing air." *Voice of Youth Advocates* reviewer Mary K. Chelton noted that *Stotan!* depicts "beautifully the joy, pain, and emotional strength of a male adolescent friendship" and called it a "lovely story and a model of the realistic adolescent novel." Writing in *School Library Journal*, Jerry Flack called *Stotan!* "a fine coming-of-age novel," while Anita Silvey of *Horn Book* compared it to the books of John R. Tunis and Bruce Brooks's *The Moves Make the Man*, works "that use a sports setting and competition to discuss the greater issues of being young and alive."

The Crazy Horse Electric Game takes a much different look at sports: it concerns a high school student who knows the thrill of having athletic talent, then loses it all and has to rebuild his life. As the novel begins, Willie Weaver is a sixteen-year-old amateur baseball player in small-town Coho, Montana, pitching for a team sponsored by the Samson Floral Shop. In the greatest moment of his career, Willie throws a winning game against a championship team sponsored by Crazy Horse Electric. By the standards of Coho, he is a living legend. Then a water-skiing accident leaves Willie brain-damaged; he is crippled and must struggle even to talk. His father, who was a winning college athlete, can scarcely stand the sight of him; friends feel awkward around him; and Willie hates his own life. Finally, he runs away from home and from human contact. Willie never expected life to be so flawed—he expected it to be as perfect as the Crazy Horse Electric game. "There's a lot to hate yourself for if you listen to those expectations," Crutcher told Kozikowski. "because no one ever meets them."

In the second half of *The Crazy Horse Electric Game*, Willie makes the long journey back from self-hatred to self-respect. After traveling as far as he can by bus, he finds himself in Oakland, California, at the One More

Last Chance High School, a fictionalized version of an actual school where Crutcher used to teach. The OMLC instructors encourage him to use physical therapy, and even basketball, to reclaim control of his body; with his pride restored, Willie becomes a valuable part of the school's community and earns his diploma. He then has the strength to return to Coho and face his family and friends, even though the reunion is a difficult one. A reviewer in *Publishers Weekly* said that *The Crazy Horse Electric Game* "resound[s] with compassion for people tripped up by their own weaknesses" and praised its "poetic sensibility and gritty realism." Writing in *Voice of Youth Advocates,* Pam Spencer noted that, as in his previous novels, Crutcher writes about a young man being forced "to dig deep for the stabilization offered in reaching one's inner strength"; the critic concluded, "Crutcher writes powerfully and movingly of Willie's attempts to 'become whole' again. . . . It's authors like Chris Crutcher who make our job of 'selling books' that much easier." *Horn Book* reviewer Anita Silvey claimed that *The Crazy Horse Electric Game* "magnificently portrays the thoughts and feelings of a crippled athlete and is a testimony to the . . . human spirit."

Perhaps the grittiest of Crutcher's YA novels is his fourth, *Chinese Handcuffs,* which describes the friendship between two emotionally traumatized young people. Dillon Hemmingway grew up watching his older brother Preston destroy himself, first through drugs and then through suicide. (Preston actually made a point of killing himself in Dillon's presence.) Dillon is close friends with Jennifer Lawless, who has been sexually abused for most of her life, first by her father when she was a small child, and then by her stepfather in the years since. Dillon thinks he is in love with Jennifer, but she has been too deeply wounded to reciprocate fully. Her emotional lifeline is sports, because the basketball court is the only place where she feels she can control her own fate. The title of the book refers to the efforts of Dillon and Jennifer to confront their pain. "Chinese handcuffs" are a classic basket-weaver's toy: they only loosen their grip when you stop pulling against them.

Dillon is so preoccupied with his brother's death that he writes long letters to him, letters that make up much of the narrative. Jennifer has similarly strong memories of her abuse. In particular, readers see a vivid portrait of her stepfather, T. B. Himself brutalized as a child, T. B. survived through cold cunning, and now he uses it to intimidate both Jennifer and her mother. Finally Jennifer tries to kill herself, but Dillon stops her. Moved to desperate action, he gathers videotaped evidence against T. B. and uses it to drive him out of Jennifer's life. Having confronted the painful truths of his world, Dillon finds that he is no longer haunted by his brother. "I've got better things to do with my life than spend it with a pen in my hand, writing to a man who never reads his mail," he says in his last letter. "My struggle with you is finished. I'm going to let you go, push my finger in and release us from these crazy Chinese handcuffs. I wish you'd stayed, though. God, how I wish you'd stayed."

Chinese Handcuffs received a favorable response from some critics, while others found it too extreme for teens. Writing in *Horn Book,* Margaret A. Bush claimed that Crutcher "constructs his painful web with intelligent insight, creating a painful, powerful story. . . . In the end the story is a compelling, well-paced, and even humorous one of human failing, survival, and hope." Writing in *Voice of Youth Advocates,* Randy Brough called *Chinese Handcuffs* a "rewarding novel, tough, topical, compelling, and well written." The strong subject matter, however, was also a cause for controversy. A notable example was the reaction of the American Library Association. Its own *Booklist* magazine refused to review the book and offered a column questioning its merit. Conceding that Crutcher was "a strong writer" capable of making a "powerful moral point," *Booklist*'s Stephanie Zvirin went on to suggest that parts of the work, including Preston's suicide, were unduly graphic. She concluded that *Chinese Handcuffs* is "an unsuccessful book—and a disappointment—because the overloaded plot strains the novel's structure and diminishes the vital message Crutcher is trying to convey." In addition, a *Kirkus Reviews* critic commented that his teenage characters "have been knocked around in Crutcher's other stories, but not to this extent. . . . Crutcher probes so many tender areas here that readers may end by feeling exhausted and emotionally bruised." However, Crutcher thinks that the amount of fan mail the book generated may have worked in the book's favor; although *Chinese Handcuffs* was almost not named an ALA Best Book for Young Adults, it did eventually receive that honor.

In response, Crutcher points to the reality of his experience—and the experiences of kids. "I think there's a case to be made for being careful with language, but I want a kid to read it and believe it," he said. "I don't want some kid to say, 'God, kids don't talk like this,' because that negates everything else there. It would be nice to be able to blame things on language, because that would sure be simple—we could change the language and things would be better. Language ain't the problem. I had just come out of seven years in Oakland, for cryin' out loud, when I wrote *Running Loose.*" He has a similar reaction to critics of *Chinese Handcuffs:* "My line is, 'Look, I *got* that stuff from kids. I *toned that down.*'" Crutcher knows that many of his readers are people in pain, and he suggests that he may have helped some of them through some difficult times. "Hard times are magnetic to hard times," he observed. "If I'm a kid who has had awful things happen to me, I'm going to look for other kids that have had that same experience because I want to be validated in the world. You get three or four of us together and we've got some pretty hard stories to tell. I'm not going to be running around with the quarterback on the football team or the head cheerleader." Not long after the controversy over

Chinese Handcuffs, Crutcher was in Houston speaking to a group of students. "A girl came up after everyone was gone and said, 'I read that book and I thought you knew me.'" At such a moment, the complaints of a few critics didn't seem to matter. "I thought, To hell with that—this is what it's really about."

In 1991, Crutcher published his first collection of short stories, *Athletic Shorts: Six Short Stories.* The volume features some of the characters from the author's novels as well as some new characters. The first story, which outlines how a fat, clumsy boy raised by two sets of homosexual parents finds dignity when he is chosen as a joke to be the king of the senior ball, and the final entry, in which Louie Banks, the title character of *Running Loose,* accepts a boy dying from AIDS as a friend even though his decision threatens his relationship with a fellow athlete, have been singled out as especially effective. Writing in *School Library Journal,* Todd Morning said, "These *Athletic Shorts* will appeal to YAs, touch them deeply, and introduce them to characters they'll want to know better." *Horn Book* reviewer Nancy Vasilakis noted, "One need not to have read Crutcher's novels to appreciate the young men within these pages. They stand proudly on their own," while *Voice of Youth Advocates* contributor Sue Krumbein concluded that all six stories "live up to the high expectations we've come to expect of Crutcher."

In 1992, the author published his first book for adults, the suspense novel *The Deep End.* Called an "outstanding, yet wrenching, look into child abuse" by *School Library Journal* contributor Mike Printz, the novel was directed to adults but is considered appropriate for teenage readers. The story outlines how child therapist Wilson Corder investigates the disappearance—and eventual murder—of a young girl as well as the possible abuse of a three-year-old boy by his father, an expert in domestic violence. Printz concludes that "Crutcher's superb, sensitive style coupled with the prudent use of his unique humor makes this a first-rate, 'can't-put-it-down' novel," while a *Kirkus Reviews* contributor observed that the author's "needle-sharp focus on hurting kids makes this memorably harrowing from the starting gun."

In his next novel for young adults, *Staying Fat for Sarah Byrnes,* Crutcher features Eric Calhoune, a senior nicknamed "Moby" for his swimming ability and size. His best friend, Sarah Byrnes, suffered terrible facial burns as a small girl and has recently retreated into silence. After Sarah escapes from the psychiatric unit of a local hospital, her psychotic father Virgil—whom readers discover was the cause of his daughter's disfigurement and who refused to let her have reconstructive surgery—stabs Eric and hijacks his car when he refuses to reveal Sarah's hiding place. Eric brings in his sympathetic coach as his ally, and with his help manages to set things aright. At the end of the novel, Eric gets a new stepfather, Sarah a new set of parents, and Virgil a beating and a jail sentence. "This is a book that punches you in the stomach and never gives you a moment to breathe," wrote Susan R. Farber in *Voice of Youth Advocates,* who concluded that the novel is Crutcher's "darkest and most riveting work to date." Writing in *Horn Book,* Nancy Vasilakis called Sarah Byrnes "one of [Crutcher's] strongest female characters to date." A *Kirkus Reviews* critic praised the novel as "pulse-pounding, on both visceral and emotional levels—a wild, brutal ride," and Janice M. Del Negro of *Booklist* considered it "strong on relationships, long on plot" and with "enough humor and suspense to make it an easy booktalk with appeal across gender lines."

In *Ironman* Crutcher chronicles the senior year of Bo Brewster, who has been assigned to an anger management group after quitting the football team and calling the coach a rude name. The group's instructor, Mr. Nak, a Japanese American from Texas, gives Bo the tools to come to realizations about himself and his relationship with his vicious father. At the same time, Bo trains rigorously for an upcoming triathlon event. Bo's determination to train as hard as he can is intensified by the fact that his father is trying to fix the event by bribing his son's main competitor. At the end of the novel, Bo competes in the triathlon with the support of the anger management group and discovers his personal strength and self-respect. Crutcher presents the story as both a third-person narrative and in the form of letters from Bo to talk-show host Larry King, the only adult the boy feels will listen to him. Writing in *School Library Journal,* Tom S. Hurlburt said, "Crutcher has consistently penned exceptional reads for YAs, and *Ironman* is one of his strongest works yet." Roger Sutton, writing in *Bulletin of the Center for Children's Books,* claimed, "If you like Crutcher, this is vintage stuff . . . [If] you haven't succumbed before, you aren't likely to now, but fans will welcome the winning formula." Writing in the *New York Times Book Review,* James Gorman noted, "The heart of the story is small and painful, and rings thoroughly true," while *Horn Book* reviewer Peter D. Sieruta concluded that *Ironman* is a novel that "doesn't strive for easy answers, but does ask many intriguing questions of both its characters and its readers."

In 1995, Crutcher became a full-time writer, although he continued to work on the Child Protection Team in Spokane, Washington. He told Heather Vogel Frederick of *Publishers Weekly,* "When it came down to it, I could not give up writing. . . . What's known can't be unknown. As a writer and a human being . . . I have to keep myself in a position where I can scream and yell and be just obnoxious about getting something done." In an interview with Christine McDonnell in *Horn Book,* Crutcher remarked, "I want to be remembered as a storyteller, and I want to tell stories that seem real so that people will recognize something in their own lives and see the connections. We are all connected. That's what I like to explore and put into stories." Quoted in *Twentieth-Century Children's Writers,* Crutcher concluded, "My mission is to write truths as I see them, reflect the world as it appears to me, rather than as others

would have it. I would like to tell stories so 'right on' that they punch a hole in the wall between young adult and adult literature." In his collection *Athletic Shorts,* Crutcher wrote, "There are a significant amount of people who . . . think kids should not be exposed in print to what they are exposed to in their lives. But I believe what I believe, and so I write my stories."

Crutcher has found that some of the most gratifying comments he gets about his works come in the mail. "I get a lot of responses from kids who don't read very much," he told Kozikowski, "and that's great because I didn't read—it's like me writing to me." He described a recent batch of letters: "One said, 'My mom's dying of cancer and this book helped me come out of my shell. I've just been saying that what's happening isn't true, but it is true. And the things that Louie Banks went through tell me a way that I can let it be true, and then go on. Things *will* go on.' There were letters from kids who had just lost people, whether it was a death or not, and they learned that there is another way to look at a loss. I was astonished at these letters—that's the feedback I like."

Returning to the subject of racism, Crutcher's 2001 novel *Whale Talk* focuses on close-minded individuals and features the familiar Crutcher underdogs who must deal directly with social issues, including hatred toward multiracial children. A gifted but uninterested athlete, senior high school student T. J. Jones, of black, white, and Japanese heritage, is finally persuaded by a favorite teacher to organize a swim team at the school. The reluctant teen agrees, but instead of turning to popular athletes to join the squad, T. J. looks for those students on the fringes of school society. As the season progresses, the students become a unusually competitive bunch, all the while working out individual problems with the newfound support of teammates. A *Publishers Weekly* reviewer called *Whale Talk* "a gripping tale of small-town prejudice [that] delivers a frank, powerful message about social issues and ills," noting that the book "will force readers to re-examine their own values and cause them to alter their perception of individuals pegged as 'losers.'" In *Horn Book,* a reviewer noted, "Crutcher knows his stuff, and he pumps adrenaline throughout the sport scenes while honestly acknowledging the personal struggles of his adolescent readers."

In 2003, Crutcher broke form by writing *King of the Mild Frontier: An Ill-Advised Autobiography.* A *Horn Book* reviewer praised the new venture: "Crutcher, best known for his novels and short stories, has discovered his most effective voice in this collection of episodic, autobiographical essays." Crutcher, whose work has at times been censored by librarians, parents, and teachers for his real-to-life dealing with the complexities—humorous and tragic—of teenage life, addresses these issues and shares stories from his growing-up years, which Joel Shoemaker, writing in *School Library Journal,* described as "tough and tender reminiscences [which] focus primarily on family, social, and school conflicts, but lessons derived from his career as a teacher, therapist, and writer are also described." It is his humility, wrote a *Publishers Weekly* reviewer, "that allows readers to laugh with young Chris, rather than at him" when he constantly makes trouble under his older brother's tutelage, gets hit in the mouth with a softball bat showing off for the girls' team, and trembles as "a terrified 123-pound freshman ('with all the muscle definition of a chalk outline')."

Crutcher once shared the following thoughts on writing: "It is a joy to write a tale that is believable, that is real. Writing is also a way to express humor and to present different human perspectives. I like to explore the different ways in which people make sense of what goes on around them—ways in which they respond to the wide range of random things that happen, and to the situations they create.

"Working in the mental health field provides me with some unique perspectives on the human drama—how people get stuck and how they grow. Every client—man, woman, or child, no matter how damaged—has shown me at least a small glimpse of how we're all connected."

Biographical and Critical Sources

BOOKS

Children's Literature Review, Gale (Detroit, MI), Volume 28, 1992, pp. 98-108.

Crutcher, Chris, *Athletic Shorts: Six Short Stories,* Greenwillow (New York, NY), 1991.

Crutcher, Chris, *Chinese Handcuffs,* Dell (New York, NY), 1991.

Crutcher, Chris, *Running Loose,* Greenwillow (New York, NY), 1983.

Crutcher, Chris, *Stotan!,* Dell (New York, NY), 1988.

Crutcher, Chris, telephone interview with Thomas Kozikowski for *Authors and Artists for Young Adults,* Volume 9, Gale (Detroit, MI), 1992.

Davis, Terry, *Presenting Chris Crutcher,* Twayne/Prentice-Hall (New York, NY), 1997.

Gallo, Donald R., editor, *Speaking for Ourselves: Autobiographical Sketches by Notable Authors of Books for Young Adults,* National Council of Teachers of English (Urbana, IL), 1990, p. 59.

Silvey, Anita, editor, *Children's Books and Their Creators,* Houghton Mifflin (Boston, MA), 1995, pp. 181-182.

Twentieth-Century Children's Writers, St. James Press (Detroit, MI), 1994.

PERIODICALS

Booklist, August, 1989, Stephanie Zvirin, "The YA Connection: *Chinese Handcuffs,*" p. 1966; March 15, 1993, Janice M. Del Negro, review of *Staying Fat for Sarah Byrnes,* p. 1313.

Bulletin of the Center for Children's Books, May, 1983, Zena Sutherland, review of *Running Loose,* p. 165; April, 1995, Roger Sutton, review of *Ironman,* p. 269.

Emergency Librarian, January-February, 1991, Dave Jenkinson, "Portraits: Chris Crutcher," pp. 67-71.

Horn Book, September-October, 1986, Anita Silvey, review of *Stotan!,* p. 596; November-December, 1987, Anita Silvey, review of *The Crazy Horse Electric Game,* p. 741; May, 1988, Christine McDonnell, "New Voices, New Visions: Chris Crutcher," p. 332; July-August, 1989, Margaret A. Bush, review of *Chinese Handcuffs,* p. 487; September-October, 1991, Nancy Vasilakis, review of *Athletic Shorts,* pp. 602-603; May-June, 1993, Nancy Vasilakis, review of *Staying Fat for Sarah Byrnes,* p. 337; October, 1995, Peter D. Sieruta, review of *Ironman,* p. 606; May, 2001, review of *Whale Talk,* p. 320; May-June, 2003, Betty Carter, review of *King of the Mild Frontier: An Ill-Advised Autobiography,* p. 368.

Idaho Statesman (Boise, ID), July 28, 1983, Lori Montgomery, "Idaho Novelist: First Book Wins Raves."

Journal of Youth Services in Libraries, summer, 2000, Chris Crutcher, "The 2000 Margaret A. Edwards Award Acceptance Speech," pp. 17-19.

Kirkus Reviews, April 15, 1983, review of *Running Loose,* p. 461; February 15, 1989, review of *Chinese Handcuffs,* p. 290; November 15, 1991, review of *The Deep End,* p. 1436; March 15, 1993, review of *Staying Fat for Sarah Byrnes,* p. 369.

New York Times Book Review, July 2, 1995, James Gorman, review of *Ironman,* p. 13.

Publishers Weekly, May 29, 1987, review of *The Crazy Horse Electric Game,* p. 79; February 20, 1995, Heather Vogel Frederick, "Chris Crutcher: 'What's Known Can't Be Unknown', " pp. 183-184; March 12, 2001, review of *Whale Talk,* p. 91; March 3, 2003, review of *King of the Mild Frontier,* p. 77.

School Library Journal, May, 1983, Trev Jones, review of *Running Loose,* p. 80; May, 1986, Jerry Flack, review of *Stotan!,* p. 100; September, 1991, Todd Morning, review of *Athletic Shorts,* p. 278; September, 1992, Mike Printz, review of *The Deep End,* p. 189; March, 1995, Tom S. Hurlburt, review of *Ironman,* p. 222; June, 2000, Betty Carter, "Eyes Wide Open," pp. 42-45; April, 2003, Joel Shoemaker, review of *King of the Mild Frontier,* p. 176.

Voice of Youth Advocates, April, 1983, Mary K. Chelton, review of *Running Loose,* p. 36; April, 1986, Mary K. Chelton, review of *Stotan!,* p. 29; June, 1987, Pam Spencer, review of *The Crazy Horse Electric Game,* p. 76; June, 1989, Randy Brough, review of *Chinese Handcuffs,* p. 98; April, 1992, Sue Krumbein, review of *Athletic Shorts,* p. 26; August, 1993, Susan R. Farber, review of *Staying Fat for Sarah Byrnes,* p. 150.

ONLINE

Chris Crutcher's Authorized Web Site, http://www.about crutcher.com/ (November 27, 2003).

Teenreads.com, http://www.teenreads.com/ (April 2, 2001), interview with Crutcher.*

DAVIS, (A.) Aubrey 1949-

Personal

Born August 5, 1949; son of Milton Davis (a businessman) and Edith Cohen; married Sandra Carpenter-Davis; children: Nathanael, Olwyn. *Education:* University of Toronto, B.A., 1974; University of Western Ontario, B.Ed., 1975; University of Toronto, M.Ed., 1987, specialist certificates in special education and drama education, 1990. *Hobbies and other interests:* Reading, hiking, canoeing, fishing, biking, Tai Chi.

Addresses

Home and office—15 Graham Gardens, Toronto, Ontario, Canada M6C 1G6. *E-mail*—aubrey.davis@ sympatico.ca.

Career

Grey County board of education, Canada, grade school teacher, 1975; Northumberland and Newcastle board of education, Canada, special education teacher, 1976-78; self-employed in antique restoration and sales, logging, farming, gardening, and nursery work, 1978-80; "Lateral and Creative Thinking" teacher for adults, 1981-82; Metropolitan Toronto board of education, Toronto, Ontario, special education teacher, 1980-87; North York Board of Education, Toronto, Ontario, teacher in oral language program for developmentally handicapped students, 1987-2004; writer and storyteller. Has made author and storyteller appearances throughout Canada and the United States. Adult literacy volunteer in nursing homes and jails.

Member

Writers' Union of Canada, Storytellers of Canada, Canadian Society of Children's Authors, Illustrators and Performers, Storyteller's School of Toronto, Canadian Children's Book Centre, IBBY Canada, Elementary Teachers Federation of Ontario, Elementary Teachers of Toronto.

Awards, Honors

Notable Canadian Fiction for Children citation, Canadian School Library Association, 1995, Alcuin Society Book Design Award, 1996, Tiny TORGI Award shortlist for most popular children's Braille book, CNIB Library for the Blind, and IBBY Honour List citation for illustration, 1998, all for *Bone Button Borscht;* Mr. Christie's Book Award shortlist citation, Governor General's Literary Award shortlist citation, both 1996, and Amelia Frances Howard-Gibbon Award shortlist citation, 1997, all for *Sody Salleratus;* Children's Media Award,

In a variation on the Stone Soup folktale, Aubrey Davis relates the story of a beggar who convinces the unfriendly and miserly inhabitants of a town to donate ingredients to make a kettle of borscht. (From Bone Button Borscht, *illustrated by Dusan Petricic.)*

Parent's Guide, and Communication-Jeunesse, Palmares des livres préférés des jeunes, both 1999, both for *The Enormous Potato.*

Writings

Bone Button Borscht, illustrated by Dusan Petricic, Kids Can Press (Toronto, Ontario, Canada), 1995.

Sody Salleratus, illustrated by Alan and Lea Daniel, Kids Can Press (Toronto, Ontario, Canada), 1996.

The Enormous Potato, illustrated by Dusan Petricic, Kids Can Press (Toronto, Ontario, Canada), 1997, Scholastic (New York, NY), 1998.

Bagels from Benny, illustrated by Dusan Petricic, Kids Can Press (Toronto, Ontario, Canada), 2003.

Contributor, *Tales for an Unknown City,* edited by Dan Yashinsky, McGill-Queen's University (Toronto, Ontario, Canada), 1990; contributor to books retold by Idries Shah, including *Thinkers of the East,* Octagon Press (London, England), 1982; *The Subtleties of the Inimitable Mulla Nasrudin,* Octagon Press (London, England), 1983; *The Pleasantries of the Incredible Mulla Nasrudin,* Octagon Press (London, England), 1983; *The Exploits of the Incomparable Mulla Nasrudin,* Octagon Press (London, England), 1983. Davis's books have been translated into French, Hebrew, Portuguese, and Korean.

Adaptations

Bone Button Borscht was performed in Toronto, Ontario, December 4, 2003, with the Toronto Symphony Orchestra and a guest group, Finjan, narrated by Barbara Budd. A version performed by the Winnipeg Symphony is available on compact disc.

Sidelights

Aubrey Davis is a writer, storyteller and oral language teacher for developmentally challenged children. He drifted into writing when he was asked to tell a Chanukah story to very young children and couldn't find one that suited him. He told *SATA:* "In desperation I wrote one myself. *Bone Button Borscht* was born of necessity. The children loved it and so did the publisher to whom I sent it."

Davis added: "I'm not really sure why I became a writer. I always loved to read. As a boy I had a passion for myths, Bible stories, science fiction and *Mad Magazine.* My neighbor was a writer for CBC. Maybe I caught the writing bug from him. I loved to write funny stories. My grade six teacher liked them. But my eighth-grade teacher hated them. So I stopped writing creatively until I was forty-two.

"Perhaps my writing began in a non-linear way. One day a supply teacher waltzed into our grade twelve English class. He taught me how to think for myself, to question my assumptions, and to consider what might

In his rendition of a nineteenth-century American folktale, Davis's rousing story depicts the many people who are devoured by a savage bear when, one by one, they cross a bridge to buy the baking soda an old woman needs for her biscuits. (From Sody Salleratus, *illustrated by Alan and Lea Daniel.)*

be really important. The following year I joined a theatre group, volunteered with mentally handicapped children, learned to speed-read, and served as president of the student council. Two years later I quit university to travel in Europe and Africa. Maybe it was that teacher's doing, or maybe it was simply the sixties.

"On the Canary Islands I opened a copy of *The Sufis* by Idries Shah. Because Omar Khayyam was a favorite film from my childhood and because his name appeared in the index I began to read. Lively and intensely thought provoking, this book introduced me to the idea of storytelling. I have always been interested in performance. My mother was very involved in amateur theatre, as was my wife.

"In any case, I became a storyteller. At first I told stories to my own children, then at a weekly gathering in Toronto. I told in nursing homes, festivals and jails. In time I told on national radio and television. I created an oral language program for mentally challenged children. I taught them language through story. And they taught me how to tell and to write simply and dramatically.

"I have worked as a lab technician, logger, and house painter. I've sold antiques and I've raised goats. How

In a humorous, cumulative folktale, **The Enormous Potato,** *a farmer calls more and more people to help him unearth his prized spud. (Retold by Davis and illustrated by Dusan Petricic.)*

did I become a writer? Perhaps it happened by chance or through necessity. Perhaps I was influenced by others or merely guided by my own interests and abilities. But I feel that something within, beneath consciousness led me down strange pathways plucking what it needed from the people and experiences it met along the way. And the insignificant, the unexpected, even the distasteful have proved to be as valuable as the significant, deliberate and pleasing."

Davis has provided his own novel spin on several beloved European folk tales. *Bone Button Borscht,* one of three Davis picture books illustrated by Dusan Petricic, re-tells the old "Stone Soup" story using an imaginative beggar and a shtetl peopled by miserly folk who learn community spirit from the beggar's offer to make soup from his coat buttons. The story begins in a colorless mode, but as each villager adds an ingredient to the "button soup," the rich hues of the borscht unfold, and all the various characters feast upon it. "*Bone Button Borscht* truly exploits the dynamic potential of the picture-book medium," wrote Sarah Ellis in *Horn Book.* "The whole thing moves like an animated short or like a piece of music." Ellis concluded that the work shows "a lovely satisfying shape."

Sody Salleratus is a re-telling of an old mountain tale. A boy sets off to buy some "sody salleratus" (baking soda) at the store, but he is accosted and eaten by a bear before he can bring it home. One by one his family members go looking for him, only to fall victim to the same hungry bear. Finally, the crafty squirrel on the mantelpiece seeks out the bear and plays a trick that frees the whole family. Stephanie Zvirin in *Booklist* noted that Davis adds "a storyteller's tempo" to the work. Zvirin likewise characterized the book as "a good read-aloud" and a "lively tale." In a similar vein, *The Enormous Potato,* adapted from an original version in-

volving a turnip, demonstrates the value of teamwork. A farmer has grown the biggest potato anyone has ever seen—but how can he unearth it? He calls upon his wife, daughter, dog, and cat for help, and each push and pull to no avail. Finally, with the help of a lowly mouse, the potato rolls free, providing sustenance for the entire town. Helen Rosenberg in *Booklist* cited *The Enormous Potato* for its "freshness and vitality."

Benny's grandfather makes and sells bagels in *Bagels from Benny.* Every day Benny's grandfather thanks God for the ingredients that go into the bagels, but Benny wants to go a step further. When no one is looking, Benny stashes a sack of bagels in the Ark at his local synagogue. A week later, they have disappeared, and Benny is sure that God has taken them. To his intense disappointment, however, some weeks later he discovers that a poor member of the congregation has been removing them and eating them. Benny's grandfather explains that helping others gives God the greatest pleasure of all. In *Booklist,* Hazel Rochman praised *Bagels for Benny* as "the story of how a small gesture can make a difference . . . a moving drama of generosity and faith." A *Publishers Weekly* reviewer felt that the work displays a welcome use of Davis's "fluid prose," which "increases the folktale's accessibility to young readers."

Biographical and Critical Sources

PERIODICALS

Booklist, November 1, 1997, Kay Weisman, review of *Bone Button Borscht,* p. 480; March 15, 1998, Stephanie Zvirin, review of *Sody Salleratus,* p. 1246;

November 1, 1998, Helen Rosenberg, review of *The Enormous Potato,* p. 498; October 1, 2003, Hazel Rochman, review of *Bagels from Benny,* p. 333.

Horn Book, September-October, 1995, Sarah Ellis, review of *Bone Button Borscht,* p. 643.

Publishers Weekly, February 2, 1998, review of *Sody Salleratus,* p. 88; October 27, 2003, review of *Bagels from Benny,* p. 66.

School Library Journal, November, 1997, Susan Pine, review of *Bone Button Borscht,* p. 106; April, 1998, Lisa Falk, review of *Sody Salleratus,* p. 115; November 1, 1998, Maryann H. Owen, review of *The Enormous Potato,* p. 77.

Toronto Star, December 11, 2003, Richard Ouzounian, "Heaping Serving of Bone Button Borscht."

E-F

EDWARDS, Julie
See ANDREWS, Julie

* * *

EDWARDS, Julie Andrews
See ANDREWS, Julie

* * *

ELLIOTT, (Robert) Scott 1970-

Personal

Born September 12, 1970, in Lexington, KY; son of Robert Bruce (a radiologist) and Elizabeth (a teacher and horse breeder) Elliott. *Education:* Vanderbilt University, B.A. (with honors), 1993; University of Colorado at Boulder, M.A., 1996; Columbia University, M.F.A., 1999. *Hobbies and other interests:* Fly fishing, backpacking, songwriting, film.

Addresses

Home—4815 Graustark, Houston, TX 77006. *Agent*—Alice Tasman, Jean Naggar Literary Agency, 216 E. 75th St., 1E, New York, NY 10021. *E-mail*—clearstream@mail.com.

Career

Teachers and Writers Collaborative, New York, NY, writer-in-residence, 1997-2000; Hofstra University, New York, NY, adjunct writing instructor, 1999-2000; Writers in the Schools, Houston, TX, writer-in-residence at Long Middle School and High School for the Performing and Visual Arts, 2001—; University of Houston, Houston, TX, teaching fellow, 2000—; writer.

Awards, Honors

Columbia University Writing Division fellowship; C. Glenn Cambor fellowship, University of Houston; finalist, PEN Northwest Margery Davis Boyden Residency.

Writings

Coiled in the Heart (novel), Putnam (New York, NY), 2003.

Author of short stories, including "The Second Salmon," published in the *Vanderbilt Review,* 1993; "A Fishing Tale," published in *Sniper Logic,* 1996; and "My Injury," published in *Samsara,* 2002.

Work in Progress

In the Olympics, a novel set in and around the Olympic National Park in Washington State; a collection of short stories; nonfiction essays.

Sidelights

Scott Elliott told *SATA:* "Though it sounds strange to say it, I write because writing affords me a place where I have the opportunity to be better than myself, or at least the messy, incomprehensible self I inhabit on a daily basis. This is a place where I can use the advantage of extra time for contemplation and multiple drafts to discover and approach what I truly think and feel about life, about being human, and about the best way to live. It is a place where I can search for, build, and vivify images, characters, and actions that embody truths and evoke a multiplicity of responses from intelligent readers who are also on quests for truths and for the best, richest kind of life. As a writer, you are a quiet creator of an evocative world. A book should be a living thing, as Henry James has said—'an immense, exquisite, correspondence with life.' If the writer is successful, the reader can inhabit a book and find multiple pathways within it, different living strands with each read, just as an imaginative person can discover and countenance multiple ways of living a life."

Elliott's debut novel examines the long-term consequences of a boy's rash act that leads to the sudden death of another youngster. Tobia Caldwell is seven years old when a subdivision begins sprouting on the land that has been in his family for two hundred years. Tobia realizes that his family has had to sell the land due to financial reverses, but he still suffers when a bully about his age moves into one of the new homes and begins tormenting him. Tobia tells the boy that there's a silver dollar hidden in the roots of an old tree on the edge of the creek that runs through the Caldwell property. In reality, the tree offers refuge to a cotton-mouth snake that bites Tobia's rival and kills him. The remainder of *Coiled in the Heart* explores Tobia's coming into adulthood with the guilt and pain he feels over the death.

In interviews, Elliott has said that *Coiled in the Heart* is fiction, not at all based upon his own experiences, except for the fact that he liked to play along a rural creek when he was young, and he once saw a worker kill a poisonous snake. From these two incidents—as well as an ongoing fascination with the New Madrid earthquake, computers, and suburban sprawl—grew a novel about the deep South and how its legacy affects its most recent generations. Mark Coomes in the *Louisville Courier-Journal* noted that Elliott, born and raised in Kentucky, "possesses a Louisvillian's ability to see Dixie from an intimate distance. Elliott, like Louisville itself, possesses Southern sensibilities without all the Southern entanglements."

Novelist Pat Conroy was one of the prominent authors who provided a dust jacket endorsement for *Coiled in the Heart* on its release in 2003. A *Publishers Weekly* reviewer commended the novel as "richly atmospheric" and added that Elliott has proven himself to be "a solid, assured stylist." In his feature on Elliott, Coomes called *Coiled in the Heart* "a quintessential work of Southern fiction."

Biographical and Critical Sources

PERIODICALS

Library Journal, June 1, 2003, Ann H. Fisher, review of *Coiled in the Heart,* p. 164.
Louisville Courier-Journal, October 11, 2003, Mark Coomes, "A Sense of Place."
Publishers Weekly, June 2, 2003, review of *Coiled in the Heart,* p. 30.

ONLINE

Fun with Spot Reading Guides, http://books.funwithspot. com/ (June 10, 2004), synopsis of *Coiled in the Heart,* with author commentary and discussion questions.

* * *

FARJEON, (Eve) Annabel 1919-2004
(Sarah Jefferson)

OBITUARY NOTICE—See index for *SATA* sketch: Born March 19, 1919, in Bucklebury, Berkshire, England; died February 8, 2004, in London, England. Dancer and

author. The daughter of critic Herbert Farjeon and artist Joan Farjeon, Annabel grew up well versed in literature and the theater. Her first passion was dance, though, and she began studying ballet at the age of eleven. Her early performances were with the Vic-Wells Ballet and, later, the Sadler's Wells Ballet Company. When World War II began, Farjeon became an ambulance driver in London, and after the war worked with refugees in Italy and Egypt. She then began her writing and criticism career, first as an assistant literary editor for *Time & Tide* from 1946 to 1948, then as a ballet critic for the *New Statesman* until 1964. Her knowledge of ballet also led to fourteen years as a dance critic for the London *Evening Standard* during the 1960s and early 1970s. Besides becoming a respected critic, sometimes contributing to periodicals under the pseudonym Sarah Jefferson, Farjeon was known for her books for children, including *The Siege of Trapp's Mill* (1972), *The Poetry of Cats* (1974), and *The Unicorn Drum* (1976). In addition, she completed a biography of her aunt titled *Morning Has Broken: A Biography of Eleanor Farjeon* (1986). The journal that she kept while working as a dancer in the 1930s was later published in the 1980s in *American Dance Chronicle* and adapted as a BBC documentary titled *Ballet behind the Borders* (2002).

OBITUARIES AND OTHER SOURCES:

PERIODICALS

Independent (London, England), February 13, 2004, p. 41.

* * *

FATHER GOOSE
See GHIGNA, Charles

* * *

FEARNLEY, Jan 1965-

Personal

Born February 19, 1965, in South Shields, Tyne and Wear, England; married, husband's name Paul. *Education:* Holds degrees in education and graphic design. *Hobbies and other interests:* Walking in wilderness areas and on the beach, gardening, cycling.

Addresses

Agent—David Higham Associates, 5-8 Lower John St., Golden Square, London W1F 9HA, England.

Career

Writer and illustrator. Has also worked as an early childhood educator in England.

Jan Fearnley

Awards, Honors

Children's Book Award shortlist citations for *A Perfect Day for It, Billy Tibbles Moves Out!,* and *Mr. Wolf's Pancakes;* Stockport Children's Book Award for *Just Like You;* Gold Award for Illustration, Association of Illustrators, for *Mr. Wolf and the Three Bears;* Oppenheim portfolio gold award for *A Perfect Day for It.*

Writings

SELF-ILLUSTRATED

Little Robin's Christmas, Little Tiger Press (Waukesha, WI), 1998, published in England as *Little Robin Red Vest,* Egmont Books (London, England), 1998.

Mabel and Max, Mammoth Books (London, England), 1998.

Mr. Wolf's Pancakes, Mammoth Books (London, England), 1999, Tiger Tales (Wilton, CT), 2001.

A Special Something, Hyperion Books for Children (New York, NY), 2000.

Just Like You, Mammoth Books (London, England), 2000, Candlewick Press (Cambridge, MA), 2001.

Colin and the Curly Claw, Mammoth Books (London, England), 2001, Crabtree Publishing (New York, NY), 2002.

A Perfect Day for It, Egmont Children's Books (London, England), 2001, Harcourt (San Diego, CA), 2002.

Mr. Wolf and the Three Bears, Harcourt (San Diego, CA), 2002.

Billy Tibbles Moves Out!, Collins (London, England), 2003, HarperCollins (New York, NY), 2004.

Watch Out!, Candlewick Press (Cambridge, MA), 2004.

Work in Progress

More picture books.

Sidelights

Jan Fearnley worked as a preschool teacher before devoting herself to her first love—writing and illustrating books for children. With dual degrees in early childhood education and graphic art, Fearnley has learned how to entertain young listeners with brightly-colored and engaging tales, many of which feature animals acting like people. The youngest of six children, Fearnley sometimes found herself left behind while her older brothers played together. She entertained herself by drawing and making up stories, and by reading. In an interview for the *Year of Reading* Web site, the author-illustrator said: "A book can help you deal with emotions or problems, comfort you, make you laugh or move you to tears. They're powerful things. Have you got a favorite old book that you read over and over again, especially when you're feeling down? I rest my case!"

Fearnley broke into publishing with a Christmas story, released in England as *Little Robin Red Vest* and in America as *Little Robin's Christmas.* Little Robin has seven warm, red vests—one for each day of the week. But as he sees other animals suffering from the cold, he gives his vests away one by one, until he is the one left shivering in the snow. Santa Claus rides to the rescue, endowing the little bird with a new vest made from a thread from his famous red coat. "Little Robin's unhesitating generosity will also kindle a response in young readers at any time of year," noted John Peters in *Booklist.*

One of Fearnley's most popular characters is Mr. Wolf, an affable sort who knows how to get a job done. In *Mr. Wolf's Pancakes,* he cannot seem to get any help from his neighbors—including a snobbish Chicken Little—in his quest to create a batch of warm pancakes. Undaunted, Mr. Wolf sets to work in his kitchen, and when his neighbors smell the tantalizing results, they try to join him in the feast. He turns the tables on them with a comic twist. A *Publishers Weekly* reviewer felt that youngsters would enjoy Fearnley's "sympathetic wolf and the savory surprise ending." A contributor to *Horn Book* praised Mr. Wolf as "likably drawn" with a "gentle smile" that belies his quirky appetite.

Mr. Wolf makes another appearance in *Mr. Wolf and the Three Bears.* This time he is hosting a birthday party for Baby Bear, and Grandma Wolf is providing the feast. The party is on the verge of ruin when Goldilocks crashes it and misbehaves, bringing Baby Bear to tears and ignoring every plea to curb her nastiness. Grandma Wolf solves the problem by forbidding Goldilocks to go into the kitchen—and a short time later, Grandma emerges from that very room, carrying a steaming hot pie. "Fearnley tells the story with enough of a wink and a nod so as not to alarm children," observed Rosalyn Pierini in *School Library Journal.* A *Publishers Weekly* reviewer deemed the book "archly hilarious" for Mr. Wolf's "take-no-prisoners approach to etiquette."

Other Fearnley picture books include *Just Like You, A Perfect Day for It,* and *Billy Tibbles Moves Out!* In each story, likable animals provide chances for children to learn important messages about parental guidance, friendship, and sharing. The little mouse in *Just Like You* wonders what his mother can do for him after seeing and hearing bigger, more powerful animals making promises to their children. Mother mouse assures him that her tiny size does not diminish the amount of love she holds for him. Martha Topol in *School Library Journal* observed that Fearnley's book "reminds readers of the daily expressions of unconditional love that make their relationship so unique." In *A Perfect Day for It,* curious animals follow Bear to a mountaintop because he declares it is "a perfect day for it," while not specifying what "it" is. At the top, all the animals receive a great treat. Billy Tibbles, a cat with attitude, finds his

comfortable world threatened in *Billy Tibbles Moves Out!* Told he must share his room with his brother, Billy rebels—until he discovers that a roommate brings rowdy pillowfights and a chance to sleep with Dad. "Kids will immediately connect with Billy Tibbles," maintained Ilene Cooper in *Booklist.* "Here's a book that gets it all right."

Fearnley lives in England, where her books have sold more than 300,000 copies in the past several years. In her spare time she enjoys walking, cycling, and caring for her Cornish Rex cats.

Biographical and Critical Sources

PERIODICALS

Booklist, September 15, 1998, John Peters, review of *Little Robin's Christmas,* p. 236; July, 2001, Cynthia Turnquest, review of *Just Like You,* p. 2019; February 15, 2004, Ilene Cooper, review of *Billy Tibbles Moves Out!,* p. 1062.
Horn Book, March, 2000, review of *Mr. Wolf's Pancakes,* p. 184.
Publishers Weekly, January 10, 2000, review of *Mr. Wolf's Pancakes,* p. 67; June 12, 2000, review of *A Special Something,* p. 71; March 25, 2002, review of *Mr. Wolf and the Three Bears,* p. 62; January 26, 2004, review of *Billy Tibbles Moves Out!,* p. 252.
School Library Journal, August, 2000, Martha Topol, review of *A Special Something,* p. 154; April, 2001, Martha Topol, review of *Just Like You,* p. 108; June, 2002, Rosalyn Pierini, review of *Mr. Wolf and the Three Bears,* p. 94; December, 2002, Olga R. Kuharets, review of *A Perfect Day for It,* p. 95; March, 2004, Bina Williams, review of *Billy Tibbles Moves Out!,* p. 157; April, 2004, Jane Barrer, review of *Watch Out!,* p. 110.*

ONLINE

David Higham Associates, http://www.davidhigham.co.uk/ (February 3, 2004), "Jan Fearnley."
Hungry Wolf, http://www.hungry-wolf.com/ (June 2, 2004), author's home page.
Year of Reading, http://www.yearofreading.org.uk/reading/ writers/fine/ (October 1, 2004), "Jan Fearnley."

A big bad wolf unsuccessfully requests the help of several well-known fairy tale characters when he attempts to cook in Fearnley's funny picture book with a surprise ending. (From Mr. Wolf's Pancakes, *written and illustrated by Fearnley.)*

*　　*　　*

FOREMAN, Wilmoth 1939-

Personal

Born July 24, 1939, in Columbia, TN; daughter of Clement (a machinist) and Pauline (a homemaker; maiden name, Phillips) Marshall; married Jesse F. Foreman (an advertising consultant), 1963; children: Jesse

A little mouse learns that his tiny mother has a big heart when she expresses her love in Fearnley's touching, simple tale of maternal devotion. (From Just Like You, *written and illustrated by Fearnley.)*

Walter, Ellen Ruth, Mary Kathleen. *Education:* George Peabody College for Teachers, B.A., 1961; Vermont College of Norwich University, M.F.A., 2002; attended University of Tennessee—Knoxville, 1990, and University of Tennessee—Martin, 1998. *Religion:* Presbyterian. *Hobbies and other interests:* Reading, fishing, gardening, traveling.

Addresses

Home—931 Camellia Dr., Columbia, TN 38401. *E-mail*—wilmothforeman@yahoo.com.

Career

Duluth High School, Duluth, GA, teacher of English, 1961-62; *Daily Herald,* Columbia, TN, worked in ad-

vertising department, 1962-65, reporter, 1988, weekly columnist, 1999—; adult education teacher, 1990-94; teacher of English as a second language, 1991-92; Central High School, Columbia, special education teacher, 1992-94, teacher of English and social studies in Optional High School at-risk program, 1993-99; Columbia State Community College, Columbia, instructor in developmental writing, 1994. First Presbyterian Church, Columbia, organist, 1966-96, music coordinator, 1980-87; First United Methodist Church, Pulaski, TN, organist, 1999—. Tennessee Arts Commission, Arts in Education program, teacher of writing, 1990—; has also taught non-credit courses in reminiscence writing and creative writing at Columbia State Community College, Columbia.

Member

Society of Children's Book Writers and Illustrators, Tennessee Writers' Alliance, Maury County Community Chorus.

Writings

Summer of the Skunks, Front Street Books (Asheville, NC), 2003.

Sidelights

Summer of the Skunks, Wilmoth Foreman's first novel, offers a warm tale of sibling bickering and bonding set in the mid-twentieth-century rural South. Told from the point of view of ten-year-old Jill, *Summer of the Skunks* features "a strong heroine who is likeable for her spirit and earnest nature," wrote Alison Grant in *School Li-*

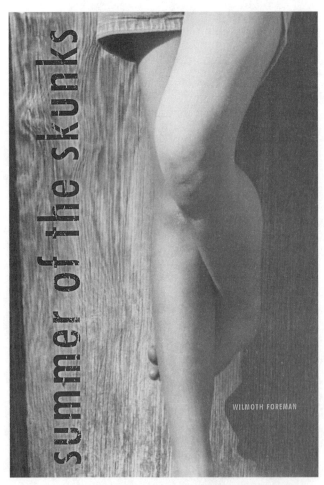

Ten-year-old Jill and her teenage siblings, raised in a loving family during the 1940s, find a new closeness when they face several challenges one summer, including a family of skunks who move in under the family's farmhouse.

brary Journal. A *Kirkus Reviews* contributor noted as well that it is Jill's voice, "with its emotional honesty and growing understanding of her family's dynamics," which shines through the novel. Jill's family includes sixteen-year-old Margo, thirteen-year-old Calvin, five-year-old Josh, and the children's hard-working parents. The children labor hard as well, helping with chores like canning and struggling to milk their temperamental cow, but during the long summer, they find plenty of time for adventures. The summer begins with a family of skunks taking up residence under the family's house, a problem that falls to the children to solve. Jill, Margo, and Calvin also team up to get rid of another unwanted house guest, their mother's lazy cousin, and to provide shelter and support to a family friend who needs their help to defeat his alcohol problem. Along the way, the children indulge in "plenty of lively bickering, along with an array of minor mishaps," John Peters wrote in *Booklist.*

Foreman told *SATA:* "My mother always said I needed to have a self-starter installed. Well, it didn't happen. But writing kept inviting me back. Finally, finally I learned a few things about how to write fiction. Or at least one fictional story that one editor deemed worthy of publication.

"Events and people in my first novel, *Summer of the Skunks,* though fiction, were triggered by memories from a childhood that was basically a happy one. For most of my writing life, I considered that 'normal' childhood to be useless as writing material. But advisors in the Vermont MFA program kept urging me to 'go there.' So I did, and am glad of it, and hope readers are glad, too."

Biographical and Critical Sources

PERIODICALS

Booklist, May 1, 2003, John Peters, review of *Summer of the Skunks,* p. 1591.
Kirkus Reviews, May 15, 2003, review of *Summer of the Skunks,* p. 750.
Publishers Weekly, May 5, 2003, review of *Summer of the Skunks,* p. 222.
School Library Journal, August, 2003, Alison Grant, review of *Summer of the Skunks,* p. 159.

ONLINE

Front Street Books Web Site, http://www.frontstreetbooks. com/ (November 11, 2003), "Wilmoth Foreman."
TeenReads.com, http://www.teenreads.com/ (November 11, 2003), Ashley Hartlaub, review of *Summer of the Skunks.*

G

GALLAGHER, Diana G. 1946-
(Diana G. Burke; Diana Gallagher Burke)

Personal
Born March 14, 1946, in Paterson, NJ; daughter of Ralph O. Grubel and Beryl M. Ledgard; married Martin R. Burke, December 30, 1994; children: Jay R. Gallagher, Chelsea Ann Streb. *Education:* High school graduate, 1964. *Politics:* Democrat.

Addresses
Home—10020 N.W. Highway, 225A, Ocala, FL 34482.
Agent—Ricia Mainhardt, 612 Argyle Rd, L5, Brooklyn, NY 11230.

Career
Writer. Has also worked as instructor in horse riding, artist, and folk singer.

Awards, Honors
Hugo Award for best fan artist, 1988.

Writings

The Alien Dark (novel), TSR, 1990.
(With husband, Martin R. Burke) *The Chance Factor* (novel; "Star Trek: Voyager" series), Minstrel Books (New York, NY), 1997.
Invasion (novel; "The Journey of Alan Strange" series), Minstrel Books (New York, NY), 1999.
Shadows (novel; "Smallville" series), Warner Books (New York, NY), 2003.

"THE SECRET WORLD OF ALEX MACK" SERIES

Alex, You're Glowing!, Minstrel Books (New York, NY), 1995.
Bet You Can't!, Minstrel Books (New York, NY), 1995.

Witch Hunt, Minstrel Books (New York, NY), 1995.
Mistaken Identity, Minstrel Books (New York, NY), 1996.
Go for the Gold, Minstrel Books (New York, NY), 1996.
Poison in Paradise, Minstrel Books (New York, NY), 1996.
Zappy Holidays, Minstrel Books (New York, NY), 1996.
Frozen Stiff, Minstrel Books (New York, NY), 1997.
Milady Alex, Minstrel Books (New York, NY), 1997.
New Year's Revolution, Minstrel Books (New York, NY), 1997.
Canine Caper, Minstrel Books (New York, NY), 1998.
Gold Fever, Minstrel Books (New York, NY), 1998.
Paradise Lost, Regained, Minstrel Books (New York, NY), 1998.

"STAR TREK: DEEP SPACE NINE" SERIES

Arcade, Minstrel Books (New York, NY), 1995.
Honor Bound, Minstrel Books (New York, NY), 1997.

"ARE YOU AFRAID OF THE DARK?" SERIES

The Tale of the Curious Cat, Minstrel Books (New York, NY), 1996.
The Tale of the Pulsating Gate, Minstrel Books (New York, NY), 1998.

"THE MYSTERY FILES OF SHELBY WOO" SERIES

Takeout Stakeout, Minstrel Books (New York, NY), 1997.
Cut and Run, Minstrel Books (New York, NY), 1998.

"SABRINA THE TEENAGE WITCH" SERIES

Showdown at the Mall, Archway (New York, NY), 1997.
Halloween Havoc, Archway (New York, NY), 1997.
Lotsa Luck, Archway (New York, NY), 1998.
Now You See Her, Now You Don't!, Archway (New York, NY), 1998.
Shamrock Shenanigans, Archway (New York, NY), 1999.

Bridal Bedlam, Archway (New York, NY), 1999.
Reality Check, Archway (New York, NY), 2000.
Wake-Up Call, Archway (New York, NY), 2001.
From the Horse's Mouth, Archway (New York, NY), 2001.

"BUFFY THE VAMPIRE SLAYER" SERIES

Obsidian Fate, Pocket Books (New York, NY), 1999.
Prime Evil, Pocket Books (New York, NY), 2000.
Doomsday Deck, Pocket Pulse (New York, NY), 2000.

"SALEM'S TALES" SERIES; FOR YOUNG READERS

Dog Day Afternoon, Minstrel Books (New York, NY), 1999.
Worth a Shot, Minstrel Books (New York, NY), 2000.

"FULL HOUSE: SISTERS" SERIES

(Under pseudonym Diana G. Burke) *Will You Be My Valentine?,* Parachute Press (New York, NY), 2000.
Substitute Sister, Parachute Press (New York, NY), 2000.
Matchmakers, Parachute Press (New York, NY), 2000.
A Dog's Life, Parachute Press (New York, NY), 2001.

"CHARMED" SERIES

Beware of What You Wish, Pocket Pulse (New York, NY), 2001.
Spirit of the Wolf, Pocket Pulse (New York, NY), 2002.
Dark Vengeance, Pocket Pulse (New York, NY), 2002.
Of Mist and Stone, Pocket Pulse (New York, NY), 2003.

"TWO OF A KIND" SERIES

Santa Girls, Parachute Press (New York, NY), 2003.
Prom Princess, Parachute Press (New York, NY), 2004.

OTHER

Contributor of short story "Tipping Is Not a City in China," to *I, Vampire,* Longmeadow Press (Stamford, CT), 1995; contributor of "The Interview," to *Eight Spells a Week: Sabrina Anthology Novel,* 1998, and "The Wizard of OR," to *Millennium Madness: Sabrina Anthology Novel,* 1999.

Work in Progress

More novels tied to television series.

Sidelights

Diana G. Gallagher has two talents. She can devise plots and adventures for popular television characters, and she can craft these into novels *on deadline.* This ability has earned Gallagher as much work as she can handle writing novels based on such television shows as *The Secret World of Alex Mack, Smallville,* and *Sab-*

rina, the Teenage Witch. Gallagher broke into publishing with a science fiction novel for adults, *The Alien Dark.* That book, and her work as a visual artist, helped to establish her in the writing community. Assignments for the television tie-in titles followed, and she enjoys the special challenges of that particular line of work.

"The requirements for writing in someone else's universe are fairly simple," Gallagher said in an interview for the Web site *Writers Write.* "The writer must know the show: background, episode storylines, characters, etc. It's also imperative to maintain the flavor of the particular series." She added that with tie-in fiction, the production company must approve each novel that presents the characters from a given show. "I've never found this to be a difficulty, just a necessary consideration," Gallagher added.

Gallagher was drawn to fiction writing by her interest in the *Star Wars* and *Star Trek* films. She has written *Star Trek* novels based on both the "Voyager" and the "Deep Space Nine" series, as well as *Shadows,* a tale based on the *Smallville* television show about the younger years of Superman. In *Shadows,* young Clark Kent becomes suspicious when a farmer he knows dies from unexplained causes. Other people begin dying mysteriously as well, and the strange malady seems to affect animals too. Clark and his friend Chloe investigate, but their progress is closely followed by the daughter of a scientist who is new in town and who may have ties to secret experiments. According to Kristine Huntley in *Booklist,* "The satisfying tale builds to an exciting climax that *[Smallville]* fans . . . definitely will want to read."

Gallagher told *SATA* that she lives in Florida with her husband, writer Martin Burke, "five dogs, five cats, and a cranky parrot." She still enjoys attending science fiction conventions, and she once turned her garage into a Halloween bookstore and gave away signed copies of her Halloween titles.

Biographical and Critical Sources

PERIODICALS

Booklist, September 15, 2003, Kristine Huntley, review of *Shadows,* p. 217.
Publishers Weekly, November 2, 1990, Penny Kaganoff, review of *The Alien Dark,* p. 70.

ONLINE

Writers Write: The Internet Writing Journal, http://www.writerswrite.com/journal/ (January, 2000), Jan McDaniel, "Diana G. Gallagher on Media Tie-In Books."

GATES, Susan 1950-

Personal

Born 1950, in Grimsby, England; married; children: one daughter, two sons. *Education:* Attended Warwick University. *Hobbies and other interests:* Live music, journalism, good wine, long walks.

Addresses

Home—County Durham, Ireland. *Agent*—c/o Author Mail, Oxford University Press, Educational Division, Great Clarendon Street, Oxford OX2 6DP, England.

Career

Writer. Previously taught at schools in Africa and England.

Awards, Honors

Carnegie Medal, and *Guardian* Fiction Prize shortlist, both 1995, both for *Raider;* Sheffield Children's Book Award, 1995, for *Beware the Killer Coat* and 1999, for *Cry Wolf;* Stockport Children's Book Award, 1997, for *Ironheads.*

Writings

FICTION

The Burnhope Wheel, Holiday House (New York, NY), 1989.

The Lock, Oxford University Press (Oxford, England), 1990.

Dragline, Oxford University Press (Oxford England), 1991.

African Dreams, Oxford University Press (Oxford, England), 1993.

Deadline for Danny's Beach, Oxford University Press (Oxford, England), 1993.

Beware the Killer Coat (also see below), illustrated by Josip Lizatović, Walker (London, England), 1994.

Beetle and the Biosphere, illustrated by Thelma Lambert, Walker (London, England), 1994.

Runners, Bodley Head (London, England), 1995.

Raider, Oxford University Press (Oxford, England), 1995.

William's Workshop: A One-Act Play in Five Scenes, illustrated by Nick Ward, Ginn (Aylesbury, England), 1995.

Pet Swapping Day, illustrated by Lucy Keijser, Hippo (London, England), 1996.

Whizz Bang and the Crocodile Room, illustrated by Sami Sweeten, Hippo (London, England), 1996.

Well Dazzled, Bodley Head (London, England), 1996.

Firebug, Oxford University Press (Oxford, England), 1996.

Ironheads, Oxford University Press (Oxford, England), 1997.

Don't Mess with Angels, Walker (London, England), 1997.

Criss Cross, Scholastic (London, England), 1997.

Esther and the Baby Baboon, illustrated by Rhian Nest James, Hippo (London, England), 1997.

Humanzee, Oxford University Press (Oxford, England), 1998.

Attack of the Tentacled Terror, Puffin (London, England), 1998.

Sea Hags, Suckers, and Cobra Sharks, Puffin (London, England), 1998.

Fisherwitch, illustrated by Rhian Nest James, Hippo (London, England), 1998.

(Reteller) *The Three Heads in the Well,* illustrated by Sue Heap, Scholastic (London, England), 1998.

Return of the Killer Coat (sequel to *Beware the Killer Coat*), Walker (London, England), 1998.

Revenge of the Toffee Monster, Puffin (London, England), 1999.

The Terrible Power of the Rabbit House, illustrated by Martin Remphry, Oxford University Press (Oxford, England), 1999.

Batty the Hero, illustrated by Rhian Nest James, Scholastic (London, England), 1999.

The Hummingbird Secret, Scholastic (London, England), 1999.

Cry Wolf, Scholastic (London, England), 1999.

Pagans, Scholastic (London, England), 2000.

Killer Mushrooms Ate My Gran, Puffin (London, England), 2000.

White Stranger, Oxford University Press (Oxford, England), 2000.

Night of the Haunted Trousers, Puffin (London, England), 2001.

Dad's Story, illustrated by Lisa Smith, Oxford University Press (Oxford, England), 2001.

Dinosaur Garden, illustrated by Georgie Birkett, Oxford University Press (Oxford, England), 2001.

The Magician's Pigeon, Scholastic (London, England), 2001.

Edward's Magic Paintbox, illustrated by Sue Robinson and Helen Leach, Lothian (Melbourne, Australia), 2002.

I Want to Play!, illustrated by Any Beckett, Children's Corner (London, England), 2002.

Invasion of the Vampire Spiders, Puffin (London, England), 2002.

Return of the Mad Mangler, illustrated by Tony Blundell, Puffin (London, England), 2002.

Eric's Talking Ears, illustrated by Martin Remphrey, Oxford University Press (Oxford, England), 2002.

Sugar Bag Baby, illustrated by Sebastien Braun, Orchard (London, England), 2003.

A Brief History of Slime!, illustrated by Tony Blundell, Puffin (London, England), 2003.

FOR BEGINNING READERS

Dangerous Trainers, illustrated by Martin Remphrey, Oxford University Press (Oxford, England), 1996.

Waiting for Goldie, illustrated by Jane Cope, Oxford University Press (Oxford, England), 1996.

Danny's Secret Fox, illustrated by Alicia Garcia de Lynam, Oxford University Press (Oxford England), 1996.

The Lie Detector, illustrated by Ivan Bates, Oxford University Press (Oxford, England), 1996.

The Clowns Next Door, illustrated by Bill Piggins, Oxford University Press (Oxford, England), 2001.

Bill's Baggy Pants, illustrated by Anni Axworthy, Picture Window Books (Minneapolis, MN), 2003.

"REVOLTING RABBLES" SERIES; ILLUSTRATED BY LEO BROADLEY

Toffs and Toshers, Scholastic (London, England), 2002.
Boils and Blisters, Scholastic (London, England), 2002.
Ruffs and Ruffians, Scholastic (London, England), 2002.
Crocs and Curses, Scholastic (London, England), 2002.

OTHER

English at Nelson Street (for adults), three volumes, Blacket (Glasgow, Scotland), 1987.

Lifescope (nonfiction), two volumes, Oxford University Press (Oxford, England), 1989.

(With Ann Jungman and Cecelia Lenagh) *The Big Wicked Witch Book* (stories), Hippo (London, England), 1998.

(With Marilyn Watls and Aiden Chambers) *More Cool School Stories,* Red Fox (London, England), 1999.

(With Sylvia Green and Kara May) *The Big Bad School Book* (stories), Hippo (London, England), 1999.

Adaptations

"Stupid Trousers" was adapted for theater by David Calcutt.

Sidelights

In 1989 Susan Gates published her first novel, *The Burnhope Wheel,* and she has been writing ever since. Being a writer was not what she had planned for her life, however; when she was only eighteen, Gates became a teacher in Malawi, Africa. She returned home to England after teaching there, studied American literature at Warwick University, and then continued on as a teacher in England. "When I was growing up in Grimsby, it never occured to me [to be a writer]," the author noted in an interview for *Schoolsnet.com.* "Writing seemed to be a different world that kids like me could never be part of—but I was wrong." Though she didn't start off writing comedy, Gates's best-known novels have a comedic and sometimes horrific bent; whether including killer coats, vampire spiders, or killer mushrooms, Gates knows how to make readers both laugh and wait in suspense to see what will happen next.

The Burnhope Wheel tells the story of Ellen and Dave, two teens who have a strange attraction to the abandoned Burnhope lead mine. Ellen finds a photograph of two miners who were killed in an accident, and soon after begins hearing the voice of one of the miners in her head. Together, Ellen and Dave find the treasure that had led to the deaths of the two miners, and almost meet the same fate themselves when the mine suddenly seems to come alive and the dead miner gains control over Ellen's mind. "The novel has some very exciting moments and will attract readers of the supernatural," wrote Susan F. Marcus in a review for *School Library Journal.*

Beware the Killer Coat was Gates's first novel to earn the Sheffield Children's Book Award. Far more silly than *The Burnhope Wheel, Beware the Killer Coat* tells the story of Andrew, who is convinced the coat he got from a "jumble-sale" isn't quite right. The way the zippers look like sharp teeth and the way the coat clings to him while he's wearing it lead Andrew to believe that his coat is actually out to get him! Andrew's coat troubles continue in *Return of the Killer Coat,* in which he must save his friend Alice from falling prey to the killer coat—which has disguised itself by becoming a different color.

With *Cry Wolf,* Gates returns to a slightly more serious story. Danny has disappointed his mother by skipping school and not having what his mother considers to be good friends. In order to appease his mother, Danny invents an imaginary friend, Sebastian, who fills all his mother's requirements. But in doing so, he discovers that his brother Tid also has an imaginary friend, one he calls Wolf, who has creepy yellow eyes and silver teeth; Tid seems to be warning Danny of some danger as well, and Danny suspects that there's more to Wolf than just imagination. Bette D. Ammon called *Cry Wolf* "Good scary stuff," in her review for *Kliatt.* Brian E. Wilson, writing for *Booklist,* pointed out that Gates also spins a "humorous, clever story."

Instead of a killer coat, fatal fungi appear in *Killer Mushrooms Ate My Gran.* Young Maggot and his superpowered Gran have to save the world from an invasion of mutant mushrooms. It seems that the only thing that can stop them is a powerful and repulsive green tea. Gran falls to the mushrooms, and Maggot manages to save her and destroy the mushrooms, only to find out that several of the mushrooms have escaped! Louise L. Sherman, writing for *School Library Journal,* called *Killer Mushrooms Ate My Gran* a "mildly scary, humorous story" that "will please elementary graders." In her interview with *Schoolsnet.com* Gates explained that Gran "is based on my Great Gran who lived to be 102 and was a very formidable lady. . . . I was scared stiff of her!"

Gates also wrote the "Revolting Rabbles," a series of chapter books for younger readers that features the Rabble family. When Mr. Rabble no longer has work as a historian, he forms a company that will hire out to do historical reenactments—and coerces his family into joining him. The Rabbles are hired to perform various time periods, from the Elizabethan and Victorian eras to the Dark Ages to ancient Egypt, but things never go quite as planned. Story narrator Rae Rabble tells how things go awry, and worries constantly about what else might go wrong. In *Toffs and Toshers,* for example, while Mr. Rabble researches the Dark Ages, Rae's older brother Ryan, an inventor, tries to develop a superior suit of armor, and her younger brother obsesses about the Black Plague.

In *Return of the Mad Mangler* Gates again combines silliness and horror. Leon's favorite tree is reputed to be haunted by a ghost of a washerwoman known as the Mad Mangler. When the tree is stolen, Leon gathers a crew to help him recover it, including his siblings, Donny and a sister known only as Leather Girl, and Bernard, who also had a tree stolen. The four trace the tree to the home of an aging rock star, and there encounter the Mad Mangler herself. Cindy Lombardo, reviewing the audio version of *Return of the Mad Mangler* for *School Library Journal,* commented that "Listeners who relish wacky humor and unusual settings will delight in this tale of science run amok."

In her interview with *Schoolsnet.com,* Gates offered the following advice to young writers: "I'm tempted to say, just do it. Don't listen to advice or at least don't listen to too much as it tends to cramp your style. Despite what I've just said I'm going to give some advice—just open your mind, be alert to the world around you and generally be a nosy parker—I know I am."

Biographical and Critical Sources

PERIODICALS

Booklist, December 15, 2002, Brian E. Wilson, review of *Cry Wolf,* p. 774.

Kliatt, September, 2002, Bette D. Ammon, review of *Cry Wolf,* p. 51.

School Library Journal, December, 1989, Susan F. Marcus, review of *The Burnhope Wheel,* p. 118; July, 2001, Louise L. Sherman, review of *Killer Mushrooms Ate My Gran,* p. 60; December, 2003, Cindy Lombardo, review of *Return of the Mad Mangler,* p. 75.

Times Educational Supplement, December 8, 1989, Penelope Farmer, review of *The Burnhope Wheel,* p. 27.

ONLINE

Northern Children's Book Festival Web site, http://www.ncbf.org.uk/ (March 29, 2004), profile of Gates.

Oxford University Press Web site, http://www.oup.co.uk/ (March 29, 2004), profile of Gates.

Schoolsnet.com, http://www.schoolsnet.com/ (March 29, 2004), interview with Gates.*

*   *   *

GHIGNA, Charles 1946-
(Father Goose, a pseudonym)

Personal

Surname is pronounced *Geen*-ya; born August 25, 1946, in Bayside, NY; son of Charles Vincent and Patricia

Charles Ghigna

Ghigna; married Nancy Minnicks, June 24, 1967 (divorced June 5, 1973); married Debra Holmes (a writer), August 2, 1975; children: (first marriage) Julie Ann; (second marriage) Chip. *Education:* Florida Atlantic University, B.A., 1968, M.Ed., 1969; also attended Edison Community College, 1964-66, University of South Florida, 1968-69, and Florida State University, 1973.

Addresses

Agent—c/o Author Mail, Random House Children's Books, 1745 Broadway, New York, NY 10019. *E-mail*—PaGoose@aol.com.

Career

High school English teacher in Fort Myers, FL, 1967-73; Edison Community College, Fort Myers, instructor in creative writing, 1973; National Council of Teachers of English, Urbana, IL, poetry editor of *English Journal,* 1974; Alabama School of Fine Arts, Birmingham, poet-in-residence, 1974-93; Samford University, instructor in creative writing, 1979. Creator, director, performer on *Cabbages and Kings* (children's television series), Alabama Education Television, 1976. Correspondent for *Writer's Digest* magazine, 1989—. Author of nationally syndicated light verse feature "Snickers" for Tribune Media Services, 1993-98. Has given hundreds of readings at colleges and secondary schools and has made hundreds of visits to elementary and middle schools.

Awards, Honors

Fellowship grants from the National Endowment for the Arts, the Library of Congress, the Mary Roberts Rinehart Foundation, and the Rockefeller Brothers Fund; First Place, *Writer's Digest* National Poetry Writing Competition, 1977, for "Divers"; Pulitzer Prize nomination, 1990, for *Returning to Earth;* Helen Keller Literary Award, 1993; First Place, International Sakura Haiku Writing Competition, 1993, for "October"; Pick of the Lists, American Booksellers Association, 1994, for *Tickle Day: Poems from Father Goose,* and 1995, for *Riddle Rhymes.* Ghigna performed his poetry at the Library of Congress in 1978 and at the Kennedy Center for the Performing Arts in 1984; his poetry was featured on the American Broadcasting Corporation (ABC-TV) program *Good Morning America* in 1991.

Writings

FOR CHILDREN

Good Dogs, Bad Dogs, illustrated by David Catrow, Hyperion (New York, NY), 1992.

Good Cats, Bad Cats, illustrated by David Catrow, Hyperion (New York, NY), 1992.

The Day I Spent the Night in the Shelby County Jail, Best of Times (New York, NY), 1994.

Tickle Day: Poems from Father Goose, illustrated by Cyd Moore, Hyperion (New York, NY), 1994.

Riddle Rhymes, illustrated by Julia Gorton, Hyperion (New York, NY), 1995.

Animal Trunk: Silly Poems to Read Aloud, illustrated by Gabriel, Harry N. Abrams (New York, NY), 1999.

Mice Are Nice, illustrated by Jon Goodell, Random House (New York, NY), 1999.

See the Yak Yak, illustrated by Brian Lies, Random House (New York, NY), 1999.

(With wife, Debra Ghigna) *Christmas Is Coming,* illustrated by Mary O'Keefe Young, Talewinds (Watertown, MA), 2000.

The Alphabet Parade, illustrated by Patti Woods, River City Publishing (Montgomery, AL), 2002.

Halloween Night: Twenty-One Spooktacular Poems, illustrated by Adam McCauley, Running Press Kids (Philadelphia, PA), 2003.

One Hundred Shoes: A Math Reader, illustrated by Bob Staake, Random House (New York, NY), 2003.

My Country: Children Talk about America, Crane Hill Publishers (Birmingham, AL), 2003.

A Fury of Motion: Poems for Boys, Boyds Mills Press (Honesdale, PA), 2003.

Animal Tracks: Wild Poems to Read Aloud, illustrated by John Speirs, Harry N. Abrams (New York, NY), 2004.

If You Were My Valentine, Simon & Schuster (New York, NY), 2004.

Dylan the Smokey Dragon, Maris, West & Baker (Jackson, MS), 2004.

Oh My, Pumpkin Pie!, Simon & Schuster (New York, NY), 2005.

FOR ADULTS; POETRY, EXCEPT AS NOTED

Plastic Tears, Dorrance (Philadelphia, PA), 1973.

Stables: The Story of Christmas (chapbook), Creekwood Press (Birmingham, AL), 1976.

Cockroach (one-act play), Contemporary Drama Service (New York, NY), 1977.

Divers and Other Poems, Creekwood Press (Birmingham, AL), 1978.

Circus Poems, Creekwood Press (Birmingham, AL), 1979.

Father Songs, Creekwood Press (Birmingham, AL), 1989.

Returning to Earth, Livingston University Press (Livingston, AL), 1989.

Wings of Fire, illustrated by Patricia See Hooten, Druid (Birmingham, AL), 1992.

The Best of "Snickers," Best of Times (New York, NY), 1994.

Speaking in Tongues: New and Selected Poems, 1974-1994, Livingston University Press (Livingston, AL), 1994.

Plastic Soup: Dream Poems, Black Belt (Montgomery, AL), 1999.

Love Poems, Crane Hill Publishers (Birmingham, AL), 1999.

Haiku: The Travelers of Eternity, River City Publishers (Montgomery, AL), 2001.

Works represented in anthologies, including *Confront, Construct, Complete,* Hayden Book Co. (Rochelle, NJ), 1979; *Contemporary Literature in Birmingham,* Thunder City Press (Birmingham, AL), 1983; *Anthology of Magazine Verse,* Monitor Book Co. (Beverly Hills, CA), 1985; *Italian-American Poets,* Fordham University (Bronx, NY), 1985; *This Sporting Life,* Milkweed Editions (Minneapolis, MN), 1987; *American Sports Poems,* Orchard Books (New York, NY), 1988; *Light Year,* 1985, 1986, 1987, 1988, 1989, Bits Press (Cleveland, OH), 1989; *North of Wakulla: Poets of Florida State,* Anhinga Press (Tallahassee, FL), 1989; *Alabama Poets: A Contemporary Anthology,* Livingston University Press (Livingston, AL), 1990; *Creative Writer's Handbook,* Prentice Hall (Englewood Cliffs, NJ), 1990; *Mixed Voices: Poems about Music,* Milkweed Editions (Minneapolis, MN), 1991; *A New Geography of Poets,* University of Arkansas Press (Fayetteville, AR), 1992; (With X. J. Kennedy and Richard Kostelanetz) *Sticks,* Sticks Press, 1992; *Poetry Works!: The First Verse Idea Book,* Simon & Schuster (New York, NY), 1992; *If We'd Wanted Quiet,* Meadowbrook Press (Deephaven, MN), 1994; *The Funny Side of Parenthood,* Meadowbrook Press (Deephaven, MN), 1994; *Familiarity Breeds Children,* Meadowbrook Press (Deephaven, MN), 1994; *The Runner's Literary Companion,* Breakaway Books (Halcottsville, NY), 1994; *For Better or*

Worse, Meadowbrook Press (Deephaven, MN), 1995; *Fighting Words,* Black Belt Press, 1995; *Age Happens,* Meadowbook Press (Deephaven, MN), 1996; *Holidays and Seasonal Celebrations,* Teaching & Learning Co. (New York, NY), 1996; *Enjoy!: Invitations to Literacy,* Houghton Mifflin (Boston, MA), 1996; *My Buddy,* Houghton Mifflin (Boston, MA), 1996; *Leading Kids to Books through Puppets,* American Library Association (Chicago, IL), 1997; *Work and Other Occupational Hazards,* Meadowbrook Press (Deephaven, MN), 1998; *Advent Cookbook,* Advent Episcopal School, 1997; *McDonald's Cookbook,* Ronald McDonald House (New York, NY), 1998; *Lighten Up!,* Meadowbook Press (Deephaven, MN), 1998; *Creative Writer's Handbook,* 3rd edition, Prentice Hall (Englewood Cliffs, NJ), 1999; *A Twentieth Century Treasury of Poetry for Children,* Alfred A. Knopf (New York, NY), 1999; *Leading Kids to Books through Crafts,* American Library Association (Chicago, IL), 1999; *Laugh Twice and Call Me in the Morning,* Meadowbrook Press (Deephaven, MN), 1999; *Knock at a Star: A Child's Introduction to Poetry,* Alfred A. Knopf (New York, NY), 1999; *Harcourt Brace Reading Program,* Harcourt Brace (New York, NY), 2000; *Urban Nature,* Milkweed Editions (Minneapolis, MN), 2000; *Hidden Surprises, Grade 3,* Harcourt Brace (New York, NY), 2000; *Becoming One with the Lights,* National Council of Teachers of English (Urbana, IL), 2001; *Books Day by Day: Anniversaries and Anecdotes,* Heinemann (New York, NY), 2001; *Our Bundle of Joy,* Meadowbrook (Deephaven, MN), 2001; *Eat Their Words: Southern Writers and Recipes,* Fairhope Literary Council, 2001; *Rolling in the Aisles: Kids Pick the Funniest Poems,* Meadowbrook Press (Deephaven, MN), 2002; *Language Arts Program, Grade 1,* Harcourt Brace (New York, NY), 2002; *Stories from the Blue Moon Café II,* MacAdam/Cage (San Francisco, CA), 2003; and *Read a Rhyme, Write a Rhyme,* Alfred A. Knopf (New York, NY), 2005.

Contributor of hundreds of adult and children's poems to magazines and newspapers, including *Harper's, McCall's, Good Housekeeping, Ladies Home Journal, Kansas Quarterly, Texas Quarterly, Christian Science Monitor, Highlights for Children, Cricket, Ranger Rick, Jack and Jill, Children's Digest, Hopscotch, Children's Playmate, Crayola Kids, Guideposts for Kids, Humpty Dumpty, Ladybug, Lollipops, New York Times, Pockets, Poem Train, Pre-K Today, Turtle,* and *Child Life.* Some of Ghigna's poems have been translated into Italian, German, French, and Russian.

Sidelights

Charles Ghigna, sometimes known as Father Goose, is a popular poet for children and adults. Ghigna divides his time between writing poetry and making personal appearances at schools from the elementary level through college. He is equally adept at entertaining the youngest listeners and enlightening adult would-be writers who solicit his advice on creating and publishing books. In the realm of juvenile literature, he is best known for his rhyming books that offer amusing portraits of animals and holidays. In an interview published on his Web site, he said: "Writing, especially for children, is one of the most honorable professions in the world. It is one of the few professions that allows you to dream, that encourages you to dream, and to capture those dreams on paper and to make them come alive in the minds and hearts of others."

Ghigna was born on Long Island but moved to Fort Meyers, Florida as a five-year-old and has lived in the South ever since. In his interviews he describes himself as a happy child who earned notice for his writing skills as early as third grade, when he wrote an essay about a talking freckle on a boy's face. He began keeping a journal as a teen but told no one, so that when he began publishing poetry many years later he seemed like an overnight success. In fact he wrote obsessively for years before seeing any of his work in print, and his first sales were of adult poetry to magazines such as *Harper's.* Between 1967 and 1993 he worked as a school teacher. Since 1993, "Father Goose" has primarily been a full-time writer.

Ghigna's verse for adults is free-form, but when he writes for children he employs rhyme. His first two books, *Good Dogs, Bad Dogs* and *Good Cats, Bad Cats,* are upside-down books. If a reader chooses to read about the good dogs first, the good dogs and their behavior comprise the first half of the book. At the center the reader must turn the book upside down to continue with the other half, depicting the bad dogs. The same form animates the volume about cats. Ghigna's rhymes work in concert with illustrations by David Catrow that literalize the humorous absurdity of such commonplace notions as the ideas that dogs defend those they love and cats always land on their feet. A *Publishers Weekly* reviewer found both volumes "witty," adding: "By turns slapstick and sophisticated, the humor here will snare adults as well as children."

Tickle Day: Poems from Father Goose collects some of the many poems Ghigna has contributed to children's magazines. The collection reveals its author's interests that will find further coverage in future books: animal behavior, holidays, weather, and childhood antics. A *Publishers Weekly* critic liked the book's "flashes of personality." *Riddle Rhymes* combines two popular genres of children's literature to "appealing" effect, according to Julie Corsaro in *Booklist.* By joining the fun of riddles to the playfulness of rhymes, Ghigna has produced "a lighthearted guessing game about everyday objects in a young child's life," noted Pamela K. Bomboy in *School Library Journal.* The topics covered by Ghigna's riddles include shadows, mirrors, leaves, rainbows, and kites. "And because they are in verse, the riddles are especially fun to read out loud," remarked Campbell Geeslin in the *New York Times Book Review.*

The holidays offer children's writers ample ideas for picture books, and Ghigna has written two rhyming texts on the subject. *Halloween Night: Twenty-One*

Spooktacular Poems takes a holiday that frightens some youngsters and makes it silly, reassuring children that the goblins and ghosts are made larger by the imagination. *Christmas Is Coming!,* co-authored with wife Debra Ghigna, describes how a family prepares for the favorite holiday, from readying decorations and buying gifts to packing all away again at the season's end. Shelley Townsend-Hudson in *Booklist* concluded that the verses and illustrations by Mary O'Keefe Young "reflect the holiday excitement."

Ghigna has also written *A Fury of Motion: Poems for Boys,* recognizing that boys sometimes have a difficult time enjoying verse. The spare rhymes in this volume aim at a young adult audience, covering such topics as sports, feelings, vacation activities, and even haircuts. In her *School Library Journal* review of the work, Donna Cardon noted that the poems would be appropriate for the intended age group as well as younger boys. Cardon praised *A Fury of Motion* as "the perfect book for boys who might not want to advertise the fact that they are reading poetry."

Animal Tracks: Wild Poems to Read Aloud searches through the animal kingdom for silly behavior and word-games that relate to familiar creatures. Some of the poems rely upon puns for their humor, while others describe the animals in question with light verse, easily read or memorized. Carolyn Phelan in *Booklist* liked the way Ghigna's poems "draw connections between animals and people or things," and Susan Scheps in *School Library Journal* called the title "charming," with ". . . significant appeal."

In an interview with Tracy Hoffman in *Word Museum* online, Ghigna commented: "My ideas [for poems] come from everywhere! They pop into my head when I least expect them. Many poem and story ideas come to me while I am driving or mowing or taking a shower! I also do 30-40 school visits each year. Sometimes ideas come to me while I'm around children, especially while I'm playing with my son and his friends. Ideas also come to me while looking out the window of my upstairs office. My son and I often spend time after school jumping on his trampoline. Sometimes after jumping we collapse on the trampoline and lie still looking up at the clouds and watching Mother Nature's movie screen. We always find something new to think about while looking toward the sky. Other ideas for poems and stories also come from memories of my childhood—which still hasn't ended!"

Ghigna once commented: "I hope my poems offer children the opportunity to explore and celebrate the joys of childhood and nature, and to see some of the wondrous ironies all around them. I also hope my humorous poems tickle the funny bone of their imaginations. I usually do not sit down to write a poem with a preconceived 'goal.' I like to enter each poem with a sense of wonderment and discovery. My favorite poems are those that contain little surprises that I did not know were there until I wrote them."

In his spare time, Ghigna enjoys collecting things. In addition to baseball cards, letter openers, and kaleidoscopes, he has a growing collection of geese that fans have sent him over the years in honor of "Father Goose." In an interview published on his Web site, he said of his geese miniatures: "At night when I turn out the lights and go downstairs they sneak around the room and visit each other. . . . Most of the time they are well-behaved."

Biographical and Critical Sources

PERIODICALS

Booklist, November 15, 1995, Julie Corsaro, review of *Riddle Rhymes,* p. 562; October 1, 1999, Hazel Rochman, review of *Mice Are Nice,* p. 364; September 1, 2000, Shelley Townsend-Hudson, review of *Christmas Is Coming!,* p. 132; May 1, 2004, Carolyn Phelan, review of *Animal Tracks: Wild Poems to Read Aloud,* p. 1560.

New York Times Book Review, April 7, 1996, Campbell Geeslin, review of *Riddle Rhymes,* p. 21.

Publishers Weekly, August 24, 1992, review of *Good Cats, Bad Cats* and *Good Dogs, Bad Dogs,* p. 78; September 12, 1994, review of *Tickle Day: Poems from Father Goose,* p. 91; September 27, 1999, review of *Animal Trunk: Silly Poems to Read Aloud,* p. 103; August 4, 2003, review of *Halloween Nights: Twenty-One Spooktacular Poems,* p. 78; March 29, 2004, "Earth Day," p. 65.

School Library Journal, September, 1994, Kathleen Whalin, review of *Tickle Day: Poems from Father Goose,* p. 208; November, 1995, Pamela K. Bomboy, review of *Riddle Rhymes,* p. 89; October, 2000, review of *Christmas Is Coming!,* p. 59; October, 2003, Donna Cardon, review of *A Fury of Motion: Poems for Boys,* p. 192; April, 2004, Susan Scheps, review of *Animal Tracks,* p. 132.

Writer's Digest, August, 1999, Brad Crawford, "Charles Ghigna: Our Baseball Coach Made Us Take Ballet," p. 6.

ONLINE

Charles Ghigna Home Page, http://charlesghigna.com/ (June 2, 2004), includes interviews, bibliography, and book reviews.

Ink Spot, http://www.inkspot.com/ (June 2, 2004), interview with Ghigna.

Word Museum, http://www.wordmuseum.com/ (June 2, 2004), Tracy Hoffman, "An Exclusive Interview with Father Goose, Charles Ghigna."

*   *   *

GOODHART, Pippa 1958-

Personal

Born 1958; married, 1986; husband's name, Mick; children: three. *Education:* Attended Leeds University and Durham University.

Addresses

Home—45 Elms Rd., South Knighton, Leicester, Leicestershire LE2 3JD, England.

Career

Writer. Heffers Children's Bookshop, Cambridge, England, bookseller and manager, 1974-1979; Rhyme and Reason Bookshop, Leicester, England, bookseller, 1986; Oxford University Press, Oxford, England, reader of children's book submissions, 1986—; tutor, Leicester Adult Education College, 1999—.

Awards, Honors

Smarties Prize shortlist, and Kathleen Fidler Award shortlist, both for *Flow;* East Midlands Arts' Writers' Award, 2000.

Writings

Flow, illustrated by Anthony Lewis, Heinemann (London, England), 1994.

Ginny's Egg, illustrated by Aafke Brouwer, Heinemann (London, England), 1995.

Hamper's Great Escape, illustrated by Caroline Holden, Oxford University Press (London, England), 1996.

Lie Spider, illustrated by Rian Hughes, Mammoth (London, England), 1997.

Milly, illustrated by Jason Cockcroft, Hodder (London, England), 1997.

Play Time, illustrated by Brita Granström, Watts (London, England), 1997.

Shopping Time, illustrated by Brita Granström, Watts (London, England), 1997.

Morning Time, illustrated by Brita Granström, Watts (London, England), 1997, published as *My Morning Time,* 2002.

Bed Time, illustrated by Brita Granström, Watts (London, England), 1997, published as *My Bed Time,* 2002.

Pest Friends, illustrated by Louise Armour-Chelu, Mammoth (London, England), 1997.

Noah Makes a Boat, illustrated by Bernard Lodge, Houghton Mifflin (Boston, MA), 1997.

Row, Row, Row Your Boat, illustrated by Stephen Lambert, Crown (New York, NY), 1997, published as *Row Your Boat,* Mammoth (London, England), 1998.

Snooty Prune, Oxford University Press (Oxford, England), 1998.

Flying Lessons, illustrated by Sharon Lewis, Hodder (London, England), 1998.

Alona's Story, Mammoth (London, England), 1999.

All that Glitters, Hodder (London, England), 1999.

Catnapped, illustrated by Joanna Harrison, Mammoth (London, England), 1999.

Time Swing, illustrated by Mark Robertson, Mammoth (London, England), 1999.

Jack's Mouse, illustrated by Stephen Lambert, Mammoth (London, England), 1999.

Happy Sad, illustrated by Stephen Lambert, Mammoth (London, England), 1999.

Me and My Newt, illustrated by David Mostyn, Oxford University Press (Oxford, England), 1999.

Frankie's House-Tree, illustrated by Leonie Shearing, Mammoth (London, England), 2000.

The House with No Name, illustrated by Peter Kavanagh, Barrington Stoke (Edinburgh, Scotland), 2000.

Sister Ella, illustrated by Jane Bottomley, Oxford University Press (Oxford, England), 2000.

Peter and the Waterwolf, illustrated by Ian Beck, Corgi Pups (London, England), 2001.

Kind of Twins, illustrated by Ailie Busby, Egmont (London, England), 2001.

Molly and the Beanstalk, illustrated by Brita Granström, Walker (London, England), 2001.

Slow Magic, illustrated by John Kelly, Red Fox (London, England), 2002, Crabtree (New York, NY), 2004.

Friends Forever, illustrated by Ailie Busby, Egmont (London, England), 2003.

Pam's Maps, illustrated by Katherine Lodge, Red Fox (London, England), 2003.

In Pippa Goodhart's lively retelling of the Noah legend, the Biblical hero crafts his famous ark with the help of his grandson Little Noah. (From Noah Makes a Boat, *illustrated by Bernard Lodge.)*

Dragon Boy, illustrated by Martin Ursell, Egmont (London, England), 2003.

Pudding, illustrated by Caroline Jayne Church, Chicken House (London, England), 2003, published as *Pudgy: A Puppy to Love,* Scholastic (New York, NY), 2003.

Arthur's Tractor: A Fairy Tale with Mechanical Parts, illustrated by Colin Paine, Bloomsbury (New York, NY), 2003.

You Choose, illustrated by Nick Sharratt, Doubleday (London, England), 2003.

Ratboy, illustrated by Polly Dunbar, Barrington Stoke (Edinburgh, Scotland), 2004.

Sidelights

Pippa Goodhart began working with books as a bookseller at the age of sixteen. It was not until much later that she began to write for children. "I loved books, particularly children's books, and have been a bookseller and a teacher and a mother and a publisher's reader, but I had never dared to think of trying to write books myself," Goodhart told interviewers at the *Bloomsbury Publishing* Web site. Not until 1994, with encouragement from her husband Mick, did Goodhart publish her first book. *Flow* was well received and was shortlisted for both the Smarties Prize and the Kathleen Fidler Award.

Goodhart has written more than thirty books since then, published in both England and the United States. Her titles cover a wide range of topics: *Pam's Maps,* for example, tells a pirate story, while *Peter and the Waterwolf* features a folktale from the Netherlands about a boy who saves his country by plugging a leak in a dyke with his finger. *Noah Makes a Boat* retells the story of Noah and the ark, but features Noah's grandson, Little Noah, as the brains behind the building of the ark.

Pudding, published as *Pudgy: A Puppy to Love* in the United States, is a story of two loners who manage to find each other and become friends. No one wants to play with Pudgy the puppy; the girl Lucy has no one to play with either. Eventually, Pudgy runs away from home, finds Lucy, and forms a lasting bond with the girl. Goodhart tells the story in only six sentences, which Sally R. Dow called "playful" in her review of *Pudgy* for *School Library Journal.* A critic for *Kirkus Reviews* noted that in a small amount of text, "Goodhart addresses a range of universal emotions."

Goodhart used fairy tales for her inspiration in such books as *Sister Ella,* a twist on the Cinderella story, and *Molly and the Beanstalk,* an adaptation of the traditional English story about Jack and his magic beans. In *Arthur's Tractor: A Fairy Tale with Mechanical Parts,* Goodhart used a different fairy tale strategy, one with two stories happening at the same time. As a knight tries to save a princess from a dragon, a nearby farmer hears the noises they make and becomes convinced that his tractor is broken. When the princess shrieks, Arthur is sure that he needs to oil his "sprocket spring sprig-

get." Arthur continues this way through the tale, completely oblivious to the ruckus behind him. However, by story's end, the farmer finally notices the interested princess joining him under the tractor's hood in an unusual happily-ever-after ending. "The book bubbles with delightful British colloquialisms," noted Karin Snelson in *Booklist,* and a reviewer for *Publishers Weekly* praised Goodhart's "snappy storytelling." G. Alyssa Sadler complimented Goodhart's "clever tale" in her review for *School Library Journal,* concluding that *Arthur's Tractor* "will appeal to children who love a tale with a twist."

In an interview on the *Word Pool* Web site, Goodhart explained that she enjoys writing for children "because they are a fresh, honest, interested audience open to almost anything." Goodhart told her interviewers at the *Bloomsbury Publishing* Web site that she gets her ideas from "everything around me and inside me, from the past, the present, and my imagination."

Biographical and Critical Sources

BOOKS

Goodhart, Pippa, *Arthur's Tractor: A Fairy Tale with Mechanical Parts,* illustrated by Colin Paine, Bloomsbury (New York, NY), 2003.

PERIODICALS

Booklist, October 1, 1997, Ilene Cooper, review of *Noah Makes a Boat,* p. 323; February 15, 2003, Karin Snelson, review of *Arthur's Tractor: A Fairy Tale with Mechanical Parts,* p. 1074.

Guardian (London, England), January 15, 2002, Lindsey Fraser, review of *Peter and the Waterwolf,* p. 69; October 25, 2003, Julia Eccleshare, review of *You Choose,* p. 33.

Horn Book, September-October, 1997, Martha V. Parravano, review of *Noah Makes a Boat,* p. 557.

Kirkus Reviews, January 1, 2003, review of *Arthur's Tractor,* p. 60; April 1, 2003, review of *Pudgy: A Puppy to Love,* p. 534.

New York Times Book Review, February 15, 1998, review of *Noah Makes a Boat,* p. 25.

Publishers Weekly, August 25, 1997, review of *Noah Makes a Boat,* p. 65; December 23, 2002, review of *Pudgy,* p. 69, and review of *Arthur's Tractor,* p. 70.

School Library Journal, September, 1997, Kathy Piehl, review of *Noah Makes a Boat,* p. 182; December, 1997, Maria B. Salvadore, review of *Row, Row, Row Your Boat,* p. 90; March, 2003, G. Alyssa Sadler, review of *Arthur's Tractor,* p. 193; April, 2003, Sally R. Dow, review of *Pudgy,* p. 120.

Times Educational Supplement, April 25, 2003, Geraldine Brennan, "Read It Any Way You Want," p. 37.

ONLINE

Bloomsbury Publishing Web Site, http://www.bloomsbury.com/ (February 12, 2004).

Word Pool Web Site, http://www.wordpool.co.uk/ (February 12, 2004).*

*   *   *

GORELICK, Molly C(hernow) 1920-2003

OBITUARY NOTICE—See index for *SATA* sketch: Born September 19, 1920, in New York, NY; died December 17, 2003, in Los Angeles, CA. Psychologist, educator, and author. Gorelick was a noted psychologist, professor, and researcher who specialized primarily in the educational and developmental needs of children ranging from those with special needs to those who were considered gifted. She attended both undergraduate and graduate courses at the University of California at Los Angeles, where she completed her Ed.D. in 1962. Gorelick began her career as a Los Angeles teacher from 1948 to 1962, also working as a counselor from 1957 to 1958. Conducting research at UCLA, she joined the faculty there as an instructor in psychology and education in 1957, and also worked as a research assistant and supervisor of the psychology clinic at the university during the early 1960s. During the late 1960s, she was chief of guidance services at the Exceptional Children's Foundation in Los Angeles and an assistant professor at the University of Southern California's School of Education. The last twenty-one years of her career were spent as a professor at California State University at Northridge, where she retired in 1991. During her career, Gorelick continuously demonstrated her concern for the mental and physical well-being of children, performing such tasks as researching children's nutritional needs and training Los Angeles area teachers on how to handle the many different challenges of that city's multi-ethnic student population. She was also the author of books for children and adults. Her children's books, written with Jean Boreman, include such titles as *Fire on Sun Mountain* (1967) and *Snow Storm at Green Valley* (1968); her nonfiction works were designed for educators and include *Careers in Integrated Early Childhood Settings* (1975) and *Recipes for Teaching* (1975). Gorelick's interest in children also led her to cowrite the documentary *A Child Is a Child* (1981) with Al Levitt, a film that won third place at the Montevideo, Uruguay, film festival.

OBITUARIES AND OTHER SOURCES:

PERIODICALS

Los Angeles Times, December 24, 2003, p. B11.

GRAY, Kes 1960-

Personal

Born 1960, in Chelmsford, England; married; children: three. *Education:* University of Kent, B.A.

Addresses

Agent—David Higham Associates, 5-8 Lower John St., Garden Square, London W1F 9HA, England.

Career

Advertising copywriter for firms in England, c. 1982-97; writer and freelance advertising copywriter, 1997—.

Awards, Honors

Received numerous awards for advertising campaigns in United Kingdom; overall prize, Federation of Children's Book Awards, Stockport Schools Book Award, overall prize, Sheffield Book Award, and Experian Big Three Award, all 2001, all for *Eat Your Peas.*

Writings

Eat Your Peas, illustrated by Nick Sharratt, Dorling Kindersley Publishing (New York, NY), 2000.

Who's Poorly Too?: The 'Get Well Soon' Book, illustrated by Mary McQuillan, Bodley Head (London, England), 2000, published in America as *The "Get Well Soon" Book: Good Wishes for Bad Times,* Millbrook Press (Brookfield, CT), 2000.

Really, Really, illustrated by Nick Sharratt, Bodley Head (London, England), 2002.

(With Linda M. Jennings) *Toffee and Marmalade: Two Pet Stories,* Oxford University Press (Oxford, England), 2002.

Billy's Bucket, illustrated by Garry Parsons, Candlewick Press (Cambridge, MA), 2003.

Our Twitchy, illustrated by Mary McQuillan, Henry Holt (New York, NY), 2003.

You Do!, illustrated by Nick Sharratt, Bodley Head (London, England), 2003.

Cluck O'Clock, illustrated by Mary McQuillan, Hodder Children's Books (London, England), 2003, Holiday House (New York, NY), 2004.

Baby on Board, illustrated by Sarah Nayler, Hodder Children's Books (London, England), 2003, Simon & Schuster (New York, NY), 2004.

Also author of *Vesuvius Poovius,* Hodder Children's Books (London, England). Contributor to the "Treetops" reading series published by Oxford University Press.

Sidelights

A background as an award-winning advertising copywriter prepared Kes Gray to become a picture book writer. The British author learned how to keep his

When small bunny Twitchy finds out he's adopted, his horse and cow parents teach him about familial love in Kes Gray's tender picture-book story. (*From* Our Twitchy, *illustrated by Mary McQuillan.*)

thoughts concise and phrased in a way to make an influence, and that has translated nicely into his more recent creative endeavors. Since winning the overall prize from the Federation of Children's Book Awards in 2001 with *Eat Your Peas,* Gray has written a number of titles that have made a quick transit from England to America. *Booklist* reviewer Tim Arnold described Gray's work as "absurdly funny."

Eat Your Peas introduces Daisy, "a veritable icon of juvenile intransigence," to quote a *Publishers Weekly* reviewer. It is dinnertime, and Daisy doesn't want to eat her peas. Mom resorts to bribery, promising ice cream if Daisy eats the vegetables. When Daisy won't budge, Mom keeps upping the ante until Daisy's reward for eating peas includes Africa, seventeen swimming pools, the moon, the stars, and the sun. Then Daisy makes a counter offer. She'll eat peas if Mom eats brussels sprouts. Tim Arnold in *Booklist* particularly liked the resolution of Gray's plot because it "does not involve some sort of punishment." The *Publishers Weekly* critic praised the multiple award-winning title for its "escalating silliness" and "bold graphics." Daisy makes her second appearance in *You Do!,* another story in which she engages Mom in a battle of wills. Gray has hinted that more Daisy titles may lie in the future.

Among Gray's most popular titles on both sides of the Atlantic is *The "Get Well Soon" Book: Good Wishes for Bad Times,* published in England as *Who's Poorly Too?: The 'Get Well Soon' Book.* Picture books aimed specifically at ailing youngsters are relatively rare, and

Gray approaches the subject with equal doses of humor and sympathy. A series of animals are coping with various illnesses in the book: Cynthia Centipede sprains ninety-eight ankles, Delia the Dragon burns herself when she sneezes, and Katie the Cat winds up in bandages after an over-zealous mouse chase. The book's message is that all will recover, a reassuring thought for a youngster confined to bed. In her *Booklist* review, Ilene Cooper noted that the title would certainly appeal to sick children, "but even kids who are as healthy as a horse will enjoy this." Jane Marino in *School Library Journal* likewise felt that young listeners would be "sure to giggle at the inventive plights these creatures experience." And Jennifer Mangan in *Christian Parenting Today* concluded that the book "promotes compassion for others."

Our Twitchy is another Gray picture book that examines a difficult issue for young children. Twitchy the rabbit can't understand why he looks so different from his parents. Clearly something is amiss. His mother is a cow, and his father is a horse. When his parents explain that he is adopted, Twitchy runs away. He returns home only after he has tried to alter his appearance to look more like them, feeling that they won't love him with long ears and a puffy tail. They quickly explain that "being in a family is about love and acceptance," according to Kristin de Lacoste in *School Library Journal.* A *Publishers Weekly* critic liked the way *Our Twitchy* "presents authentic childhood concerns about a sometimes difficult-to-approach topic without using a heavy hand."

Cluck O'Clock takes a popular subject, telling time, and spins it into a funny tale about chickens. The lives of Freda, Frye, and the other feathered denizens of a family farm begin at "four o'clock" in the morning and continue through the day to a dust bath at "seven o'cluck," followed by a fox scare just before midnight. "This energetic and silly story has a lilting rhyme that sets a frolicking pace," observed Martha Topol in *School Library Journal.* Connie Fletcher in *Booklist* characterized the story as "winsome . . . to be sure, as well as a great way to learn about time."

Many people are familiar with the "Baby on Board" signs that hang in some cars. Gray used the concept for a picture book on pregnancy. A young girl describes the changes in her mother's appearance, and temperament, month by month as the family anticipates the arrival of a new baby. The girl also charts the baby's development from a tiny blob to a moving phenomenon, and finally to a healthy sibling. Connie Fletcher in *Booklist* praised *Baby on Board* as "a delightful choice" for children whose parents are expecting another infant.

Gray has been known to describe himself as a child who never grew up. He has been a collector since his youth and especially likes items related to Pokemon and Sonic the Hedgehog.

Biographical and Critical Sources

PERIODICALS

Booklist, September 1, 2000, Tim Arnold, review of *Eat Your Peas,* p. 122; December 15, 2000, Ilene Cooper, review of *The "Get Well Soon" Book: Good Wishes for Bad Times,* p. 826; August, 2003, Carolyn Phelan, review of *Billy's Bucket,* p. 1989; April 1, 2004, Connie Fletcher, review of *Cluck O'Clock,* p. 1368; May 15, 2004, Connie Fletcher, review of *Baby on Board,* p. 1625.
Christian Parenting Today, July, 2001, Jennifer Mangan, review of *The "Get Well Soon" Book,* p. 53.
Publishers Weekly, September 18, 2000, review of *Eat Your Peas,* p. 111; October 20, 2003, review of *Our Twitchy,* p. 53; March 15, 2004, review of *Cluck O'Clock,* p. 74.
School Library Journal, September, 2000, Lisa Dennis, review of *Eat Your Peas,* p. 198; February, 2001, Jane Marino, review of *The "Get Well Soon" Book: Good Wishes for Bad Times,* p. 100; December, 2003, Kristin de Lacoste, review of *Our Twitchy,* p. 114; March, 2004, Martha Topol, review of *Cluck O'Clock,* p. 169.*

*   *   *

GRIFFIN, Adele 1970-

Personal

Born July 29, 1970, in Philadelphia, PA; daughter of John Joel Berg (a business manager) and Priscilla Sands

Adele Griffin

Watson (a school principal); married Erich Paul Mauff (an investment banker). *Education:* University of Pennsylvania, B.A., 1993. *Politics:* Democrat. *Hobbies and other interests:* Movies.

Addresses

Office—215 Park Ave. S., New York, NY 10003. *Agent*—Charlotte Sheedy, c/o Sterling Lord Literistic, 65 Bleecker St., New York, NY 10012.

Career

Writer. Clarion Books, New York, NY, assistant editor, 1996-98, freelance manuscript reader, 1996—.

Member

Society of Children's Book Writers and Illustrators, "Young Penn Alum," Friends of the New York Public Library, 92nd Street Young Men's Christian Association (YMCA) of New York.

Awards, Honors

National Book Award nomination, National Book Foundation, 1997, and Notable Book citation, American Library Association (ALA), 1997, both for *Sons of Liberty;* Books for the Teen Age, New York Public Library, 1997, and *Parenting Magazine* Award, 1997, both for *Split Just Right;* Blue Ribbon designation, *Bulletin of the Center for Children's Books,* Best Books, *Publish-*

ers *Weekly* and *School Library Journal,* Notable Book, ALA, Best Books for Young Adults, ALA, and 100 Titles for Reading and Sharing, New York Public Library, all 1998, all for *The Other Shepards;* Best Books, ALA and *Publishers Weekly,* both 2001, both for *Amandine.*

Writings

Rainy Season, Houghton Mifflin (Boston, MA), 1996.
Split Just Right, Hyperion (New York, NY), 1997.
Sons of Liberty, Hyperion (New York, NY), 1997.
The Other Shepards, Hyperion (New York, NY), 1998.
Dive, Hyperion (New York, NY), 1999.
Amandine, Hyperion (New York, NY), 2001.
Hannah, Divided, Hyperion (New York, NY), 2002.
Overnight, G. P. Putnam's Sons (New York, NY), 2003.
Where I Want to Be, G. P. Putnam's Sons (New York, NY), 2004.

"WITCH TWINS" SERIES

Witch Twins, Hyperion (New York, NY), 2001.
Witch Twins at Camp Bliss, Hyperion (New York, NY), 2002.
Witch Twins and Melody Malady, illustrated by Jacqueline Rogers, Hyperion (New York, NY), 2003.

Sidelights

Adele Griffin once told *SATA:* "One of my most treasured childhood memories is the excitement I felt going book shopping before summer vacation. I looked forward to our family's annual visit to New York City and trip to Brentano's, where I was allowed to purchase as many books as I wanted, a joyful extravagance. I knew what I liked: stories about princesses, tough heroines who, defying all odds, would rise from a garret or cottage adjacent to the requisite bog to become a mogul—usually of a department store. I did *not* like science fiction, fantasy, or books about boys.

"While my books are not science fiction or fantasy, I do like to write about both girls *and* boys. (Perhaps age and marriage have helped with that particular aversion.) The voices in my writing are those of the children I have listened to hear and have strained to remember, voices that speak from the secret world we too soon leave. My goal, as I continue my career, is to write books for all young people, even boys, who look forward to a trip to the library or bookstore with great joy, and who are companioned by the friendship of a favorite book."

Since the late 1990s Griffin has emerged as a novelist who explores teen behavior in all its variety, good and bad. Some of her novels, such as *Overnight* and *Amandine,* offer realistic portraits of manipulative, selfish

young women and the friends they attract. Other books, including *Dive* and *Hannah, Divided* introduce unconventional young adults who must come to terms with their uniqueness. On the lighter side, Griffin's "Witch Twins" series wraps lessons on sibling rivalry and cooperation around stories of magic, spell-casting, and the supernatural. According to Ilene Cooper in *Booklist,* "Griffin elevates every genre she writes," whether it be fantasy or straight realistic fiction.

Griffin's well-received debut novel, *Rainy Season,* was lauded in a *Publishers Weekly* review as "ambitiously conceived and sharply observed." The story follows Lane Beck, a fearful twelve-year-old girl, and her belligerently bold younger brother Charlie through a single transformative day. The Beck family is living on an army base in the Panama Canal Zone in 1977, when resentment of American imperialism is at its peak. The story's setting is key mainly for its contribution of danger and suspense, but the history and politics relevant to the Canal Zone are also discussed in an author's note. *Horn Book* reviewer Nancy Vasilakis wrote that the Panama setting "adds a faint aura of decadence to the narrative." Janice M. Del Negro of the *Bulletin of the Center for Children's Books* maintained that the story's atmosphere is "strongly evoked but never intrusive," adding that "the politics are present but always in the background." In anticipation of a battle with the children on the opposite side of the Zone, the Beck children and their friends begin building a fort. Tensions escalating outside the family are paralleled by the strains existing within the family. Lane is prone to panic attacks, Charlie to bully-like behavior, and both children's problems are being deliberately ignored by their parents. Lane's concern for her brother forces her to break the family's pathological silence about the grief they feel over older sister Emily's death in a car accident. *School Library Journal* contributor Lucinda Lockwood commented favorably on Griffin's "evocative" writing and the author's ability to "capture the setting and the nuances of adolescent relationships." A *Publishers Weekly* critic commended the way Griffin "unfolds the events of the day and lets the reader make sense of them," revealing the nature of the tragedy "deep into her story without resorting to melodrama or otherwise manipulating the characterizations." Del Negro concluded that certain images in the work "will remain with readers long after the book is closed."

In an interview with Elizabeth Devereaux for *Publishers Weekly,* Griffin explained that *Rainy Season* was not an autobiographical novel. Griffin did, however, make frequent summer visits to Panama as a child, after her parents divorced and her father moved to Central America. She tackled the subjects of divorce and a girl's experience of life without her father in her next book, *Split Just Right. Horn Book* reviewer Nancy Vasilakis noted that the "sunny" tones of this novel "differ markedly from the somber, interior voice that characterized Griffin's first novel." *Bulletin of the Center for Children's Books* reviewer Janice M. Del Negro also commented on the "more relaxed, humorous tone" of *Split Just Right,* commending the "natural easy flow" with which Griffin portrays central protagonist Danny's interpersonal relationships.

A well-grounded fourteen-year-old who enjoys writing, Danny (otherwise known as Dandelion Finzimer) lives with her flamboyant, single, part-time waitress/actress/drama-teacher mother. With no memory of her father, Danny is unsure whether she should trust her mother's view of him and longs to learn about—or perhaps even meet—him. By way of a mix-up, Danny does get to meet her father, and in the process discovers much about her parents, her work as a burgeoning writer, and the line between fact and fiction. *School Library Journal* contributor Carol A. Edwards asserted that in this work, Griffin "takes one of the most tired plots in current fiction and gives it fresh zip." *Booklist* correspondent Ilene Cooper praised the book for successfully tackling "a number of interesting issues, including class distinction and family relationships."

Griffin's next book, *Sons of Liberty,* again adopts the more serious tone of her first novel. Through seventh-

Bubble, bubble, boil and . . . *double* trouble!

Identical twin witches Claire and Luna try to concoct a plan using their often ill-fated magic to dissuade their father from remarriage in Griffin's beguiling novel for young readers. (Cover illustration by Jacqueline Rogers.)

Two sisters are caught in the depressing environment of their parents' mourning over the loss of their other three children until an enigmatic artistic stranger comes into their lives and teaches the girls to move beyond their parents' grief. (Cover illustration by Jim Carroll.)

grader Rock Kindle, Griffin seriously examines the complicated issues faced by members of a dysfunctional family. Rock has always looked up to his father, and in imitation of his father's behavior, has become a bully. Rock's older brother, Cliff, has lost patience with their father's warped sense of militancy, which prescribes regular doses of humiliation and such bizarre punishments as waking the boys up in the middle of the night to do chores and calisthenics. When the family shatters, no longer able to stand the strain, Rock is forced to choose between loyalty to his father and loyalty to his newly discovered sense of self. In a starred review, a *Publishers Weekly* critic praised Griffin's use of "pointedly jarring dialogue" and her "keen ear for adolescent jargon." *Horn Book* reviewer Kitty Flynn credited the development of Rock's character with providing "the tension in what could have been a superficial treatment of the issues."

With *The Other Shepards,* Griffin created a supernatural teen romance about a girl named Holland and her obsessive-compulsive sister Geneva. The two are passing their adolescent years in a world that is haunted by the memory of three older siblings who died before the two sisters were even born. In the guise of Annie, a mural painter, the spirit of the older sister breathes color into the Shepard family. A *Publishers Weekly* critic wrote that Griffin "spins a taut story of two girls . . . who must confront the unknown in order to liberate themselves. . . . Griffin's story offers a resounding affirmation that fears are to be faced, not denied, and life is to be lived, not mourned." In a *Booklist* review, Ilene Cooper lauded the way Griffin "paints Annie so carefully she seems as real as a kiss from a first boyfriend, and what can be more real than that?" Cooper concluded her positive assessment of *The Other Shepards* by asserting: "Carefully crafted both in plot and language, this book shows the heights that popular literature can scale."

Dive explores the difference between family ties forged by biology and those crafted from circumstance. When his irresponsible mother deserts the family, eleven-year-old Ben elects to stay with his well-grounded stepfather, Lyle. Ben's brother, Dustin, is more inclined to engage in daring behavior, so Dustin chafes under Lyle's rules. The brothers must sort out their problematic relationship after Dustin suffers a serious injury in a diving accident. Nancy Vasilakis in *Horn Book* called *Dive* "a wrenching tale of a young man struggling to find his voice in an unpredictable world."

In 2001 Griffin launched her "Witch Twins" series, introducing ten-year-old twins Claire and Luna. Although they look alike, Claire and Luna are distinct individuals with unique personalities. They must keep their magic a secret from most of their family members, with the exception of Grandy, the grandmother from whom they have inherited their witchy talents. The action in *Witch Twins* revolves around Claire and Luna's attempts to break up their father's impending marriage to a woman named Fluffy. "Griffin's modern tale bursts with everyday enchantment," noted Catherine T. Quattlebaum in her *School Library Journal* review of the book. The critic also lauded the work for its "breezy mixture of otherworldly witchcraft and ordinary activities." The twins attend summer camp in *Witch Twins at Camp Bliss*, once again proving their independence by pursuing different courses from the moment they arrive. Claire must overcome a rival to win the coveted "Camp Bliss Girl" trophy, and Luna cannot find the magic dust given to her by her grandmother. In *School Library Journal*, Debbie Whitbeck observed that in this sequel, Griffin "keeps the characters true to their personalities introduced in the first novel." Diane Foote in *Booklist* liked the "satisfying and convincing happy ending."

In their third adventure, *Witch Twins and Melody Malady,* the girls get an opportunity to meet their idol, film and television star Melody Malady. Tension erupts when Melody becomes friends with Claire, leaving Luna in the company of Melody's brainy but quiet sister, Dolores. Through a series of adventures, both sets

Shy Delia is thrilled to meet the exotic student at her new school, until she discovers that Amandine is dangerous and cruel and Delia finds herself victimized by Amandine's frightening and destructive behavior.

of siblings learn to appreciate their family ties. "Fans of the series will enjoy this offering," maintained Linda B. Zeilstra in *School Library Journal*

Griffin tackles the difficult subject of teen friendships in two realistic novels, *Amandine* and *Overnight*. Both books frankly confront the way some teenaged girls seek to manipulate their peers and to exert power. Delia, the insecure narrator of *Amandine*, is drawn into an obsessive friendship with dramatic, artistic Amandine. When Amandine's behavior toward another girl takes a dangerous turn, Delia tries to break away. Only then does she discover the full force of Amandine's wrath. According to Anita L. Burkam in *Horn Book,* "Amandine's controlling nature and Delia's weak complicity are believably and subtly developed." Ilene Cooper in *Booklist* felt that Griffin "takes well-worn stereotypes . . . and . . . makes them seem much more: more real, more vulnerable, more scary." *School Library Journal* contributor Alison Follos called *Amandine* "a powerful story with real characters."

Overnight, published in 2003, "once again penetrates the cruelty inherent in female cliques," to quote a *Pub-*

Thirteen-year-old math prodigy Hannah has to move beyond her small hometown and the narrow-minded opinions of those who think math is for boys in Griffin's emotional story of a girl trying to widen the range of opportunities available to her in 1934.

lishers Weekly critic. Griffin introduces readers to the "Lucky Seven," a tightly-knit group of girls who gather for a sleepover on Friday the Thirteenth. Certain rifts have developed amongst the girls, and these conflicts become noticeable when one of their number, Gray, disappears during the party. The group's leader, Martha, is ready to assert her control, even if it means putting Gray's life in jeopardy. B. Allison Gray in *School Library Journal* deemed the novel an "insightful version of the universal story of ostracism and manipulation among preteens." The *Publishers Weekly* contributor felt that Griffin "expertly captures the pettiness of the Lucky Seven."

One of Griffin's most popular books is the novel *Hannah, Divided.* Set in Depression-era Pennsylvania, the story centers on Hannah, a farm girl who also happens to be a math genius and an obsessive-compulsive. Hannah loves living on a farm, helping her family with the chores and attending a one-room school with children she has known all her life. But her love of math just will not go away, and with the help of a wealthy Philadelphia patron, Hannah travels to the big city to try to win a scholarship. Once there, she is torn between her

homesickness and her burning desire to work with numbers, even in an alien place full of automobiles, loud music, and strangers. "This portrait of a child struggling with symptoms of obsessive-compulsive disorder is sensitive and convincing," declared Barbara Scotto in *School Library Journal.* Scotto also found *Hannah, Divided* to be "a novel well worth savoring." A *Publishers Weekly* critic gave the book a starred review, particularly praising the way Griffin "makes inventive use of a third-person narration to demonstrate Hannah's computer-like brain and quirky personality." In her starred *Booklist* review of the work, Ilene Cooper concluded: "In other hands, this might have been a problem novel. Here it is a celebration."

In her 1996 *Publishers Weekly* interview, Griffin admitted, "I have no life. . . . I leave work, go to the gym, come home and have dinner, and I write, every night. I talk to my mother, and then I go to bed. . . . I don't even have a plant." Much has changed since those days. Griffin is now a full-time writer with numerous awards and commendations for her work—and she is married. Offering an outlook on her writing future, Griffin said in 1996: "I don't think I want to do this my whole life, but right now, while I still feel so passionate about putting all my spare time into writing, I'll do it." In a more recent interview with the *Embracing the Child* Web site, she said: "Writing is not something that just came naturally to me. There was lots of practicing—still is. So my advice would be not to feel embarrassed about playing other people's songs before you find your own style."

Biographical and Critical Sources

PERIODICALS

Booklist, June 1 and 15, 1997, Ilene Cooper, review of *The Other Shepards,* pp. 1702-1703; September 15, 1997, Carolyn Phelan, review of *Sons of Liberty,* p. 235; August, 1998, Ilene Cooper, review of *The Other Shepards,* p. 1999; April 15, 2001, Ilene Cooper, review of *Witch Twins,* p. 1552; September 15, 2001, Ilene Cooper, review of *Amandine,* p. 226; July, 2002, Diane Foote, review of *Witch Twins at Camp Bliss,* p. 1844; October 1, 2002, Ilene Cooper, review of *Hannah, Divided,* p. 323; September 15, 2003, Karin Snelson, review of *Witch Twins and Melody Malady,* p. 236.
Bulletin of the Center for Children's Books, February, 1997, Janice M. Del Negro, review of *Rainy Season,* p. 207; September, 1997, Janice Del Negro, review of *Split Just Right,* p. 11.
Horn Book, March-April, 1997, Nancy Vasilakis, review of *Rainy Season,* p. 198; July-August, 1997, Nancy Vasilakis, review of *Split Just Right,* p. 455; January-February, 1998, Kitty Flynn, review of *Sons of Liberty,* p. 72; November, 1999, Nancy Vasilakis, review of *Dive,* p. 739; September, 2001, Anita L. Burkam, review of *Witch Twins,* p. 583; November-December, 2001, Anita L. Burkam, review of *Amandine,* p. 748.

Plain Dealer (Cleveland, OH), April 13, 2003, Cheryl Stritzel McCarthy, "A Transplanted Savant Finds She Has Much to Learn off the Farm," p. J11.

Publishers Weekly, October 14, 1996, review of *Rainy Season,* p. 84; December 16, 1996, Elizabeth Devereaux, "Flying Starts: Six First-Time Children's Book Authors Talk about Their Fall," p. 32; September 8, 1997, review of *Sons of Liberty,* p. 77; September 21, 1998, review of *The Other Shepards,* p. 86; July 2, 2001, review of *Witch Twins,* p. 76; August 20, 2001, review of *Amandine,* p. 81; August 26, 2002, review of *Hannah, Divided,* p. 69; December 16, 2002, review of *Overnight,* p. 68.

San Francisco Chronicle, April 25, 1999, Susan Faust, "Haunting Novel Is Not Your Average Ghost Story," p. 9.

School Library Journal, November, 1996, Lucinda Lockwood, review of *Rainy Season,* pp. 104-105; June, 1997, Carol A. Edwards, review of *Split Just Right,* p. 117; July, 2001, Catherine T. Quattlebaum, review of *Witch Twins,* p. 82; November, 2001, Alison Follos, review of *Amandine,* p. 158; June, 2002, Debbie Whitbeck, review of *Witch Twins at Camp Bliss,* p. 96; December, 2002, Barbara Scotto, review of *Hannah, Divided,* p. 138; February, 2003, B. Allison Gray, review of *Overnight,* p. 141; July, 2003, Linda B. Zeilstra, review of *Witch Twins and Melody Malady,* p. 96.

ONLINE

Embracing the Child, http://www.embracingthechild.org/ (November, 2002), "An Interview with Adele Griffin" and synopses of the author's books.*

*   *   *

GUY, Geoffrey 1942-

Personal

Born September 2, 1942, in Gloucester, England; son of Harold Hubert (a farmer) and Kathleen Betty Guy; married Lesley Frances Irene Thornton (a secretary), September 30, 1972; children: Frances Rachel, Thomas Kenneth, Ellen Mary. *Education:* Boroun Road Training College, certificate of secondary education, 1963; Université de Poitiers, certificate d'études etrangers. *Politics:* "Conservative with Socialist Leanings." *Religion:* Christian. *Hobbies and other interests:* Singing, history, especially architecture and agriculture, gardening.

Addresses

Home—51 Carrant Rd., Tewkesbury, Gloucestershire, GL20 8AA, England. *E-mail*—lesgeoff@tinyworld.co.uk.

Career

School teacher in Birmingham and Gloucestershire, 1963-70; postal worker in London, England, 1970-72; Ministry of Defence, London and Malvern, England,

Geoffrey Guy

foreign currency finance clerk, 1972-75; Customs and Excise Office, Droitwich, Birmingham, and Gloucester, England, executive officer and senior officer, 1975-95; self-employed gardener, 1995-2003.

Member

Tewkesbury Amateur Dramatic Society.

Writings

Hannibal's Rat, illustrated by Douglas Carrel, Hodder Children's Books (London, England), 2003.

Hannibal and Cleopatra, Hodder Children's Books (London, England), in press.

Work in Progress

A third "Hannibal" story, tentatively titled *Mice on the Move;* an adventure novel for young adults, *Accelerator.*

Sidelights

Geoffrey Guy told *SATA:* "Over the years, I've written various articles, hopefully humorous, for local papers. Indeed, the first chapter of *Hannibal's Rat* is derived from one of these. However I was unable to concentrate on extended writing while working for Customs and Excise and it was only after retiring to become a gardener that I had the time to think about it.

"*Hannibal's Rat* is a children's book, but I did not write it with children in mind, or indeed with anyone particular in mind: in effect, for my own enjoyment. Nor is there any consciously-expressed moral message or lesson in the three books which, if the remaining two are published, will make up what might be called the "Scratchbelly Trilogy." However, on considering them after completion I can discern a sort of moral theme: When a character cheats and breaks the ethical rules he eventually receives his comeuppance, though it may be delayed until a later book.

"The books are about mice, cats, dogs, rats, etc., with the action perceived from the mice's point of view. I make no attempt to be 'true' to the lives of real mice, which are almost certainly nasty, brutish, and short. There are nevertheless a lot of deaths in my stories; in fact the number increases with the second book, and in the third, *Mice on the Move,* the mouse deaths reach apocalyptic proportions. I feel that this is inevitable if you are going to write about animals which are the main food source for a great many creatures.

"I usually think of the stories' plots while gardening and, indeed, construct many of the actual sentences in my head at the same time. This considerably reduces the time spent actually putting pen to paper. I always hand-write the words because I find it easier to note something wrong with a sentence when it is hand-written: typing is too neat.

"Terry Pratchett's trilogy *Truckers, Diggers,* and *Wings* is, I think, one of the funniest and most attractive series of 'fantasy' books. Richard Adams' *Watership Down* is a fine book which I suppose mine might be said to resemble in terms of the animal/fantasy element, but I've consciously tried to avoid similarities. To my mind, his rabbits get off too lightly. And I've never quite understood why *Wind in the Willows* is a good children's book. It is a brilliant social commentary on Britain between the wars but as a child I found it mightily inconsistent and confusing.

"I know little or nothing about illustrators but I was immensely impressed by the work of Douglas Carrel who created the pictures for *Hannibal's Rat.* I certainly wouldn't presume to offer advice to anyone aspiring to be a writer, although I might be able to help him with his gardening."

In *Hannibal's Rat,* mice are not given names until they survive to adulthood—before that, they are numbered. Scratchbelly and his family are living comfortably behind the walls in a house until a new family moves in, and Number Three, Scratchbelly's son, is spotted by the newcomers. The mice avoid the traps and poison set out for them, but the greatest menace is Hannibal, a cat recruited specifically to catch the mice. Fearing for his life, Scratchbelly negotiates a truce with Hannibal. If Scratchbelly can provide a rat for Hannibal to catch, Hannibal will leave the mice alone. Scratchbelly must go outside, literally, to find a suitable rat. Andrea Rayner in the *School Library Association Journal* described *Hannibal's Rat* as "an appealing and convincing fantasy where the animal characters really do come to life." Julia Jarman in *Carousel* liked the "believable characters, humor and . . . exciting plot."

Biographical and Critical Sources

PERIODICALS

Carousel, summer, 2003, Julia Jarman, review of *Hannibal's Rat,* p. 17.

School Library Association Journal, summer, 2003, Andrea Rayner, review of *Hannibal's Rat.*

H

HARRIS, Dorothy Joan 1931-

Personal

Born February 14, 1931, in Kobe, Japan; emigrated to Canada, 1938; daughter of Hubert and Alice Langley; married Alan Harris (a company secretary-treasurer), October 8, 1955; children: Kim, Douglas. *Education:* University of Toronto, B.A. (with honors), 1952. *Religion:* Anglican.

Addresses

Home—159 Brentwood Rd. N., Toronto, Ontario, Canada M8X 2C8. *Agent*—Dorothy Markinko, McIntosh & Otis, 475 Fifth Ave., New York, NY 10017.

Career

Elementary school teacher in Kobe, Japan, 1954-55; editor for Copp Clark Publishing Company, 1955-60; writer.

Writings

The House Mouse, illustrated by Barbara Cooney, Frederick Warne (New York, NY), 1973.
The School Mouse, illustrated by Chris Conover, Frederick Warne (New York, NY), 1977.
The School Mouse and the Hamster, illustrated by Judy Clifford, Frederick Warne (New York, NY), 1979.
Don't Call Me Sugarbaby!, Scholastic Canada (Richmond Hill, Ontario, Canada), 1983.
Goodnight, Jeffrey, illustrated by Nancy Hannans, Frederick Warne (New York, NY), 1983.
Four Seasons for Toby, Scholastic Canada (Richmond Hill, Ontario, Canada), 1987.
Even If It Kills Me, Scholastic Canada (Richmond Hill, Ontario, Canada), 1987.
Speedy Sam, Scholastic Canada (Richmond Hill, Ontario, Canada), 1989.

No Dinosaurs in the Park, Scholastic Canada (Richmond Hill, Ontario, Canada), 1990.
Annabel the Detective, HarperCollins Canada (Scarborough, Ontario, Canada), 1991.

Sidelights

Dorothy Joan Harris once told *SATA:* "*The House Mouse* sprang from the doings of my own children, for Kim had a doll's house which she never played with (just as Elizabeth had in the book) and Douglas at the age of three liked it (just as Jonathan did in the book). The mouse, though, was purely imaginary, because our house was ruled by a very bossy Siamese cat called Samitu—and Sam would never tolerate any other animal on his property.

"*The School Mouse,* too, came from my children's experience, arising from the various fears and worries they had about school. Adults tend to forget how real and overpowering fears are to them, even when they seem trivial to grown-ups.

"But though much of my writing springs from actual children, editors do not always believe it. In *The House Mouse* I originally made Jonathan three years old, and one of the first criticisms I received from editors was that Jonathan did not talk like a three-year-old and should be a six-year-old. I felt like replying that my own three-year-old talked in *exactly* that way—but instead I compromised and made Jonathan four years old.

Now that my own children are growing up I try to strike up friendships with the children of neighbours and friends, so as to keep in touch with the world of childhood. And I never lose any chance to strike up a friendship with animals, wild or tame—especially with any cat. It takes me a long time to walk along our street because I have to stop and have a word with each cat I meet.

"My own cat, Sam, absolutely hates the sight of me sitting at my typewriter. Even if he is sound asleep under his chair he wakes at the first tap and goes into his act:

First he jumps up on the mantelpiece or buffer (so that I have to get up and lift him down), then he jumps up on the typewriter table, drapes his tail over the keyboard, and finally settles on my lap, with both paws firmly clamped on my wrist—which make typing extremely difficult. Someday I'm going to dedicate a book 'To Sam, without whose help I could have finished this darned book in half the time!'"

Jonathan's mouse is special. In all three of his titles, *The House Mouse, The School Mouse,* and *The School Mouse and the Hamster,* the little rodent talks to Jonathan and helps the youngster through trying situations. In *The School Mouse and the Hamster,* for instance, the mouse persuades Jonathan that the other class pet, a hamster, needs goodies and visits. Jonathan and his mouse feed the hamster, and the mouse exercises with the hamster. Confusion develops when the hamster has no appetite or energy during the day. In *Goodnight, Jeffrey,* a little boy fights going to sleep by playing with his daytime toys, until he finds a trusty stuffed animal that lulls him into inactivity. Harris's *Don't Call Me Sugarbaby!* is based on the true-life story of a friend's daughter who developed childhood onset diabetes. The book explores the life-altering changes for the girl and her family as she copes with a chronic condition. A *Maclean's* reviewer felt that the story "rings true in its detailing of the disease."

Biographical and Critical Sources

PERIODICALS

Maclean's, July 4, 1983, review of *Don't Call Me Sugarbaby!,* p. 50.
Publishers Weekly, September 9, 1983, review of *Goodnight, Jeffrey,* p. 65.
School Library Journal, March, 1980, Patricia Smith Butcher, review of *The School Mouse and the Hamster,* p. 121; December, 1983, Margaret C. Howell, review of *Goodnight, Jeffrey,* p. 56.*

*   *   *

HOFFMAN, Elizabeth P(arkinson) 1921-2003

OBITUARY NOTICE—See index for *SATA* sketch: Born March 23, 1921, in Pittsburgh, PA; died of a neurological disease July 16, 2003. Librarian, educator, and author. Hoffman was a librarian whose interest in ghosts led to her writing several books for children and young adults. Finishing her undergraduate degree at Dickinson College in 1942 and her library-science degree at Drexel University in 1961, Hoffman actually started out as an elementary-school teacher in Pennsylvania during the late 1950s and early 1960s. She was then hired as coordinator of the division of school libraries for the Pennsylvania Department of Education in 1966. In 1975 she joined the faculty at Villanova University as an associate professor of library science and chair of the department until 1978, and the next year she became director of the Havertown Township Free Library in Pennsylvania until her retirement in 1991. During the 1970s Hoffman began publishing books for young readers, several of which were inspired by the house she lived in, which was supposedly haunted. Her works include *This House Is Haunted* (1977), *Here a Ghost, There a Ghost* (1978), and *In Search of Ghosts: Haunted Places in the Delaware Valley* (1992), as well as the somewhat less spooky *Palm Reading Made Easy* (1971) and *Palm Reading* (1977).

OBITUARIES AND OTHER SOURCES:

PERIODICALS

Library Hotline, August 11, 2003, p. 6.

*   *   *

HOLADAY, Bobbie 1922-

Personal

Born August 5, 1922, in Pocontico Hills, NY; daughter of Coe Smith (a pastor and writer) and Ethel May (a teacher) Hoyne; married George Barfoot, 1950 (divorced); married Earl Holaday (a mechanic), 1959 (divorced); children: Bonnie, Bettie. *Education:* Denison University, B.A., 1944; graduate study at Arizona State University, 1987-90. *Politics:* Democrat. *Religion:* Episcopalian.

Addresses

Home—Phoenix, AZ. *Agent*—c/o Author Mail, University of Arizona Press, 355 S. Euclid Ave., Suite 103, Tucson, AZ 85719-6654. *E-mail*—azwolflady1@cox. net.

Career

Whirlpool, Inc., St. Joseph, MI, secretary, 1950-56; Arizona Industrial Council, Phoenix, AZ, secretary, 1956-57; Motorola, Inc., Phoenix, AZ, secretary, 1957-59; General Electric Co., Phoenix, AZ, secretary, 1959-60, technical writer, 1960-66, programmer, 1966-70; Honeywell, Inc., Phoenix, AZ, system analyst, 1970-83, staff engineer, 1983-86; writer and environmentalist, 1980—. Program chairperson, Palo Verde Group, Grand Canyon Chapter of Sierra Club, c. 1970-80. Founder and executive director, Preserve Arizona's Wolves (P.A. W.S.), 1988-98.

Member

Sierra Club.

Bobbie Holaday

Awards, Honors

Volunteer service award, Arizona Heritage Alliance, 1994; environmentalist of the year award, Arizona Game and Fish Commission, 1995; Arizona Cactus-Pine Girl Scout Council World of Outdoors award, 1995; award for excellence, Defenders of Wildlife Conservation, 1998; award of appreciation for outstanding achievement, Sierra Club, 2001.

Writings

Wild Places (poems), Horlo Press, 1985.
Return of the Mexican Gray Wolf: Back to the Blue, University of Arizona Press (Tucson, AZ), 2003.

Work in Progress

The Poster Wolf, a children's picture book.

Sidelights

Bobbie Holaday told *SATA:* "Throughout my life I had written poems, and was voted class poet in my senior years in high school and college. I dreamed of becoming a professional writer, but shelved such dreams when faced with raising two daughters on my own. Employment with large corporations ensured a stable income not found with freelance writing. Following retirement in 1986, my involvement with environmental causes excluded my pursuit of serious writing other than poetry until 1998 when I began my narrative of the return of the Mexican wolf. It is my hope that *Return of the Mexican Gray Wolf: Back to the Blue* will not only provide an accurate account of my work to bring back this wolf, but will also show others, particularly seniors, that one persistent person's efforts can make a difference.

"Most of my first draft of the book was written in long hand while I was camped at Luna Lake, near Alpine, Arizona. With no phone or television to distract me, I could focus my thoughts to putting on paper my experi-

ences of the preceding eleven years. I later entered the book's text onto my computer, where it underwent a series of revisions over the next two years. My most creative writing efforts took place during daytime hours when I would work in two-hour bursts.

"No one had recorded the struggle faced by biologists and wolf advocates when they attempted to return the Mexican gray wolf from near extinction to his historic habitat. I felt such a book was needed to let people know the obstacles that had to be overcome to enable wolf recovery. Authors like L. David Mech, Rick McIntyre, and Mike Phillips have written excellent wolf books. However, no ordinary citizen who voluntarily supported wolf recovery had previously documented his/her experiences. There are many authors who have researched wolf projects like the placement of Canadian wolves into Yellowstone National Park and Idaho wilderness, and have produced enjoyable books on the subject. The majority of these authors were wildlife biologists or employees of wildlife conservation organizations. Their books provide valuable information with perspectives quite different from a non-professional senior citizen.

"For anyone wanting to become a published author, you must enjoy the creative exercise of writing. You must endure many hours of isolation devoted to writing your story. With nonfiction you must be prepared to conduct research and interviews to complete your text. Once written, finding a publisher for your work is no easy chore. Most publishers reject more queries and proposals than they accept, so it is important that you produce a compelling query letter and a winning proposal. Worthwhile correspondence courses are available to teach you how to produce these important documents. As a first-time author, when you snag a publisher, you will face a new set of challenges, both painful and educational. Just swallow your pride and accept the fact that the editors are usually right in their decisions. Once your book is printed and you find yourself signing copies for eager readers, you'll reap the rewards for all of your efforts."

Holaday has been cited by the Sierra Club and the Defenders of Wildlife Conservation for her work as an environmentalist. At a time when many people retire to a sedentary lifestyle, Holaday took up hiking and discovered an avocation that led her to work tirelessly to compromise the interests of farmers and ranchers with that of the wild wolves and wilderness areas that were needed for their survival. Her first success was to spearhead the designation of Arizona's Hellsgate region as a wilderness area. She later worked to have the Eagletail Mountains included in the Bureau of Land Management's Desert Wilderness Act of 1990. Holaday's most visible work, however, has been that of restoring Mexican wolves to their former habitat in eastern Arizona. It is this effort that she chronicles in her first-person account, *Return of the Mexican Gray Wolf: Back to the Blue.* Holaday was the founder of Preserve

Arizona's Wolves (P.A.W.S.), a nonprofit organization dedicated to returning wolves to certain wilderness preserves. The organization raised money for lobbying purposes and also helped to educate Arizona's residents about wolves, their needs, and their place in the ecosystem. It was not necessarily easy to convince the livestock ranchers to live with wolves near their properties. On the *Arizona Wild* Web site, Holaday recalled: "Working to get that wilderness was mild compared to what I put myself through with the wolves. The challenges with that campaign very often brought me to tears, but this critter needs a voice, and I was determined to be that voice."

In 1998 Holaday helped to carry the cages of three Mexican wolves to an acclimatization pen in Arizona. She was there when they entered the preserve and has charted their efforts to survive in the wild ever since. *Return of the Mexican Gray Wolf* ends on a hopeful note, as the wolves begin to breed and to prey upon wild species within their wilderness area. As Sandy Bahr observed of the book in the *Sierra Club* magazine, "The story [Holaday] tells demonstrates how one person really can make a difference, punctuated with examples of how people working together can make an even bigger difference." In her *Booklist* review of *Return of the Mexican Gray Wolf*, Nancy Bent concluded: "Teen wolf lovers will be fascinated by the endangered species story."

Holaday is in her eighties but still working hard for the wolves and other Arizona environmental issues. "The fire is still there," she said on the *Campaign for America's Wilderness* Web site. "I always try to keep focused on any goal I'm trying to achieve. I'm passionate and feel driven to achieve my goals. It makes me feel good to know that I will be leaving a heritage— something far more valuable than monetary treasures— these wilderness areas and having wolves in our forests. You can't put a price on hearing a wolf howl."

Biographical and Critical Sources

PERIODICALS

Booklist, September 1, 2003, Nancy Bent, review of *Return of the Mexican Gray Wolf: Back to the Blue,* p. 35.

Columbian, January 27, 1998, Kate Hunger, "Mexican Gray Wolf Reintroduced to the Wild Decades after Demise."

Sierra Club, January/February, 2004, Sandy Bahr, "A Noble Goal and a Good Story," p. 8.

ONLINE

Arizona Wild, http://www.AZWild.org/ (June 2, 2004), "Redefining the Radical Environmentalist."

Campaign for America's Wilderness, http://www.leave itwild.org/newsletter/ (March, 2004), "Bobbie Holaday: A Natural Wilderness Champion."

HORSFIELD, Alan 1939- (David Alan, a pseudonym)

Personal

Born January 22, 1939, in Sydney, Australia; married; wife's name, Elaine. *Education:* Bathurst Teachers' College, teaching certificate, 1959; University of New England, B.A., 1969; Deakin University, B.Ed., 1987; University of New South Wales, M.Ed., 1989. *Hobbies and other interests:* Theatre, travel, reading, jogging, walking, environmental issues, swimming, jazz, wine festivals.

Addresses

Home—P.O. Box 627, Savusavu, Fiji Islands. *E-mail*— horsfield@connect.com.fj.

Career

School teacher in New South Wales, 1960-70; deputy master, deputy principal, and acting principal at schools in Australia, 1970-79; Bambusi St. International School, Papua, New Guinea, principal, 1980-81; Mandang International School, Papua, New Guinea, principal, 1982-87; classroom teacher, New South Wales, 1988; The Emanuel School, Randwick, assistant head of primary, 1989, head of primary, 1990-94; Children's Book Council, New South Wales, development officer, 1994-97; University of New South Wales, English and math research officer, 1998-99; writer, 2000—.

Member

Australian Society of Authors, Children's Book Council, New South Wales Writers Centre.

Writings

NONFICTION

Year 4 Selective Schools Scholarship English, Book 1, Pascal Press (Glebe, New South Wales, Australia), 1996.

Year 6 Selective Schools Scholarship English, Book 2, Pascal Press (Glebe, New South Wales, Australia), 1996.

Selective Schools Maths Tests Year 6, Pascal Press (Glebe, New South Wales, Australia), 1997.

Rusting, Rotting, and Reactive, Thomson Nelson Science Infotexts (Victoria, New South Wales, Australia), 1997.

Public Sector Recruitment Tests, Pascal Press (Glebe, New South Wales, Australia), 1998.

Comprehension Skills Year 3, Pascal Press (Glebe, New South Wales, Australia), 1998.

Comprehension Skills Year 4, Pascal Press (Glebe, New South Wales, Australia), 1998.

Alan Horsfield

Comprehension Skills Year 5, Pascal Press (Glebe, New South Wales, Australia), 1998.

Comprehension Skills Year 6, Pascal Press (Glebe, New South Wales, Australia), 1998.

Year 4 Placement Test Practice Numeracy, Pascal Press (Glebe, New South Wales, Australia), 1998.

Year 4 Placement Test Practice Literacy, Pascal Press (Glebe, New South Wales, Australia), 1998.

English Literacy Skills Year 2, Pascal Press (Glebe, New South Wales, Australia), 1999.

Comprehension Skills Year 7, Pascal Press (Glebe, New South Wales, Australia), 1999.

Narrative Writing for Students, two volumes, Pascal Press (Glebe, New South Wales, Australia), 2004.

FICTION

The Rats of Wolfe Island, Lothian (Sydney, Australia), 2002.

Dr awkwarD, Macmillan (Sydney, Australia), 2002.

Great Hair Robbery, Lothian (Sydney, Australia), 2003.

Cadaver Dog, Lothian (Sydney, Australia), 2004.

NO Signs (picture book), Peranga Post Press (Darling Downs, Queensland, Australia), 2004.

Contributor of short stories to collections, including "So Much for Aliens," *Thomas Nelson Buzz Words,* Series 1 (Victoria, New South Wales, Australia), 1996, "The Big Race," *Thomas Nelson Buzz Words,* Series 2 (Victoria, New South Wales, Australia), 1997; "The Ghost Writer," *Crackers,* Macmillan Educational (Sydney, Australia), 1997; "Lemming Run," *Then and Now,* Wannabee Publishing (California Gully, Victoria, Australia), 1997; "Monopillar," *BlitzIt,* Thomas Nelson Educational (Vic-

toria, New South Wales, Australia), 1997; "Bubble Buster," *Sparklers,* Blake Education (Glebe, New South Wales, Australia), 1998; "The Aitutaki Phantom," Nelson ITP (Victoria, New South Wales, Australia), 1999; "My Sad Skeleton," *Galaxy Kids,* 2002; "The Strange Story of Elmer Floyd," *Just Kids,* Longman Pearson (Sydney, Australia), 2002; "Daily Bread," *Gigglers,* Blake Education (Glebe, New South Wales, Australia), 2002; "Dream On, Brian," *Dreams,* Ginninderra Press (Charnwood, Australia), 2002; "The Brahmin and the Ungrateful Tiger," Nelson ITP (Victoria, New South Wales, Australia), 2003.

WITH WIFE, ELAINE HORSFIELD; UNDER PSEUDONYMS DAVID ALAN AND PATRICIA ANN TURNER

Primary Basic Skills Numeracy Practice Year 3, Nightingale Press (Victoria, New South Wales, Australia), 1998.

Primary Basic Skills Numeracy Practice Year 5, Nightingale Press (Victoria, New South Wales, Australia), 1998.

Primary Basic Skills Literacy Practice, Year 3, Nightingale Press (Victoria, New South Wales, Australia), 1998.

Primary Basic Skills Literacy Practice, Year 5, Nightingale Press (Victoria, New South Wales, Australia), 1998.

Primary Basic Skills Numeracy Practice, Year 2, Nightingale Press (Victoria, New South Wales, Australia), 1998.

Secondary Basic Skills Literacy Practice Year 7, Nightingale Press (Victoria, New South Wales, Australia), 2000.

Primary Basic Skills Literacy Practice Year 6, Nightingale Press (Victoria, New South Wales, Australia), 2001.

Primary Basic Skills Numeracy Practice Year 6, Nightingale Press (Victoria, New South Wales, Australia), 2001.

Contributor of articles to magazines and newspapers, including *Magpies* and *Australian Multicultural Book Review.*

Sidelights

Alan Horsfield is an Australian-based author who has published more than fifty books, many of them educational texts in literacy and numeracy. His early writing was for children's magazines, newspapers, and journals. Later he began writing textbooks and factual books. His first children's fiction was published in 1996. Since then he has had more than fifteen works of fiction published, three of which are with Lothian Books. His works have been published in a number of English-speaking countries, including Australia, New Zealand, Canada, and the United States.

Horsfield is a former teacher who has worked in state and private schools across New South Wales. He and his wife, Elaine, enjoy traveling and many of his stories reflect the places that he has visited.

Horsfield conducts writing workshops in schools in Australia and New Zealand for primary and secondary students. His main focus is on gifted and talented writers. In 2004 he served as writer in residence for Domremy College in Sydney. He is a past president of the New South Wales Children's Book Council and is a former judge for the New South Wales Premier's Book Awards. Since retiring from the educational field, he has devoted himself to writing. He told *SATA* that he "shuttles between Sydney and Fiji," where he has an office "overlooking a tranquil, tropical lagoon. A perfect place for inspiration."

J

JEFFERSON, Sarah
  See FARJEON, (Eve) Annabel

*   *   *

JONES, Carol 1942-

Personal

Born August 17, 1942, in Oldbury Birmingham, England; immigrated to Australia, 1972; daughter of William Henry (a business manager) and Dorothy Irene (a homemaker; maiden name, Pritchard) Jones; married Ronald Patterson Johnston (a primary school teacher), 1972; children: Mark, Sally. *Education:* Birmingham College of Art, national design diploma (book illustration), 1963. *Hobbies and other interests:* "Gardening, trying to grow old fashioned English cottage flowers, cross-stitch embroidery (no time of late for that), following Mark's cricket games each season and daughter Sally's hockey career."

Addresses

Home and office—17 Matthews St., Wollowgong 2500, New South Wales, Australia. *Agent*—Margaret Connoly, 37 Ormond St., Paddington 2021, New South Wales, Australia.

Career

Illustrator and author.

Member

Australian Society of Authors, Society of Book Illustrators.

Writings

RETELLER AND ILLUSTRATOR

Old MacDonald Had a Farm, Houghton (Boston, MA), 1988.
This Old Man, Houghton (Boston, MA), 1990.

Hickory Dickory Dock and Other Nursery Songs, Angus & Robertson (Sydney, New South Wales, Australia), 1991, published as *Hickory Dickory Dock and Other Nursery Rhymes,* Houghton (Boston, MA), 1992.
Town Mouse, Country Mouse, Houghton (Boston, MA), 1995.
The Hare and the Tortoise, Houghton (Boston, MA), 1996.
The Lion and the Mouse, Houghton (Boston, MA), 1997.
What's the Time, Mr. Wolf?, Houghton (Boston, MA), 1999.
The Gingerbread Man, Houghton (Boston, MA), 2002.

ILLUSTRATOR

Ronald Melzack, reteller, *The Day Tuk Became a Hunter and Other Eskimo Stories,* Dodd (New York, NY), 1967.
Alan Boucher, *The Hornstranders,* Meredith Press (New York, NY), 1969.
Sally Farrell Odgers, *Drummond: The Search for Sarah,* Holiday House (New York, NY), 1990.
Ann Jungman, *Honest Mum, I've Looked Everywhere,* Angus & Robertson (Sydney, New South Wales, Australia), 1992.
Alice Cameron, *The Cat Sat on the Mat,* Houghton (Boston, MA), 1993.

Sidelights

Illustrator Carol Jones began her career with a title retold by Ronald Melzack, *The Day Tuk Became a Hunter and Other Eskimo Stories,* and her work on folk-tales has continued from there. After providing illustrations for two books written by other authors, Jones began to choose stories on her own, retelling them and illustrating them at the same time. Whether using nursery rhymes, childhood songs, children's games, or fables, Jones's retellings are generally considered straightforward, and her illustrations well suited to each tale. She also uses a unique technique in the format of her books: she creates a die-cut window in every other page to allow readers to see where the characters are going, or where they've been. Jones began using this technique with *Old MacDonald Had a Farm,* and has continued using it in her retellings ever since.

One book that uses Jones' die-cut technique is *Town Mouse, Country Mouse.* Jones' retelling of the well-known Aesop fable allows readers to see how different the worlds of the two mice are by giving hints through her mouse-hole-like windows. A critic for *Publishers Weekly* called the book "charmingly illustrated, engagingly straightforward," and Mary Harris Veeder in *Booklist* praised Jones's illustrations for "bear[ing] up to long and pleasant scrutiny." Jones's retelling of Aesop's *The Hare and the Tortoise* again uses the window technique so that readers can always see both hare and tortoise, even when hare is far ahead of the slow tortoise. Kay Weisman, in her *Booklist* review, noted that "The cluttered pen-and-ink with watercolor illustrations . . . perfectly compliment the text."

Instead of turning to Aesop's fables for inspiration in *What's the Time, Mr. Wolf?,* Jones bases her picture book on a playground game. In the story, the wolf, whom readers can tell is ready to make trouble, invites all his barnyard "friends" over for a special dinner. Every two hours one of Mr. Wolf's guests arrives to ask what time it is, and Mr. Wolf tells them to get something else to add to the dinner celebration. When the wolf finally has all of his guests assembled at his house, he blows his cover, and the barnyard animals flee, having their own celebration without him in what a contributor to *Publishers Weekly* called "an enjoyable romp." Writing for *Booklist,* Marta Segal assured parents that "the cheerful, well-detailed silliness of the illustrations will prevent even the smallest child from being scared."

In *The Gingerbread Man* Jones retells the traditional folktale, but with "two nifty twists" according to a reviewer for *Publishers Weekly.* The first twist is the use of her die-cut windows. The second is that among the

Young readers get a secret glimpse of each step of Mr. Wolf's planned feast in Carol Jones's peephole book about the devious wolf and his unsuspecting guests/main course. (*From* What's the Time, Mr. Wolf?, *written and illustrated by Jones.*)

In Jones's self-illustrated retelling of the tale of the feisty Gingerbread Man, he is pursued by several well-known characters from nursery rhymes in his flight from the Little Old Man and the Little Old Woman into the clutches of a cunning fox. (*From* The Gingerbread Man.)

Gingerbread Man's pursuers are characters from Mother Goose rhymes, including Little Miss Muffett, Humpty Dumpty, and Little Boy Blue. She stays true to the story, however, with the Gingerbread Man's familiar rhyme, allowing readers to chant it back whenever the Gingerbread Man calls it out. She also adheres to the traditional ending: the ultimate demise of the Gingerbread Man in the mouth of the fox. "Readers will find something new with each look at the wonderfully detailed drawings" in *The Gingerbread Man,* praised a critic from *Kirkus Reviews.* Judith Constantinides in *School Library Journal* commented favorably on Jones's "minutely detailed and intriguing illustrations," and Hazel Rochman wrote in *Booklist* that readers "will be drawn into the pictures, especially since a small circular cutout shows where the cheeky run away has been and hints at what's waiting for him." Jones includes a recipe for gingerbread at the end of the book, so readers can bake their own gingerbread men.

Although Jones has developed a following with her original, self-illustrated retellings, she uses her die-cut technique when illustrating works by other writers as well. With Alice Cameron, she produced *The Cat Sat on the Mat,* a picture book following a cat from sitting place to sitting place, starting its day out on a mat and returning there by the end of the book. Designed for early readers, each object on which the cat is sitting is printed in red letters, to help children learn to read by associating with the pictures. "Jones' pen-and-watercolor illustrations have a warm, cozy feel," wrote Annie Ayers in *Booklist.*

"I was educated at the Bournville Primary School on the Cadbury estate on the outskirts of Birmingham," Jones once told *SATA.* "Father worked at Cadburys and our family lived on a factory estate. After primary school, I went to Moseley Secondary Art School. Then at sixteen, I attended Birmingham College of Art. I spent 1958-63 obtaining the National Design Diploma, specialising in book illustration. After a post graduate year working at a printers and Penguin Books, I moved to London, freelanced, and taught art two-and-a-half days a week at Clapham Girls Grammar, which paid the rent and living costs.

"I moved to Toronto, Canada, in 1967, my most successful assignment being *The Day Tuk Became a Hunter and Other Eskimo Stories.* I returned to London in 1968, and worked for the BBC on the children's programmes *Play School* and *Jackanory,* and did freelance work. I immigrated to Australia in 1972. After living in Sydney for six months, I settled in Wollowgong. I married a primary school teacher, Ron Johnston, and had two children, Mark and Sally." Selling water colour pictures inspired by her favorite book, *The Wind in the Willows,* through art shows and galleries was the step that took Jones to her renewed career as a children's book illustrator.

Biographical and Critical Sources

PERIODICALS

Booklist, December 15, 1994, Annie Ayers, review of *The Cat Sat on the Mat,* p. 756; April 15, 1995, Mary Har- ris Veeder, review of *Town Mouse, Country Mouse,* p. 1506; September 1, 1996, Kay Weisman, review of *The Hare and the Tortoise,* p. 139; October 15, 1999, Marta Segal, review of *What's the Time, Mr. Wolf?,* p. 454; February 15, 2002, Hazel Rochman, review of *The Gingerbread Man,* p. 1017.

Kirkus Reviews, February 15, 2002, review of *The Gingerbread Man,* p. 259.

Publishers Weekly, March 27, 1995, review of *Town Mouse, Country Mouse,* p. 85; October 4, 1999, review of *What's the Time, Mr. Wolf?,* p. 74; January 21, 2002, review of *The Gingergread Man,* p. 90.

School Library Journal, June, 1992, Rachel Fox, review of *Hickory Dickory Dock,* p. 94; October, 1994, Heide Piehler, review of *The Cat Sat on the Mat,* p. 86; June, 1994, Denise Anton Wright, review of *Town Mouse, Country Mouse,* p. 102; September, 1996, Heide Piehler, review of *The Hare and the Tortoise,* p. 198; November, 1997, Karen James, review of *The Lion and the Mouse,* p. 85; December, 1999, Amy Lilien-Harper, review of *What's the Time, Mr. Wolf?,* p. 100; April, 2002, Judith Constantinides, review of *The Gingerbread Man,* p. 134.*

K

KIRK, Daniel 1952-

Personal
Born May 1, 1952, in Elyria, OH; son of Donald (a puppeteer) and Connie (a puppeteer; maiden name, Porch) Kirk; married Julia Gorton (an author and illustrator), 1986; children: Ivy, Raleigh, Russell. *Education:* Ohio State University, B.A. (summa cum laude), 1974. *Politics:* Left Democrat. *Religion:* "Nature worship."

Addresses
Home and office—207 Baldwin St., Glen Ridge, NJ 07028.

Career
Author and illustrator. *Exhibitions:* Work has been shown at Storyopolis Gallery, Los Angeles, CA.

Awards, Honors
Received various awards from the American Institute of Graphic Arts and the Society of Illustrators.

Writings

SELF-ILLUSTRATED

Skateboard Monsters, Rizzoli (New York, NY), 1992.
Lucky's Twenty-four Hour Garage, Hyperion (New York, NY), 1996.
Trash Trucks!, Putnam (New York, NY), 1997.
Breakfast at the Liberty Diner, Hyperion (New York, NY), 1997.
Bigger, Putnam (New York, NY), 1998.
Hush, Little Alien, Hyperion (New York, NY), 1999.
Moondogs, Putnam (New York, NY), 1999.
Humpty Dumpty, Putnam (New York, NY), 2000.

The Snow Family, Hyperion (New York, NY), 2000.
Bus Stop, Bus Go!, Putnam (New York, NY), 2001.
Go! (includes audio CD), Hyperion (New York, NY), 2001.
Dogs Rule! (includes audio CD), Hyperion (New York, NY), 2003.
Jack and Jill, Putnam (New York, NY), 2003.
Lunchroom Lizard, Putnam (New York, NY), 2004.
Rex Tabby, Orchard (New York, NY), 2004.

ILLUSTRATOR

Maida Silverman, *Dune: Pop-Up Panorama Book,* Grosset & Dunlap (New York, NY), 1984.
Santa Claus the Movie Pop-Up Panorama Book, Grosset & Dunlap (New York, NY), 1985.
Michael Lipson, *How the Wind Plays,* Hyperion (New York, NY), 1994.
Margaret Wise Brown, *The Diggers,* Hyperion (New York, NY), 1995.
Kevin Lewis, *Chugga-Chugga Choo-Choo,* Hyperion (New York, NY), 1999.
Kevin Lewis, *My Truck Is Stuck!,* Hyperion (New York, NY), 2002.
Miriam Schlein, *Hello, Hello!,* Simon & Schuster (New York, NY), 2002.

Sidelights
Author and illustrator Daniel Kirk told *SATA* that he knew at the age of five that he would one day be an artist. Fittingly, he found in his own kids the inspiration to fulfill his childhood dream. "I started writing stories when my children were very small," he recalled, "and I get lots of good ideas for books based on the funny things my kids say and do. I have always been a painter, and I used to write a lot of songs, but I never thought of putting my writing and my picture-making together until I spent a lot of time reading books to my own children. Now I try all my ideas out on my two sons and daughter, and get their feedback on which of my characters are interesting, how I should end stories, and which of my stories are worth writing down."

One story that was well worth writing down is Kirk's self-illustrated debut book, *Skateboard Monsters,* in which a group of playing children rush to get out of the way as a gang of zany monsters on skateboards takes over the sidewalk. In a *Booklist* review, Ilene Cooper praised the book's "in-your-face artwork that uses unusual perspectives, elongated shapes, and the boldest of colors to match the feverish, skateboarding mood." *School Library Journal* contributor Carolyn Noah also commended Kirk's illustrations, which "[burst] off the pages with energy and wild good cheer," and his text, "jet-propelled verse [that] is graphically integrated."

Kirk told *SATA* that he likes to try different techniques when he paints. "My books *Breakfast at the Liberty Diner* and *Lucky's Twenty-four Hour Garage* are both set in the 1930s," he said, "so I chose a painting style that looks reminiscent of art from that time period." *Booklist* reviewer Cooper commented favorably on Kirk's approach, noting that *Breakfast at the Liberty Diner* "captures the [1930s] feeling in both the subject matter and the style of the art." Bobby and his family are waiting for Uncle Angelo at the Liberty Diner when they are surprised by a visit from President Roosevelt. "Filled with bustling, sipping, munching, smiling people, the scenes at the Liberty Diner come alive," re-

In Daniel Kirk's self-illustrated version of **Humpty Dumpty,** *a clever young king who loves puzzles saves Humpty from ruin after his fall.*

In Kirk's expanded self-illustrated version of **Jack and Jill,** *a hungry crocodile living in the well forces the hero and heroine to be brave and resourceful.*

marked a *Kirkus Reviews* critic. *Lucky's Twenty-four Hour Garage* tracks the customers and cars that visit a 1939 New York City garage in the wee hours of the morning. A *Publishers Weekly* contributor called the book "a captivating slice of Americana." In a review for *Booklist,* Cooper declared, "Kirk's art . . . is absolutely terrific. The glowing oils that fill the pages bring you right into the twenty-four-hour world of Lucky's garage."

Kirk employs another medium for his artwork in *Trash Trucks!,* which tells of Kim and Pete's adventures helping out on garbage day. "I used collage and mixed media technique, and a much wilder design style," he once explained, "because the story is about wild and fanciful garbage trucks who come to life and roam around." "Sesame Street's Oscar would be hard pressed to match the enthusiasm that Kirk . . . shows for garbage collection," a *Publishers Weekly* critic remarked in a review of the book. A *Kirkus Reviews* critic noted that "the bright colors, inventive design, and in-your-face perspective present a diverting visual cacophony," while Michael Cart of *Booklist* maintained that "Kirk's singsong, rhyming text is infectious . . . but the main attraction is the rambunctious art."

Compared to his earlier efforts, "*Bigger* is a very straightforward kind of book," said Kirk to *SATA,* "and the pictures are direct to match the text." *Bigger* fol-

lows one boy's development inch by inch, from embryo to school age. *School Library Journal* contributor Jody McCoy thought that Kirk's "writing is appropriately simple and utilitarian," and "point of view is handled beautifully." A reviewer for *Publishers Weekly* declared: "The stylized pictures match the idealized account of growing up, which bubbles with satisfaction and wonder."

Kirk has also written twisted, modernized adaptations of the nursery rhymes "Humpty Dumpty" and "Jack and Jill." *Humpty Dumpty* provides a happy ending to the story of the shattered egg: although all of the king's horses and all of the king's men cannot put Humpty Dumpty together again, the king himself—a shy young boy who enjoys putting together puzzles—can. *School Library Journal* contributor Kathleen Kelly thought that the best feature of the book was Kirk's illustrations, "a combination of oils, magazine clippings, and computer printouts that gives the pictures a busy, textured look." In Kirk's version of *Jack and Jill,* the siblings are foiled in their attempts to draw water from the well by a giant talking crocodile who turns out to be their missing father. Kirk's retro illustrations for this tale were widely commented upon. They are "quirky but somehow work with the rhyming story," thought *School Library Journal*'s Kristin de Lacoste, while *Booklist*'s Cart predicted, "high-school kids who peruse picture books for art ideas will think they're a hoot."

Bus Stop, Bus Go! is an energetic story of a particularly crazy school bus ride, told in "a bongo-beat rhyming text," as a reviewer wrote in *Publishers Weekly.* The normal chaos of young children doing their homework, playing games, and chewing gum is heightened on this morning when Tommy's hamster escapes from its cage and scampers through the vehicle. "The rhyming text nicely conveys the stop-and-go motion (and commotion) of the bus," commented *Booklist*'s Helen Rosenberg, and as Robin L. Gibson wrote in *School Library Journal,* Kirk's "brightly colored illustrations complement the noisy atmosphere."

Kirk returned to his hobby of song-writing for the books *Go!* and *Dogs Rule!,* both of which come with CDs of Kirk singing the verses contained in the book. Dogs' lives "have never been captured with more slobbery exuberance" than they are in *Dogs Rule!,* John Peters declared in *Booklist.* The lyrics are written from the point of view of various dogs, from spoiled purebred lapdogs to happy-go-lucky mutts, and Kirk's caricature-like illustrations of excited, grinning dogs express the book's cheerful mood. "Kirk excels at capturing canine expressions," thought a *Kirkus Reviews* contributor.

In addition to illustrating his own texts, Kirk has also provided the pictures for works by other children's authors. Notable among these efforts is his artwork for a reinterpretation of Margaret Wise Brown's *The Diggers,* originally published in 1960 with illustrations by Clement Hurd. In a *Booklist* review, Carolyn Phelan praised the "large, brilliantly colored oil paintings [done] in a heroic style that romanticizes man and his machines." Kirk also illustrated Michael Lipson's *How the Wind Plays,* of which Anna Biagioni Hart, writing in *School Library Journal,* remarked, "this personification of wind will be fascinating to youngsters and a boon to creative teachers or librarians." Reviewing the same work for *Booklist,* Cooper called attention to Kirk's versatility of technique, noting that his oil paintings "combine a 1930s style with a modern airbrushed look that's eye-catchingly fresh."

Kirk teamed up with author Kevin Lewis on the books *Chugga-Chugga Choo-Choo* and *My Truck Is Stuck!* In the first book, a young boy's toys come alive and help to man a toy train as it carries "freight" around the boy's bedroom. "Kirk's color-saturated pictures are a feast for the eyes, with many wonderful details for little ones to explore," Lauren Peterson wrote in *Booklist.* In *My Truck Is Stuck!,* Kirk extends Lewis's story of a dump truck that gets stuck in a pothole and needs lots

of help to be pulled out. The artist creates bright, humorous illustrations, done with oil paints over sand and plaster. In Kirk's imagination, the truck drivers are all dogs, and their truck (license plate BONZ-4U) carries a huge pile of bones. At least, it does at the beginning of the story: as the dogs and their would-be rescuers work on freeing the truck, a group of prairie dogs quietly spirits away the bones. *Booklist's* Connie Fletcher described Kirk's illustrations as "sunny and funny" and commented on his "vibrant" palette, while a *Publishers Weekly* reviewer thought that "the dog characterizations are a stitch."

Kirk once told *SATA* that his work on children's books has been "the most fulfilling work I have ever done. The more I write, the more ideas occur to me. I was worried that I might just have a handful of stories inside me, but now it seems like there is a bottomless sea of great stories out there, and I just have to go fishing for them.

On the bus ride to school Tommy's hamster escapes from his cage and the excited passengers of the bus search high and low for the mischievous pet. (*From* Bus Stop, Bus Go!, *written and illustrated by Kirk.*)

"The most difficult part of my job is getting used to the fact that a picture book takes me four or five months to paint. That is a long, boring time for me, because once I have written the book and drawn the sketches, I feel ready to leave the project behind, and move on to something new and challenging. But people seem to like the way I paint, so I must slog on through all the pictures and try to be patient.

"I do not have a particular writing style that I always use. I feel that the story dictates the way it should be told, and sometimes that will be in rhyme, sometimes in prose, sometimes with lots of verbal details or dialogue, and sometimes very spare. Sometimes it is best to let the pictures tell the story themselves. There are authors who have a particular way of writing, and each book they write is instantly recognizable as their book. That would be boring for me. I like to try something a little different each time! The only constants are that I like bright colors; simple shapes; rounded, dimensional characters; and atmospheric lighting.

"I think picture books are very important to children. I hope that the books I do will encourage imagination, curiosity, playfulness, love of words and artwork, and get kids to think about things that are important to them. I love books that are unconventional and nonconformist, and in my own writing, I don't like to preach. Morals are sometimes useful, and they always help a book sell, but I feel that my job is primarily to create a sense of wonder and fun, to entertain, to suggest different ways of thinking about things; and sometimes, if it fits, teach a lesson, too!"

Biographical and Critical Sources

PERIODICALS

Astronomy, December, 2001, review of *Hush, Little Alien,* p. 102.

Booklist, January 15, 1993, Ilene Cooper, review of *Skateboard Monsters,* p. 921; May 1, 1994, Ilene Cooper, review of *How the Wind Plays,* p. 1609; May 1, 1995, Carolyn Phelan, review of *The Diggers,* pp. 1576-1577; September 1, 1996, Ilene Cooper, review of *Lucky's Twenty-four Hour Garage,* p. 143; May 15, 1997, Michael Cart, review of *Trash Trucks!,* p. 1579; November 1, 1997, Ilene Cooper, review of *Breakfast at the Liberty Diner,* p. 482; May 1, 1998, Linda Perkins, review of *Bigger,* p. 1521; March 15, 1999, John Peters, review of *Moondogs,* p. 1333; October 15, 1999, Lauren Peterson, review of *Chugga-Chugga Choo-Choo,* p. 455; November 15, 1999, Carolyn Phelan, review of *Hush, Little Alien,* p. 636; May 15, 2000, Connie Fletcher, review of *Humpty Dumpty,* p. 1757; September 1, 2000, Shelle Rosenfield, review of *Snow Family,* p. 130; June 1, 2001, Helen Rosenberg, review of *Bus Stop, Bus Go!,* p. 1891; December 15, 2001, Gillian Engberg, review of *Go!,* p. 727;

June 1, 2002, Julie Cummins, review of *Hello, Hello!,* p. 1728; November 1, 2002, Connie Fletcher, review of *My Truck Is Stuck!,* pp. 508-509; June 1, 2003, Michael Cart, review of *Jack and Jill,* p. 1787; October 15, 2003, John Peters, review of *Dogs Rule!,* p. 407.

Bulletin of the Center for Children's Books, June, 1998, p. 367.

Horn Book, March-April, 1999, Liza Woodruff, review of *Moondogs,* pp. 193-194; July-August, 2002, Lauren Adams, review of *Hello, Hello!,* p. 451.

Kirkus Reviews, August 1, 1996, p. 1154; May 1, 1997, review of *Trash Trucks!,* p. 723; August 15, 1997, review of *Breakfast at the Liberty Diner,* p. 1307; March 15, 1998, p. 406; September 15, 2001, review of *Go!,* p. 1360; May 15, 2002, review of *Hello, Hello!,* p. 740; August 15, 2002, review of *My Truck Is Stuck,* p. 1228; June 1, 2003, review of *Jack and Jill,* p. 806; October 15, 2003, review of *Dogs Rule!,* p. 1272.

New York Times Book Review, December 22, 1996, Sam Swope, review of *Lucky's Twenty-four Hour Garage,* p. 16; May 17, 1998, Amy L. Cohn, review of *Bigger,* p. 28; May 14, 2000, Sam Swope, review of *Humpty Dumpty,* p. 22; December 3, 2000, Scott Veale, review of *Snow Family,* p. 84.

Parenting, summer, 1993, Leonard S. Marcus, review of *Skateboard Monsters,* pp. 74-75.

Publishers Weekly, August 26, 1996, review of *Lucky's Twenty-four Hour Garage,* p. 97; May 12, 1997, review of *Trash Trucks!,* p. 75; October 27, 1997, review of *Breakfast at the Liberty Diner,* p. 74; April 27, 1998, review of *Bigger,* p. 65; March 15, 1999, review of *Moondogs,* p. 59; May 17, 1999, review of *Chugga-Chugga Choo-Choo,* p. 77; January 10, 2000, review of *Bigger,* p. 70; September 11, 2000, review of *Snow Family,* p. 90; June 18, 2001, review of *Bus Stop, Bus Go!,* p. 81; October 8, 2001, review of *Go!,* p. 62; April 29, 2002, review of *Hello, Hello!,* p. 68; September 2, 2002, review of *My Truck Is Stuck!,* p. 74; May 19, 2003, review of *Jack and Jill,* pp. 73-74; December 8, 2003, review of *Dogs Rule!,* p. 60.

School Library Journal, February, 1993, Carolyn Noah, review of *Skateboard Monsters,* p. 73; May, 1994, Anna Biagioni Hart, review of *How the Wind Plays,* p. 99; July, 1995, Carole D. Fiore, review of *The Diggers,* pp. 54-55; September, 1996, Carolyn Jenks, review of *Lucky's Twenty-four Hour Garage,* p. 182; November, 1997, Alicia Eames, review of *Breakfast at the Liberty Diner,* p. 85-86; May, 1998, Jody McCoy, review of *Bigger,* p. 118; March, 1999, Barbara Elleman, review of *Moondogs,* p. 177; September, 1999, Robin L. Gibson, review of *Chugga-Chugga Choo-Choo,* p. 193; December, 1999, Kathleen M. Kelly MacMillan, review of *Hush, Little Alien,* p. 102; June, 2000, Kathleen Kelly, review of *Humpty Dumpty,* p. 118; September, 2000, Sheilah Kosco, review of *Snow Family,* p. 201; September, 2001, Robin L. Gibson, review of *Bus Stop, Bus Go!,* p. 193; December, 2001, Mary Elam, review of *Go!,* p. 124; July, 2002, Maryann H. Owen, review of *Hello, Hello!,* p. 111; October, 2002, Melinda Piehler, review of *My Truck Is Stuck!,* p. 118; November, 2003, Kristin de Lacoste, review of *Jack and Jill,* p. 104.

ONLINE

Storyopolis Art Gallery, http://www.storyopolis.com/
    (January 13, 2004), "Daniel Kirk."*

*   *   *

KOSCIELNIAK, Bruce 1947-

Personal

Born July 9, 1947, in Adams, MA; son of Edwin and
Irene Koscielniak. *Education:* Vesper George School of
Art, Boston, MA, degree in commercial art, 1969; Will-
iams College, B.A., 1975. *Hobbies and other interests:*
Music, art history.

Addresses

Home—36 Summer St., Adams, MA 01220.

Career

Writer, oil painter, and illustrator. Former clerk, U.S.
Postal Service, Adams, MA. *Military service:* U.S.
Army, 1969-71, received good conduct medal.

Writings

FOR CHILDREN; SELF-ILLUSTRATED

Hector and Prudence, Alfred A. Knopf (New York, NY),
    1990.
Hector and Prudence—All Aboard!, Alfred A. Knopf (New
    York, NY), 1990.
Euclid Bunny Delivers the Mail, Alfred A. Knopf (New
    York, NY), 1991.
Bear and Bunny Grow Tomatoes, Alfred A. Knopf (New
    York, NY), 1993.
Geoffrey Groundhog Predicts the Weather, Houghton Miff-
    lin (Boston, MA), 1995.
*Hear, Hear, Mr. Shakespeare: Story, Illustrations, & Selec-
    tions from Shakespeare's Plays,* Houghton Mifflin
    (Boston, MA), 1998.
*The Story of the Incredible Orchestra: An Introduction to
    Musical Instruments and the Symphony Orchestra,*
    Houghton Mifflin (Boston, MA), 2000.
Johann Gutenberg and the Amazing Printing Press,
    Houghton Mifflin (Boston, MA), 2003.
*About Time: A First Look at Time and the Clocks That
    Measure It,* Houghton Mifflin (Boston, MA), 2004.

ILLUSTRATOR

David Fair, *The Fabulous Four Skunks,* Houghton Mifflin
    (Boston, MA), 1996.

Work in Progress

Looking at Glass through the Ages, a history of glass-
making, for Houghton Mifflin.

Bruce Koscielniak

Sidelights

Writer and illustrator Bruce Koscielniak has produced a
number of books, mostly for preschoolers and readers
in the early grades. His characters are usually animals,
and include the pigs Hector and Prudence, the mailman
Euclid Bunny, the farmers Bear and Bunny, and the
self-styled weather man Geoffrey Groundhog.

Koscielniak told *SATA:* "I began writing and illustrating
my first book projects (combining interests in writing
and art) about twenty years ago in the early 1980s. My
first book, *Hector and Prudence,* was published in 1990
by Alfred A. Knopf, and was followed by several more
fiction picture books for very young readers.

"However, in the mid-1990s I began to look at personal
interests—art, music, history—as topics for books that
were factually based. *Hear, Hear, Mr. Shakespeare* was
my transition into nonfiction topics, followed in 2000
by *The Story of the Incredible Orchestra* (I had played
violin in the public school orchestra), and in 2003 by
Johann Gutenberg and the Amazing Printing Press.
About Time looks at the mechanics of time and the various kinds of clocks people have used to measure time
with.

"In doing these books I try to present important topics,
including hard-to-find information, in a fully illustrated,
overview format. I take particular care to make sure the
writing and illustrations are accurate, and to use the
best source material available to me. For *Incredible Orchestra,* I was able to look at and handle rare and valuable antique musical instruments in the music collection

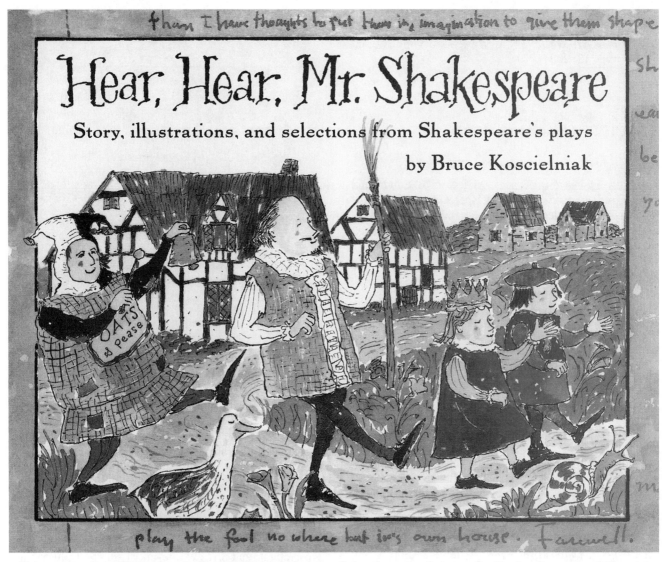

Using quotes from Shakespeare's plays, Koscielniak depicts a fictional meeting between the Bard and a group of itinerant actors who stop in Stratford on their way to London. (Cover illustration by Koscielniak.)

of the Library of Congress in Washington, DC. It was there also that I was able to look at early hand copied manuscript books, as well as Gutenberg's press-printed Latin Bible.

"Each of these recent books required more than two years of research and writing to prepare."

Koscielniak's working experience is probably most akin to that of Euclid Bunny. For years until he became a full-time author and illustrator, Koscielniak worked for the United States Postal Service, and before that he served a two-year stint in the U.S. Army during the Vietnam War. By the late 1990s, however, his writing had given him a degree of freedom which made it possible to spend part of each year in Las Vegas and part of it in his native Adams, Massachusetts.

Hence Koscielniak was reliving elements of his own experience when he wrote *Euclid Bunny Delivers the Mail.* In the story, written for pre-schoolers and first-

graders, all of the chickens who normally deliver the barnyard mail are sick with the flu. Bernie Bear, the postmaster, needs a replacement, so he calls the Euclid Bunny Speedy Delivery Service. Unfortunately, Euclid Bunny's service turns out to be a little too speedy. It takes him just 20 minutes to deliver all the mail, but he gets all the addresses wrong and takes every single letter and package to the wrong animal. The story is filled with amusing mishaps, until Euclid is asked to take the place of the most famous bunny of all: the Easter Bunny.

Hector and Prudence centers on pigs rather than bunnies. The story is written for a slightly older group of readers than *Euclid Bunny,* and the subject matter is a bit more mature. Hector and Prudence are a married couple, and at the beginning of the story, Hector thinks Prudence is acting strangely because she no longer wants to wallow in the mud, but desires a proper house for the two of them. The reason behind her sudden determination soon becomes apparent when Hector realizes that Prudence is pregnant. After their six little piglets arrive, the couple's life changes dramatically, and at the end of each day, they are worn out from caring for their new family. One scene noted by reviewers in *Publishers Weekly* and *School Library Journal* finds Harold and Prudence, exhausted after a long day, resting in a pair of lawn chairs under the night sky; unknown to them, their children are sneaking out of their upstairs bedroom by means of a rope-ladder made from bed sheets. The *Publishers Weekly* commentator praised Koscielniak's "rambunctious, jolly illustrations," adding that "children and parents alike will find his understated wit hard to resist."

Koscielniak followed his first Hector and Prudence book with *Hector and Prudence—All Aboard!* This time it's Christmas, and Hector and Prudence give their children a special present: a magical toy train that takes them on a mysterious journey. *Booklist* reviewer Ilene Cooper commented: "There's a lot going on in [Koscielniak's] ink-and-watercolor art as the train travels through forests, tunnels, and over bridges, often with near disastrous results."

Animal characters appear once again in *Bear and Bunny Grow Tomatoes,* written for preschoolers and primary graders. As a reviewer in *Publishers Weekly* pointed out, the story is related to that of "The Ant and the Grasshopper." In the original fable, the ant labors to provide for the future, while the grasshopper never thinks about tomorrow. Bear is the equivalent of the

ant, planting and tending his field with care; and Bunny is more like the grasshopper, recklessly throwing his seeds onto the ground and running off to play when it's time to weed and water the crop. Naturally, when harvest time comes, Bear has plenty to show for his efforts, whereas Bunny can't even *find* his tomatoes. In the end, of course, Bear shares some of his abundant crop with Bunny. "Far from being a tiresome exercise in preparedness," the *Publishers Weekly* critic commented, "Koscielniak imbues his story with touches of gentle humor that make the characters and their goofy antics quite irresistible."

Like the first Hector and Prudence book, *Geoffrey Groundhog Predicts the Weather* involves a grown-up theme. The title character's mother has taught him how to predict the weather as groundhogs do, and on the proper day in February he burrows out of his hole and makes a forecast that turns out to be accurate. This attracts the attention of the local paper, and Geoffrey Groundhog becomes something of a celebrity. Hence on the next February 2, his burrow is surrounded by well-wishers—and by reporters. In fact, the lights of the TV cameras are so strong that Geoffrey can't see whether or not he has a shadow. Finally he seeks assistance from his mother, who helps him make the right prediction.

Several reviewers observed that while children would enjoy the story of Geoffrey Groundhog's triumph, grownups are more apt to appreciate the portrayal of

The history of the orchestra as well as the nature of its various instruments forms the basis for Koscielniak's instructive picture book. (From The Story of the Incredible Orchestra: An Introduction to Musical Instruments and the Symphony Orchestra, *written and illustrated by Koscielniak.)*

With special emphasis on Johann Gutenberg, who invented the printing press in the fifteenth century, Koscielniak traces the evolution of modern printing and the inks and papers needed to facilitate the process. (From Johann Gutenberg and the Amazing Printing Press, *written and illustrated by Koscielniak.)*

the media feeding frenzy that surrounds the celebrity groundhog. A *Publishers Weekly* commentator remarked favorably on Koscielniak's "subdued palette of olive greens, browns, and other wintry hues," while *School Library Journal* contributor Tana Elias mentioned his "energetic watercolor and pen drawings." Elizabeth Bush in the *Bulletin of the Center for Children's Books* noted that "Koscielniak's snappy line-and-watercolor cartoons cleverly spoof the annual hoopla at Punxsutawney, Pennsylvania."

Koscielniak's skill as an illustrator also attracted notice in reviews of *The Fabulous Four Skunks,* a story written by David Fair. For young children, the book depicts a group of skunks who form a rock band: when their manager tells them "You stink," he means it literally. *Booklist* reviewer Ilene Cooper observed that Koscielniak, with his illustrations, "highlights every bit of humor in the text and adds some of his own." In the

words of *School Library Journal* contributor Lisa S. Murphy, "Koscielniak's humorous, cartoon-style illustrations invite individual browsing."

Hear, Hear, Mr. Shakespeare introduces readers to the works of William Shakespeare using familiar garden animals and a troupe of obliging actors who visit the playwright at his Stratford home. Koscielniak incorporates actual lines from Shakespeare's plays and fancifully adds definitions for some words that twenty-first century readers might not have encountered before. A *Publishers Weekly* critic concluded of the work: "To borrow a quip the author quotes from *Love's Labour's Lost,* 'Tu-who! A Merry note. . .' that Koscielniak strikes."

The author's extensive research for *The Story of the Incredible Orchestra: An Introduction to Musical Instruments and the Symphony Orchestra* filters into a text that acquaints children with the wide variety of instruments that make up a modern orchestra. Koscielniak packs a great number of facts into his book, from explanation of different styles of music to the detailed examination of individual instruments and the history of their use in classical music. Koscielniak illustrates the book with somewhat whimsical sketches that contrast with the more serious tone of the text. "Informed and lively, Koscielniak's . . . fact-filled excursion through music history is just the ticket for budding musicians," stated a *Publishers Weekly* critic in a starred review. *School Library Journal* correspondent Corinne Camarata likewise found the book "a fine complement to music-education programs."

Johann Gutenberg and the Amazing Printing Press explores the whole process of book-making from the invention of paper by the Chinese to the creation of the first printing press. Koscielniak takes readers into the workrooms of the early printers and explains how presses work using terms that children can understand. His active illustrations help to explain the whole process. According to a *Publishers Weekly* reviewer, "Motivated readers will come away with an understanding of the general process and with an appreciation for the man saluted at the end as 'Mr. G.'"

Koscielniak plans to continue writing and illustrating books about the valuable inventions that have made life easier in modern times.

Biographical and Critical Sources

PERIODICALS

Booklist, November 1, 1990, Ilene Cooper, review of *Hector and Prudence—All Aboard!,* p. 527; February 1, 1996, Ilene Cooper, review of *The Fabulous Four Skunks,* p. 937; April 15, 2000, GraceAnne A. DeCandido, review of *The Story of the Incredible Orchestra: An Introduction to Musical Instruments and the Symphony Orchestra,* p. 1549.

Bulletin of the Center for Children's Books, November, 1995, review of *Geoffrey Groundhog Predicts the Weather,* pp. 95-96.

Publishers Weekly, April 13, 1990, review of *Hector and Prudence,* p. 62; May 10, 1993, review of *Bear and Bunny Grow Tomatoes,* p. 71; August 21, 1995, review of *Geoffrey Groundhog Predicts the Weather,* p. 65; January 15, 1996, review of *The Fabulous Four Skunks,* p. 461; April 3, 2000, review of *The Story of the Incredible Orchestra,* p. 79; August 18, 2003, review of *Johann Gutenberg and the Amazing Printing Press,* p. 78.

School Library Journal, August, 1990, Ellen Fader, review of *Hector and Prudence,* p. 132; October, 1995, Tana Elias, review of *Geoffrey Groundhog Predicts the Weather,* p. 105; April, 1996, Lisa S. Murphy, review of *The Fabulous Four Skunks,* p. 108; May, 1998, Sally Margolis, review of *Hear, Hear, Mr. Shakespeare,* p. 118; June, 2000, Corinne Camarata, review of *The Story of the Incredible Orchestra,* p. 134; September, 2003, Laurie Edwards, review of *Johann Gutenberg and the Amazing Printing Press,* p. 200.

L

LANTZ, Fran
See LANTZ, Francess L(in)

*   *   *

LANTZ, Francess L(in) 1952-
(Fran Lantz)

Personal

Born August 27, 1952, in Trenton, NJ; daughter of Frederick W. (an architect) and Dorothea (a secretary and housewife; maiden name, Lingrell) Lantz; married Craig Shaw Gardner (a science fiction author), January, 1981 (divorced, 1983); married John M. Landsberg (a physician), April 30, 1984; children: Preston. *Education:* Dickinson College, B.A., 1974; Simmons College, M.L.S., 1975. *Politics:* Democrat.

Addresses

Agent—Kendra Marcus, Bookstop Literary Agency, 67 Meadow View Rd., Orinda, CA 94563.

Career

Dedham Public Library, Dedham, MA, children's librarian, 1976-79; writer, 1979—. Semi-professional musician in Boston, MA, 1974-79; "nanny" for babies in Boston, 1979-83. Santa Barbara City College, Adult Extension, Santa Barbara, CA, teacher, 1989-93.

Member

Authors Guild, Society of Children's Book Writers and Illustrators.

Writings

YOUNG ADULT NOVELS

Good Rockin' Tonight, Addison-Wesley (Boston, MA), 1982.

Francess L. Lantz

A Love Song for Becky, Berkley Publishing (New York, NY), 1983.
Surfer Girl, Berkley Publishing (New York, NY), 1983.
Rock 'n' Roll Romance, Berkley Publishing (New York, NY), 1984.
Senior Blues, Berkley Publishing (New York, NY), 1984.
Can't Stop Us Now ("Overnight Sensation" series), Dell (New York, NY), 1986.
Making It on Our Own ("Overnight Sensation" series), Dell (New York, NY), 1986.

Varsity Coach: Take Down, Bantam (New York, NY), 1986.

Swept Away: Woodstock Magic, Avon (New York, NY), 1986.

Varsity Coach: Double Play, Bantam (New York, NY), 1987.

Swept Away: Star Struck, Avon (New York, NY), 1987.

Swept Away: All Shook Up, Avon (New York, NY), 1987.

Sweet Valley Twins: Center of Attention, Bantam (New York, NY), 1988.

Sweet Valley Twins: Jessica's Bad Idea, Bantam (New York, NY), 1989.

The Truth about Making Out, Bantam (New York, NY), 1990.

Dear Celeste, My Life Is a Mess, Bantam (New York, NY), 1992.

Mom, There's a Pig in My Bed!, Avon (New York, NY), 1992.

Turn It Up: Everything You Need to Know to Start Your Own Rock Band or Rap Group, Avon (New York, NY), 1992.

Rock, Rap, and Rad: How to Be a Rock or Rap Star, Avon (New York, NY), 1992.

Randy's Raiders, Rainbow Bridge (Mahwah, NJ), 1994.

Be a Star!, Rainbow Bridge (Mahwah, NJ), 1996.

Neighbors from Outer Space, Troll (Mahwah, NJ), 1996.

Someone to Love, Avon (New York, NY), 1997.

Spinach with Chocolate Sauce, Troll (Mahwah, NJ), 1997.

Stepsister from the Planet Weird, Random House (New York, NY), 1997.

Fade Far Away, Avon (New York, NY), 1998.

Lights! Camera! Love!, Aladdin (New York, NY), 2000.

Love Song, Aladdin (New York, NY), 2000.

A Royal Kiss, Aladdin (New York, NY), 2000.

Letters to Cupid, American Girl (Middleton, WI), 2001.

"LUNA BAY: A ROXY GIRL SERIES"

Pier Pressure, HarperCollins (New York, NY), 2003.

Wave Goodbye, HarperCollins (New York, NY), 2003.

Weather or Not, HarperCollins (New York, NY), 2003.

Hawaii Five-Go!, HarperCollins (New York, NY), 2003.

Oh Buoy, HarperCollins (New York, NY), 2003.

Heart Breakers, HarperCollins (New York, NY), 2004.

Contributor of articles and reviews to *Kliatt.* Restaurant and movie reviewer for *Santa Barbara Independent,* 1989-91.

Adaptations

Stepsister from the Planet Weird was adapted by Disney as a television film, 2000.

Work in Progress

A middle grade novel for Dutton.

Sidelights

Author Francess L. Lantz got her start writing for children as a librarian. Her first title, *Good Rockin' Tonight* was published in 1982, and Lantz has written a variety of books since, from serious young adult novels to funny middle grade stories to series books like "Hardy Boys" and "Sweet Valley Twins."

Born in 1952 in Trenton, New Jersey, and raised in Bucks County, Pennsylvania, Lantz displayed a passion for writing at a young age. Her father, an architect, would draw with her as she wrote and illustrated her own stories. As she grew up, she gained a reputation as a tomboy among her friends. "My stories were usually about war, or spies, and they were always violent," she once commented. "Despite this, my fifth-grade teacher encouraged my talent and allowed me to stay inside during recess to tape record my stories with my friends." While her early dreams involved growing up to become a famous writer, the Beatles' coming to the United States in 1964 changed everything for the twelve-year-old budding author. Lantz continued to write, but now wrote songs, accompanying herself on the guitar. After college, she moved to Boston, hoping to become a famous rock star. Despite many performances and lots of good times, she never landed an album deal, and she went back to school to become a children's librarian.

As a children's librarian, Lantz would take the children from her story hour to a local graveyard once a year to read them scary stories. "Yes, I took the kids to a nearby graveyard and scared the pants off them," Lantz told *SATA.* She continued, "After a couple of years I was having trouble finding new stories that were short, easy to read aloud, and really scary. In desperation, I wrote some myself. They were a big hit with the kids and that was when I first thought, hey, maybe I could write children's books." Her first attempts were picture-book texts, followed by a scary fantasy novel and two mysteries. Although none of these sold, Lantz continued to write, and her next novel, *Good Rockin' Tonight,* a title for young adults, was published.

While Lantz began her career by writing young adult novels loosely based on her own life, she eventually switched to middle-grade books, where she could add more humorous elements to her stories. In *Mom, There's a Pig in My Bed!,* Lantz tells the story of Dwight Ewing, who hopes that the earth will swallow him up, so he won't have to endure his embarrassing family. After moving them to a small town, Dwight's father draws all sorts of attention to the family through his determination to raise seeing-eye pigs for blind people who are allergic to dogs. As a way of saving face, Dwight convinces everyone that his father is really wealthy and is engaged in his present porcine pursuits in an attempt to educate his children as to the ways of regular folks. Along with the predicted backfire to Dwight's misrepresentation, *Mom, There's a Pig in My Bed!* contains "some very funny scenes" involving swine, as well as insight into the problems that can spring from even an innocent lie, according to *School Library Journal* contributor Nancy P. Reeder. In *Stepsister from the Planet Weird,* Lantz introduces readers to Megan, who is in despair over her mother's upcoming marriage because it will mean having a "perfect" stepsister, Ariel. The truth, however, is that Megan's new step-family are aliens. Though Ariel is popular at school, she misses her home planet, where she can be in her native gaseous form. Though Megan and Ariel hate each other, they team together in an effort to keep their parents from getting married. Lantz tells her tale in the form of diary entries from both Megan and Ariel, and the book's "zany humor" combines with the author's "wit . . . [and] character development" to result in a novel that appeals to even reluctant readers, in the opinion of *School Library Journal* reviewer Cheryl Cufari. A critic for *Publishers Weekly* called the novel "a light, fast read."

Although Lantz concentrated on writing for preteens during the 1980s and much of the 1990s, she returned to her focus on young adults with *Someone to Love* and *Fade Far Away*. In *Someone to Love,* published in 1997, fifteen-year-old Sara finds that her liberal ideals conflict with her parent's materialistic lifestyle. As her parents plan to adopt the baby of Iris, an unmarried mother who is extremely poor, Sara is drawn to Iris, who represents the independence, romance, and adulthood Sara dreams of. Sara encourages Iris to be a part of the child's life even after her parents adopt the baby; her parents disagree and threaten not to adopt the child. Hearing this, Sara convinces Iris to run away, and the two of them will raise the baby together. "The novel explores all sides of adoption very well," wrote Anne O'Malley in *Booklist*. Again focusing on a fifteen-year-old protagonist, *Fade Far Away* is narrated by Sienna, the artistic daughter of a famous sculptor and his wife, a woman obsessed with her husband's advancement in the arts community to the exclusion of all else, including her daughter. In a novel that *Kliatt* reviewer Claire Rosser called "intense and challenging," Sienna must contradict her mother and support her father's efforts to reevaluate his priorities after he is diagnosed with a brain tumor. "This emotionally charged coming-of-age story borrows the glamorous trappings of the art world," showing Sienna coming to terms with her father's failings and her own growing sense of self, according to a *Publishers Weekly* critic.

Lantz was selected by Roxy, a fashion brand, to launch a series of books about surfer girls called "Luna Bay." As author of the first several books, Lantz launched the world of five surfer girls living in Southern California and working as junior counselors at a surf camp run by one of the girl's parents. Roxanne Burg, writing for *School Library Journal* considered the series "Gidget for the 21st century." Lantz, a surfer herself, uses surf slang to make the world of the girls more real. "Some 7,200 people have signed up for an online book club where readers discuss the characters and their own lives," noted a reporter for *Knight Ridder/Tribune Business News*. The reporter added, "Lantz discusses the story lines with Roxy surf-team members, which helps keep the books authentic."

Lantz once told *SATA:* "I was an only child with loving parents who encouraged my creative impulses. When I was ten, I wanted to be a writer, an artist, and a boy. At thirteen I discovered the guitar, decided it was okay to be female, and spent the next years making music.

"My novels are about contemporary kids trying to discover who they are and what they believe in. My protagonists often feel pressured by their parents and their peers to behave in certain ways. In the course of the novel, the main character struggles to do what she or he thinks is right, despite outside influences.

"Most of my novels are set in the present and contain references to current clothes, movies, music, etc. The reasons are two-fold: (1) I find it natural to write about what I know. I was a consumer of popular culture (rock 'n' roll, fashion, movies, etc.) as a teenager and I still enjoy it (especially rock 'n' roll) so I include it in my books. (2) Kids like to read about their world and their problems, especially if the author is close enough to their world to write realistically about it. I think I can do that.

"For some reason I find it very easy to remember my pre-teen and teenage years. I can vividly recall my feelings when I first heard a rock 'n' roll record, when my mother caught me rolling around on the sofa with my boyfriend, when I learned that my father had died. At the same time, I can now view these events from an adult perspective.

"Both these views, I feel, are required to write juvenile novels. If the author can see the world through a child's eyes and nothing more, his book will be one-dimensional and claustrophobic. If he can only view kids from an adult perspective, his story will be manipulative and didactic. So far I think I've been able to integrate both perspectives. If I ever lose that ability, it will be time to stop writing juvenile novels and move on to something else."

In addition to continuing to write fiction, Lantz contributes articles to magazines and newspapers, and has dabbled in nonfiction with *Rock, Rap, and Rad: How to Be a Rock or Rap Star,* which *Voice of Youth Advocates* contributor Patrick Jones praised as "an interesting book aimed at all the teens who ever wanted to see their faces on MTV." She and her family live in Santa Barbara, California, where she enjoys visiting local schools to talk to budding authors.

Biographical and Critical Sources

PERIODICALS

Booklist, July, 1993, p. 1955; April 15, 1997, Anne O'Malley, review of *Someone to Love,* p. 1420; March 15, 1998, p. 1216; September 1, 2001, Lolly Gepson, review of *Stepsister from the Planet Weird,* p. 128.

Kirkus Reviews, February 1, 1997, p. 224.

Kliatt, May, 1998, Claire Rosser, review of *Fade Far Away,*
p. 7; January, 2002, Claire Rosser, review of *Letters
to Cupid.*

Knight Ridder/Tribune Business News, September 24,
2003, Catrine Johansson, "Huntington Beach, Calif.,
Apparel Brand Rides Book Series Wave."

New York Times, June 11, 2000, Laurel Graeber, "Somewhere Between Big Bird and Buffy," p. 4L.

Publishers Weekly, June 8, 1990, Diane Roback and Richard Donahue, review of *The Truth about Making Out,*
p. 55; November 22, 1991, review of *Dear Celeste,
My Life Is a Mess,* p. 57; January 6, 1997, review of
Someone to Love, p. 74; November 10, 1997, review
of *Stepsister from the Planet Weird,* p. 74; June 29,
1998, review of *Fade Far Away,* p. 60; January 3,
2000, review of *Love Song,* p. 76; June 23, 2003, review of *Pier Pressure,* p. 68.

School Library Journal, January, 1993, Nancy P. Reeder,
review of *Mom, There's a Pig in My Bed!,* pp. 100-01;
February, 1998, Cheryl Cufari, review of *Stepsister
from the Planet Weird,* p. 109; May, 2000, Elaine Ba-
ran Black, review of *Love Song,* p. 172; August, 2000,
Joanne K. Cecere, review of *A Royal Kiss,* p. 186;
March, 2001, Darlene Ford, review of *Stepsister from
the Planet Weird,* p. 88; February, 2004, Roxanne
Burg, review of *Pier Pressure,* p. 148.

Voice of Youth Advocates, April, 1993, Patrick Jones, review of *Rock, Rap, and Rad: How to Be a Rock or
Rap Star,* p. 55.

ONLINE

Francess Lantz's Home Page, http://www.silcom.com/
~writer (July 30, 2004).

Autobiography Feature

Francess L. Lantz

Francess L. Lantz contributed the following autobiographical essay to *SATA:*

Whohen I was born, the trumpets blared, the red carpet was rolled out, and the stars in the sky spelled
out FRANCESS.

Well, not quite, but my birth was definitely greeted
with delight at 55 Fairway Drive, Yardley, Pennsylvania.
That's because my mother was in her forties and had
suffered through three miscarriages before she became
pregnant with me. There had been no guarantee the
fourth pregnancy would be any different. The only cer-
tainty was that it would be her last.

And yet, despite the odds, there I was. The world's
most wanted child. Darling Francess, spelled with two
s's, just like princess.

Not surprisingly, I grew up feeling pretty special.
My parents and grandparents paid lots of attention to
me. They cooed and clapped when I walked, talked, or
stuck a green bean up my nose. So you can imagine
what they did when I drew pictures, made up stories,
sang and danced. The applause was deafening!

Children respond to praise, and I responded by doing more of what came naturally—being creative. My
father was an accomplished artist, and we spent many

happy hours drawing "tattoos" on each other's hands
and arms with ballpoint pens. My mother had written
poems and plays in her youth, and she eagerly typed up

*Lantz, age three, and her "glamourous" mother on the
sofa, 1955.*

Lantz, age six, with her father, grandparents, and cat, Jeepers, Christmas, 1958.

my stories with the correct spelling and punctuation. My grandfather was a wonderful fiddle player, and he never tired of playing "Turkey in the Straw" while I danced.

Life was good—except for one thing. My mother was a very fashionable woman. Her blond hair was always perfectly coiffed; her clothes were stylish. She thought I would be a junior version of her—a feminine little angel who loved pretty clothes and ribbons in her hair. But noooo. I hated having my hair combed, I chose pants over dresses, and I liked cap guns better than dolls.

Then, when I was four years old, I had a revelation. The activities I liked (playing Army, writing stories about war, climbing trees) were considered boy activities; the clothes I liked (shorts, T-shirts and Army helmets) were considered boy clothes. Therefore, I could not be a girl. I had to become a boy.

Okay, I know that sounds kind of crazy. But remember, this was the 1950s, when male and female roles were clearly defined and quite distinct. Boys were supposed to be strong and brave and athletic, and they could grow up to be anything they wanted. Girls were

docile and demure, and they were supposed to grow up to be wives and mothers, or (if you absolutely had to get a job) teachers, librarians, nurses, or secretaries.

I wanted to be strong, brave, and athletic, and join the Marines. In my little four-year-old head, that meant I had to be a boy. So I set out to become one. I insisted my parents stop calling me Francess and start calling me Tommy. I begged my mother for a short haircut and boy clothes. My Christmas list was filled with boy toys like plastic soldiers, race cars, and baseball cards.

To my parents' credit, they didn't go ballistic. They humored me and told themselves it was just a phase. I was allowed to get a short, pixie haircut. I had to wear dresses to school and church, but I could wear shorts or pants at home. At Christmas, I got all the boy toys I requested, plus a few girl toys I hadn't. My parents even called me Tommy, although they couldn't keep the amused smile off their faces.

Well, the years passed and my tomboy phase didn't go away. I hung out with three boys in my neighborhood. Their names were Johnny, Artie, and Richard, and they used my lowly wannabe status to make my life miserable. They were constantly daring me to do rotten things, like smash the neighbor's jack-o-lantern or drag the nerdy kid from down the street into the bushes and pull down his pants. I did everything they asked me to (and usually got in trouble for it) because I desperately wanted to be accepted as one of them—a macho, rule-breaking, take-no-prisoners boy.

There were good times too. We lived across from a golf course and most of our adventures happened there. We found old golf balls in the bushes, cleaned them up, and sold them to the golfers for a dime or twenty-five cents. We bought Cokes and candy bars at the pro shop. We played King of the Hill on the greens, caught frogs in the water trap, and sledded down the hill behind the seventeenth hole.

We did lots of rowdy things too, like soap our neighbors' windows and toilet paper their bushes on Mischief Night (the night before Halloween). Once we climbed a tall maple tree on the golf course, waited until a golfer got ready to tee off, and screamed just as he connected with the ball. The guy hit into the rough, then cursed and looked around, wondering where the heck that sound had come from. We hid among the leaves, snickering with malevolent delight.

I had female friends too. My best friend was a classmate named Dottie, and I loved her because when we played Army, she let me be the Drill Sergeant and boss her around. That sounds mean, I know, but after being lorded over all weekend by the neighborhood boys, I needed someone who would let me lord over her. We did other activities together, too, like Girls Scouts and school band.

Fifth grade was the height of my tomboy phase. Like the ten-year-old boys who were my friends, I was mesmerized by blood and guts and war and violence. I read anthologies of horror stories and drew pictures of people in black hoods torturing unwilling victims. I watched the movie *West Side Story* and completely missed the anti-violence message. All I saw was a bunch of really cool dudes carrying switchblades and acting tough. Inspired, I decided to create my own fictional gang, the Ravens, and write stories about them. In every story, at least one person was violently murdered.

My poor parents, who up to now had been extremely tolerant of my weirdness, were getting nervous. If this tomboy thing was just a phase, why wasn't it passing? My mother told me later that she and my father considered sending me to a psychiatrist. They might have done it, too, if it wasn't for the influence of my wonderful fifth grade teacher.

When I walked into her classroom, Jane Anstine was twenty-four years old and in her second year of teaching. She was fun-loving, enthusiastic, and eager to do whatever it took to get her kids excited about learning. She took one look at me and realized right away I was a good kid. I got *A*s and *B*s, I had friends, I didn't pull the wings off flies. In short, the odds were good that I wasn't going to grow up to be a sniper. So instead of being shocked by my stories of death and de-

Lantz as a tomboy, 1961.

struction, she encouraged me to write more. She even let my friends and me stay in at recess and record my stories on the school tape recorder (with background music and gory sound effects).

Even though my parents tried to tolerate my tomboy craziness, I knew they were hoping it would soon be over with. Miss Anstine didn't feel that way. She liked me just the way I was. In fact, she made me feel that my writing and artwork were something special, that *I* was something special—not just to my immediate family, but to an objective outside observer. She made me want to keep writing, keep drawing, keep creating.

Miss Anstine was such a positive influence on me that I stayed in touch with her through the years. In fact, we're now good friends. I even dedicated one of my novels, *Mom, There's a Pig in my Bed,* to her. And, I'm pleased to report, she's still a teacher and still encouraging kids to laugh, learn, and be themselves.

The next three years were just as critical to my development as Ms. Anstine's class was, but in a completely different way. For starters, I entered adolescence. My body was changing and I could no longer ignore the fact that I was, in reality, a girl. Then I discovered boys, and suddenly I didn't mind so much.

It's not as if I turned into the feminine princess my mother wanted me to be. Far from it! I still wrote gory stories, although now they were about spies (the subject of my favorite TV show, *The Man from U.N.C.L.E.*), not street gangs. But the big difference was that there were male spies *and* female spies in my new stories, and when they weren't assassinating enemy agents, they were making out.

I wasn't making out in real life—not yet—but I sure was interested. I was interested in fashion now too, and the latest rock music, and everything that was hip and happening and cool.

In order to study coolness at close range, my best friends and I decided to spy on a group of popular tenth graders at our school. We followed them around, eavesdropped on their conversations, taking notes on everything we found out. Pretending to be tenth graders ourselves, we wrote them love letters which we shoved in their lockers when no one was looking. We continued our deception until Bill, the leader of the clique, figured out our real identities. Uh-oh, payback time. One day, while I was following him down a crowded hallway, he suddenly stopped, smiled condescendingly, and patted me on the head. Needless to say, that was the end of our coolness fact-finding mission.

I was a big reader in junior high, and not a very discriminating one. I read any paperback that caught my eye at the drugstore—*The Guinness Book of World Records, Black Like Me* (the true story of a white journalist who masqueraded as a black man to study race relations in America), *Mad* magazine, an anthology of science fiction stories by Harlan Ellison called *I Have No Mouth and I Must Scream,* Marvel Comics, and lots of James Bond novels. High culture, low culture—it was all the same to me. If a book moved me in some way, I liked it.

Even more important to me than books, however, was music. I was already playing the clarinet in school, and I'd gone through a brief infatuation with the drums. Then, when I was in seventh grade, Beatlemania hit America. Like every other red-blooded American girl, I was madly, passionately in love with the Beatles (John was my favorite, then Paul) and all the other bands that followed in their wake. My bedroom walls were plastered with photos of the Fab Four, the Rolling Stones, Herman's Hermits, Paul Revere and the Raiders. I spent countless hours in front of the stereo, ear plastered to the speaker, trying to figure out the lyrics to my favorite songs.

But there was one difference between me and my girlfriends. Like them, I swooned over the Beatles and

With Darren the dog, 1962.

dreamed of meeting them. But unlike my friends, I also wanted to *be* a Beatle. I wanted to play the guitar, I wanted to write songs, I wanted to perform in a stadium filled with screaming, love-struck fans.

So I asked my parents for a guitar and I got one for my thirteenth birthday. It was acoustic, not electric, but I wasn't complaining. Soon I was taking lessons at the local music store, learning folk songs from the *Joan Baez Songbook*. As soon as I could play two chords, I wrote my first song, "Why, Peter, Why?" Okay, the lyrics—about my latest crush—weren't exactly deathless, but they definitely were heartfelt.

Looking back, I wish I'd had the chutzpah to demand electric guitar lessons. I wish I'd started a band and learned to rock out. Who knows? I might have become the first female heavy metal star. But girls just didn't *do* that back in 1965. And at the self-conscious age of thirteen, with my "call me Tommy" days behind me, I didn't have the courage to buck the system. Besides, I was too busy making music.

Soon I had stopped writing stories, and I rarely took out my drawing pad. All my creative energy went into songwriting. I discovered that I liked minor chords and major sevenths, and I experimented with interesting, unusual chord changes. Along with the British invasion groups, I was listening to folk singers like Tom Paxton, Donovan, Bob Dylan, Simon and Garfunkel, and the Chad Mitchell Trio.

When I wasn't doing schoolwork, playing music, or watching TV (*Wild, Wild West, I Spy, Mission: Impossible, The Avengers*) I was skateboarding. Then my family went on a vacation to the New Jersey shore and I discovered surfing. My friend Nanette and I begged my parents to let us rent a board, and soon we were paddling out into the shorebreak. All we caught was whitewater, but when I stood up and felt the wave push me forward, my life was changed.

I must have been the only teenage girl in Pennsylvania who subscribed to *Surfer* magazine. I knew the names of all the surf stars—Greg Noll, Mark Doyle, Mickey Dora, Nat Young—and I dreamed of moving to California and visiting the famous surf spots I'd read about, places with exotic names like San Onofre, Rincon, and Malibu.

Then, in tenth grade, something happened that turned my world upside down. My father began to mysteriously lose weight. He spent a lot of time going to doctors and finally, he went into the hospital for a big operation. When he came home, he started to get better—but only a little. Soon, he was losing weight again. Meanwhile, my grandmother, who lived with us, had a stroke and died.

After my grandmother's funeral, my mother moved my father's architectural office into the spare bedroom. But Dad spent very little time at his drafting table. Mostly, he just lay in bed.

Lantz (on right) surfing at the New Jersey shore with friend, Nanette, 1967.

Something horrible was happening, I knew it. My mother, however, continued to act very normal and upbeat, and she seemed to expect me to do the same. My role, as best as I could discern it, was to continue living my life as if nothing unusual was happening.

I did my best, but inside I was freaking out. My father never got out of bed anymore; my mother spent her nights sleeping in a reclining chair by his side. I lay in my bed, eyes wide open, body coiled like a snake. Every time my mother walked into the hallway, my stomach clenched into a painful knot. *She's coming to tell me he's dead,* I thought. I held my breath and waited. When she walked back into his room, I let myself breathe again.

One day my mother sat me down and said, "Your father has cancer. He isn't going to get better." But by then I was in denial myself. "Yes, he will," I insisted. Before she could respond, I got up and walked away.

Six months after my father's operation, an ambulance took him to the hospital. He didn't look like my father anymore. He had sunken cheeks, glazed eyes, and the body of a concentration camp victim. I couldn't bear to look at him.

Dottie and I were still friends, but she lived at the Jersey shore now. One day she called me up and invited me down for the weekend. My mother said, "I don't think you should go. Your father isn't going to live much longer."

I didn't want to hear that, and I definitely didn't want to see it. So I talked my mother into letting me go to the shore. I arrived at Dottie's house in giddy high spirits, like someone who had just been released from prison. We had a great evening together, talking, giggling, and listening to music.

The next morning, Dottie's mother walked into the room and kissed me. She had barely even touched me before. What was *that* about?

"Your father died this morning," she said quietly.

I cried, but only for a minute. I had learned my mother's lesson well. Act normal, stay upbeat. Deny, deny, deny. So I slipped my psyche into a set of emotional armor that would take me years to shed.

Eleventh grade was my rebellious year. I didn't want to be home with my grieving mother, so I hung out with my new friends, the freaks. This was the hippie era, 1968, and the freaks were the long-haired kids who listened to psychedelic music, protested the Vietnam War, and took drugs. They were a motley crew—male and female, rich and poor, college-bound kids and future drop-outs. But we had one thing in common—we didn't like our lives and we were looking for an escape.

I could have gotten heavily into drugs and screwed up my life completely, but luckily for me, a new, positive influence arrived just when I needed it most. The church I attended, St. Andrew's Episcopal, had recently hired a new priest. In fact, my father had served on the vestry that selected him. Frank T. Griswold, III, or Father G., as I called him, started on the job only a few months before my father died. He was young, handsome, energetic, and ready to shake things up.

One day, Father G. saw me sitting with the youth group kids, morosely strumming my guitar. He asked me if I wanted to play and sing in church on Sunday, and in that instant, the dark clouds began to part. Soon I was performing folk songs (religious and secular) at the ten o'clock service, and, eventually, writing songs with Father G. I also created posters to decorate the parish house, and even wrote some prayers that were recited in church.

Father Griswold gave me more than a place to perform. He and his wife Phoebe also gave me their friendship. When I was feeling sad about my dad or angry at my mom, they welcomed me into their home and lent a sympathetic ear. They took me seriously and treated me like an adult. They listened to my thoughts on life and love, religion and politics, and they didn't laugh.

Father G. encouraged me to attend a program for teens at an Episcopal conference center outside of Philadelphia. It was a fabulous experience! I worked with disadvantaged kids in the inner city, met a lot of liberal-thinking, creative teenagers just like me, and found a new audience for my songs.

When I came back, I shared my deepest longing and my secret fear with Father G. "I want to find a way to make a living doing something creative when I grow up," I told him. "If I don't succeed—if I have to settle for a regular job—I don't think I'll be able to stand it." How I was going to make that happen was still unclear to me. I just knew I wanted it with all my heart.

Like Jane Anstine, Father Griswold was a huge influence in my life. Today Father G. is the Presiding Bishop of the Episcopal Church in United States. When I visit New York, he always finds time to see me. I dedicated one of the "Overnight Sensation" books to him, which he claims raised his "coolness quotient" considerably.

The summer of eleventh grade brought a new adventure. I applied to be an American Field Service exchange student and, after much essay-writing and many interviews, I was chosen. AFS matches students and families by interests, not by country. I had to be open to going almost anywhere in the world, and I was. In fact, I remember telling everyone I hoped I'd be sent somewhere really exotic, like Africa or India.

Well, I got my wish. I was matched with a theater- and music-loving family in Bombay, India. And I have to give my mother a lot of credit. She was still getting over the death of her husband, and now her daughter was leaving her, going halfway around the world for the entire summer. But after her initial shock ("India? Are you sure they didn't mean Indiana?"), she was completely encouraging. I'm sure she spent the summer biting her nails, wondering if she'd ever see her only child alive again, but she never let me see that. She was always positive and enthusiastic.

My summer was very challenging and very wonderful. AFS encourages its exchange students to immerse themselves in their new culture. I wasn't a tourist—far from it. I was supposed to eat with my new family, dress like my new sister, join in with my new family's daily activities. For me, that meant eating spicy foods after a lifetime of bland American cuisine. It also meant brushing my teeth with water that was far from clean by U.S. standards. As a result, I had diarrhea on and off the entire summer! But when I wasn't in the bathroom, I was having lots of new and exciting experiences. I took sitar lessons. I visited the Taj Mahal. I watched my Indian family act in a play (directed by my Indian dad). I visited a Bollywood movie set. I taught my rock 'n' roll-loving Indian brother some new guitar chords. I got my ears pierced. I learned how to wear a sari. I also saw overpopulation and poverty like I'd never imagined.

By the end of the summer, I'd come to realize that the United States isn't the center of the universe. There's a big world out there filled with fascinating people, amazing cultures, beautiful sites and scenery. I wanted to see more of it!

The first day of twelfth grade, I ate lunch with my old friends, the freaks. I tried to tell them about my ex-

Wearing a sari in Bombay, India, 1969.

periences in India, but their only response was, "Man, you must have smoked some great dope over there!" I looked around the table and saw a bunch of burned-out losers who couldn't see beyond their next toke. It was time to move on.

My mother says I complained a lot during my senior year of high school, and that I was more than ready to go to college. Looking back, however, I remember it as a great year. Instead of belonging to a clique like so many high school students, I had friends from every group. I kept a few of my freaky friends, the ones who weren't major druggies. I was also friends with the brainiacs who were in my honors classes. Then the president of the student council appointed me to be head of the Human Relations Committee (a committee created to do community service projects) and suddenly I was hanging out with the popular crowd as well.

Meanwhile, I was still singing at church and at local coffeehouses. My songs were becoming more sophisticated, my guitar playing was improving, my voice was growing richer and stronger. I was listening to music by singer-songwriters like James Taylor, Joni Mitchell, and Crosby, Stills, and Nash. More and more, I was thinking that music was my calling.

When it came time to apply to college, I really didn't know what I wanted. My mother was pushing for

a traditional school that was close to home. I probably would have preferred a funky, alternative college in California. But my mother was paying, so I ended up at Dickinson College, a small liberal arts school in central Pennsylvania.

I knew I wanted to major in English or music, but I wasn't sure which. I still loved to write, and I'd learned a lot from my high school teachers. Miss Tindall, my eleventh grade teacher, had been strict and serious. She'd taught us how to write essays that were well-organized, logical, and grammatically correct. Mr. Corbett, my twelfth grade teacher, had been sensitive and creative. He'd read us poetry and given us lots of creative writing assignments.

But when I walked into my first Survey of English Literature class, I knew I wasn't an English major. The class was huge, the professor droned on endlessly (when he wasn't snorting a Vicks Nasal Inhaler), and the papers we were expected to churn out weekly were long and dull. The more quotes from the book you could cram into your paper, the better your grade. Whether or not you actually understood what you were reading—that seemed to be secondary.

Then I walked into History of Music 101. Talk about a mind-blowing experience! The professor was practically jumping up and down with excitement as he talked about Gregorian chant and Medieval madrigals. And when he played the music—oh my god! It sounded like nothing I had every heard before. Weird open harmonies, strange high-pitched voices, bizarre song structures—I loved it! I knew then and there I had to major in music.

During my four years at Dickinson I was introduced to hundreds of new, brain-expanding ideas, both in and out of class. I studied music, philosophy, art, and history. I learned to play the flute and the piano. I took creative writing courses, wrote poetry, and helped to edit the school literature review. I performed in a live theater show that was a combination talk show and comedy review. I attended dozens of blow-your-socks-off rock concerts. I fell in love; I fell out of love. I had my heart broken; I broke a few hearts. I wrote dozens of new songs and played my guitar at the weekly school coffeehouse.

But there was something missing in my life. As an only child, I think I secretly yearned for an intense, sibling-style relationship. And losing my father at age fifteen made me long for a father figure. I solved both problems—or so I thought—by falling in love and getting married between my junior and senior years.

My new husband and I soon left Pennsylvania and moved to Boston, Massachusetts. After twenty years in small towns, Boston was a thrill. I loved the old brick houses, the cluttered bookstores, the movie theatres showing foreign films, the rock clubs and coffeehouses. Skateboarding, surfing, sledding at the seventeenth hole—all that seemed very long ago and far away. I was a city girl now.

I finished my last semester of college at Boston University, where I took music courses that weren't offered at Dickinson. My favorite was a composing seminar in which I wrote the first movement of a string quartet. Meanwhile, I dreamed of being discovered by a famous music producer who would turn me into the next Joni Mitchell or Janis Joplin. It didn't happen, but I did meet a talented guitar player named Jeff who liked my music enough to want to perform with me.

Soon we were performing at every coffeehouse, club, and art gallery that would have us. To make money, I was working at a succession of boring temp jobs, typing, filing, answering phones. More than ever, I felt I had to find a way to make a living by being creative. I was sure that if I had to work in an office full-time, I would die.

I thought about starting an actual band—drums, bass, electric guitars—and moving on to bigger venues. But it seemed like a daunting task. I'd never played electric guitar before, never jammed with a group of musicians. It seemed so much easier to just keep playing acoustic music with Jeff and waiting for my big break.

With Jeff producing, I eventually recorded a number of my songs with a full band. It was so much fun to sing with all that sound and intensity behind me! Eagerly, I mailed my demos off to record companies (yep, they still made vinyl records back then). Then I sat back and waited . . . and waited . . .

Well, as you probably guessed, I never became a famous rock star. Looking back, it's easy to see why. I loved to write songs and sing them, but everything else about the music business left me cold. I didn't like practicing every day, and I wasn't serious about improving my skills. I hated hanging out in dark, smoky clubs at night. I didn't understand the importance of networking with music industry types. Heck, I didn't even *like* most of the music people I met. They weren't bad people, just awfully one-dimensional. They ate, drank, and breathed rock 'n' roll. I was into everything—books, food, movies, art, squash (the game, not the vegetable), travel, and more.

Finally, just when I thought I couldn't stand another temp job, my mother announced that she would pay for me to go to graduate school. Great idea, I thought, but what should I study? Music? No, I didn't love classical music enough to devote my life to it. Teaching? No, I didn't feel committed enough to take on a classroom of unruly elementary school children.

Then I remembered a woman I'd known who'd gotten her master's in Library Science. Perfect! It only took a year, you didn't have to take a big exam to get in, and you didn't have to write a thesis. Plus, you got to hang out in libraries and read books all day. What could be bad?

I applied to Simmons College's School of Library Science and I got in. Piece of cake! But when I showed up for my first class, reality set in. Most of the students were middle-aged working librarians who wanted to further their careers by getting an M.L.S. They were quiet, reserved, serious—the total opposite of twenty-four-year-old, rock 'n' roll Fran. Plus, the classes (with titles like Reference Methods and Beginning Cataloging) were a big snooze.

Luckily, I found the few other students who were my age and we quickly formed the young, hip librarians clique. Then I took a Children's Literature course and realized that I liked children's books, and—come to think of it—I'd always liked children too. In fact, looking back over my life, it seemed I'd always been around kids. I babysat. I taught guitar lessons to ten-year-olds. I was a volunteer music teacher in the Boston schools.

Hey, maybe being a children's librarian wouldn't be half bad!

A year and a half later, I had my degree and a job as the children's librarian in Dedham, Massachusetts, a suburb of Boston. Boy, had my life changed! Instead of spending my nights in cramped, smoky rock clubs, I was spending my days in a spacious, sunny library. Instead of hanging out with moody musicians, I was surrounded by exuberant children. I was still playing my guitar, but now I was teaching folk songs to preschoolers.

I spent three years at the Dedham Public Library, and I loved it. I wasn't one of those shy, fingers-to-the-lips librarians. I liked action! I gave book talks in the schools. I brought authors into the library to speak to the kids. I planned huge, circus-like summer reading programs. I ran a fourth through sixth grade after-school club in which we sang folk songs, went on scavenger hunts, made craft projects, and rode horses. And every

Playing guitar, 1971.

Halloween, I put on a Graveyard Storyhour. We met at the library after dark and, with only a kerosene lantern to light our way, we trooped down to the local church graveyard. The children sat on the grass; I sat on a gravestone and told stories to scare their little pants off! It was a huge success!

Working at the library taught me a number of things. I found out I loved kids, but I hated the monotony and lack of autonomy that comes with a full-time, forty hour a week job. I also realized that being a librarian wasn't enough for me. I kept thinking about what I'd told Father Griswold all those years ago: "I want to find a way to make a living doing something creative when I grow up. If I don't—if I have to settle for a regular job—I don't think I'll be able to stand it."

Being a children's librarian *was* creative, in a way. I'd describe it as a cross between a teacher and an events planner. But I wanted to be an artist. The only problem was I still didn't know what kind of artist I wanted to be, or how I was going to make it happen. But, as it turns out, the answer was right in front of me.

At library school and at my job, I was constantly reading children's books. I especially enjoyed the wacky science fiction of Daniel Pinkwater, the spooky fantasies of John Bellairs, the funny contemporary stories of Judy Blume and Paula Danzinger, and the angst-filled teen fiction of Paul Zindel and M. E. Kerr. Gradually, it dawned on me: Once upon a time, I liked to write stories. Maybe I could write stories again. Hey, maybe I could be a children's book author!

My first attempts at children's fiction were the scary stories I created for the annual Graveyard Storyhour. That was easy—I just thought back to the gross, gore-filled stories of my youth and let my imagination run wild. Then I tried to write picture books. That was harder. The ideas didn't come as easily, the words didn't flow as freely. Still, I churned out a couple. *Roger the Rock* was about a boy so lazy he decided on a career as a boulder. *Sweet Pea and the Road Rodents* was a tall tale about a six-inch-tall girl who gets kidnapped by biker rats.

I typed up my scary stories and my picture books, and sent them off to a few well-respected publishing houses. Soon I was the proud owner of a large pile of rejection slips. But I also got a letter from an editor at Little, Brown and Company telling me she liked *Sweet Pea* and was showing it to her boss.

Oh my gosh! I was being considered by a major publisher! Undoubtedly, I would receive an acceptance phone call any minute.

But it never came. Instead, I received a polite rejection letter informing me that ultimately they'd decided to pass on my manuscript. I was disappointed, but not defeated. An editor had liked my story. Certainly, other editors would like it too. And if I wrote another story, and another, eventually one of them was bound to sell.

Next, I wrote a novel, a mystery set in a town like Yardley, starring a group of kids who hang out at the local golf course. Then I wrote a fantasy novel about a thirteen-year-old girl who learns her grandmother is a sorceress.

More submissions, more rejections. I had amassed over fifty by now. But some of the rejections praised my kid-friendly writing style and my believable dialogue. I knew I could sell something, I just *knew* it. If only I had more time to devote to my writing . . .

That problem was solved when my friends Morris and Elaine had a baby. They needed a nanny, and I begged them to hire me. Never mind that I had never fed, changed, or even held an infant in my life. I was great with kids, so I was sure I'd be great with babies too. Besides, I was dying to leave the library.

Luckily for me, Morris and Elaine said yes, and soon I was spending every afternoon caring for baby Benjamin. Turns out I *was* good with babies, and I loved my new role as Assistant Mommy. Plus, I had my mornings free to write.

But write what? More picture books? Another fantasy novel? No, it was time for something new.

I'm sure that at some point in my life I'd heard the phrase "write what you know." I'm sure you've heard it too. Well, take it from me—it's good advice, especially for beginners.

Many people think their real life is too dull, too ordinary to make a gripping novel. But if you base your book on places, people, situations, and/or emotions you've intimately experienced, it will make your writing flow. Suddenly, your stories will be more honest, more natural, more believable, more . . . well, *real*.

Notice I said *base* your novel on your real life. That doesn't mean write your autobiography. Fiction—especially children's fiction—is more intense, more structured, and more compact than real life. Think of it as starting with your feet on the ground and your head in the clouds. You've got the real life setting and situations (in your feet—feel them?); now use your imagination (your head) and ask yourself "what if?"

Anyway, that's what I did. I started with a character—a fifteen-year-old girl who wants to take guitar lessons. She dreams of someday joining a full-on rock band, but her parents will only spring for folk guitar lessons. Meanwhile, she's spending the summer babysitting a neighbor's toddler.

Sound familiar? It sure did to me. It was my life as a teen mixed with my current life as a nanny.

Next, I let my imagination fly. What if this girl decides to sneak behind her parents' back and take electric guitar lessons? What if she secretly joins a rock band led by a charismatic but self-centered lead guitarist (loosely based on a boyfriend I had in high school)? And what if this guy starts pressuring her to take a walk on the wild side because (as he puts it), "You have to be a rebel to play rock 'n' roll"?

Lantz and best friend, Dottie, Santa Barbara, CA, 1987.

I was inspired and started writing. Back then, there weren't personal computers. I wrote the novel in a loose-leaf binder and then typed the final draft on a typewriter. The end result was *Good Rockin' Tonight,* my first novel for young adults. I sent it out and received a couple of encouraging rejections, but no offers.

Then I learned another important lesson about writing—the business side, that is. It's good to network. At the time, I was writing book reviews for a library publication called *Kliatt*. I told the editors that I was trying to get published and they suggested I call their friend, an editor at Addison-Wesley. Soon I was sitting in the editor's office, showing her my manuscripts. A few weeks later, she bought *Good Rockin' Tonight.*

I was in ecstasy! At last I had found a way to make money by being creative. I was a professional writer! I called everyone I knew, starting with my mother and Father Griswold, and told them the good news.

The book was published in the fall of 1982. It was so thrilling to read my name on the cover! And there on the back flap was my photograph. It was just as good as seeing my photo on an album cover—maybe better, because I didn't have to hang out in any dark, smoky rock clubs to make it happen.

I couldn't wait to start my next book. I wanted to write about a teenage boy with a fatal brain tumor who decides to commit suicide. This book wouldn't be based on my real life, but who cared? I was ready to sink my teeth into something deep, serious, and philosophical.

Naturally, I planned to discuss my proposal to my new editor. But then I received a letter informing me that Addison-Wesley had decided to stop publishing children's books. The fall list—the one *Good Rockin' Tonight* was on—would be their last.

I didn't know it then, but this was a harbinger of things to come. Almost every time I've found a publisher that likes my work, they either get bought by a larger conglomerate or change their business plan. Either way, I get left behind in the wreckage. Same with editors. I hook up with one who likes my work and after a book or two she leaves the company—or even worse, quits the business!

Well, at least *something* was going my way—I now had an agent. She pointed out that teen romance novels were selling and suggested I write one. It looked easy and fun, so I put my suicide novel on hold and wrote a romance—then another, and another, and another.

But writing teen romances wasn't exactly challenging. I wanted to work on a story that asked deeper questions than, "Does he think I'm cute?" I trotted out my suicide novel, but my agent thought it would be hard to sell with just a proposal. She suggested I write the entire novel and get back to her.

I'd sold my romance novels from only one chapter and an outline. It was so simple that I'd become spoiled. So I came up with Plan B. I wrote an outline for a series. It was called *Birds of a Feather,* and it was about four girls who audition to be in a New York rock band. They soon discover that the mastermind behind the band is a Svengali-like producer who wants to turn them into a teeny-bopper hit machine. Will the girls sell out—and possibly become mega-stars—or hang onto their ideals and make music that comes from the heart?

When a publisher decided to buy my proposal, I was over the moon. I was going to write something serious, something real, something meaningful, right? Wrong!

I was assigned an editor who, I'm sure, had never been to a rock concert in her life. The first thing she asked me to do was change one of the main characters. C.C. is a rich girl who hates her life. At the end of book one, she skips out of her debutante ball to perform with the band. But my editor wanted to tone down her rebellion. "What if she goes to her debutante ball and finds out it's actually kind of fun?" she suggested.

Soon, my editor and I were fighting about everything. I, seeing myself as the misunderstood artist, dug my heels in. My editor, who viewed this series as a commercial venture, not a great work of art, thought I was being a royal pain. The truth lay somewhere in between.

Two books in the series (retitled "Overnight Sensation") were published, but neither the publisher nor I were very happy with them. Well, at least I'd learned another valuable lesson about the publishing business: find out the company's plans for your book before you sign on the dotted line. This is especially true if you're selling a proposal. Who will be your editor? Does he have the same vision for the book that you do? Does he want changes, and are they changes you can live with?

When "Overnight Sensation" fizzled, I panicked. Would I ever sell another book? When I was asked to write a *Sweet Valley Twins* novel, I jumped at it. Soon, I was writing for other established series. I was a hired hand, working on a deadline. My name didn't even appear on the title page.

Series writing wasn't all bad, however. I learned how to craft a tight outline, how to write fast, and how to work with an editor. But I was starting to feel like the girls in "Overnight Sensation." I was writing for money, not love. It was time to produce something from my heart.

So I returned to the childhood pond and threw in my line. Soon I was reminiscing about my seventh grade adventures, spying on the popular kids to learn how to be cool. There had to be a book in there somewhere . . .

There was and it became my first novel for middle grade readers, *The Truth about Making Out.* It had a tight plot and lots of humor. Why, I wondered, hadn't I written humor before? I'd grown up reading *Mad* magazine, watching *Laugh-In,* and listening to Jonathan Winters and Bill Cosby albums. I loved to laugh, and I loved to make other people laugh. Now I could do both with my writing.

If you've written as many books as I have (thirty-five and counting), you eventually have to look beyond your real life for ideas. I keep my eyes and ears open, always on the lookout for characters and situations that can be developed into novels. Once, for example, I read an article in *The Smithsonian Magazine* about the popularity of pigs as pets. According to some scientists, pigs are smarter than dogs.

Suddenly, a character popped into my head—a wacky, eccentric father who wants to train seeing-eye pigs for blind people who are allergic to dogs. His two younger children love the idea, but his oldest son, thirteen-year-old Dwight, is so embarrassed by his weirdo family that he tells his friends a big, whopping lie. The idea turned into the novel *Mom, There's A Pig in My Bed!*

A news article about an Ohio restaurant that served adults in one room and children in another led to *Spinach with Chocolate Sauce.* I dreamed up a couple who owns a hip Hollywood restaurant that caters to babies and toddlers. Puck, the family's twelve-year-old son, is forced to work there, feeding and entertaining the screaming brats.

Some books are inspired by reading other authors. I adored *The Hitchhiker's Guide to the Galaxy* by Douglas Adams, and Bruce Coville's *My Teacher Is an Alien.* So I decided to write my own funny alien story. I came up with two—*Neighbors from Outer Space* and *Stepsister from the Planet Weird,* which was made into a Disney Channel Original Movie.

Many authors have horror stories about selling their books to Hollywood, but I'm not one of them. Maybe because I'm a big movie fan (I've written screenplays, and I've reviewed movies for a weekly newspaper), I knew what to expect. A movie company options your book. Then they change it into something that only vaguely resembles your original story. Hey, folks, that's Hollywood.

So I wasn't alarmed when I saw the TV movie of *Stepsister.* In fact, I was ecstatic! Sure, they'd changed plenty of things—the surfing scenes in my novel had become windsurfing scenes, my explanation of why the aliens had come to Earth had been altered, and the climax of the story had been changed to add more conflict and zaniness. But the characters were just as I'd written them, and the actors played them perfectly. The humor was still there, and the theme was in tact. And it certainly was a thrill to see the words "Based on the novel by Francess Lantz" flashing across my TV screen!

Surfing in Malibu, 2002.

Every once in awhile, the idea for a book appears out of nowhere. I was walking to a Starbucks in Palm Springs, California, when some words suddenly popped in my consciousness. *I'm looking for love. Mind-bending, heart-thumping, soul-stirring love.* Since I wasn't actively looking for love at the time, I didn't know what to make of such an unusual declaration. Then it hit me—this is one of my characters talking.

I stopped and listened. "The kind you read about in romance novels," she continued. "The kind you see on TV and in the movies. I'm talking sweep-you-off-your-feet, too-excited-to-eat Love with a capital L."

I ran to Starbucks, borrowed a pen, and wrote the words on a napkin. But when I returned home, my character didn't have anything more to say. So I put the napkin in a file folder and forgot about it. A few months later, an editor at American Girl asked me if I had any good ideas for a middle grade novel. I retrieved the napkin and asked myself why this girl was so desperate to find love. The answer—and the many plot twists that followed—became the novel *Letters to Cupid.*

Not all my books have been funny middle grade novels. I've written two nonfiction books too. The first, *Rock, Rap, and Rad,* tells everything you need to know

to start your own rock band. The second, *Be a Star!,* explains how to make it as a child actor. My research strategy was simple; I just asked myself what I'd want to know if I was a twelve-year-old aspiring musician or actor. Then I sought out people who knew the answers, including producers, agents, professional rock and rap performers, and TV stars. My credentials as an author got me into some very cool places, including behind the scenes at a major rock concert, and onto the set of a hit TV show.

I finally returned to young adult fiction with my novel, *Someone to Love.* It's the story of Sara, a rebellious fifteen-year-old whose parents decide to adopt a baby. Sara befriends the eighteen-year-old birthmother, Iris—a move that threatens to sabotage the fragile adoption process. Like all my books except my first, I sold *Someone to Love* on the strength of a proposal. Then I panicked.

I was about to write a hardcover young adult novel. It needed to be longer than my previous books, more complex, with richer characters and top-notch writing. Furthermore, the issues I wanted to raise in this novel—about the challenges and ultimate benefits of open adoption—were of special importance to me. I'm the mother of an adopted child, my wonderful son, Preston. I wanted to write a book he could read someday, a book that would make him feel good about himself and his origins.

Could I pull it off? Could I write a novel that was better than anything I'd ever written before?

It wasn't easy, and much of the time, I had no idea if I would succeed—or I would even finish. In fact, I had to ask for more time, and the novel's publication date was postponed. Ultimately, however, I think *Someone to Love* is one of the best books I've written.

Interestingly, the novel didn't receive very good reviews. Many reviewers felt that Sara was unsympathetic, and that readers wouldn't identify with her self-centered world view. Teens, however, seemed to understand Sara completely, and I felt vindicated when the novel was selected as an ABA "Best Book for Young Adults" *and* an IRA "Young Adult Choice."

Remember that book I wanted to write about the teenage brain tumor patient who commits suicide? Almost fifteen years after I first had the idea, I finally returned to it. By the time I sat down to write *Fade Far Away,* however, I had made major changes in the storyline. The boy had become a man, a world-famous sculptor named Hugh Scully, and the main character had become his fifteen-year-old daughter, Sienna. Although suicide is still an essential element of the novel, the real story is the relationship between Sienna and her dad.

The plot of *Fade Far Away* has nothing to do with my real life. However, the emotions Sienna feels when her father is diagnosed with cancer are based on the confused emotions I experienced when my father grew ill. Like me, she's on the outside looking in, unable to find a way to help.

Writing the novel was an intense experience. In the past, I had viewed fiction writing as a godlike profession. I created a world and populated it with characters who thought what I told them to think and did what I wanted them to do. But writing *Fade Far Away* was a bit like acting. Each day when I sat down at my computer, I *became* Sienna. Then I took a walk through her world, feeling her pain, fear, and isolation.

For the first time I understood what authors mean when they say, "The characters don't always do what I expect." Although I was working from an outline, I found the story changing as Sienna reacted to each new situation. In fact, the process felt more like transcribing than writing. The characters were that real to me.

Unlike my father and me, Sienna and Hugh have a very troubled relationship. Still, in some ways, Sienna's story is the one I *wish* I'd lived. Unlike me, she ultimately finds a way to connect with her father in his last days, to help him and learn from him. In *Fade Far Away,* I've given Sienna a feeling of resolution and acceptance that took me decades to achieve in my real life.

Speaking of real life, mine changed dramatically when I remarried and left Boston for California. The natural beauty of Santa Barbara rekindled my childhood passions. I gave up my urban lifestyle and began hiking through the foothills above the city and the bluffs overlooking the beach. I took up bodyboarding, learned how to kayak and scuba dive, and finally got back into surfing.

I also found a way to satisfy my performing bones. I put together a slide show about my life and began visiting schools to talk about my writing career. It's a kick to meet kids who have read my books, and I love getting reluctant readers excited about books and writing. I've also begun singing again with my friend Bruce Hale, author of the "Chet Gecko" books. Performing as our alter egos, the Savage Bunnies, we sing funny, rocking songs for kids.

The year 2003 has been a busy one for me. When the popular clothing company Roxy decided to partner with HarperCollins to publish a series of novels for girls, they hired me to write them. Once again, I was able to use my real life adventures in my fiction. The series, "Luna Bay," is about five best friends who live and surf in the fictional California town of Crescent Cove. When I wasn't writing the novels, I was doing research—surfing, that is.

With son, Preston (age 11), 2003.

Before the "Luna Bay" books were published, some people wondered if they could possibly be worthwhile. After all, Roxy is a clothing company, not a publisher. Maybe the books would be nothing but one long ad for surfer chick clothes.

But I knew differently. I wouldn't have taken the job if I'd had to compromise my writing to please the Roxy Girl execs. And I didn't. From the start, the books were intended to be engrossing stories about real girls with well-rounded lives and believable problems. Fortunately, the reviewers and (most importantly) my readers feel I've succeeded, and the series has inspired surfers and eager wannabes from coast to coast.

Twenty years after my first book was published, there's still more childhood gold to mine. In 2003, two stories I wrote about tomboys were published in short story anthologies. "Standing on the Roof Naked" is about a teenage girl who's confused about her sexuality. She finds solace and direction when she hooks up with a male DJ and performs a cathartic rap at the school dance. "The Day Joanie Frankenhauser Became a Boy" follows a basketball-loving girl who masquerades as a boy for twenty-four hours.

After the stories were published, my agent suggested that Joanie deserved her own book, and I agreed.

I set to work on a novel version that sold to Dutton and will be published in 2005.

When *Letters to Cupid* was published, my editor at American Girl told me the company was planning to produce a bookmark to promote the novel. One side would feature a photo of me as a thirteen-year-old and the other side would show a photo of me now. My editor asked me to answer some questions—first as my thirteen-year-old self and then as my current self—to accompany the photos.

Thirteen-year-old Fran was asked, "What is your greatest wish?"

That's easy. "To someday live by the beach and make a living doing something creative," I replied.

Then adult Fran was asked, "What is your biggest accomplishment?"

That's when it hit me. I'm living in California, just a few blocks from the beach. I'm surfing. I'm a professional writer. *My childhood dreams have come true!*

Okay, maybe I'm not as special as my doting parents once led me to believe. But when I look at those bookmarks, I hear trumpets blare, I feel the red carpet between my toes, and the stars in the sky arrange themselves into something that looks a whole lot like FRANCESS.

LEVETE, Sarah 1961-

Personal

Born December 9, 1961, in United Kingdom; married Keith Newell (a designer), May 29, 1997; children: Jack, Eliza. *Education:* Sussex University, B.A. (with honors), 1985.

Addresses

Agent—c/o Author Mail, Aladdin Books, 2-3 Fitzroy Mews, London W1T 6DJ, England. *E-mail*—sarah@levete.fsnet.co.uk.

Career

British Council Public Theatre Network, arts administrator, 1986-94; Aladdin Books, Two-Can, and Dorling Kindersley, London, England, senior editor, 1994-2001; writer and editor, 2001—.

Member

Society of Authors.

Awards, Honors

Editor's choice citation, *Books for Keeps,* 1996, for *How Do I Feel about Loneliness and Making Friends.*

Writings

NONFICTION

How Do I Feel about Looking after Myself, Franklin Watts (London, England), 1996, Copper Beech Books (Brookfield, CT), 1998.

How Do I Feel about Loneliness and Making Friends, Franklin Watts (London, England), 1996, Copper Beech Books (Brookfield, CT), 1998.

How Do I Feel about Being Jealous, Copper Beech Books (Brookfield, CT), 1999.

Ladders ("Mighty Machines" series), Two-Can Press (London, England), 1999.

How Do I Feel about When People Die, Copper Beech Books (Brookfield, CT), 1998.

Rivers and Lakes, Copper Beech Books (Brookfield, CT), 1999.

I Can Smile, Franklin Watts (London, England), 2001, Copper Beech Books (Brookfield, CT), 2002.

A Closer Look at Rivers and Lakes, Franklin Watts (London, England), 2001.

I Can Speak Up, Franklin Watts (London, England), 2001, Copper Beech Books (Brookfield, CT), 2002.

Talking about Alcohol, Franklin Watts (London, England), 2004.

Talking about Drugs, Franklin Watts (London, England), 2004.

Talking about Step Families, Franklin Watts (London, England), 2004.

Talking about Health and Eating, Franklin Watts (London, England), 2004.

Mean Machines: Monster Trucks, Raintree (London, England), 2004.

OTHER

Tommy's Working Pregnancy Guide (adult nonfiction), Tommy's Baby Charity, 2004.

Spider-Man Annual 2004 (fiction), Alligator Books (London, England), 2004.

Spider-Man Sticker Book, Alligator Books (London, England), 2004.

Sidelights

Sarah Levete told *SATA:* "I find it particularly rewarding to write about feelings and personal and social issues. Childhood is full of pleasure and fun, but it is also full of difficult and painful feelings. It is reassuring for a child to know that his or her feeling or situation is not uncommon—reading about it doesn't make the difficulty disappear—but it can offer some support and reassurance. On a higher note, I have just finished writing a 'Spider-Man' annual which was great fun."

Levete has written a series of easy-to-read nonfiction titles on some of the most difficult issues facing children: the death of a loved one, drug and alcohol abuse, loneliness, peer pressure, and self-assertiveness. The books set up scenarios and then ask the reader to come up with solutions, realizing that many questions have no easy answers. *Booklist* contributor Susan Dove Lempke characterized the "How Do I Feel About" series as "useful, attractive books." Stephani Hutchinson in *School Library Journal* liked the fact that the series is "accessible to readers." Hutchinson called the books "useful resources for classroom units."

Biographical and Critical Sources

PERIODICALS

Booklist, September 15, 1999, Susan Dove Lempke, review of *How Do I Feel about Being Jealous,* p. 264.

School Library Journal, August, 1998, Stephani Hutchinson, reviews of *How Do I Feel about Loneliness and Making Friends* and *How Do I Feel about Looking after Myself,* p. 152.

*   *   *

LIBBY, Barbara M.

Personal

Born March 7, 1947, in Kearny, NJ; daughter of Samson (a butcher) and Muriel Marcus; married Mort Libby

Barbara M. Libby

(a businessman), September 26, 1980; stepchildren: Daniel, Elizabeth, Brent. *Education:* Pratt Institute, B.F.A., 1970; also attended courses at Baltimore Institute of Art, University of Cincinnati, Art Academy of Cincinnati, and workshops with Uri Shulevitz, Marcia Brown, and Marion Dane Bauer. *Hobbies and other interests:* Environmental issues, children's literacy, dog training.

Addresses

Agent—c/o Author Mail, Eclipse Press, 3101 Beaumont Centre Circle, Lexington, KY 40513.

Career

South-Western Publishing Co., Cincinnati, OH, book designer, 1978-89; freelance book designer, 1989-2000; writer and illustrator, 1992—. Artist-in-residence, James E. Biggs Early Childhood Education Center, Covington, KY, 2000-01.

Member

Society of Children's Book Writers and Illustrators.

Awards, Honors

National Press Club "bookfest" selection, and "top 10 youth sports books" citation, *Booklist,* both 2003, and second place citation for equine-related books, American Horse Publications, 2004, all for *I Rode the Red Horse: Secretariat's Belmont Race.*

Writings

SELF-ILLUSTRATED

Old Cat, Gramercy Press (New York, NY), 1993.
I Rode the Red Horse: Secretariat's Belmont Race, Eclipse Press (Lexington, KY), 2003.

Work in Progress

A true story of the mascot of the China Marines in World War II, the Philippines; research on Jimmy Winkfield, the last African American jockey to win the Kentucky Derby.

Sidelights

Barbara M. Libby told *SATA:* "The idea to write about the racehorse Secretariat was my husband's. He'd been reading an article by William Nack for *Sports Illustrated,* entitled "Pure Heart," which was a eulogy for the horse. It was a beautiful tribute, and sparked my interest as a potentially great subject. The first time I saw videotape of Secretariat running, I burst into tears. It is so rare to see that kind of physical perfection.

"Initially, I intended to write a full biography with lots of illustrations. And I did, complete with footnotes about jockey silks, and so on. But something happened along the way. I had quotes from the jockey (Ron Turcotte) running through my head, and realized there was an entirely different book there, much shorter, much more poetic, and focusing on the Belmont race, which defined his place in the history of the Triple Crown. I sat down one afternoon and began to type, and it almost came out all of a piece. This was after reading, thinking and writing for eighteen months, so it didn't come out of a vacuum.

"I may not have been born on a horse, but I was close to being born with a pencil in my hand. There is no memory of not drawing. However, doing *these* drawings gave me great anxiety! This wasn't some old nag, this was 'The Horse of the Century!' All that musculature! With my first book, *Old Cat,* people said, 'You really know your cats. This is just like my (old, black and white, one-eyed, etc.) cat.' We lived with the cat, so we did know him, all his postures and expressions.

"And here I was taking on this Myth-in-Life of a horse! I visited the Kentucky Horse Park, and several horse farms, saw the grooming and breaking to a saddle, watched horse movies (*The Black Stallion* is a favorite. It also plays on the idea of horse as mythological symbol), watched the Secretariat videos over and over, collected as many photos as I could find, and finally jumped in. In the end, you can only do what you can do. Whew!

"When Secretariat ran, in 1973, the country was in distress over Watergate and Vietnam. His image, blazing red in blue and white, represented what we wanted to be. There was such a purity to him. His records still stand, thirty years later. I fell in love with him. He should be remembered."

Libby's book, *I Rode the Red Horse: Secretariat's Belmont Race* was voted one of the top ten sports books for young readers by *Booklist* magazine in 2003. The self-illustrated title tells the story of Secretariat from the point of view of his jockey, Ron Turcotte, and introduces children to racing lore and a history of the times in which Secretariat ran. In citing the title for the honor, *Booklist* correspondent Gillian Engberg particularly praised the "vivid, realistic artwork." In his *Booklist* review, Todd Morning concluded that *I Rode the Red Horse* "beautifully captures a memorable sports moment."

Biographical and Critical Sources

PERIODICALS

Booklist, July, 2003, Todd Morning, review of *I Rode the Red Horse: Secretariat's Belmont Race,* p. 1895; September 1, 2003, Gillian Engberg, "Top 10 Youth Sports Books," p. 124.

ONLINE

Eclipse Press, http://www.equinepress.com/ (June 7, 2004), interview with Libby and information about *I Rode the Red Horse.*

*   *   *

LINDSEY, Kathleen D(orothy) 1949-

Personal

Born June 13, 1949, in Clayton, NJ; daughter of William Henry (a railroad worker and clergyman) and Mae Williams; married David L. Lindsey (a systems administrator), June 25, 1966; children: David II, Donald, Dean, Natasha Sade, Jaquille, Darrell (deceased). *Education:* Graduated from high school in Clayton, NJ. *Religion:* Church of Christ. *Hobbies and other interests:* Quilting, camping, gardening, cooking, and reading.

Addresses

Home—506 Elm Ave., Clayton, NJ 08312. *E-mail*—katdl@comcast.net.

Career

Writer. Performer, with sisters, of *Seven Quilts for Seven Sisters,* a historical treatment of African American quilting with music and drama, live and on television for

To save their farm from foreclosure, Sadie and her family band together to turn Mama's delectable pies into a source of income. (From Sweet Potato Pie, *written by Kathleen D. Lindsey and illustrated by Charlotte Riley-Webb.)*

Public Broadcasting stations and the syndicated network show *Visions*. Member and leader of quilting guilds; teacher of quilting and other folk art crafts. Keynote speaker, "Remembering Black History," Black History Month in New Jersey, 2004; also shared podium at a lecture event with Miss America 2004, Erika Dunlap.

Member

Needle Little Love.

Awards, Honors

Has received numerous awards for individual quilts; New Jersey General Assembly Award for *A Stitch in Time;* ceremonial proclamation from Mayor of Clayton, NJ, 2004.

Writings

A Stitch in Time (play), first performed in New Jersey, 1992.
Sweet Potato Pie (picture book), illustrated by Charlotte Riley-Webb, Lee & Low (New York, NY), 2003.

Work in Progress

Fish to Fry, a picture book; *Pa Pa's Working Tools,* a picture book; *Run Faredy Run,* the story of a slave girl who finds her way to freedom by the use of coded quilts and song.

Sidelights

Through her many contributions to the understanding of African American history, Kathleen D. Lindsey has come to be known as "Miss Kat." Lindsey and her sis-

ters created a stage performance called *Seven Quilts for Seven Sisters* that uses their own quilts, music, and drama to show how African Americans have communicated through this art form from the earliest days of slavery to the present era. Their show has been featured on the Public Broadcasting System and other television programs, and they present it live as well. Lindsey was led to this creative endeavor after the death of her son Darrell, who was the victim of a drunken driver in 1988.

Quilting plays a large part in all of Lindsey's work. She teaches the craft to adults and children and has done extensive research on the role quilts played as secret maps for the Underground Railroad. She even features a self-created quilt in her children's book, *Sweet Potato Pie.*

Set around the turn of the twentieth century, *Sweet Potato Pie* tells the story of a family that turns a potential tragedy into a triumph. Drought kills all of Papa's crops except the sweet potatoes. Faced with the possibility of losing the family farm, Papa and Mama decide to bake sweet potato pies and sell them at a harvest celebration. The whole family pitches in to make the pies, and the tasty confections prove to be a best-seller at the fair. This gives Mama the idea to begin a business baking pies.

Lindsey has said that *Sweet Potato Pie* is based on her own experiences selling homemade pies at a festival in Southern New Jersey when she was young. Her work has a higher goal, however. She told *SATA:* "My stories convey a message that families who work together have greater knowledge of love and sound family values."

Lindsey is also the author of a play, "A Stitch in Time," that won a New Jersey General Assembly Award. The play depicts life for African Americans in the Civil War era and its immediate aftermath. A lifetime resident of New Jersey, Lindsey lives in the same town in which she was born.

Biographical and Critical Sources

PERIODICALS

Booklist, September 15, 2003, Terry Glover, review of *Sweet Potato Pie,* p. 247.
School Library Journal, December, 2003, Susan M. Moore, review of *Sweet Potato Pie,* p. 118.

ONLINE

Kat Lindsey Home Page, http://www.katlindsey.com/ (June 2, 2004).
Lee & Low Books, http://www.leeandlow.com/booktalk/ katlindsey.html/ (June 2, 2004), "Book Talk with Kathleen D. Lindsey."

*   *   *

LOEHFELM, Bill

Personal

Male.

Addresses

Home—New Orleans, LA. *Agent*—c/o Author Mail, Lucent Books, 10911 Technology Place, San Diego, CA 92127. *E-mail*—bloehfelm@aol.com.

Career

Freelance journalist and writer in New Orleans, LA; teaching assistant in English, University of New Orleans.

Writings

Osama Bin Laden ("Heroes and Villains" series), Lucent Books (San Diego, CA), 2003.

Sidelights

Bill Loehfelm is a journalist and educator in New Orleans who specializes in that city's vibrant music scene. His book *Osama Bin Laden* attempts to explain the life of an international terrorist to early readers. Loehfelm gives details of Bin Laden's early life and his dedication to the most radical forms of Islam. The book also explores the founding of al-Qaeda and how Bin Ladin

A volume from the "Heroes and Villians" biography series, Osama bin Laden *tracks the reasons for Bin Laden's religious fanaticism and his role as a leader of al-Qaeda as well as outlining the acrimonious relationship between the United States and the Middle East.*

has inspired a generation of young fighters to give their lives for his agenda. *Osama Bin Ladin* is an entry in the "Heroes and Villains" series published by Lucent Books. As John Peters noted in *School Library Journal,* "few readers are likely to sleep easily" after reading about this zealot's power and the scope of his influence.

Biographical and Critical Sources

PERIODICALS

School Library Journal, July, 2003, John Peters, review of *Osama Bin Ladin,* p. 144.

*   *   *

LUXBACHER, Irene M. 1970-

Personal

Born December 10, 1970, in Toronto, Ontario, Canada; daughter of Frank (a tailor) and Sophia (a nurse) Luxbacher. *Education:* Queen's University, B.A., 1992; also studied at Emily Carr College of Fine Art and Design, Vancouver, British Columbia, Canada, and University of Toronto.

Addresses

Agent—c/o Author Mail, Kids Can Press Ltd., 29 Birch Ave., Toronto, Ontario, Canada M4V 1E2. *E-mail*—iluxbacher@rogers.com.

Career

Avenue Road Arts School, Toronto, Ontario, visual arts instructor, 1992-2002; Royal Conservatory of Music, Toronto, Ontario, visual arts consultant, 1999-2001; Propeller Centre for the Visual Arts, Toronto, Ontario, 2000-01; Arts for Children of Toronto, curator, 2001-02; writer and illustrator, 1997—. *Exhibitions:* Queen's University, Kingston, Ontario, 1992; Emily Carr College of Fine Art and Design, Vancouver, British Columbia, 1993; A Space, Vancouver, British Columbia, 1994; Avenue Road Art School, Toronto, Ontario, 1996; Area Space, Propeller Gallery, Red Head Gallery, Open Studio, and Avenue Road Art School, all 1997; Toronto Convention Centre, Propeller Gallery, and Art Gallery of Mississauga, all Toronto, Ontario, all 1998; Propeller Centre for the Visual Arts, University of Toronto, and Artsystem, all 2001; BCE Place and Canadian Broadcasting Corporation, both 2002.

Writings

The Jumbo Book of Art, Kids Can Press (Toronto, Ontario, Canada), 2003.

Sidelights

Irene M. Luxbacher puts her experience as an artist and teacher to work in her title *The Jumbo Book of Art.* Luxbacher told *SATA* that the book was inspired by the work done at the Avenue Road Arts School in Toronto, Canada. "The unique artwork and teaching methods of the instructors at the school was the source for many of the projects found within *The Jumbo Book of Art,*" she said. As its name suggests, the book is a huge compilation of art projects for youngsters, from lessons on basic drawing and coloring techniques, to sculpture, paper arts, mixed-media projects, stenciling, dioramas, and mask-making. Luxbacher includes illustrations and step-

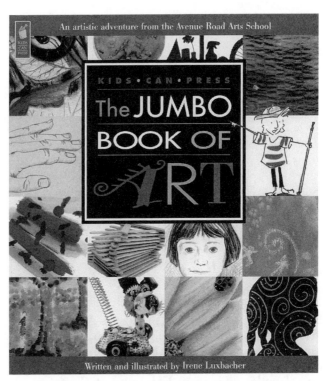

Irene M. Luxbacher's self-illustrated book purports that anyone with imagination can be an artist and offers many suggestions for artistic endeavors, along with information on materials, technique, and detailed instruction.

by-step instructions, and most of the items she uses are inexpensive and readily available. "This volume makes a terrific case for the argument that everyone can be an artist," enthused Sophie R. Brookover in *School Library Journal.* Brookover went on to recommend *The Jumbo Book of Art* as a "must-have" title "for every art and elementary school classroom."

Biographical and Critical Sources

PERIODICALS

School Library Journal, November, 2003, Sophie R. Brookover, review of *The Jumbo Book of Art,* p. 162.

M

MacGREGOR, Carol Lynn

Personal

Born in Boise, ID; daughter of Gordon Angus (a contractor and rancher) and Nellie Alene (a homemaker) MacGregor; married Gayle Brian Allen (a pilot and property manager), 1996; children: J. G., Laura, Catherine, Janelle. *Education:* University of California at Berkeley, B.A., 1964; Georgetown University, M.A., 1987; Boise State University, M.A., 1991; University of New Mexico, Albuquerque, Ph.D., 1999. *Hobbies and other interests:* Raising Quarter horses, reading, art, opera, needlework, travel, skiing, swimming.

Addresses

Home—1109 Warm Springs Ave., Boise, ID 83712. *E-mail*—cmacgregorphd@ctcweb.net.

Career

Research assistant to U.S. Senator Len B. Jordan, Washington, DC, 1964-67; Alaska Airlines, Seattle, WA, executive secretary, 1968-69; Secretary of State, Boise, ID, microfilm programmer, 1969; Emmett Independent School District, director of pilot program to integrate Mexican children into mainstream classrooms, 1970-72; Office of Economic Opportunity, teacher of English as a second language and of preparation for G.E.D. tests, 1972-73; Boise State University, Boise, ID, adjunct professor of Spanish, political science, and humanities, 1970-2001. Owner of Black Canyon Ranch, Emmett, ID, 1988-97; owner of "Carol's Collection," a jewelry boutique, 1992-96; owner of Belvedere Ranch, Cascade, ID, 1997—. Owner of other ranches in Cascade and Emmett, ID. Speaker for Idaho Humanities Council, 1998—, and presenter at numerous conferences, school visits, symposia, and seminars. Leader of interpretive tours on the Lewis and Clark Expedition.

Awards, Honors

Joel E. Ferris Award, Cheney-Cowles Museum, 1991, for *The Journals of Patrick Gass: Member of the Lewis*

Carol Lynn MacGregor

and Clark Expedition; Professional development awards, Boise State University, 1997 and 1999.

Writings

The Journals of Patrick Gass: Member of the Lewis and Clark Expedition, Mountain Press (Missoula, MT), 1997, 5th edition, 2003.

Shoshoni Pony, Caxton Press (Caldwell, ID), 2003.
Lewis and Clark's Bitter-Sweet Crossing, Caxton Press (Caldwell, ID), 2004.

Contributor, *The American West in 2000,* University of New Mexico Press (Albuquerque, NM), 2003. Contributor to periodicals, including *We Proceeded On, Journal of the West, Boise Magazine, Western Historical Quarterly, New Mexico Historial Review, Montana: The Magazine of Western History,* and *Idaho Yesterdays.*

Work in Progress

Prosperity in Isolation: Boise, Idaho, 1882-1910.

Sidelights

Carol Lynn MacGregor told *SATA:* "Operating a ranch in Valley County, Idaho, and writing, teaching, and lecturing on the history of the American West occupy much of my time and bring my life good rewards. Add to those time in minding accumulated things and keeping abreast of the various interests of my husband, four of my children and two of his, and our travel. I am never bored.

"My study of history began at Wellesley College and the University of California at Berkeley in the sixties. I majored in European history because I wanted to know what had happened, even though I did better in English and foreign language classes (Spanish and French). Later, as a single mother in the eighties, I returned to school, probing deeper into the thought, writing, and analysis of history. I completed an M.A. in liberal studies at Georgetown University, an M.A. in history at Boise State University, and a Ph.D. in American history at the University of New Mexico at Albuquerque. Meanwhile, my children finished high school and university studies. Three of them pursued graduate degrees.

"My book, *The Journals of Patrick Gass: Member of the Lewis and Clark Expedition* began as a master's thesis and languished several years until I found Gass's original account book for years spent in Wellsburg, West Virginia, after the famous expedition. It was still owned by descendants who gave me publication rights. Editing without working for a publisher or newspaper brought 'baptism by fire.' Another new experience was writing for children. I saw that audiences of Idaho fourth graders listened attentively to an interesting non-fiction story, asked good questions, and deserved a book with Native Americans as protagonists. Since I always loved horse stories, the story about how Shoshonis brought horses to the Northwest, *Shoshoni Pony,* was a natural for me. Its sequel, *Lewis and Clark's Bitter-Sweet Crossing,* tells the whole story of the expedition, but the centerpiece is the meeting with Sacagawea's people from whom they got horses, crossing the Bitter-root Mountains with their Shoshoni guide, Toby, and returning to Nez Perce country to stay a month next to them on the Clearwater River in 1806.

"The next publication came from an easier beginning, my graduate studies with Dr. Gerald Nash, who asked me to contribute to a *festenscrift* celebrating his career, along with other colleagues and students. My essay on Boise's cultural life in *The American West in 2000* traces Boise's growth from 1950 to 2000, using the thesis that the prosperity of citizens in a relatively isolated area makes Boise unique, bringing cultural amenities beyond expectation for a city its size.

"During the Bicentennial of the Lewis and Clark expedition, I was not active as an adjunct professor of history at Boise State University, using my time instead as a lecturer for the Idaho Humanities Council. I have spoken throughout Idaho and also in many other states, including Kansas, Montana, Virginia, Missouri, North Dakota, New Mexico, and West Virginia.

"The future provides time for more adventures, and time to record some of those of my past. It beckons me to prepare my dissertation on Boise from 1882-1910 for publication, to write several more historical articles about our region, and to stretch toward writing a memoir. I look forward to more time to dream, to reflect, and to create."

*   *   *

MANN, Elizabeth 1948-

Personal

Born 1948; married Stuart Waldman (an editor and publisher); children: Lucas. *Education:* Bank Street College of Education, M.S.E.

Addresses

Home—New York, NY. *Office*—c/o Mikaya Press, 12 Bedford St., New York, NY, 10014. *E-mail*—mann@ mikaya.com.

Career

Former teacher in the New York, NY, public schools; writer, Mikaya Press, New York, NY, cofounder, 1995—.

Awards, Honors

Informational Book of the Year, International Reading Association, Young Readers Book Award, *Scientific American,* Jefferson Cup Award Honor Book, Virginia Library Association, One Hundred Books to Read and Share selection, New York Public Library, Best Books of the Year selection, Child Study Children's Book Committee, and named Outstanding from a Learning Perspective, Parent Council, all for *The Brooklyn Bridge;* Children's Books of Distinction selection, *Hungry Mind Review,* for *The Great Pyramid;* Best Books of the Year selection, Child Study Children's Book

Committee, and named Outstanding from a Learning Perspective, Parent Council, both for *The Great Wall;* Notable Children's Book in the Field of Social Studies, National Council for the Social Studies/Children's Book Council, and named a Top Choice Book, *Children's Literature,* both 1999, both for *The Panama Canal;* Nonfiction Honor Book selection, *Voice of Youth Advocates,* 2000, for *Machu Picchu.*

Writings

"WONDERS OF THE WORLD" SERIES

The Brooklyn Bridge, illustrated by Alan Witschonke, Mikaya Press (New York, NY), 1996.

The Great Pyramid, illustrated by Laura Lo Turco, Mikaya Press (New York, NY), 1996.

The Great Wall, illustrated by Alan Witschonke, Mikaya Press (New York, NY), 1997.

Machu Picchu, illustrated by Amy Crehore, Mikaya Press (New York, NY), 1997.

The Panama Canal, illustrated by Fernando Rangel, Mikaya Press (New York, NY), 1998.

The Roman Colosseum, illustrated by Michael Racz, Mikaya Press (New York, NY), 1998.

Hoover Dam, illustrated by Alan Witschonke, Mikaya Press (New York, NY), 2001.

Tikal: The Center of the Maya World, illustrated by Tom McNeely, Mikaya Press (New York, NY), 2002.

Empire State Building: When New York Reached for the Skies, illustrated by Alan Witschonke, Mikaya Press (New York, NY), 2003.

Adaptations

A sound recording of *The Great Wall* was produced by Cutting Corporation (Bethesda, MD), 1999.

Sidelights

Elizabeth Mann's experience as a schoolteacher led her to write her first book, *The Brooklyn Bridge,* a well-regarded account about how the massive structure was built during the late 1800s. Mann was teaching her second-grade class in Brooklyn, New York, about the famous landmark and could tell that she was not generating any interest, as she remarked on the *Mikaya Press* Web site. She had worked hard to make the subject interesting, covering the classroom walls with illustrations and diagrams and planning a walk across the bridge for her students. Nevertheless, the students seemed bored, and Mann was stumped as to how to bring the story of the bridge to life. Only when she found some information on the Roebling family, who had invested nearly a decade and a half in building the bridge, and then related their story of struggle, failure, and triumph did her students begin to pay real attention.

Out of this experience, Mann developed the idea for her book about the Brooklyn Bridge. She and her husband, Stuart Waldman, agreed that children need attention-grabbing stories in their nonfiction books if they are to become truly interested in them. As a result, the couple formed Mikaya Press in 1995. With an emphasis on books with compelling narratives and striking illustrations, maps, charts, and timelines, Mikaya Press began publishing factual books for young readers. At first the press concentrated solely on Mann's work, but more recently it has published books by other authors as well.

The first book published by Mikaya Press was *The Brooklyn Bridge,* in which Mann tells the story of the bridge's construction. The author "effectively conveys the human drama of this great construction feat and provides lucid explanations of the technology and the building phases," wrote reviewer Margaret A. Bush in *Horn Book.* Susan Dove Lempke, writing in *Booklist,* praised the book for relating "the stories as adventures without ever resorting to melodrama."

Mann eventually retired from teaching to focus on writing. Like *The Brooklyn Bridge,* her subsequent books have all targeted young readers and focused on man-made wonders, including the Great Pyramids, the Great Wall of China, the Panama Canal, the Roman Colosseum, the South American Inca city of Machu Picchu, the Hoover Dam, the ancient Mayan city of Tikal, and the Empire State Building. She has said that her main goal is tell a good story, as she remarked on the *Houghton Mifflin Education Place* Web site. To help her in that goal, children, including her son, often critique her work paragraph by paragraph, marking them with a "G" for good or a "C" if the information is unclear. "It's very good feedback," she commented.

Mann's research for each book usually begins at the library or bookstore as she gathers a wide range of information, from the politics and cultures of the time of the man-made wonder to the machines and tools available to build it. For example, in *The Great Wall* readers learn not only about the Great Wall's construction but also about the history behind the decision to build it in the first place. This history behind the concept of the wall is "surprisingly accessible" in Mann's account, according to Stephanie Zvirin in *Booklist.*

As a former teacher, Mann has learned how to capture and maintain her young readers' attention. As a result, each of her titles provides a central resource for teachers of younger grade-school children. The books have also been received favorably by reviewers. For example, Joy Fleishhacker, writing a review of *The Brooklyn Bridge* and *The Great Pyramid* for *School Library Journal,* noted that the books "feature an informative mix of historical reproductions, striking illustrations, and clearly presented texts." In a review of *Machu Picchu* that appeared in *Booklist,* reviewer Ilene Cooper commented, "It is Mann's comfortable text that makes this [book] so special. She ably brings the Incas' complicated society into focus." Mara Alpert, writing in *School Library Journal,* may have summed up Mann's writing efforts best when she called *Hoover Dam,* "A wonderfully readable, well-organized book filled with fascinating detail."

Empire State Building: When New York Reached for the Skies continues Mann's exploration of amazing works of human craftsmanship. Not only does the author describe how the use of steel made tall buildings such as the Empire State Building possible, she also details how rapidly it was constructed and its impact on a nation reeling in the depths of the Great Depression. Begun in 1929 and finished in 1931, the skyscraper changed Manhattan forever. "Mann writes clearly and concisely, never sacrificing the drama of the story," wrote Kay Weisman in a *Booklist* review of the work. In *School Library Journal,* Delia Fritz called *Empire State Building* an "ideal resource" and promised that it "will capture the imaginations of report writers and general readers alike."

It is that goal that Mann has in mind when she writes. She knows that children are often *required* to read nonfiction books in school for reports and projects, but she has higher ambitions to satisfy. Her challenge, she says

The thirty year construction of the Brooklyn Bridge during the second half of the 1800s is documented in Elizabeth Mann's book from the "Wonders of the World" series. (From The Brooklyn Bridge, *illustrated by Alan Witschonke.)*

In her book from "Wonders of the World" series, Mann not only describes the erection of the Great Wall but the history of Chinese struggles that led up to the decision to create an invincible barrier. (From The Great Wall, *illustrated by Alan Witschonke.)*

on the *Houghton Mifflin Education Place* Web site, is to create books that youngsters will read "not just for homework but for the sheer pleasure of it."

Biographical and Critical Sources

PERIODICALS

Booklist, February 1, 1997, Susan Dove Lempke, review of *The Brooklyn Bridge* and *The Great Pyramid,* p. 937; January 1, 1998, Stephanie Zvirin, review of *The Great Wall,* p. 806; December 15, 1998, Stephanie Zvirin, review of *The Roman Colosseum,* p. 746; February 1, 1999, Sally Estes, review of *The Panama Canal,* p. 971; July, 2000, Ilene Cooper, review of *Machu Picchu,* p. 2033; December 15, 2000, Gillian Engberg, review of *The Roman Colosseum,* p. 810; December 1, 2001, Carolyn Phelan, review of *Hoover Dam,* p. 656; December 15, 2002, Kay Weisman, review of *Tikal: Center of the Mayan World,* p. 757;

February 1, 2004, Kay Weisman, review of *Empire State Building: When New York Reached the Skies,* p. 973.

Children's Digest, December, 1997, review of *The Brooklyn Bridge,* p. 12; June, 1999, "It's a Wonderful World," p. 10.

Horn Book, May-June, 1997, Margaret A. Bush, review of *The Brooklyn Bridge,* p. 342; March-April, 2002, Betty Carter, review of *Hoover Dam,* p. 229.

Kirkus Reviews, November, 1, 1998, review of *The Panama Canal,* p. 1601; December 1, 2002, review of *Tikal,* p. 1770.

Publishers Weekly, November 11, 1996, review of *The Brooklyn Bridge,* p. 75; December 1, 1997, review of *The Great Wall of China,* p. 53; February 2, 2004, "Uncovering History," p. 79.

School Library Journal, June, 1997, Joy Fleishhacker, review of *The Brooklyn Bridge* and *The Great Pyramid,* p. 140; December, 1997, Shirley N. Quan, review of *The Great Wall,* p. 140; December, 1998, Carol Fazioli, review of *The Panama Canal,* p. 140; February, 1999, Cynthia M. Sturgis, review of *The Roman Colosseum,* p. 121; June, 2000, Daryl Grabarek, review of *Machu Picchu,* p. 168; December, 2001, Mara Alpert, review of *Hoover Dam,* p. 167; January, 2003, Ann Welton, review of *Tikal,* p. 165; April, 2004, Delia Fritz, review of *Empire State Building,* p. 174.

Science News, December 13, 2003, review of *Empire State Building,* p. 383.

Scientific American, December, 1997, Phylis Morrison and Philip Morrison, review of *The Brooklyn Bridge,* p. 126.

ONLINE

Houghton Mifflin Education Place, http://www.eduplace.com/kids/hmr/ (August 10, 2003), "Meet Elizabeth Mann."

Mikaya Press, http://www.mikaya.com/ (August 10, 2003), "About Mikaya."*

*   *   *

McCORMICK, Kimberly A. 1960-

Personal

Born April 15, 1960, in New Castle, PA; daughter of J. Russell (in auto sales) and Sydney R. (an elementary schoolteacher; maiden name, Rodgers) Shumaker; married Rodney W. McCormick (a director of construction and manufacturing), August 25, 1979; children: Kaycee Lane, Nicolette Frances. *Education:* Slippery Rock State University, B.S., 1987; Westminster College (New Wilmington, PA), M.Ed., 1992. *Politics:* Republican. *Religion:* Baptist.

Addresses

Home—2022 Eastbrook Rd., New Castle, PA 16101. *E-mail*—Rokikani2022@aol.com.

Career

New Castle Playhouse, member, 1987-90; Wilmington Area School District, New Wilmington, PA, elementary teacher, 1988—; Lawrence County Reading Council, board member, 1997-2003; secretary, 2000-03; Nail Art and Tanning Boutique, New Castle, PA, owner and nail technician, 2002—.

Awards, Honors

Sallie Mae Outstanding First Year Teacher Award, 1989; Gift of Time Award, 1995; Literacy Award, International Reading Association, 2001.

Writings

Plays to Ponder, Good Apple/Frank Schaffer Publishing (Torrance, CA), 1999.

The Way I See It: Fifty Values-Oriented Monologues for Teens, Meriwether Publishing (Colorado Springs, CO), 2001.

Author of church school curriculum materials. Author of "What's Your Opinion," a playkit collection of ten monologues, Contemporary Drama Services (Colorado Springs, CO), 2000. Contributor to books and periodicals, including *Teacher Tips, Instructor, Mailbox, Home Life, Our Little Friend, Primary Treasure,* and *Sunshine.*

Sidelights

Kimberly A. McCormick told *SATA:* "I like to say I first became interested in writing during my 'BC' days, Before Children and Before College! I was leisurely enjoying a copy of *Women's Day* magazine when I ran across a contest asking you to write about your 'favorite Christmas tradition.' With nothing else to do, I typed up my favorite tradition and, surprisingly, won an honorable mention award. Sadly to say, only the top five entries were published, and I didn't even make a copy of my entry before I mailed it! Nevertheless, this small bit of success inspired me to pursue my writing.

"My grandmother used to tell me that my writing talent was a gift from God. Because of this I try to write material which I believe is for the betterment of children. Most of my writing success has come in the area of education. I like to write plays, skits, and monologues that teachers can use to generate positive classroom discussions about lessons in life. A lot of what I write is inspired by my own two daughters, Kaycee and Nicolette.

"I have definitely learned the lesson of 'never giving up' through my writing. It takes hard work and determination to be a published author. I still have many goals for my writing career, one of which is to have a children's story book published. Hopefully, this dream will one day be fulfilled.

"Until that time, I enjoy all types of activities. I teach school, sing, and own a nail and tanning salon where I work part-time as a nail technician. I love to exercise, taking brisk walks as often as the weather permits, and spend as much time as possible with my husband and children. Finally, I will learn to play the piano before I turn fifty!

"No matter how long I have the privilege of living, I plan to learn new and different things. Education keeps my life interesting and exciting!"

O

OBERMAN, Sheldon 1949-2004

OBITUARY NOTICE—See index for SATA sketch: Born May 20, 1949, in Winnipeg, Manitoba, Canada; died of cancer March 26, 2004, in Winnipeg, Manitoba, Canada. Educator, artist, and author. Oberman, a diverse talent whose interests included creating found-art objects and song writing, composed books for all ages but was best known for his award-winning children's books, a number of which drew on his experiences growing up in a Jewish family. After studying literature at the University of Winnipeg, where he earned a B.A. in 1972, and at the University of Jerusalem, he completed a B.Ed. at the University of Manitoba and started a career as a high school English and drama teacher at Joseph Wolinsky Collegiate in Winnipeg. His routine of telling bedtime stories to his children evolved into an interest in writing his own stories, which include award-winning works such as *The Lion in the Lake/Le Lion dans le Lac* (1988), *This Business with Elijah* (1993), and *The Always Prayer Shawl* (1994). Oberman enjoyed performing these stories live in front of young audiences, and to keep his acting talents honed he took on small movie roles; he also wrote screenplays and directed short films. In addition, he wrote lyrics for the popular Canadian children's entertainer Fred Penner, and five of the albums released by Penner featuring Oberman's songs received Juno nominations. More recently, Oberman gained critical acclaim for his 1999 title, *The Shaman's Nephew: A Life in the Far North,* written with Simon Tookoome, which was shortlisted for the Governor-General's Award and won the Norma Fleck Award, and 2000's *The Wisdom Bird: A Tale of Solomon and Sheba.* Though he developed inoperable cancer in his throat, Oberman continued working in his last months, publishing *Island of the Minotaur* in 2003 and completing a two-volume set of Jewish folk tales, which will be published posthumously. Other honors earned by Oberman include the National Jewish Book Award and the Sydney Taylor American Librarians Awards; after his death, the Manitoba Writers' Guild named their writing program for emerging authors after Oberman.

OBITUARIES AND OTHER SOURCES:

PERIODICALS

Globe & Mail (Toronto, Ontario, Canada), May 25, 2004.
Winnipeg Free Press (Winnipeg, Manitoba, Canada), June 10, 2004.

*   *   *

OPPEL, Kenneth 1967-

Personal

Born August 31, 1967, in Port Alberni, British Columbia, Canada; son of Wilfred (a lawyer) and Audrey (a visual artist; maiden name, Young) Oppel; married Philippa Sheppard (a university professor), September 8, 1990; children: Sophia Marie. *Education:* University of Toronto, B.A. (English and cinema), 1989. *Hobbies and other interests:* Sailing, swimming, travel, airships, movies, theater.

Addresses

Office—HarperCollins Canada, 2 Bloor S. East, 20th Fl., Toronto, Ontario M4W 1A8, Canada. *E-mail*—kenneth.oppel@sympatico.ca.

Career

Writer, 1985—; Scholastic Canada, Richmond Hill, Ontario, associate editor, 1989; *Quill & Quire,* Toronto, Ontario, Books for Young People editor, 1995-96.

Member

Canadian Society of Children's Authors, Illustrators and Performers.

Awards, Honors

Canadian Library Association (CLA) Notable Book selection, 1991, for *The Live-forever Machine,* and 1993 for *Dead Water Zone;* City of Toronto Book Awards fi-

Kenneth Oppel

nalist, 1992, and Our Choice selection, Canadian Children's Book Centre, 1992-93, both for *Cosimo Cat;* CLA Notable Book designation, 1993, and Choice designation, Canadian Children's Book Centre, 1995-96, for *Follow That Star;* Air Canada Award, Canadian Authors Association, 1995, for "outstanding promise" demonstrated by a young (under thirty years) Canadian writer; Pick of the List, American Booksellers Association, and Quick Pick for Reluctant Readers, American Library Association, both 1997, shortlist, Ruth Schwartz Award, shortlist, Silver Birch Award, Blue Heron Award, Mr. Christie's Book Award, and Book of the Year for Children, CLA, all 1998, and Maud Hart Lovelace Award, and Prix SNCF du Livre Jeunesse, both 2002, all for *Silverwing; Booklist* Editor's Choice, and Canadian Children's Book Centre Choice, both 2000, both for *Peg and the Whale;* Ruth Schwartz Children's Book Award, Mr. Christie Book Award, CBA Libris Award for Best Specialty Book of the Year, Canadian Library Association Book of the Year for Children, and *Smithsonian* Notable Book, 2000, Manitoba Young Readers' Choice designation, 2002, and New Jersey Garden State Award shortlist, all 2003, all for *Sunwing;* Toronto Public Library Celebrates Reading Award, 2002; CLA Book of the Year award, Mr. Christie's Book award, and Red Maple award, all 2003, and Manitoba Young Reader's Choice award, 2004, all for *Firewing.*

Writings

PICTURE BOOKS

Cosimo Cat, illustrated by Regolo Ricci, Scholastic Canada (Markham, Ontario, Canada), 1990.

Follow That Star, illustrated by Kim LaFave, Kids Can Press (Toronto, Ontario, Canada), 1994.

Peg and the Whale, illustrated by Terry Widener, Simon & Schuster (New York, NY), 2000.

Peg and the Yeti, illustrated by Barbara Reid, HarperCollins Canada (Toronto, Ontario, Canada), 2004.

FICTION

Colin's Fantastic Video Adventure, illustrated by Kathleen C. Howell, Dutton (New York, NY), 1985.

The Live-forever Machine, Kids Can Press (Toronto, Ontario, Canada), 1990.

Dead Water Zone, Kids Can Press (Toronto, Ontario, Canada), 1992, Little, Brown (Boston, MA), 1993.

Cosmic Snapshots, illustrated by Guy Parker-Reese, Penguin, 1993.

Galactic Snapshots, illustrated by Guy Parker-Reese, Penguin, 1993.

Emma's Emu, illustrated by Carolyn Crossland, Penguin, 1995.

The Devil's Cure (adult novel), HarperCollins (Toronto, Ontario, Canada), 2000.

Airborn, HarperEos (New York, NY), 2004.

"SILVERWING" TRILOGY

Silverwing, Simon & Schuster (New York, NY), 1997.

Sunwing, HarperCollins Canada (Toronto, Ontario, Canada), 2000.

Firewing, HarperCollins Canada (Toronto, Ontario, Canada), 2002.

"BARNES AND THE BRAINS" SERIES

A Bad Case of Ghosts, illustrated by Peter Utton, Penguin (New York, NY), 1993.

A Bad Case of Magic, illustrated by Peter Utton, Penguin (New York, NY), 1993, published as *A Strange Case of Magic,* illustrated by Sam Sisco, Scholastic Canada (Markham, Ontario, Canada), 2001.

A Bad Case of Robots, illustrated by Peter Utton, Penguin (New York, NY), 1994, published as *A Crazy Case of Robots,* illustrated by Sam Sisco, Scholastic Canada (Markham, Ontario, Canada), 2001.

A Bad Case of Dinosaurs, illustrated by Peter Utton, Penguin (New York, NY), 1994, published as *An Incredible Case of Dinosaurs,* Scholastic Canada (Markham, Ontario, Canada), 2001.

A Bad Case of Super-Goo, illustrated by Peter Utton, Penguin (New York, NY), 1996, published as *A Weird Case of Super-Goo,* illustrated by Sam Sisco, Scholastic Canada (Markham, Ontario, Canada), 2001.

A Creepy Case of Vampires,, Scholastic Canada (Markham, Ontario, Canada), 2002.

OTHER

Oppel's books have been translated into Spanish, French, German, Dutch, Italian, Danish, Chinese, Japanese, Portuguese, Serbian, Czech, and Slovakian.

Adaptations

Silverwing was adapted as an animated television program by Bardel Entertainment.

Work in Progress

A sequel to *Airborn.*

Sidelights

Kenneth Oppel has written several books for young people, ranging from picture books and first readers to young-adult fiction, as well as authoring several screenplays. What is most impressive about Oppel's body of work is the amount he published before age twenty-nine. In recognition of this accomplishment, the Canadian Authors Association awarded him the 1995 Air Canada Award for promise demonstrated by a young Canadian writer.

Born in the small mill town of Port Alberni, British Columbia, in 1967, Oppel grew up mostly in Victoria, British Columbia, and on the opposite coast of Canada, in Halifax, Nova Scotia. Oppel's father, who worked in a furniture factory when his second son was born, decided to go back to college, which necessitated the move to Victoria. Then, graduating from the University of Victoria, he decided to go to law school, which took the family to Nova Scotia. "As kids, we hated being moved and went kicking and screaming, but subsequently we loved Halifax," Oppel told Dave Jenkinson in a *Canadian Review of Materials* profile. Once his father finished law school, Oppel and his family then returned to Victoria, where he completed junior high school and went to high school.

One constant in these years was books. "As kids," Oppel explained to Jenkinson, "we were surrounded by books and, when you grow up in an environment like that, you just are automatically more interested in words and in telling stories." Studying at private schools, Oppel found that he most enjoyed creative writing assignments, but as actual creative writing—creating short stories and novels—was not emphasized in schools the young Oppel began working on these in his own time at home. By the sixth grade he was already writing lengthy manuscripts with a distinct *Star Wars* influence. "These big science fiction epics rarely got finished because I'd get five chapters in and then have no idea of what happened next," he told Jenkinson. Fantasy tales came next, inspired by the role-playing game "Dungeons and Dragons." As a young reader, Oppel, like such distinguished Canadian authors as Alice Munro and children's novelist Kit Pearson, was inspired by L. M. Montgomery's "Emily of New Moon" series. He related strongly to Emily's dream of becoming a published writer and by grade seven determined that he, too, would write. He commented in the Canadian Children's Book Centre anthology *Writing Stories, Making Pictures:* "I remember making a vow to my father when I was thirteen, that I wanted to have something

published before I'd turned fourteen." Although that may not have been an uncommon goal for ambitious young teens with a flair for writing, it was definitely uncommon that Oppel published a novel before he was out of high school. The story behind that accomplishment is almost too good to be true.

Oppel's first work, *Colin's Fantastic Video Adventure,* wasn't published until he was seventeen years old, though he did write the first draft at age fourteen. Oppel earned his lucky break when a family friend who knew British children's author Roald Dahl agreed to show him the young boy's story. Dahl was impressed enough to pass it on to his own literary agent. The agent agreed to represent the book and promptly sold it to publishers in London and New York.

Oppel's inspiration for *Colin's Fantastic Video Adventure* resulted from another of his passions—playing video games. In the story, eleven-year-old Colin wins video game contests with the help of two spacemen who escaped from the boy's favorite video game "Meteoroids." Colin eventually realizes that cheating isn't fair and goes on to play a third contest by himself. "Writing it was good therapy," Oppel told the Canadian Children's Book Centre of his work on the book, "a withdrawal technique if you will, enabling me to experience video games vicariously without spending huge amounts of money." As Susan Roman noted in *Booklist,* "the theme is very trendy and has appeal—especially to reluctant readers."

After his first book, Oppel had trouble getting a second one published. So he stopped writing and focused on his studies. While at the University of Toronto, he majored in English literature and cinema. Fascinated by his cinema studies, Oppel began making student films. When he returned to writing children's books in his final year of undergraduate study, *The Live-forever Machine,* written for an independent studies course in creative writing, demonstrated the new cinematic influence. The story of fourteen-year-old Eric, who stumbles upon two men who discovered the secret of immortality in 391 A.D. and have been chasing each other through history ever since, reads as though a camera is mounted on Eric's shoulders. The reader sees a dank underworld where the Live-Forever machine is jealously guarded, a deceptively bland urban upper world melting under a ferocious sun, and a cool museum that offers refuge from the heat and a passageway into the past. The cinematic technique and themes introduced in this novel became a trademark of Oppel's later efforts.

Dead Water Zone, Oppel's next YA novel, details the relationship between two brothers possessing opposite characteristics. Paul, who is strong physically, travels to Watertown, in search of his missing brother Sam, who is the brainier half of the two. When he gets there, Paul suspects that his brother has discovered a secret hidden in the waters surrounding the eerie town. *Horn Book* contributor Elizabeth S. Watson, Lucinda Lockwood of

School Library Journal, and Elizabeth MacCallum of the Toronto *Globe & Mail* all described *Dead Water Zone* as "Dickensian" in scope and flavor. *Voice of Youth Advocates* contributor Deborah Dubois wrote that "Teens who like science fiction will find this a gripping novel that will leave them with much food for thought."

Geared for a younger audience, Oppel's "Barnes and the Brains" chapter books provide plenty of action and dialogue for newly independent readers, typically between the ages of six and nine. In *A Bad Case of Ghosts,* Giles Barnes discovers ghosts in an old house newly occupied by Giles and his family. With the help of two young ghost-hunters, Kevin and Tina, the harmless ghosts eventually leave the family alone. According to *School Librarian* contributor Cathy Sutton, "This is a well-written story with good character development." The trio's mystery-solving services are needed once again in *A Bad Case of Magic,* when books mysteriously float off the local library's shelves and right out the door. "The stories move along smartly, and they are full of fun, action, and the occasional deliciously scary bit," noted Fred Boer in *Quill & Quire.* Other titles within the series, including *A Bad Case of Robots,* and *An Incredible Case of Dinosaurs,* were also received favorably.

Oppel is best known for his "Silverwing" series, in which he introduces his readers to yet another world, one of bats. "I said I'd never write a talking animal story," Oppel told Dave Jenkinson in *Canadian Review of Materials* online. "I've always had a slightly condescending attitude toward them and thought they were somehow cutesy." But he was drawn to the idea of basing a novel—or trilogy, as it turned out—around such an unlikable animal. For Oppel, part of the fun of the story was the challenge of making this creature so often associated with horror and scary novels into an endearing and appealing protagonist. Another challenge was the fact that a bat's world is largely auditory, rather than visual. Oppel's writing then, needed to rely heavily on auditory images.

The first novel in the series, *Silverwing,* tells the story of the bat Shade, the smallest of the Silverwing community of bats. Loved and protected by his mother, Shade is often taunted by other bats his age because of his physical weakness. But Shade compensates for this in his acute intelligence as well as with a stubborn, self-willed streak. His intellectual curiosity, however, gets him into trouble, as when he tries to see the sun—something forbidden to bats from the time when they refused to take a stand in the battle between birds and beasts—and brings down the punishment of the night owls on his fellow bats. As the colony migrates to its winter home, Shade again gets into trouble, losing track of the flight-path during a storm. He then must search for his colony, and is helped by another bat, Marina Brightwing, who has been ostracized by her own colony because of the silver band on her leg. These two set about upon a voyage of discovery, searching not only

When a young Silverwing bat named Shade sets off for migration and gets separated from his colony, he encounters several fascinating bats in his adventurous journey. (Cover illustration by Troy Howell.)

for Shade's colony, but also for the secret of the silver band, and for the whereabouts of Shade's father. *Silverwing* won critical praise and honors from many quarters. A critic for *Publishers Weekly* found that this "epic journey is gripping, and details of bat life are inventively and convincingly imagined." Writing in *Horn Book,* Lauren Adams also commended Oppel for creating an "intriguing microcosm of rival species, factions, and religions," and further noted that the author "has left enough unsolved mystery to entice readers into the apparently planned sequel." *Quill & Quire* reviewer John Wilson commented that "*Silverwing* creates a complete culture with its own mythology, lore, and rationale. Like all books in this genre, its success depends upon the convincing portrayal of a plausible world. This Kenneth Oppel has achieved."

Silverwing was a publishing success, and its sequel came with the publication of *Sunwing* in 2000. Oppel continues the saga of Shade and the Silverwings in this novel, with Shade and Marina continuing the search for Cassiel, Shade's father. Accompanied by a small group of bats, Shade finds a huge indoor forest filled with bats. Once inside, however, he and the others cannot escape. While many of the bats take this new home as a fulfillment of legend—that they will be able to fly in daylight without any fear of owls—Shade is suspicious. Captured and tagged, and loaded onto crates, Shade and the other bats are dropped as living bombs over a distant jungle. Shade and a few others survive this, only to do battle with Goth, an enemy bat. Again, the critical response was favorable for Oppel's bat book. Anne St. John, writing in *Horn Book,* declared that Shade's "dangerous adventures make a memorable impact," and *Booklist*'s Carolyn Phelan lauded the book as "action packed and suspenseful." Sarah Ellis, writing in *Quill & Quire,* noted that with *Sunwing* "Oppel admirably fulfills his promise of a sequel." Ellis went on to conclude that the second novel in the series "is a book of big effects."

Firewing, the third novel in the series, focuses on Griffin, son of Shade and Marina. This young bat is as self-willed as his father, and when he tries to steal fire from humans he burns his friend and then is sent on a frightening journey into the Underworld. Shade, meanwhile,

In Oppel's second book about young Shade, the Silverwing bat is joined by Marina, a Brightwing, in tracking down his father, and their search culminates with a heroic rescue. (Cover illustration by Troy Howell.)

attempts to save his son, but soon he discovers that his old nemesis, Goth, is also on hand to complicate matters. A critic for *Kirkus Reviews* thought this third installment a "fine tale" despite some "inelegant writing." *Horn Book* contributor Anita L. Burkam had greater praise for the novel, commenting that "this new adventure, with its compelling geography and cosmology of the underworld, takes [readers] places *Silverwing* and *Sunwing* never dreamed of." And Susan Perren, reviewing the title in the *Globe & Mail,* wrote that Oppel "constructs a wonderfully florid and richly imagined world, a bat world in which life and death, goodness and evil, heaven and hell, and the notion of giving up one's own life so that another might live, are there for the reading—and the feeling. Hats off to Oppel for a hat trick!" So popular did the "Silverwing" books become that they spawned an animated television series.

Speaking with a contributor for *Achuka,* Oppel posited the possibility of continuing with the series. "I never set out to write a series. I wrote very much one book at a time. I always tell myself I won't proceed unless I've got a really good idea I'm really excited about. And I really felt that with each book. *Silverwing* ended and I kind of liked the way it ended. It had quite an open ending. A lot of the kids who wrote to me didn't agree. They wanted to know if Shade found his father. And luckily I had an idea for the second book, as I was revising *Silverwing*. So *Sunwing* was easy to write. *Firewing* was harder really, because everything was pretty well wrapped up at the end of *Sunwing*. But then I had the idea of a child in the underworld—a sort of Orpheus descent. I'm open to a fourth book. I don't think I'm quite done with Shade. But I don't have that big idea yet."

Oppel's fantasy novel *Airborn,* set in an imaginary world where giant airships rule the skies, has been compared to the works of Jules Verne and Robert Louis Stevenson. *Airborn* follows the adventures of fifteen-year-old Matt Cruse, a cabin boy aboard the luxury ship Aurora. As the Aurora crosses the Pacificus on its way to Lionsgate City, Matt spies a tattered balloon and rescues its sole passenger, an elderly man whose tales of majestic, catlike winged creatures are quickly dismissed. When Matt later meets Kate de Vries, the man's grand-daughter, he becomes convinced of the existence of the cloud cats.

In addition to his novels and short chapter books, Oppel has written a couple of picture books as well as a number of screenplays. The author's 1990 picture book *Cosimo Cat,* described as a "charming and magical" story by Terri L. Lyons in *Canadian Children's Literature,* features a young boy in search of an intriguing cat. Oppel has also written the award-winning picture book *Peg and the Whale* as well as the chapter book *Emma's Emu.* In spite of his success in the field of juvenile literature, he hasn't confined his writing exclusively to children's books either. He has also published an adult medical thriller, *The Devil's Cure,* dealing with a pos-

Shade, young hero of other Oppel books, now a father, courageously plunges into the Underworld when his newborn son is drawn into the land of the dead by a menacing adversary. (Cover illustration by Troy Howell.)

sible cure for cancer found in the white cells of a death-row inmate who will stop at nothing to keep the world from profiting from his blood. Reviewing the novel in *Library Journal,* Linda M. G. Katz found *The Devil's Cure,* "engaging and nicely paced."

Biographical and Critical Sources

BOOKS

Egoff, Sheila, and Judith Saltman, *The New Republic of Childhood: A Critical Guide to Canadian Children's Literature in English,* Oxford University Press (New York, NY), 1990, p. 270.
"Meet Kenneth Oppel" (booklet), Kids Can Press, 1994 (unpaged).
Writing Stories, Making Pictures: Biographies of 150 Canadian Children's Authors and Illustrators, Canadian Children's Book Centre, 1995, pp. 245-247.

PERIODICALS

Booklist, July, 1985; January 1, 2000, Carolyn Phelan, review of *Sunwing,* 927; November 15, 2000, Connie Fletcher, review of *Peg and the Whale,* p. 639; May 15, 2001, Gilbert Taylor, review of *The Devil's Cure,* p. 1737; *Colin's Fantastic Video,* pp. 1558-1559.

Book Report, November-December, 1993, pp. 47-48.
Books for Keeps, January, 1996, p. 13.
Bulletin of the Center for Children's Books, October, 1985, p. 34; January, 1998, p. 170.
Canadian Book Review Annual, 1993, pp. 6174-6175.
Canadian Children's Literature, number 65, 1992, pp. 106-107; number 71, 1993, Terri L. Lyons, review of *Cosimo Cat,* pp. 87-88; number 86, 1997, pp. 52-54; spring, 2001, review of *Sunwing,* p. 182.
Canadian Review of Materials, January, 1991, p. 35; May, 1991, p. 174; November, 1992, p. 312.
Globe & Mail (Toronto, Ontario, Canada), September 19, 1992, Elizabeth MacCallum, "Journey through the Underworld Kindles a Glowing Novel," p. C19; May 11, 2002, Susan Perren, review of *Firewing.*
Horn Book, November-December, 1993, Elizabeth S. Watson, review of *Dead Water Zone,* p. 747; November-December, 1997, Lauren Adams, review of *Silverwing,* p. 684; March-April, 2000, Anne St. John, review of *Sunwing,* p. 199; July-August, 2000, review of *Peg and the Whale,* p. 442; March-April, 2003, Anita L. Burkam, review of *Firewing,* pp. 215-217.
Journal of Adolescent and Adult Literacy, May, 1997, Ronald Jobe, review of *Silverwing,* p. 137; December, 2003, Michael Jung, review of *Firewing,* p. 349.
Junior Bookshelf, August, 1994, p. 138.
Kirkus Reviews, September 1, 1997, review of *Silverwing,* p. 1394; December 1, 2002, review of *Firewing,* p. 1772.
Library Journal, May 1, 2001, Linda M. G. Katz, review of *The Devil's Cure,* p. 128.
Maclean's, July 17, 2000, review of *The Devil's Cure,* p. 129.
Presbyterian Record, December, 1995, p. 47.
Publishers Weekly, May 24, 1993, review of *Dead Water Zone,* p. 89; October 20, 1997, review of *Silverwing,* p. 76; January 17, 2000, "Fiction Sequels," p. 58; June 4, 2001, review of *The Devil's Cure,* p. 57; December 16, 2002, "The Story Goes On," p. 70.
Quill & Quire, November, 1990, p. 14; March, 1991, pp. 20-21; July, 1992, p. 48; August, 1994, p. 33; April, 1995, Fred Boer, review of *A Bad Case of Ghosts* and *A Bad Case of Magic,* p. 41; May, 1995, p. 48; April, 1997, p. 37; October, 1998, Andrew Pyper, "Taking Flight: Kenneth Oppel Talks about Life after *Silverwing,*" pp. 41-42; April, 1999, review of *The Devil's Cure,* pp. 38-39; August, 1999, Sarah Ellis, review of *Sunwing,* p. 38; April, 2000, review of *The Devil's Cure,* pp. 38-39; December, 2000, review of *Peg and the Whale,* pp. 30-31.
Resource Links, December, 1999, review of *Emma's Emu,* pp. 8-9, and review of *Sunwing,* p. 29; April, 2000, Gail Lennon, review of *The Live-forever Machine,* p. 50; December, 2000, review of *Peg and the Whale,* pp. 7-8; February, 2001, review of *A Bad Case of Ghosts* and *A Strange Case of Magic,* pp. 17-18; April, 2001, Krista Johansen, review of *Dead Water Zone,* p. 25, and Gail Lennon, review of *The Live-forever Machine,* p. 50; June, 2001, Judy Cottrell, review of *A Crazy Case of Robots,* p. 39; December, 2001, Johal Jinder, review of *An Incredible Case of Dinosaurs,* pp. 19-20; April, 2002, Evette Signarowski, review of

A Weird Case of Super Goo, pp. 24-25, and Odile Rollin, review of *Silverwing,* pp. 54-55; February, 2003, Judy Cottrell, review of *A Creepy Case of Vampires,* pp. 13-15; June, 2003, Odile Rollin, review of *Sunwing,* pp. 45-47.

School Librarian, August, 1993, Cathy Sutton, review of *A Bad Case of Ghosts,* p. 109.

School Library Journal, October, 1985, Li Stark, review of *Colin's Fantastic Video Adventure,* p. 175; May, 1993, Lucinda Lockwood, review of *Dead Water Zone,* p. 127; October, 1997, Beth Wright, review of *Silverwing,* p. 137; February, 2000, Susan L. Rogers, review of *Sunwing,* p. 124; November, 2000, Kathleen Kelly, review of *Peg and the Whale,* p. 129; February, 2002, Louise L. Sherman, review of *Silverwing* (audiobook).

Voice of Youth Advocates, June, 1993, Deborah Dubois, review of *Dead Water Zone,* p. 104; April, 1998, Nancy Eaton, review of *Silverwing,* p. 58.

ONLINE

Achuka, http://www.achuka.co.uk/ (April 16, 2003), "Kenneth Oppel."

Airborn Web site, http://www.airborn.ca/ (March 15, 2004).

Canadian Review of Materials Online, http://www.umanitoba.ca/outreach/cm/ (March 15, 2004), Dave Jenkinson, "Kenneth Oppel."

Canadian Society of Children's Authors, Illustrators, and Performers Web site, http://www.canscaip.org/ (March 15, 2004), "Kenneth Oppel."

CBC4Kids, http://www.cbc4kids.ca/ (April 16, 2003), "Author Profile: Kenneth Oppel."

HarperEos Web site, http://www.harpercollins.com/hc/eos/ (March 15, 2004), "Kenneth Oppel."

Kenneth Oppel Homepage, http://www.kennethoppel.ca/ (March 15, 2004).

Mystery Ink Online, http://www.mysteryinkonline.com/ (March 15, 2004), interview with Oppel.

Red Cedar Book Awards Web site, http://redcedar.swifty.com/ (March 15, 2004), "Kenneth Oppel."

Scholastic Canada Web site, http://www.scholastic.ca/ (March 15, 2004), "Kenneth Oppel."

Silverwing Web site, http://www.silverwing.tv/index2.php/ (March 15, 2004).

Trades, http://www.the-trades.com/ (January 16, 2003), Howard Price, review of *Firewing.*

P

PALMER, Judd 1972-

Personal
Born 1972, in Calgary, Alberta, Canada. *Education:* Earned degree from Trinity College, University of Toronto.

Addresses
Agent—c/o Author Mail, Bayeux Arts, Inc., 119 Stratton Crescent S.W., Calgary, Alberta T3H 1T7, Canada; fax: 403-249-2477.

Career
Puppeteer, illustrator, and writer. Puppeteer for Disney, YTV, and *Whoopi's Littleburg;* founding member of the Old Trout Puppet Workshop theater company, Alberta, Canada, 1999—; Agnostic Mountain Gospel Choir, lead singer and slide banjo. *Exhibitions: Drawings of the Preposterous,* University of Calgary, 2003.

Awards, Honors
Governor General's Literary Award for English text shortlist, Canada Council, 2003, for *The Maestro.*

Writings

"PREPOSTEROUS FABLES FOR UNUSUAL CHILDREN" SERIES; SELF-ILLUSTRATED

The Tooth Fairy, Bayeux Arts (Calgary, Alberta, Canada), 2002.
The Maestro, Bayeux Arts (Calgary, Alberta, Canada), 2002.
The Wolf King, Bayeux Arts (Calgary, Alberta, Canada), 2003.
The Sorcerer's Last Words, Bayeux Arts (Calgary, Alberta, Canada), 2003.

Abigail is determined to go to the castle of the Tooth Fairy even though her eccentric grandfather tries to prevent her. (From The Tooth Fairy, *written and illustrated by Judd Palmer.)*

Also the author of a play version of *The Tooth Fairy,* first performed by the Old Trout Puppet Workshop in Calgary, Alberta, Canada, in 2001.

ILLUSTRATOR

Victor Mintz, *Musical Cheers: A Music & Opera Lover's Guide to Humorous Verse*, Bayeux Arts (Calgary, Alberta, Canada), 2001.

Sidelights

Judd Palmer has reworked several classic fairy tales into slightly twisted picture books in the "Preposterous Fables for Unusual Children" series. These books sprang from Palmer's work with the puppet company that he founded, Old Trout Puppet Workshop. *The Tooth Fairy* began its life as a play that Palmer wrote and the Old Trout Puppet Workshop performed, and only later did Palmer write the story down and provide illustrations for it.

Palmer's Tooth Fairy is not the sweet, elderly, coin-dispensing lady of most children's imaginations. Instead of wings, this fairy uses a hot-air balloon, and the aviator goggles that this mode of transportation requires make "its eyes look huge and watery." Abigail is determined not to surrender her perfect smile, still composed entirely of baby teeth despite the fact that the girl is twelve years old, to this creature. She decides to fight the Tooth Fairy to keep them forever, but while chasing after the Tooth Fairy she has a series of perilous adventures involving pirates and a sea monster who writes poetry. Susan Miller praised the book's tone in *Resource Links,* calling it "almost like a 'penny dreadful' novel written in Victorian times."

Other books in the series take up the question of what happened after the purported end of the story in fairy tales including "The Pied Piper of Hamelin" and "The Boy Who Cried Wolf." In *The Maestro,* the orphan Hannah moves in with her aunt and uncle in Hamelin. Because there are no other children in town to play with (having all been lured away by the Pied Piper), Hannah becomes friends with a ghostly rat named Oskar—ghostly, of course, because all of the rats in town were killed by the Pied Piper. With the rat's help, Hannah discovers the abducted children, who are imprisoned in caves and forced to perform in the Pied Piper's orchestra. A whole pack of rats and the adults of Hamelin free the children, but Hannah, who loves to sing, asks to stay and study with the Maestro. The book "is well written (almost in a lyrical manner) and is a wonderful story," Antonia Gisler wrote in *Resource Links,* while *Canadian Materials* critic Mary Thomas suggested that both *The Tooth Fairy* and *The Maestro* would appeal to readers "particularly keen on the sound and feel of language."

Biographical and Critical Sources

BOOKS

Palmer, Judd, *The Tooth Fairy,* Bayeux Arts (Calgary, Alberta, Canada), 2002.

Hannah wants to learn about music and tries to join the Pied Piper's School of Music for Children, led by a mysterious, somewhat menacing instructor. (From The Maestro, *written and illustrated by Palmer.)*

PERIODICALS

Canadian Materials, November 14, 2003, Mary Thomas, review of *The Tooth Fairy* and *The Maestro.*

FFWD Weekly (Calgary, Alberta, Canada), October 9, 2003, Wes Lafortune, "More Than Fairy Tales: Judd Palmer Brings the Preposterous to Life."

Resource Links, April, 2003, Antonia Gisler, review of *The Maestro,* p. 20, and Susan Miller, review of *The Tooth Fairy,* pp. 20-21; February, 2004, Carolyn Cutt, review of *The Sorcerer's Last Words,* p. 56, and Evette Berry, review of *The Wolf King,* p. 56.

ONLINE

Bayeux Arts Web Site, http://www.bayeux.com/ (March 17, 2004).

Old Trout Puppet Workshop Web Site, http://theoldtrouts.org/ (January 14, 2004).*

PIERCE, Tamora 1954-

Personal

Born December 13, 1954, in Connellsville, PA; daughter of Wayne Franklin and Jacqueline S. Pierce; married Timothy Erving Liebe, 1985. *Education:* University of Pennsylvania, B.A., 1976.

Addresses

Home—New York, NY. *Agent*—Craig R. Tenney, Harold Ober Associates, 425 Madison Ave., New York, NY 10017. *E-mail*—tampierce@aol.com.

Career

City of Kingston, NY, tax data collector, 1977-78; towns of Hardenburgh and Denning, NY, tax clerk, 1978; McAuley Home for Girls, Buhl, ID, social worker and housemother, 1978-79; Harold Ober Associates, New York, NY, assistant to literary agent, 1979-82; creative director of ZPPR Productions, Inc. (radio producers), 1982-86; Chase Investment Bank, New York, NY, secretary, 1985-89; freelance writer, 1990—. Former instructor, Free Woman's University, University of Pennsylvania.

Member

Authors Guild, Science Fiction and Fantasy Writers of America.

Awards, Honors

Author's Citation, Alumni Association of the New Jersey Institute of Technology, 1984, for *Alanna: The First Adventure;* Schüler-Express ZDF Preis (Germany), 1985, and South Carolina Children's Book Award nomination, 1985-86, both for *In the Hand of the Goddess;* Children's Paperbacks Bestseller, *Australian Bookseller and Publisher,* 1995, for *Wolf-Speaker;* Best Books for Young Adults list, Hawaii State Library, Best Science Fiction, Fantasy, and Horror list, *Voice of Youth Advocates,* both 1995, and Best Books for Young Adults list, American Library Association (ALA), 1996, all for *The Emperor Mage;* Best Science Fiction, Fantasy, and Horror list, *Voice of Youth Advocates,* 1996, and Best Books for the Teen Age list, New York Public Library, 1997, both for *The Realms of the Gods;* Best Books for Young Adults list, ALA, 2004, for *Trickster's Choice.*

Writings

"SONG OF THE LIONESS" QUARTET

Alanna: The First Adventure, Atheneum (New York, NY), 1983.
In the Hand of the Goddess, Atheneum (New York, NY), 1984.

Tamora Pierce

The Woman Who Rides like a Man, Atheneum (New York, NY), 1986.
Lioness Rampant, Atheneum (New York, NY), 1988.

"IMMORTALS" QUARTET

Wild Magic, Atheneum (New York, NY), 1992.
Wolf-Speaker, Atheneum (New York, NY), 1994.
The Emperor Mage, Atheneum (New York, NY), 1995.
The Realms of the Gods, Atheneum (New York, NY), 1996.

"CIRCLE OF MAGIC" QUARTET

Sandry's Book, Scholastic (New York, NY), 1997.
Tris's Book, Scholastic (New York, NY), 1998.
Daja's Book, Scholastic (New York, NY), 1998.
Briar's Book, Scholastic (New York, NY), 1999.

"PROTECTOR OF THE SMALL" QUARTET

First Test, Random House (New York, NY), 1999.
Page, Random House (New York, NY), 2000.
Squire, Random House (New York, NY), 2001.
Lady Knight, Random House (New York, NY), 2002.

"CIRCLE OPENS" QUARTET

Magic Steps, Scholastic (New York, NY), 2000.
Street Magic, Scholastic (New York, NY), 2001.

Cold Fire, Scholastic (New York, NY), 2002.
Shatterglass, Scholastic (New York, NY), 2003.

OTHER

Trickster's Choice, Random House (New York, NY), 2003.
Trickster's Queen (sequel to *Trickster's Choice*), Random House (New York, NY), in press.

Contributor to *Digital Deli,* edited by Steve Ditlea, Workman (New York, NY), 1984; *Planetfall,* edited by Douglas Hill, Oxford University Press (New York, NY), 1985; *Flights of Fantasy,* Perfection Learning (Logan, IA), 1999; *Lost and Found,* edited by Helen and M. Jerry Weiss, Tor (New York, NY), 2000; and *Half-Human,* edited by Bruce Coville, Scholastic (New York, NY), 2001. Contributor to periodicals including *Christian Century* and *School Library Journal.* Author of radio scripts aired on National Public Radio, 1987-89. Pierce's works have been translated into German, Danish, Swedish, and Spanish.

Adaptations

Several of Pierce's novels have been recorded as audio books. Many of Pierce's series have been sold in boxed sets.

Work in Progress

Terrier, the first book in the "Provost's Dog" trilogy; other titles in the "Provost's Dog" trilogy; novels set in the "Circle" universe; a novel about the character Numair, set before the "Immortals" series.

Sidelights

Tamora Pierce's fantasy novels for young readers are noted for their strong female protagonists and their imaginative, well-drawn plots. In her "Song of the Lioness" quartet, Pierce features the character Alanna, a young woman who disguises herself as a man in order to train as a knight, and then uses her physical strength and her capabilities as a healer to serve Prince Jonathan and engage in numerous medieval adventures. "I enjoy writing for teenagers," Pierce once commented, "because I feel I help to make life easier for kids who are like I was."

Born in Pennsylvania, Pierce and her family moved often in the 1960s and 1970s, traveling between San Francisco and Fayette County in Pennsylvania. Pierce has noted that her father got her started writing when she was six, inspired by his storytelling skills. By the time she was in college at the University of Pennsylvania, Pierce was writing short stories, and on the advice of one her professors, she began writing a novel, a sword and sorcery tale. Once out of college, Pierce supported herself with jobs to pay the rent and continued writing her fantasy stories.

Alanna is introduced to readers in *Alanna: The First Adventure,* published in 1983. The first novel in the "Song of the Lioness" quartet, *Alanna* focuses on the title character's determination to avoid the traditional fate of young noble women her age—life in a secluded convent. Instead, she cuts her hair, binds her breasts, and, as "Alan," changes identities with her brother and begins training to become a knight in the service of her country's king. During her grueling education, she learns hand-to-hand combat from George Cooper, the King of Thieves, and she becomes close friends with Prince Jonathan, who does not know that his favorite knight-in-training is, in fact, a young woman. Only during a battle in the forbidding Black City does the prince discover Alanna's true gender; on the pair's return to the palace, he makes her his squire regardless.

In Pierce's second novel, the highly praised *In the Hand of the Goddess,* Alanna, now a squire, struggles to master the skills she will need to survive her test for knighthood in the Chamber of the Ordeal. She goes to war against a neighboring country and clashes repeatedly with Duke Roger, an urbane and devious mage who is determined to usurp the throne from his cousin, Prince Jonathan. She is successful in her efforts to protect Jonathan despite the duke's attempts to get rid of her. Once she is knighted, she decides to leave royal service and journey out into the world in search of further adventures. In a *School Library Journal* review, Isabel Soffer praised Pierce's first two books about Alanna as "sprightly, filled with adventure and marvelously satisfying."

In *The Woman Who Rides like a Man,* the third installment of "Song of the Lioness," Alanna is on her own. With her servant Coram Smythesson and Faithful, her cat, she encounters a tribe of desert warriors called the Bazhir. Proving her worth in physical combat, she is accepted by the Bazhir and ultimately becomes their shaman, or wizard. Alanna broadens the outlook of these desert people, raising a few women of the tribe to an equal level with the men before moving on to other adventures. And in the final volume of the quartet, *Lioness Rampant,* the stubborn heroine has become legendary for her skills in battle and for her magical powers; now she goes on a quest for the King of Tortall. Ascending to the Roof of the World after encountering numerous trials and challenges, she attempts to claim the Dominion Jewel, a precious stone said to give its bearer the power to do good. In addition to adventure, she also encounters love in the person of Liam, a warrior known far and wide as the Shang Dragon; however, his dislike of her magical powers makes their relationship a fragile one. Liam is not her only suitor, and *Lioness Rampant* resolves previous questions about Alanna's relationships with her friends Prince Jonathan and George Cooper. Calling Pierce "a great story-teller" in a review of *The Woman Who Rides like a Man,* a *Junior Bookshelf* contributor praised the series' inventive characters in particular, noting that the multitalented heroine's "sword, her companion, and her cat will always be ready to rise to any emergency."

Pierce followed her popular "Song of the Lioness" novels with a second series, "The Immortals," which began in 1992 with the novel *Wild Magic*. Although Alanna makes an appearance in the series, the new protagonist is thirteen-year-old Daine, an orphaned teen who has an unexplained empathy with wild creatures and a second sense that allows her to foresee danger. In fact, she is in danger of reverting to a wild creature herself until the wizard Numair teaches her to control and channel her "wild magic." Daine then uses her powers to stop evil humans from coercing the newly arrived Immortals—dragons, griffins, spidrens, and Stormwings—into helping them accomplish destructive purposes. Called "a dynamic story sure to engross fantasy fans" by Sally Estes in *Booklist, Wild Magic* was praised by Anne A. Flowers, who maintained in her *Horn Book* review that readers will "find in Daine a strong heroine whose humble beginning makes her well-deserved rewards even more gratifying."

Wolf-Speaker continues the adventures of Daine as the fourteen year old and her mentor, the mage Numair, join a pack of wolves that are at odds with humans. Men working for an evil wizard named Tristan have discovered opals in the wolves' hunting lands in Dunlath Valley. The scramble for the precious gems result in mine pollution and a destroyed ecosystem. Hunted by Stormwings controlled by Tristan, Daine and her companions must use all their powers, including shape changing, to stop the impending ecological catastrophe. "Daine is a super new heroine who makes this action-packed fantasy a joy to read," Mary L. Adams wrote in *Voice of Youth Advocates,* while Bonnie Kunzel noted in her *School Library Journal* article that *Wolf-Speaker* "is a compulsively readable novel that YAs won't be able to put down until the final battle is over and good triumphs. Pierce's faithful readers as well as any action-adventure or animal fantasy fans will be delighted with this new series." Daine's adventures continue in other "Immortals" novels, which include *The Emperor Mage*, published in 1995, and 1996's *The Realms of the Gods,* the concluding novel of the series in which Pierce's young female protagonist convinces dragons and other Immortal creatures to fight on her side against the powers of evil.

Magic once again plays an important role in Pierce's fantasy series "Circle of Magic." Unlike Pierce's two previous series, which take place in the country of Tortall, the "Circle of Magic" books are set in the land of Emelan. In *Sandry's Book,* "a rich and satisfying read," according to a *Kirkus Reviews* critic, Sandry, Daja, Briar, and Trisana—four young people from various walks of life—meet and become friends while living in Winding Circle Temple. Each of the four protagonists has a different form of inherent magic: Sandry's magic has to do with weaving, Briar's has to do with plants, Daja's magic involves fire, and Tris's magic deals with weather. The four overcome the negative aspects of their lives as they struggle to learn to control their newfound abilities. When they are caught together in an earthquake, Sandry has to use her magic to protect them. The action continues the summer after the earthquake

in *Tris's Book,* in which Tris and the other mages try to protect Winding Circle Temple from a pirate attack after its defenses are weakened. *Booklist*'s Chris Sherman felt that the second book in the series was "just as dramatic and engaging as *Sandry's Book,*" a "cut above many fantasies for this age group." The third book in the series, *Daja's Book,* features the "danger and prejudice," according to *Booklist*'s Sherman, that Daja must face as the sole survivor of her family's shipwreck. She is marked as *trangshi,* or a bringer of bad luck. "Pierce's magic and the customs and rituals of her world continue to fascinate," Sherman further remarked. In *Briar's Book,* the young mage-in-training and his teacher must combine magic to battle a deadly plague threatening Summersea. "An entirely satisfying, carefully crafted fantasy," concluded Sherman in another *Booklist* review.

Pierce returns to Tortall in the "Protector of the Small" quartet, inaugurated in 1999 with *First Test.* The series begins with the tale of Keladry of Mindelan, a ten-year-old girl who desperately wants to emulate the feat of her hero, Alanna the Lioness, and thereby win her knight's shield. As the first girl allowed to become a page, Kel faces a different set of challenges than Alanna did when trying to win the approval of her peers—they knowingly have to accept her as a girl trying to become a knight. Not only must she tackle the opinions of others her age, but she soon learns that Lord Wyldon of Cavall has added a beginning year onto the training program that only girls must take. Though outraged at the unfair treatment of girls by the system—and the unfair hazing of young pages—Kel manages to keep her temper in check and show her determination to become a knight. Susan Dove Lempke, writing in *Booklist,* called *First Test* a "splendidly rousing feast." A reviewer for *Publishers Weekly* praised, "old and new readers alike will be won over by Kel."

After surviving her first year, Kel continues her training in *Page.* Her three years as a page are no less challenging than her start; Kel takes on a maid to protect her from nobles who have been molesting her, and also finds some friends among the other knights-in-training. When one of them is kidnapped, Kel and the others must go to the rescue. Lempke, writing in *Booklist,* felt "Pierce's legions of fans will love" *Page* and "anxiously await the next in the . . . series." Heather Dieffenbach, in a *School Library Journal* review of *Page,* wrote "Readers will appreciate this true example of grrrl power." In *Squire,* Kel is chosen to squire not Alanna the Lioness, as she had hoped, but Raoul, Knight Commander of the elite King's Own. Raoul proves to be a good match for her temperament, and Kel's challenges in *Squire* deal more with unruly centaurs and magical creatures than finding acceptance. Patricia A. Dollisch, reviewing *Squire* in *School Library Journal,* noted that "Kel's fans will delight in seeing the parallels in their own lives, and Alanna and Daine's fans will enjoy seeing their favorites, if only in cameo roles." Also reviewing *Squire,* Anne St. John commented in *Horn Book,* "Kel's determination to succeed, her compulsion to stand up for those weaker than herself, and her exploration of what it means to be both a knight and a woman make her a compelling character."

Kel's story concludes in *Lady Knight.* While facing her final test to become a knight, Kel is granted a vision of an evil magic being used by an enemy nation. She knows that she is to face the evil wizard behind it, known as the Nothing Man, but instead of being allowed to take up her quest, her first station as a knight is to run a refugee camp. The Nothing Man's machines are being used against the knights fighting the war, and Kel is torn between her post and aiding her friends. However, when the Nothing Man's followers kidnap refugees from her camp, she takes her quest head on. Called "appropriately larger in scope" than its predecessors, *Lady Knight* offers a "gripping climax," according to a critic for *Kirkus Reviews.* Noting that Kel possesses but does not heavily depend upon her magical skills, Lempke of *Booklist* commented that Kel "taps her courage, cleverness, and moral outrage to fight evil." Sharon Rawlins, in a review for *School Library Journal,* claimed, "This is an essential book for anyone who enjoyed the others in the series," while Paula Rohrlick of *Kliatt* wrote, "It's satisfying to see Kel growing into her new role as knight and succeeding in her destiny as Protector of the Small."

With *Magic Steps,* the first volume in the "Circle Opens" series, Pierce takes readers back to Emelan and the four young mages of "Circle of Magic." This quartet of novels picks up four years after the events of "Circle of Magic," and has a new twist: the mages of Winding Circle discover and train others who possess unrealized magical talents. *Magic Steps* features Sandry and how this witch of weaving takes on a student of her own in a "fast-paced, engrossing read, sure to satisfy fantasy fans," according to *Booklist*'s Shelle Rosenfeld. *Street Magic* continues the adventures with young Briar leaving Winding Circle with his teacher Rosethorn to spread magical plant lore to people in distant areas. On his venture, he meets young Evvy, a street urchin, who is unknowingly the possessor of strong magical abilities which Briar helps to cultivate. Eva Mitnick, reviewing the book in *School Library Journal,* found it to be a "solid addition to this enthralling series."

The third book in the series, *Cold Fire,* features Daja, who encounters twins with powers that need nurturing and a mysterious arsonist whose identity she must discover. Considered darker by some critics, *Cold Fire* was dubbed "An absolute must for fans of the series" and a "thoughtful stand-alone fantasy" by a critic for *Kirkus Reviews. Shatterglass,* the final volume in the quartet, features Tris as she travels to Tharios, a land dominated by a rigid caste system. She encounters Keth, a glassblower with the magical ability to harness lightning when creating his works. Though she is years younger, Tris helps to teach Keth how to control his talents as both of them become involved in trying to stop a serial killer. "In lively prose laced with wry humor,

Pierce creates realistic, dimensional characters," wrote Shelle Rosenfeld in *Booklist.* Beth L. Meister praised *Shatterglass* in her review for *School Library Journal* as "a successful combination of fantasy and mystery." A critic for *Kirkus Reviews* claimed Pierce's "fans will undoubtedly clamor for future updates on her likeable young mages and their fascinating world."

The heroine of Pierce's *Trickster's Choice,* the first in a duo set in Tortall, has large shoes to fill. As the daughter of the most famous knight in the country—Alanna the Lioness—Alianne (called Aly) struggles to become her own person. More like her father, the one-time King of Thieves, than her warrior mother, Aly's dream is to become a spy, but her parents forbid it. After a fight with her mother, Aly goes sailing to cool off and is captured by pirates and sold into slavery. The family of Duke Balitang, who now owns her, is in bad standing with the royalty of the Copper Isles, and they are all sent into exile. In a bargain with the god Kyprioth, the Trickster of the title, Aly agrees to protect Duke Balitang's two daughters in exchange for the Trickster's aid in returning her home and convincing her parents to

In a novel which combines fantasy with mystery, Pierce portrays two teenage mages with remarkable powers that help them track down a serial killer in a medieval city of Thalios. (Cover illustration by Peter Scanlan.)

Alianne, teenage daughter of Pierce's well-loved pro-tagonist Alanna, has her mother's prowess which she uses when she is enslaved and must barter her skills for her safe return home. (Cover illustration by Joyce Tenneson.)

allow her to be a spy. Aly learns that her charges are of greater import than just the daughters of a banished noble; one of the girls is the "One Who Is Promised," a true heir to the throne of the Copper Isles. Through Aly's skills in diplomacy and her own spy craft, she must find a way to bring the girls to safety and enable the One Who Is Promised to take on her true destiny. "The new Tortall page-turner will delight existing fans and create many more," promised a writer for *Kirkus Reviews.* Though noticing the slower pace of the novel, a reviewer for *Publishers Weekly* suggested that the pace "will be just right to her legion of devotees."

In a review of *Lady Knight,* a writer for the *Cincinnati Enquirer* said of the Tortall novels, "Even if you are late to this world, you'll quickly become immersed in it." Commenting on Pierce's heroines, Elizabeth Devereaux of the *New York Times* wrote, "The lure of the Tortall heroines is not in their infinite variety nor is it in their verisimilitude. Rather, they faithfully reiterate an ideal—of feminine power that relies on brains, not beauty; of feminine attractiveness that relies on competence, not helplessness; and of feminine alliances that grow stronger, not weaker, in the face of conflicts." Pierce herself has commented that she is devoted to bringing female heroines (also called "sheroes") to life.

"When I was growing up," she told Cecelia Goodnow of the *Seattle Post-Intelligencer,* "I was looking for female warriors. So I was writing what I wanted to read, which was girls kicking butt in medieval times." She also told Goodnow that while there are many girl heroines not conforming to stereotypical girl roles, "I think I'm just about the only one who has girls going through military training. Girls as knights—that's a very powerful image."

"I owe my career as a writer and my approach to writing to people like my writing mentor, David Bradley, who taught me that writing is not an arcane and mystical process, administered by the initiate and fraught with obstacles, but an enjoyable pastime that gives other people as much pleasure as it does me," Pierce once commented. "I enjoy telling stories, and, although some of my topics are grim, people get caught up in them."

A woman with wide-ranging interests, Pierce continues to focus her research in specific areas, many of which eventually become incorporated into her fantasy novels for teens. "I am interested in medieval customs, life, and chivalry," she once said. "I study Japanese, Central Asian, and Arabic history and culture; wildlife and nature; crime; the American Civil War; and the conflicts between Islam and Christianity in the Middle Ages and the Renaissance. Occasionally I rescue hurt or homeless animals in a local park . . ., visit schools as often as I can, and read, read, read."

Biographical and Critical Sources

BOOKS

Authors and Artists for Young Adults, Volume 26, Gale (Detroit, MI), 1998.
Beacham's Guide to Literature for Young Adults, Volume 8, Beacham Publishing (Osprey, FL), 1994.
Encyclopedia of Fantasy, St. Martin's Press (New York, NY), 1997.
St. James Guide to Young Adult Writers, 2nd edition, St. James Press (Detroit, MI), 1999.
Speaking for Ourselves II: More Autobiographical Sketches by Notable Authors of Books for Young Adults, National Council of Teachers of English (Urbana, IL), 1993.

PERIODICALS

Booklist, October 15, 1992, Sally Estes, review of *Wild Magic,* p. 419; March 15, 1994, Mary Harris Veeder, review of *Wolf-Speaker,* p. 1344; June 1, 1995, Sally Estes, review of *The Emperor Mage,* p. 1757; October 15, 1996, Sally Estes, review of *The Realms of the Gods,* p. 414; August, 1998, Chris Sherman, review of *Tris's Book,* p. 1991; December 1, 1998, Chris Sherman, review of *Daja's Book,* p. 662; February 15,

1999, Chris Sherman, review of *Briar's Book*, p. 1060; May 15, 1999, Sally Estes, "Top Ten Fantasy Novels for Youth," p. 1691; June 1, 1999, Susan Dove Lempke, review of *First Test*, p. 1832; March 1, 2000, Shelle Rosenfeld, review of *Magic Steps*, p. 1236; August, 2000, Susan Dove Lempke, review of *Page*, p. 2141; April 15, 2001, Shelle Rosenfeld, review of *Street Magic*, p. 1557; September 1, 2001, Susan Dove Lempke, review of *Squire*, p. 97; September 1, 2002, Chris Sherman, review of *Cold Fire*, p. 2002; October 1, 2002, Susan Dove Lempke, review of *Lady Knight*, p. 313; March 1, 2003, Shelle Rosenfeld, review of *Shatterglass*, p. 1193.

Book Report, March-April, 1993, Holly Wadsworth, review of *Wild Magic*, p. 43; September-October, 1994, Kathryn Whetstone, review of *Wolf-Speaker*, p. 43; November-December, 1995, Ruth Dishnow Cox, review of *The Emperor Mage*, p. 43; November-December, 1997, Carol Sinofsky, review of *Sandry's Book*, p. 41.

Bulletin of the Center for Children's Books, November, 1984, p. 53; April, 1986, p. 156; November, 1997, pp. 97-98.

Childhood Education, fall, 2002, Elsa L. Geskus, review of *Cold Fire*, p. 52.

Cincinnati Enquirer, October 15, 2002, review of *Lady Knight*, p. C3.

Horn Book, October, 1983, Ethel R. Twichell, review of *Alanna: The First Adventure*, pp. 577-578; September-October, 1984, review of *In the Hand of the Goddess*, pp. 598-599; May-June, 1986, Ann A. Flowers, review of *The Woman Who Rides Like a Man*, pp. 333-334; March-April, 1989, p. 234; January-February, 1993, Ann A. Flowers, review of *Wild Magic*, p. 93; September-October, 1994, Ann A. Flowers, review of *Wolf-Speaker*, p. 613; July-August, 1995, p. 485; May, 2000, Anne St. John, review of *Magic Steps*, p. 319; March, 2001, Anne St. John, review of *Street Magic*, p. 211; July, 2001, Anne St. John, review of *Squire*, p. 460; May-June, 2003, Anita L. Burkam, review of *Shatterglass*, p. 353; January-February, 2004, Anita L. Burkam, review of *Trickster's Choice*, p. 90.

Junior Bookshelf, October, 1989, review of *The Woman Who Rides like a Man*, p. 243.

Kirkus Reviews, August 1, 1988, pp. 1154-1155; October 15, 1992, p. 1314; July 15, 1997, review of *Sandry's Book*; May 1, 2002, review of *Cold Fire*, p. 665; July 15, 2002, review of *Lady Knight*, p. 1041; March 15, 2003, review of *Shatterglass*, p. 475; September 1, 2003, review of *Trickster's Choice*, p. 1129.

Kliatt, March, 2002, Paula Rohrlick, review of *Cold Fire*, p. 11; November, 2002, Paula Rohrlick, review of *Lady Knight*, p. 14; November, 2003, Paula Rohrlick, review of *Trickster's Choice*, p. 8.

New York Times, November 16, 2003, Elizabeth Devereaux, "Woman Warrior," review of *Trickster's Choice*, p. 39.

Publishers Weekly, May 24, 1999, review of *First Test*, p. 80; February 21, 2000, review of *Magic Steps*, p. 88; September 15, 2003, review of *Trickster's Choice*, p. 66.

Roanoke Times, April 3, 1997, Cassandra Spratling, "Young Readers Are Giving Prince Charming the Brush Off," p. 1.

School Library Journal, December, 1984, Isabel Soffer, review of *In the Hand of the Goddess*, p. 94; July, 1995, Patricia A. Dollisch, review of *The Emperor Mage*, p. 80; August, 1995, Bonnie Kunzel, "The Call of the Wild: YAs Running with the Wolves," pp. 37-38; November, 1996, p. 124; April, 1998, Beth Wright, review of *Tris's Book*, p. 136; December, 1998, Carrie Schadle, review of *Daja's Book*, pp. 129-130; March, 1999, Eva Mitnick, review of *Briar's Book*, pp. 213-214; July, 1999, Kathleen Isaacs, review of *First Test*, p. 99; August, 2000, Heather Dieffenbach, review of *Page*, p. 188; July, 2001, Eva Mitnick, review of *Street Magic*, p. 112; August, 2001, Patricia A. Dollisch, review of *Squire*, p. 186; August, 2002, Lisa Prolman, review of *Cold Fire*, p. 196; December, 2002, Sharon Rawlins, review of *Lady Knight*, p. 146; July, 2003, Beth L. Meister, review of *Shatterglass*, p. 134; December, 2003, Connie Tyrrell Burns, review of *Trickster's Choice*, p. 158.

Seattle Post-Intelligencer, November 4, 2003, Cecelia Goodnow, "Pierce's Skill at Spinning Yarns Has Paid Off," p. E1.

Voice of Youth Advocates, April, 1985, p. 56; December, 1988, p. 248; August, 1994, Mary L. Adams, review of *Wolf-Speaker*, p. 159.

ONLINE

Tamora Pierce Web Site, http://www.tamora-pierce.com/ (January 21, 2004).*

*   *   *

PORTO, Tony 1960-

Personal

Born August 9, 1960, in Evergreen Park, IL; son of Joseph (owner of a wholesale produce company) and Geraldine (a high school teacher) Porto; married Mary O'Sullivan (a radiology technologist), November 10, 1984; children: John, Anne. *Education:* Illinois Institute of Technology, B.S. (visual design), 1982.

Addresses

Home—2435 West Coyle, Chicago, IL 60645. *Office*—Three Communication Design, 4507 N. Ravenswood, Suite 105, Chicago, IL 60640. *E-mail*—tony@3cd.com.

Career

Three Communication Design (graphic design firm), Chicago, IL, founding partner, 1989—; writer.

Writings

Get Red!: An Adventure in Color, Little, Brown (Boston, MA), 2002.

Blue Aliens!: An Adventure in Color, Little, Brown (New York, NY), 2003.

Tony Porto

Work in Progress

A third book in the series that began with *Get Red!,* titled *Chicken Yellow.*

Sidelights

Tony Porto is a member of a Chicago-based partnership that includes Mitch Rice and Glenn Deutsch. Together, Porto, Rice, and Deutsch founded Three Communication Design, a graphic arts company with a focus on educational publishing. *Get Red!: An Adventure in Color* and *Blue Aliens: An Adventure in Color* are collaborative efforts, but Porto is responsible for the text in both volumes. Critics consider these works cleverly humorous concept books that celebrate the many appearances of color in nature and culture.

In *Get Red!* a narrator who does not appear introduces readers to a talking red crayon who helps to get all sorts of class projects done. Unfortunately, the crayon is dwindling in size, and as it does its temper gets short. Just when the crayon is needed the most—to color a drawing of the planet Mars—it disappears. The narrator must employ psychology to persuade the crayon to give its all for the sake of a class project. In addition to the plot, readers are treated to facts about the color red and photographs of red objects. Through the book, suggested Lynda Ritterman in *School Library Journal,* youngsters "are made aware of the uses of the color in

art and nature." Ritterman found *Get Red!* "attractive" and "imaginative." A *Publishers Weekly* critic likewise praised "this creative team's eye for arresting photos and design."

"I suppose you could say that the idea for *Get Red!* was 'born' . . . at Three Communications Design," Porto told *SATA.* "My 3CD partners (Mitch Rice and Glenn Deutsch) and I decided that it would be lots of fun to design a children's book with a bunch of pictures that had only one thing in common—color. So we set about collecting images and interesting facts to go along with them. But no matter how big the pile of images grew, it always seemed incomplete. It eventually occurred to us that we needed a story to hold everything together. Ya see, we're graphic designers, we tend to get excited by visual things first.

"So anyway, I took a crack at writing the story. I really enjoyed making both the kid and his crayon a couple of smart-alecks since I'm kind of a smart-alecky guy myself.

"Oh yeah, at some point along the way, we decided *not* to let the reader see what the kid in the story looks like. We wanted to keep the attention on all the neat red

Because your tongue is red like a raspberry, and kind of shaped like one too, sticking your tongue out at someone is called giving them a raspberry.

***Inspired by his lack of a red crayon to do a school project about Mars, a boy launches into an exploration of red things.** (From* Get Red!: An Adventure in Color, *written by Tony Porto and conceived and designed by 3CD—Porto, Mitch Rice, and Glenn Deutsch.)*

stuff. Besides, he's pretty goofy, and we couldn't get a picture of him with a clean shirt on and his hair combed."

The same "goofy" kid carries the story in *Blue Aliens!* Having watched a movie about aliens who eat anything green, the frightened narrator convinces himself that blue aliens must be eating all the blue objects missing in the world. The hungry aliens steal the blue-lined paper and threaten a schoolteacher, Mrs. Sapphire, who loves blue eyeshadow and blue earrings. Marianne Saccardi in *School Library Journal* noted that readers "will be delightfully 'grossed out'" by the imaginative illustrations. Saccardi concluded that "the alien subject matter will . . . draw readers in."

Biographical and Critical Sources

PERIODICALS

Publishers Weekly, August 5, 2002, review of *Get Red!: An Adventure in Color,* p. 72; November 17, 2003, "Favorite Characters Return," p. 67.
School Library Journal, October, 2002, Lynda Ritterman, review of *Get Red!,* p. 126; November, 2003, Marianne Saccardi, review of *Blue Aliens!: An Adventure in Color,* p. 113.

*   *   *

PRYOR, Michael 1957-

Personal

Born April 23, 1957, in Swan Hill, Victoria, Australia; son of James (a builder) and Shirley (a finance manager; maiden name, Harris) Pryor; married Wendy Cracknell (a web project manager), October 9, 1982; children: Celeste, Ruby. *Ethnicity:* "Australian." *Education:* University of Melbourne, B.A., 1978, diploma of education, 1979. *Religion:* Anglican. *Hobbies and other interests:* Sport, cooking, wine, multimedia.

Addresses

Home—45 Shiers St., Alphington, Victoria 3078, Australia. *Agent*—Cherry Weiner Literary Agency, 28 Kipling Way, Manalapan, NJ 07726-3711. *E-mail*—michael@michaelpryor.com.au.

Career

Teacher and writer. Banyule High School, Melbourne, Victoria, Australia, English teacher, 1980-93; Viewbank College, Melbourne, instructor in English, 1993-97; Harcourt Education, Melbourne, electronic publisher, 1998—.

Member

Australian Society of Authors; Melbourne Football Club.

Awards, Honors

Shortlisted for the Aurealis Awards four times; three "Notable Book" citations, Children's Book Council of Australia.

Writings

The Mask of Caliban, Hodder Headline Australia (Sydney, New South Wales, Australia), 1996.
Talent, Hodder Headline Australia (Sydney, New South Wales, Australia), 1997.
The House of Many Rooms ("Doorways" trilogy), Hodder Headline Australia (Sydney, New South Wales, Australia), 1998.
The Book of Plans ("Doorways" trilogy), Hodder Headline Australia (Sydney, New South Wales, Australia), 1998.
The Unmaker ("Doorways" trilogy), Hodder Headline Australia (Sydney, New South Wales, Australia), 1999.
Cosmic Cook, Addison Wesley Longman (Melbourne, Victoria, Australia), 1999.
Blackout, Hodder Headline Australia (Sydney, New South Wales, Australia), 2000.
Air Time, Pearson Education (South Melbourne, Victoria, Australia), 2001.
Don't Make Vompa Unhappy, Barrie Publishing (Port Melbourne, Victoria, Australia), 2001.
Dog Days, Pearson Education (South Melbourne, Victoria, Australia), 2002.
Bruno Trask and the Dark Lady's Jewels, Hodder Children's Books Australia (Sydney, New South Wales, Australia), 2002.
Quentaris in Flames, Lothian Books (South Melbourne, Victoria, Australia), 2003.
Beneath Quentaris, Lothian Books (South Melbourne, Victoria, Australia), 2003.
Stones of Quentaris, Lothian Books (South Melbourne, Victoria, Australia), 2004.

Contributor of "Room for Improvement" to *Gadgets and Gizmos,* edited by Paul Collins and Meredith Costain, Addison Wesley Longman (South Melbourne, Victoria, Australia), 1999, and "Honest Harry's Used Spaceships" to *Alien Encounters,* edited by Paul Collins and Meredith Costain, Pearson Education (South Melbourne, Victoria, Australia), 2000.

Work in Progress

Blaze of Glory, a fantasy novel for teens.

Sidelights

Michael Pryor told *SATA:* "I began writing because I'd been working as a teacher of English for a dozen years, telling young people how to write, what to write, when to write. One day it struck me that I didn't know if I could do what I was expecting all my students to do.

"That night, I sat down and started a story.

"Of course, I'd always thought I could be a writer—one day. I'd loved reading from an early age (something that has never left me), and I'd felt that I'd like to do the magic that writers were doing for me. One day.

"After sweating over that initial story, drafting and re-drafting, crossing out and starting again, being assailed by doubts and second thoughts, I eventually finished. I sent it to a magazine publisher. They liked it, bought it, and published it.

"That was the beginning of my writing career.

"I'm a believer in the great tradition of storytelling. I believe the highest praise is when a reader says, 'I couldn't put your book down.' I want readers to turn pages, to be lost in the narrative, to be constantly wanting to know what's going to happen next.

"I write fantasy (and science fiction) because I believe that this is where the big questions are explored. Who are we? What are we doing here? Is there such a thing as destiny, and what about free will? What are the limits of imagination?

"I admire writers of the imagination. J. R. R. Tolkien, the master. Roger Zelazny. Paul Collins. Phillip Pullman. Robert Heinlein.

"My writing has appeared in Australia, New Zealand, Denmark, China, and the United States. Editions of my latest books are about to be published in Russia and Thailand. Several of my books have been made into 'Talking Books,' audio versions with professional actors narrating.

"I visit many schools, libraries, and conferences talking about my work and about writing and reading in general. Talking to large groups and running workshops is exciting and keeps me in touch with my readership."

Biographical and Critical Sources

PERIODICALS

Courier-Mail (Brisbane, Queensland, Australia), January 10, 2004, Jason Nahrung, review of "Quentaris" series, p. M6.

ONLINE

Michael Pryor Web Site, http://www.michaelpryor.com.au/ (March 15, 2004).

R-S

RHUE, Morton
See STRASSER, Todd

*   *   *

RODDIE, Shen

Personal
Born in Singapore; married Terence Roddie (a management consultant); children: Charles, Tanya. *Education:* Earned B.A. in history. *Religion:* Christian.

Addresses
Home—11 Rolfe Place, Oxford OX3 ODS, England. *Agent*—Eunice McMullen, Low Ibbotsholme Cottage, Off Bridgelane, Troutbeck Bridge, Windermere, Cumbria LA23 1HU, England. *E-mail*—shen@roddie.co.uk.

Career
Writer. Has also worked as a journalist, public relations director for an oil company, copywriter, and radio presenter.

Awards, Honors
Shortlist citation, Sheffield Book Prize, for *Mrs. Wolf.*

Writings

Hatch, Egg, Hatch!: A Touch-and-Feel Action Flap Book, illustrated by Frances Cony, Joy Street Books (Boston, MA), 1991.
Animal Stew: A Lift-the-Flap Surprise Book, illustrated by Patrick Gallagher, Houghton Mifflin (Boston, MA), 1991.
Mrs. Wolf, illustrated by Korky Paul, Tango Books (London, England), 1992, Dial Books for Young Readers (New York, NY), 1993.

Shen Roddie

Mini Beasty's Itch, illustrated by Maureen Roffey, Tango Books (London, England), 1993, published in America as *The Terrible Itch: A Scratch and Bite Pop-Up Book,* Simon & Schuster Books for Young Readers (New York, NY), 1993.
Chicken Pox!: A Touch-and-Feel Pull-Tab Pop-Up Book, illustrated by Frances Cony, Joy Street Books (Boston, MA), 1993.
Don't Be Silly, Mrs. Nellie, illustrated by Sonia Holleyman, Orchard Books (London, England), 1994.
Help, Mama, Help!: A Touch-and-Feel Pull-Tab Pop-Up Book, illustrated by Frances Cony, Little, Brown (Boston, MA), 1995.
Tamborina's Troubles: A Pop-Up Storybook, illustrated by Maureen Roffey, Tango Books (London, England), 1995.
Fancy That!: A First Story about Growth, illustrated by Stephen Yardley, Reader's Digest Children's Books (Bath, England), 1997.
Shipwreck!: A First Story about Sorting and Pairing, illustrated by Nadine Bernard Westcott, Reader's Digest Children's Books (Bath, England), 1997.
The House That Pig Built: A First Story about Manners, illustrated by Jan Lewis, Reader's Digest Children's Books (Bath, England), 1997.

Best of Friends!, illustrated by Sally Anne Lambert, Frances Lincoln (London, England), 1997.

The Fastest Egg and Spoon Race Ever: A First Story about Time, illustrated by Philip Norman, Reader's Digest Children's Books (Bath, England), 1997.

Best of Friends, illustrated by Sally Anne Lambert, Frances Lincoln (London, England), 1997, published in America as *Too Close Friends,* Dial Books for Young Readers (New York, NY), 1998.

Henry's Box, illustrated by Sue King, Ladybird (Loughborough, England), 1998.

Toes Are to Tickle, illustrated by Kady MacDonald Denton, Tricycle Press (Berkeley, CA), 1997.

Please Don't Chat to the Bus Driver, illustrated by Jill Newton, Bloomsbury Children's Books (London, England), 2000.

Simon Says!, illustrated by Sally Anne Lambert, Frances Lincoln (London, England), 2000.

Not Now, Mrs. Wolf!, illustrated by Selina Young, Dorling Kindersley (New York, NY), 2000.

Whoever's Heard of a Hibernating Pig, illustrated by Eleanor Taylor, Bloomsbury Children's Books (London, England), 2000.

Goodbye, Hello!, illustrated by Carol Thompson, Dorling Kindersley (New York, NY), 2001.

Sandbear, illustrated by Jenny Jones, Bloomsbury Children's Books (New York, NY), 2002.

The Gossipy Parrot, illustrated by Michael Terry, Bloomsbury Children's Books (New York, NY), 2003.

You're Too Small, illustrated by Steve Lavis, Tiger Tales (Wilton, CT), 2004.

Also author of *A Pet Please, Mama!,* Tango Books (London, England); *Caterpillar's Wedding,* Templar Books (London, England); *Helpful Henry,* Ladybird Books (Loughborough, England); *Baby Goes Too!,* Chrysalis Books (London, England); *Goatee's Pumpkin,* Victoria House; and *From This to That,* Victoria House. Publisher, *Colour Me Happy,* Macmillan (London, England); *My Name Is Mr. Fox,* Macmillan (London, England); *Peekaboo!,* Parragon; and *Oops-a-Daisy!,* Parragon.

Adaptations

Henry's Box and *Toes Are to Tickle* were adapted for a television special by the British Broadcasting Corporation (BBC-TV) and the Australian Broadcasting Corporation (ABC-TV).

Sidelights

Shen Roddie told *SATA:* "If my mother is to be believed, I started making up tales and spewing them out when I was a pesky thing of five. I would mercilessly regale her guests with peculiar stories while she fixed the coffee. This progressed to telling real-life stories as a journalist on the national daily, which memorably included interviewing the crew of Apollo 17—the last men to walk on the moon.

"I moved on to a different audience when I worked for an oil company, producing in-house journals that kept staff in touch with each other. This involved my to-ing and fro-ing in ferries between the mainland and the pretty island refinery. I then went on to freelance for radio, presenting programmes which included modern-day innovations—still my favourite subject today.

"But my best and most rewarding audience has to be the Under Fives. Get it right, and their little faces light up. Get it wrong and I've lost them!

"*Please Don't Chat to the Bus Driver* was directly triggered by a trip to London on an Oxford coach. At the last pick-up point, up hopped a large and garrulous lady who sat behind the driver and engaged him all the way to London! With all that head-bobbing going on, we were left wondering if we were *ever* going to arrive at all. But we did! Which was just as well, as any of the incidents in the story could have happened!

"Many of my texts tend to focus on short, snappy storylines which offer the young reader a different way of seeing things. I am happy with a picture book that lifts their horizons, challenges them verbally while keeping them interested and amused."

A Singaporean who lives in the United Kingdom, Roddie has drawn an international audience with her lively animal tales, some of which feature interactive pop-up features and the kind of tactile pages made popular by *Pat the Bunny.* In *Chicken Pox!,* for instance, youngsters can manipulate flaps to make the poor, suffering baby chick scratch her itches. *Hatch, Egg, Hatch!: A Touch-and-Feel Action Flap Book* combines flaps and textures as a mother hen muddles through the process of encouraging her egg to hatch. The popular *Mrs. Wolf* features a title character who rises to the occasion when a lamb accidentally tumbles into her lair. As readers help Mrs. Wolf bathe her visitor, and then work with her in a pop-up kitchen, the frightened lamb assumes the worst—right until the end.

Roddie has received enthusiastic reviews for her "touch and feel" books. "Never has an egg seemed as endearing," commented a *Publishers Weekly* reviewer of *Hatch, Egg, Hatch!* Another *Publishers Weekly* critic gave *Chicken Pox!* a starred review, calling the book "a perfect Rx for convalescents and other fractious youngsters . . . a catchy concept." Yet another *Publishers Weekly* correspondent felt that *Mrs. Wolf* "would succeed even without the clever paper engineering." The reviewer concluded that *Mrs. Wolf* is "a book to savor."

Some of Roddie's tales impart gentle lessons to the youngest listeners and are meant to be shared with a parent or other nurturing adult. In *Tamborina's Troubles: A Pop-Up Storybook* Tamborina the turtle is trying to get to her dance recital on time, but she just cannot refuse when other animals ask for a ride on her back. Before she knows it, Tamborina is carrying a dizzying array of animals, from a fox and a moose to an elephant, plus their band instruments. Needless to say, a bad spill ensues, and Tamborina finally learns to say "No"—and nicely. Baby Chick and her mother make their third appearance in *Help, Mama, Help!: A Touch-and-Feel Pull-Tab Pop-Up Book.* This time through the imaginative tabs and pop-ups, Chick learns to overcome fear by seeking out Mama's reassurance and then just simply being brave. A *Publishers Weekly* critic concluded: "Baby Chick may need some help, but Roddie and [illustrator Frances] Cony have their formula down pat."

Too Close Friends, published in England as *Best of Friends,* explores a humorous situation that might be new to young readers. Hippo and Pig live next door to one another, and they are fast friends—until they decide to cut the hedge between their houses so they can see each other all the time. That is when Pig discovers, to her horror, that Hippo chews his toenails. Hippo, for his part, is appalled by Pig's eating habits and her too-tight tutu. Good will is restored only when the hedge grows back. "The joy of friendship—and of privacy—is dramatized in this gentle, funny picture book," observed Hazel Rochman in *Booklist.* A *Publishers Weekly* critic declared that the book would leave children "chuckling while they learn a gentle lesson about respecting the privacy of even their best pals."

An impatient hare decides to craft a sand sculpture in *Sandbear.* Noticing a mound of sand that is slightly bear-shaped, Hare adds a few quick touches to make the mound more bear-like. Hare is in a hurry, though, so his efforts are slapdash: He uses grass for an arm and a piece of driftwood for a nose, and the legs he creates aren't strong enough to hold an actual bear. Nevertheless, when Hare goes on his way, the affable Sandbear comes to life and follows, just in time to save Hare's life. Realizing the value of the friendship, Hare takes more care when he rebuilds Sandbear a second time. "Sandbear is a delightful, wistful, appealing creature who will enchant children," maintained Robin L. Gibson in *School Library Journal.* A *Publishers Weekly* contributor deemed the work "a magical tale about imagination, creativity and responsibility," concluding that a "lovely, understated joy radiates from the final scene."

Toes Are to Tickle and *You're Too Small* aim at the toddler audience. In *Toes Are to Tickle,* an enterprising and curious tot and his parents find uses for everything, from trees "to hide behind," peas "for counting," and milk "to give to the cat." In *Booklist,* Hazel Rochman commented that the title "evokes the toddler's world in all its fumbling, laughter, hugs, and messy comfort." Tad the mouse, the hero of *You're Too Small,* just can't seem to do anything without being warned that he's too small by the other, larger animals. The tables are turned, however, when the animals find the barn door locked with their dinner inside. It is Tad who squeezes through a crack to unlock the door—but only after taking the biggest piece of pie. "Most youngsters are quick to welcome a tale about someone little proving the big guys

wrong," observed a *Publishers Weekly* critic. In *The Bookseller,* Sarah Amond called *You're Too Small* "a great book for younger readers."

Biographical and Critical Sources

PERIODICALS

Booklist, June 1, 1997, Hazel Rochman, review of *Toes Are to Tickle,* p. 1721; February 1, 1998, Hazel Rochman, review of *Too Close Friends,* p. 913; December 15, 2001, Ilene Cooper, review of *Goodbye, Hello!,* p. 741.

Bookseller, February 20, 2004, Sarah Amond, "May Children's Titles," p. 31.

Publishers Weekly, April 26, 1991, review of *Hatch, Egg, Hatch!: A Touch-and-Feel Action Flap Book,* p. 58; April 13, 1992, review of *Animal Stew: A Lift-the-Flap Surprise Book,* p. 56; April 5, 1993, review of *Chicken Pox!: A Touch-and-Feel Pull-Tab Pop-up Book,* p. 74; April 26, 1993, review of *The Terrible Itch,* p. 76; May 17, 1993, review of *Mrs. Wolf,* p. 80; May 1, 1995, review of *Help, Mama, Help!: A Touch-and-Feel Pull-Tab Pop-Up Book,* p. 56; May 22, 1995, review of *Tambourina's Troubles: A Pop-Up Storybook,* p. 58; May 26, 1997, review of *Toes Are to Tickle,* p. 84; March 16, 1998, review of *Too Close Friends,* p. 63; May 6, 2002, review of *Sandbear,* p. 58; March 15, 2004, review of *You're Too Small,* p. 74.

School Library Journal, December, 2000, Linda K. Kenton, review of *Not Now, Mrs. Wolf!,* p. 104; October, 2002, Robin L. Gibson, review of *Sandbear,* p. 126.

*   *   *

SAKURAI, Gail 1952-

Personal

Born February 9, 1952, in Detroit, MI; daughter of Peter Robert (an automotive parts inspector) and Virginia Evelyn (a homemaker) Kwentus; married Eric Sakurai (an executive), July 31, 1971; children: Nicholas, Cameron. *Education:* Oakland University, B.A., 1979. *Hobbies and other interests:* Spending time with family, listening to classical music, reading.

Addresses

Office—P.O. Box 1532, West Chester, OH 45071.

Career

Writer.

Member

Society of Children's Book Writers and Illustrators.

Writings

Peach Boy: A Japanese Legend, Troll Associates (Mahwah, NJ), 1994.

Mae Jemison: Space Scientist, Children's Press (Chicago, IL), 1995.

The Liberty Bell, Children's Press (Chicago, IL), 1996.

Stephen Hawking: Understanding the Universe, Children's Press (New York, NY), 1996.

The Jamestown Colony, Children's Press (New York, NY), 1997.

Paul Revere, Children's Press (New York, NY), 1997.

The Library of Congress, Children's Press (New York, NY), 1998.

The Louisiana Purchase, Children's Press (New York, NY), 1998.

Asian-Americans in the Old West, Children's Press (New York, NY), 2000.

The Thirteen Colonies, Children's Press (New York, NY), 2000.

Juan Ponce de León, Franklin Watts (New York, NY), 2001.

Japanese American Internment Camps, Children's Press (New York, NY), 2002.

Also author of "Why the Sea Is Salty" (a re-told Japanese folk tale), *Jack and Jill* magazine, 1995.

Sidelights

Gail Sakurai told *SATA* that she "always wanted to be a writer, ever since I learned to read as a child. I planned to have my first book published by the time I was thirteen! Things didn't quite work out that way, however. For many years, other interests and needs interfered with writing, but I never lost my love of books. After getting married, holding a variety of jobs, graduating from college, and having two children, I finally returned to writing. My childhood dream came true with the publication of my first book in 1994—only twenty-nine years later than originally planned."

Sakurai described her first book, *Peach Boy: A Japanese Legend,* as a retelling of a Japanese folktale. "I learned the tale years ago from my Japanese husband, who told it to our two sons as a bedtime story," she said. "When I decided to write for children, it just seemed natural to choose *Peach Boy* for my first story. I wanted American children to be able to enjoy it as much as Japanese children have for centuries.

"My second book, a biography of Dr. Mae Jemison, the first African-American woman astronaut, grew out of my lifelong interest in space exploration. I get the ideas from my books from everywhere—from things I read, from my children, and even from television. I have more ideas than I'll ever have time to use.

"I specialize in writing nonfiction and retelling folktales from many lands. Through reading I developed an interest in other countries and cultures at an early age. I have studied French, Spanish, Italian, and Japanese, and have traveled widely.

"The hardest parts of writing are finding the time to write in a busy schedule full of family obligations, and getting started. Once I start, the words usually come quickly, because I have planned them in my head before my fingers ever touch the keyboard.

"The best parts of writing are the sense of accomplishment I feel when I have finished a story to my satisfaction, and when I sell that story to a publisher. I also enjoy meeting my readers and giving presentations at schools and libraries. My advice to aspiring writers is to read. Read everything you can get your hands on!"

Most of Sakurai's books are nonfiction history and biography texts suitable for elementary-age students who want to research famous people or landmarks. Some of her work is part of the "Cornerstones of Freedom" series, published by Children's Press. Sakurai can cover broad topics, such as the founding of the nation in *The Thirteen Colonies,* or more specific subjects, as in *The Jamestown Colony, The Liberty Bell* and *The Library of Congress.* In her *School Library Journal* review of *The Liberty Bell,* Margaret C. Howell observed that Sakurai includes many facts about the national icon that might not be known even to adults. Howell praised the book as "useful."

Sakurai has profiled several notable Americans in easy-to-read biographies, from the explorer Ponce de Leó to Paul Revere and Stephen Hawking. These also fall into two series, "Cornerstones of Freedom" and "Picture-Story Biographies." She has also explored the history of Asian Americans in this nation in two books: *Asian-Americans in the Old West* and *Japanese American Internment Camps.* The latter title describes how Japanese Americans were rounded up during World War II and forced to live in camps far from home. Carolyn Angus in *School Library Journal* has found Sakurai's nonfiction work "appropriate for young readers," for its inclusion of photographs, drawings, and chronologies that help children fix events on a particular date.

Biographical and Critical Sources

PERIODICALS

Booklist, August, 1996, Ilene Cooper, review of *Stephen Hawking: Understanding the Universe,* p. 1897.

School Library Journal, August, 1996, Margaret C. Howell, review of *The Liberty Bell,* p. 150; September, 1996, Carolyn Angus, review of *Stephen Hawking,* p. 220.*

*   *   *

SALE, Tim 1956-

Personal

Born May 1, 1956, in Ithaca, NY. *Education:* Studied art at University of Washington; studied comic art with John Buscema.

Addresses

Agent—c/o Author Mail, DC Comics, 1700 Broadway, New York, NY 10019. *E-mail*—askeditors@dccomics. com.

Career

Comic book artist, 1985—; began with Warp Graphics' *Myth Adventures,* has also worked for Thieves' World Graphics, DC Comics, and Marvel Comics.

Writings

ILLUSTRATOR; GRAPHIC NOVELS

Thieves' World Graphics 1, Thieves' World, 1985.
Thieves' World Graphics 2, Thieves' World, 1986.
Thieves' World Graphics 3, Thieves' World, 1986.
Thieves' World Graphics 4, Thieves' World, 1987.
Thieves' World Graphics (compilation), Donning Co. (Norfolk, VA), 1987.
Thieves' World Graphics 6, Thieves' World, 1988.
Batman: Madness: Legends of the Dark Knight, DC Comics (New York, NY), 1994.
Batman: Ghosts: A Tale of Halloween in Gotham City, DC Comics (New York, NY), 1995.
Batman: Haunted Knight: The Legends of the Dark Knight, DC Comics (New York, NY), 1995.
Thieves's World Graphics, DC Comics (New York, NY), 1995.
Batman: The Long Halloween, DC Comics (New York, NY), 1998.
Superman for All Seasons, DC Comics (New York, NY), 1999.
Deathblow: Sinners and Saints, WildStorm Productions (La Jolla, CA), 1999.

Artist for episodic comic books, including *The Amazon; Batgirl 21; Batman: Choices; Batman: Dark Victory; Batman: Shadow of the Bat; Billi 99, 1-4; The Black Hood, 10-11; Cable 23; Challengers of the Unknown 1-8; Comico Christmas Special 1; Daredevil: Yellow 1-6; Deathblow 3-14; Excalibur 75; Grendel 20, 23, 34-40; Grendel: Black, White, and Red; Grendel Cycle; Grendel: Devil Child 1-2; Grendel: War Child 8; Hearthrobs 1; The Savage Hulk; Showcase '94 3-4; Spiderman: Blue 1-6; Total Eclipse 2;* (Contributor) *Uncanny X-Men Annual 18;* and *Wolverine/Gambit: Victims 1-4.* Contributor of cover art to numerous comic books and trade paperbacks; contributor of pinup art to comic books.

Sidelights

Comic books offer unusual opportunities for collaboration, and artist Tim Sale has paired with writer Jeph Loeb on numerous single issue comics and longer graphic novels featuring Batman, Superman, Grendel, Daredevil, Catwoman, and the Hulk. Sale is the artist for these efforts, and—amazingly—he is colorblind. His work features dramatic use of light and shadow, and he has challenged the traditional conceptions of Batman and Superman—and their villainous adversaries—in such longer works as *Batman: The Long Halloween* and *Superman for All Seasons.* Loeb's stories allow for maximum impact of the artwork, and so Sale has earned a wide following for his sometimes unique take on superheroes.

Born in New York, Sale grew up reading Marvel Comics, an irony since the vast majority of his work is for rival publisher DC Comics. He studied art in college in the Pacific Northwest, and he took a brief course on comic book art with John Buscema in New York. Sale took his time becoming deeply involved in the business. For some years he drew his art privately, only to please himself. When he found himself working at a fast-food taco stand in his late twenties, however, he decided to try to sell some work. This led to an association with Thieves' World Graphics, a fantasy anthology series, where he illustrated stories by Lynn Abbey and Robert Lynn Asprin. Sale's association with Loeb began in 1991, when they were asked to contribute to a DC Comics series called *Challengers of the Unknown.* They have been working for DC, and occasionally Marvel, ever since.

Sale became famous in comics circles for his contributions to the *Batman: Legends of the Dark Knight* series. Sale's Batman is "dark, angry, brooding, and frightening," to quote the artist himself on the *Long Halloween* Web site. Sale makes particular use of Batman's long, pointy ears and his eerie, flowing cape to suggest the hero's mystery and deep-seated anger. Even dressed in his street clothes, Sale's Bruce Wayne exudes an old-fashioned, black-and-white film star coolness, beginning with his baggy, boxy suits and ending with his trademark scowl. Sale has also become known for his creative depictions of Gotham City, in his Batman work, and Smallville in his Superman novel. "Sale's work has a haunted quality," observed Bill Jankiewicz on the *Long Halloween* Web site. "His crowded, sprawling comic-book worlds are full of pale, emaciated people who look like they wandered out of an Edward Gorey painting to live in buildings from a Fritz Lang movie." To quote Yannick Belzil on the *11th Hour Web Magazine* site, Sale "illustrates . . . marvelously. His pages, character designs, settings, and backgrounds all have one thing that makes him one of the best artists today: character. . . . His dark version of Gotham looks like no other city in comics."

One of the best known of Sale's and Loeb's collaborations is *Batman: The Long Halloween.* Published as a graphic novel, the story originated as thirteen comic books that came out once each month. The ongoing story pitted Batman against a new enemy, an anonymous murderer known only as "Holiday." In each month's comic book, "Holiday" killed someone on the best known holiday of that month. All thirteen issues, plus some supplemental material, appear in *The Long Halloween.* In his *Ninth Art* Web site review, John Connors wrote: "The art in *The Long Halloween* is nothing short of stunning. The book can be a quick read, largely due to Sale's liberal use of big panels and splash pages. Where for other artists the use of these big, show-offy images might be gratuitous, Sale wields the technique without a misstep." Connors characterized *The Long Halloween* as "a beautiful book, supreme in its quality of detail and sense of pacing."

Both *The Long Halloween* and *Superman for All Seasons* are what is known as "Year One" comics. These works take their heroes back in time to their earliest days as crime fighters, when they are first coming to know the various villains and loved ones that will be featured in their stories through the decades. This is particularly true of *Superman for All Seasons,* set in Smallville, where Clark Kent is a high school farm boy—even slightly chubby—becoming acquainted with his special powers and his need to keep them secret. Readers meet Clark's father, his high school girlfriend Lana Lang, his soon-to-be nemesis Lex Luthor, and—when Clark ventures to the big city—Lois Lane. "The story of how this alien boy grew up to be a great American hero is brilliantly shown in Jeph Loeb and Tim Sale's *Superman for All Seasons,*" declared Jason Sacks on the *Once Upon a Dime* Web site. Sacks found Sale's depiction of the teenaged Clark Kent "all awkward size and power, . . . wonderful and resonant." The critic concluded that the graphic novel "is a master collaboration between two thoughtful and insightful creators at the top of their game. . . . Don't miss it." On the *Silver Bullet Comic Books* Web site, Craig Lemon concluded that *Superman for All Seasons* is "head and shoulders above any Superman comic of the last ten years."

Speaking about his ongoing collaboration with Loeb, Sale told the *Comicon* Web site: "It was a long and often frustrating process to get to the very easy working relationship Jeph and I have now, but from the beginning we shared many of the same comics and pop cultural influences and had a fun and challenging rapport. Jeph is very smart and very funny and very different from me in many ways, and that somehow all clicks. We're good buddies. He is interested in writing stories that allow whoever is drawing them to shine, and almost unique in the field, actually can write to their strengths." Sale enjoys greeting fans at comic conventions, and the *Long Halloween* Web site includes his step-by-step instructions on how to draw Batman.

Biographical and Critical Sources

ONLINE

11th Hour Web Magazine http://www.the11thhour.com/ archives/ (June, 2000), Yannick Belzil, review of *Batman: The Long Halloween.*

Comicon, http://www.comicon.com/ (November 17, 2003), Jennifer M. Contino, interview with Sale.

DC Comics, http://www.dccomics.com/ (August 19, 2003), synopses of comic books, including *Superman for All Seasons.*

Long Halloween, http://thelonghalloween.vacuumboy9. com/ (June 2, 2004), interviews with Sale, information on drawing Batman, and reviews of *The Long Halloween.*

Ninth Art, http://www.ninthart.com/ (August 19, 2003), John Connors, review of *Batman: The Long Halloween.*

Once Upon a Dime, http://www.onceuponadime.com/ reviews/allseasons.htm/ (August 19, 2003), Jason Sacks, "Not-So-Strange Visitor."

Rambles: A Cultural Arts Magazine, http://www.rambles. net/superman_4seasons.html/ (August 19, 2003), Tom Knapp, review of *Superman for All Seasons.*

Silver Bullet Comic Books, http://www.silverbullet comicbooks.com/reviews/ (August 19, 2003), Craig Lemon, review of *Superman for All Seasons.*

Tim Sale Tribute, http://www.geocities.com/deforgeo_ thinking/bios.html/ (August 19, 2003), brief biography of Sale.*

*   *   *

SANDIN, Joan 1942-

Personal

Born April 30, 1942, in Watertown, WI; daughter of Robert L. (a teacher) and Frances K. (an interviewer; maiden name, Somers) Sandin; married Sigfrid Leijonhufvud (a journalist), April 30, 1971 (divorced, 1986); remarried; husband's name, Brian; children: Jonas, Jenny. *Education:* University of Arizona, B.F.A., 1964.

Addresses

Home—Tucson, AZ. *Agent*—c/o Author Mail, Books for Young Readers, Henry Holt and Company, 115 West 15th St., New York, NY 10011.

Career

Illustrator, author, and translator of children's books. *Exhibitions:* Solo shows in Sweden and the United States featuring illustrations from *The Long Way to a New Land.* Art represented in the Kerlan Collection.

Member

FST, Swedish Society of Illustrators.

Awards, Honors

Best Children's Books citation, American Institute of Graphic Artists, 1970, for *Crocodile and Hen;* travel and work grants from Forfattarfonden (Swedish Writers' Fund); exhibition grant from Bildkonstnarsfonden

***Jeph Loeb and Tim Sale portray a very human Superman, who, in the course of one year, performs deeds of heroism,
leaves his hometown of Smallville for big-city Metropolis, and returns home after emotional turmoil besets him.*** *(From
"Superman for All Seasons," #1 © DC Comics. All Rights Reserved. Used with Permission. By Jeph Loeb and Tim Sale with
Bjarne Hansen.)*

(Swedish Artists' Fund); Notable Children's Trade Book in the Field of Social Studies citations, National Council for the Social Studies/Children's Book Council, 1971, for *Hill of Fire,* 1975, for *The Lemming Condition,* 1981, for *The Long Way to a New Land,* and 1981, for *Time for Uncle Joe;* Georgia Children's Award, 1973, for *"Hey, What's Wrong with This One?";* Outstanding Science Trade Book for Children citation, National Science Teachers Association/Children's Book Council, 1974, for *Woodchuck;* Edgar Allan Poe Award nominee, Mystery Writers of America, 1975, for *The Mysterious Red Tape Gang;* Notable Book citations, American Library Association, 1981, for *The Long Way to a New Land,* and 1988, for translation of Christina Bjork's *Linnea's Windowsill Garden.*

Writings

SELF-ILLUSTRATED

The Long Way to a New Land, Harper & Row (New York, NY), 1981.

The Long Way Westward, Harper & Row (New York, NY), 1989.

Pioneer Bear: Based on a True Story, Random House (New York, NY), 1995.

Coyote School News, Holt (New York, NY), 2003.

ILLUSTRATOR

Carol Beach York, *The Blue Umbrella,* Watts (New York, NY), 1968.

Randolph Stow, *Midnite: The Story of a Wild Colonial Boy,* Prentice-Hall (Englewood Cliffs, NJ), 1968.

Harold Felton, *True Tall Tales of Stormalong: Sailor of the Seven Seas,* Prentice-Hall (Englewood Cliffs, NJ), 1968.

Edith Brecht, *The Little Fox,* Lippincott (Philadelphia, PA), 1968.

Eleanor Hull, *A Trainful of Strangers,* Atheneum (New York, NY), 1968.

Ellen Pugh, *Tales from the Welsh Hills,* Dodd (New York, NY), 1968.

Maia Wojciechowska, *"Hey, What's Wrong with This One?",* Harper (New York, NY), 1969.

Joan Lexau, *Crocodile and Hen,* Harper (New York, NY), 1969.

Jan M. Robinson, *The December Dog,* Lippincott (Philadelphia, PA), 1969.

Constantine Georgiou, *Rani, Queen of the Jungle,* Prentice-Hall (Englewood Cliffs, NJ), 1970.

Joan Lexau, *It All Began with a Drip, Drip, Drip,* McCall/Dutton (New York, NY), 1970.

Jean Little, *Look through My Window,* Harper (New York, NY), 1970.

Joanna Cole, *The Secret Box,* Morrow (New York, NY), 1971.

Thomas P. Lewis, *Hill of Fire,* Harper (New York, NY), 1971.

Barbara Brenner, *A Year in the Life of Rosie Bernard,* Harper (New York, NY), 1971.

Ellen Pugh, *More Tales from the Welsh Hills,* Dodd (New York, NY), 1971.

Jean Little, *From Anna,* Harper (New York, NY), 1972.

Nathaniel Benchley, *Small Wolf,* Harper (New York, NY), 1972.

Edna Mitchell Preston, *Ickle Bickle Robin,* Watts (New York, NY), 1973.

Alison Morgan, *A Boy Called Fish,* Harper (New York, NY), 1973.

Joan L. Nixon, *The Mysterious Red Tape Gang,* Putnam (New York, NY), 1974.

Hans Eric Hellberg, *Grandpa's Maria,* translated by Patricia Crampton, Morrow (New York, NY), 1974.

Faith McNulty, *Woodchuck,* Harper (New York, NY), 1974.

Kathryn Ewing, *A Private Matter,* Harcourt Brace Jovanovich (New York, NY), 1975.

Liesel Skorpen, *Michael,* Harper (New York, NY), 1975.

Liesel Skorpen, *Bird,* Harper (New York, NY), 1976.

Sandra Love, *But What about Me?,* Harcourt Brace Jovanovich (New York, NY), 1976.

Alan Arkin, *The Lemming Condition,* Harper (New York, NY), 1976.

Thomas P. Lewis, *Clipper Ship,* Harper & Row (New York, NY), 1978.

Clyde Robert Bulla, *Daniel's Duck,* Harper & Row (New York, NY), 1979.

Nancy Jewell, *Time for Uncle Joe,* Harper & Row (New York, NY), 1981.

Eleanor Coerr, *The Bell Ringer and the Pirates,* Harper & Row (New York, NY), 1983.

Doreen Rappaport, *Trouble at the Mines,* Crowell (New York, NY), 1987.

Aileen Fisher, *The House of a Mouse: Poems,* Harper & Row (New York, NY), 1988.

Aileen Fisher, *Always Wondering: Some Favorite Poems of Aileen Fisher,* HarperCollins (New York, NY), 1991.

Nancy Smiler Levinson, *Snowshoe Thompson,* HarperCollins (New York, NY), 1992.

Elaine Marie Alphin, *A Bear for Miguel,* HarperCollins (New York, NY), 1996.

Elizabeth Winthrop, *As the Crow Flies,* Clarion (New York, NY), 1998.

Illustrator of the serial story *Army of Two,* by Betty Miles, which ran in the *Boston Herald,* 2000.

TRANSLATOR

Gunilla Bergstrom, *Who's Scaring Alfie Atkins?,* Farrar, Straus & Giroux (New York, NY), 1987.

Christina Bjork and Lena Anderson, *Linnea's Windowsill Garden,* Farrar, Straus & Giroux (New York, NY), 1988.

Christina Bjork, *Elliot's Extraordinary Cookbook,* Farrar, Straus & Giroux (New York, NY), 1991.

Christina Bjork, *The Other Alice: The Story of Alice Liddell and Alice in Wonderland,* R & S Books (New York, NY), 1993.

Christina Bjork, *Big Bear's Book: By Himself*, Farrar, Straus & Giroux (New York, NY), 1994.

Olof and Lena Landström, *Boo and Baa in a Party Mood*, R & S Books (New York, NY), 1996.

Olof and Lena Landström, *Boo and Baa in Windy Weather*, R & S Books (New York, NY), 1996.

Olof and Lena Landström, *Boo and Baa at Sea*, R & S Books (New York, NY), 1997.

Olof and Lena Landström, *Boo and Baa on a Cleaning Spree*, R & S Books (New York, NY), 1997.

Lena Arro, *Good Night, Animals*, illustrated by Catarina Kruusval, R & S Books (New York, NY), 2002.

Lena Landström, *The Little Hippos' Adventure*, R & S Books (New York, NY), 2002.

Lena Landström, *The New Hippos*, R & S Books (New York, NY), 2003.

Peter Cohen, *Boris's Glasses*, illustrated by Olaf Landström, R & S Books (New York, NY), 2003.

Jeanette Milde, *Once Upon a Wedding*, R & S Books (New York, NY), 2004.

Sidelights

A prolific illustrator, Joan Sandin is also a skilled translator and a storyteller in her own right. As Sandin once told *SATA:* "I most enjoy working with folktales and books demanding research and/or travel." Indeed, Sandin's self-illustrated works have all been well-researched historical tales, often based on her ancestors' experiences. Her extensive travels in Europe and Mexico as well as the United States have also inspired her work.

Among the many books Sandin has illustrated is *A Bear for Miguel*, written by Elaine Maria Alphin. It is an unusual story for early readers, according to reviewers, but one that is effectively done and sensitively rendered in pictures and words. When Maria brings her stuffed toy bear, Paco, along to the market with her father, she has no intention of trading him. Her feelings change, however, as she begins to understand how the war in her country of El Salvador has affected her father's ability to find work. Sensing that a little boy injured in the war would love to have Paco, Maria decides to trade the toy for food for her family. "Sandin's watercolors add to the emotional impact . . . and do an effective job of setting the scene," remarked Gale W. Sherman in *School Library Journal*.

Sandin lived in Sweden for more than a decade before returning to the United States in the mid-1980s. Since her return, she has translated several children's books from Swedish into English. Many of these translations have been of picture books by Olof and Lena Landström, including their series about Boo and Baa, two hapless little sheep who find themselves in humorous jams no matter what they try to do. In *Boo and Baa in a Party Mood*, the two prepare for a birthday party by practicing their dance steps, but things get sticky when they try to wrap the present. In *Boo and Baa in Windy Weather*, the two go to the grocery store, but dragging

Young Maria sacrifices her favorite stuffed bear in order to obtain food for her struggling family during the war in El Salvador of the 1980s. (From A Bear for Miguel, *written by Elaine Marie Alphin and illustrated by Joan Sandin.)*

home a sled laden with their purchases through a snow storm presents a problem. Sandin also translated Lena Landström's books about a family of hippopotami, including *The Little Hippos' Adventure* and *The New Hippos*. In the first book, three baby hippos get bored with swimming in the safe river near their home. Instead, they want to go diving off of the forbidden Tall Cliff. But when they are finally allowed to go swimming there, catastrophe nearly strikes. In the latter book, the hippos must get used to a new family who moves into their part of the jungle, discovering that the new family does not do everything the same way they do.

Big Bear's Book: By Himself, according to *School Library Journal* contributor Marilyn Taniguchi, is not a picture book but "a whimsical reminiscence of childhood" best suited to sentimental adults. Written by Christina Bjork, *Big Bear's Book* tells the story of a toy bear's relationship to his owner, from childhood, through a sojourn in the attic, to a place in the child's adult life and a career in the movies. Sandin is also the translator of Bjork's tribute to the children's classic *Alice in Wonderland*. In *The Other Alice: The Story of Al-*

ice Liddell and Alice in Wonderland, Bjork describes the model for Lewis Carroll's main character, Alice Liddell, and explains some of the games and other trivia associated with the book. The result is "a unique pleasure," Ann A. Flowers wrote in *Horn Book.*

Sandin's own background—her ancestors immigrated to the United States from Sweden in the nineteenth century—inspired the research that went into *The Long Way to a New Land* and *The Long Way Westward,* two self-illustrated early readers which tell the story of an immigrant family's journey from Sweden to the United States in the 1860s. Told from the perspective of Carl Erik, the family's elder son, *The Long Way to a New Land* describes a drought that forces Erik's family to sell their farm and try to make a fresh start in America. The story continues with an account of their trip by boat to the United States, where bad weather, bad smells, and crowding mean long days of discomfort before they reach their destination. Critics noted that Sandin uses her illustrations effectively to augment a necessarily spare text intended for beginning readers. "It isn't always easy to make history comprehensible to younger children," remarked Zena Sutherland of the *Bulletin of the Center for Children's Books,* but "Sandin does a nice job of it." Similarly praised as "an interesting,

In the 1860s a Swedish family leaves their drought-stricken farm to immigrate to Minnesota and begin a new life full of ambition and optimism. (From The Long Way to a New Land, *written and illustrated by Sandin.)*

well-researched slice of history" by a critic for *Kirkus Reviews, The Long Way Westward* completes the story of the Erik family's journey as they travel from New York by railroad to Minnesota to live among their relatives.

Also set in the nineteenth century, *Pioneer Bear: Based on a True Story* tells the story of John Lacy, a photographer who learns that young Andrew Irwin taught a bear to dance. Lacy travels thirty miles to the Irwin farm to photograph the bear; but when he arrives, Bearly the Bear is nowhere to be found. Sandin provides a visual survey of pioneer life on a farm while the family goes from room to room, from barn to outhouse, in search of the cub. "Pioneer activities such as washing laundry in tubs . . . and smoking meats are realistically presented in warm watercolor illustrations," Mary Ann Bursk observed in *School Library Journal.* Reviewers also noted Sandin's sly infusion of humor into the story through her illustrations. "Primary schoolers will enjoy sighting Bearly . . . as he peeks from behind outbuildings and foliage," remarked Elizabeth Bush in *Bulletin of the Center for Children's Books.*

Coyote School News was inspired by actual newspapers printed by five tiny rural schools in Depression-era Arizona. Sandin stumbled across the original newspapers, titled *The Little Cowpuncher,* while doing research for a book about her high school friend who went to one of the schools which contributed to the paper. As well as writing *Coyote School News,* Sandin also got involved in a project to digitally archive the crumbling originals of *The Little Cowpuncher* so that the materials would be available to researchers in future generations.

A *Kirkus Reviews* contributor praised the "delightful authenticity" of *Coyote School News,* which follows student Monchi Ramirez and his five siblings through the 1938-39 school year. The story is partially told from Monchi's point of view and partially conveyed through nine included issues of "Coyote School News," which are printed to look like they came from an old-fashioned, purple-inked mimeograph. "Sandin's love and knowledge of this land and its history are evident," the *Kirkus Reviews* critic concluded, as she sketches with pictures and words the lives of the twelve students of the Coyote School. Observing that the book offers young readers a look at "Mexican traditions [that] have been part of the American cultural landscape for generations," *School Library Journal* reviewer Eve Ortega found *Coyote School News* "an entertaining bit of historical fiction."

Biographical and Critical Sources

PERIODICALS

Arizona Daily Star (Tucson, AZ), September 17, 2002, Bonnie Henry, interview with Sandin, p. B1.

Booklist, December 1, 1993, Carolyn Phelan, review of *The Other Alice: The Story of Alice Liddell and Alice in Wonderland,* pp. 686-687; July, 1995, Stephanie Zvirin, review of *Pioneer Bear: Based on a True Story,* p. 1885; November 1, 1996, Carolyn Phelan, review of *Boo and Baa in Windy Weather* and *Boo and Baa in a Party Mood,* pp. 507-508; April, 1998, Hazel Rochman, review of *As the Crow Flies,* p. 1334.

Boston Herald, April 24, 2000, Kristen Bradley, review of *Army of Two,* p. 16.

Bulletin of the Center for Children's Books, March, 1982, Zena Sutherland, review of *The Long Way to a New Land,* p. 138; July, 1995, Elizabeth Bush, review of *Pioneer Bear,* p. 397.

Horn Book, February, 1982, Nancy Sheridan, review of *The Long Way to a New Land,* p. 39; March-April, 1987, Hanna B. Zeiger, review of *Trouble at the Mines,* p. 212; September-October, 1989, Mary M. Burns, review of *The Long Way Westward,* p. 618; January-February, 1992, Mary M. Burns, review of *Showshoe Thompson,* p. 66; March-April, 1994, Ann A. Flowers, review of *The Other Alice,* p. 215; May-June, 1996, Maeve Visser Knoth, review of *A Bear for Miguel,* pp. 331-332.

Kirkus Reviews, November 15, 1981, pp. 1406-1407; August 15, 1989, review of *The Long Way Westward,* p. 1250; August 1, 2002, review of *Good Night, Animals,* p. 1121; July 1, 2003, review of *Coyote School News,* p. 914.

Publishers Weekly, April 10, 1987, review of *Trouble at the Mines,* p. 96; September 30, 1988, review of *Linnea's Windowsill Garden,* p. 64; August 25, 1989, review of *The Long Way Westward,* p. 63; January 19, 1990, review of *Linnea's Almanac,* p. 106; August 5, 1996, review of *Boo and Baa in Windy Weather* and *Boo and Baa in a Party Mood,* p. 440; April 8, 2002, review of *The Little Hippos' Adventure,* p. 225; July 28, 2003, review of *Coyote School News,* pp. 94-95.

Reading Teacher, October, 1989, Lee Galda, review of *The House of a Mouse,* pp. 66-71.

School Library Journal, December, 1981, review of *The Long Way to a New Land,* p. 75; April, 1987, Mary Beth Burgoyne, review of *Trouble at the Mines,* p. 102; February, 1988, Shirley Wilton, review of *Linnea in Monet's Garden,* p. 72; November, 1988, Frances E. Millhouser, review of *Linnea's Windowsill Garden,* p. 100; January, 1989, Kathleen Whalin, review of *The House of a Mouse,* p. 70; September, 1989, Sharron McElmeel, review of *The Long Way Westward,* p. 234; April, 1990, Amy Adler, review of *Linnea's Almanac,* p. 102; May, 1991, Carolyn Jenks, review of *Elliot's Extraordinary Cookbook,* p. 100; December, 1991, Barbara Chatton, review of *Always Wondering: Some Favorite Poems of Aileen Fisher,* pp. 109-110; January, 1992, Gale W. Sherman, review of *Snowshoe Thompson,* p. 104; December, 1993, Patricia A. Dollisch, review of *The Other Alice,* pp. 140-141; April, 1995, Marilyn Taniguchi, review of *Big Bear's Book: By Himself,* p. 130; October, 1995, Mary Ann Bursk, review of *Pioneer Bear,* p. 117; June, 1996, Gale W. Sherman, review of *A Bear for Miguel,* p. 92; July, 1997, Darla Remple, review of *Boo and Baa at Sea* and *Boo and Baa on a Cleaning Spree,* p. 70; June, 1998, Faith Brautigan, review of *As the Crow Flies,* pp. 124-125; April, 2002, Be Astengo, review of *The Little Hippos' Adventure,* p. 114; February, 2003, Kathy Piehl, review of *Good Night, Animals,* p. 102; April, 2003, Bina Williams, review of *The New Hippos,* pp. 130-131; September, 2003, Edith Ching, review of *Boris's Glasses,* p. 176; October, 2003, Eve Ortega, review of *Coyote School News,* p. 138.

ONLINE

Joan Sandin Web Site, http://www.authorsguild.org/ (February 27, 2004).*

*   *   *

SHARRATT, Nick 1962-

Personal

Born August 9, 1962, in London, England; son of Michael John (a brewer) and Jill Alexandra (Davison) Sharratt. *Education:* Saint Martin's School of Art (London, England), B.A. (with honors), 1984.

Addresses

Home—Gloucestershire, England. *Agent*—c/o Candlewick Press, 2067 Massachusetts Ave., Cambridge, MA 02140.

Career

Children's book illustrator and author.

Awards, Honors

Under Fives Book Prize (3-5 nonfiction category), SHE/W.H. Smith, 1995, for *Ketchup on Your Cornflakes?;* Sheffield Children's Book Award, 1997, for *A Cheese and Tomato Spider;* Gold Winner, Best First Book, *Parents* magazine, for *Twinkle, Twinkle, Little Star;* Best Children's Book selection, *Independent,* 2001, for *Vicky Angel.*

Writings

FOR CHILDREN; SELF-ILLUSTRATED

Look What I Found!, Walker (London, England), 1991, Candlewick (Cambridge, MA), 1992.

Monday Run-Day, Candlewick (Cambridge, MA), 1992.

The Green Queen, Candlewick (Cambridge, MA), 1992.

I Look Like This, Candlewick (Cambridge, MA), 1992.

Snazzy Aunties, Walker (London, England), 1993, Candlewick (Cambridge, MA), 1994.

Don't Put Your Finger in the Jelly, Nelly!, Andre Deutsch (London, England), 1993, Scholastic (New York, NY), 1997.

Mrs. Pirate, Walker (London, England), Candlewick (Cambridge, MA), 1994.

My Mum and Dad Make Me Laugh, Walker (London, England), 1994, published as *My Mom and Dad Make Me Laugh,* Candlewick (Cambridge, MA), 1994.

Caveman Dave, Candlewick (Cambridge, MA), 1994.

The Pointy-Hatted Princesses, Walker (London, England), 1994, Candlewick (Cambridge, MA), 1996.

I Went to the Zoopermarket, Scholastic (London, England), 1995.

Rocket Countdown, Candlewick (Cambridge, MA), 1995.

Stack-a-Plane (board book), Levinson, 1996.

A Cheese and Tomato Spider, Scholastic (London, England), 1996, Barron's (Hauppauge, NY), 1998.

The Animal Orchestra, Candlewick (Cambridge, MA), 1997.

(With Stephen Tucker) *My Day,* Oxford University Press (Oxford, England), 1997.

(With Stephen Tucker) *My Games,* Oxford University Press (Oxford, England), 1997.

Come and Play!, Levinson, 1997.

Ketchup on Your Cornflakes?: A Wacky Mix-and-Match Book, Scholastic (New York, NY), 1997.

What Do I Look Like?, Walker (London, England), 1998.

(With Stephen Tucker) *The Time It Took Tom,* Scholastic (London, England), 1998.

The Best Pop-Up Magic Book . . . Ever!, Orchard (London, England), 1998.

Dinosaurs' Day Out, Candlewick (Cambridge, MA), 1998.

(With Stephen Tucker) *My Days Out,* Oxford University Press (Oxford, England), 1999.

Croc with a Clock, Campbell (London, England), 1999.

Bear with a Pear, Campbell (London, England), 1999.

A Giraffe in a Scarf, Campbell (London, England), 1999.

Kangaroo in a Canoe, Campbell (London, England), 1999.

Turning Points, Hodder (London, England), 1999.

(With Stephen Tucker) *My Friends,* Oxford University Press (Oxford, England), 1999.

(With Stephen Tucker) *My Colours,* Oxford University Press (Oxford, England), 2000.

Buzz Buzz, Bumble Kitty, Barron's (Hauppauge, NY), 2000.

Split Ends, Phyllis Fogelman Books (New York, NY), 2000.

Mouse Moves House, Candlewick (Cambridge, MA), 2000.

(Reteller, with Stephen Tucker) *Cinderella,* Macmillan (London, England), 2001.

(Reteller, with Stephen Tucker) *Three Little Pigs,* Macmillan (London, England), 2001.

(Reteller, with Stephen Tucker) *Jack and the Beanstalk,* Macmillan (London, England), 2002.

(Reteller, with Stephen Tucker) *Little Red Riding Hood,* Macmillan (London, England), 2002.

Once Upon a Time, Walker (London, England), Candlewick (Cambridge, MA), 2002.

Shark in the Park, David Fickling Books (New York, NY), 2002.

(With Sue Heap) *Red Rockets and Rainbow Jelly,* Puffin (London, England), 2003.

Pirate Pete, Walker (London, England), 2003, published as *Ahoy, Pirate Pete,* Candlewick (Cambridge, MA), 2003.

(Reteller, with Stephen Tucker) *The Three Billy Goats Gruff,* Macmillan (London, England), 2004.

(Reteller, with Stephen Tucker) *Goldilocks,* Macmillan (London, England), 2004.

CHILDREN'S BOOKS; ILLUSTRATOR

Louis Fidge, *Learning to Spell 4,* Parent and Child Programme, 1987.

Carol Watson, *If You Were a Hamster,* Dinosaur, 1988.

Jill Bennett, compiler, *Noisy Poems,* Oxford University Press (Oxford, England), 1989.

Jerome Fletcher, *A Gerbil in the Hoover,* Doubleday (London, England), 1989.

Rosemary Stones, *Where Babies Come From,* Dinosaur, 1989.

Ruth Merrtens, *Adding and Subtracting,* Parent and Child Programme, 1989.

Gina Fost, *Robots Go Shopping,* Ginn (Aylesbury, England), 1990.

Jill Bennett, compiler, *People Poems,* Oxford University Press (Oxford, England), 1990.

Jill Bennett, compiler, *Machine Poems,* Oxford University Press (Oxford, England), 1991.

Jacqueline Wilson, *The Story of Tracy Beaker,* Doubleday (London, England), 1991, Delacorte (New York, NY), 2001.

Jill Bennett, compiler, *Tasty Poems,* Oxford University Press (Oxford, England), 1992, (New York, NY), 1998.

Jacqueline Wilson, *The Suitcase Kid,* Doubleday (London, England), 1992.

Tat Small, *My First Sticker Diary,* Scholastic (London, England), 1993.

Jacqueline Wilson, *The Mum-Minder,* Doubleday (London, England), 1993.

Elizabeth Hawkins, *The Lollipop Witch,* Orchard (London, England), 1994.

Valerie Bierman, editor, *Snake on the Bus and Other Pet Stories,* Methuen (London, England), 1994.

Judy Hindley, *Crazy ABC,* Walker (London, England), 1994, Candlewick (Cambridge, MA), 1996.

Judy Hindley, *Isn't It Time?,* Walker (London, England), 1994, Candlewick (Cambridge, MA), 1996.

Judy Hindley, *Little and Big,* Walker (London, England), 1994.

Judy Hindley, *One by One,* Walker (London, England), 1994, Candlewick (Cambridge, MA), 1996.

Vince Cross, compiler, *Sing a Song of Sixpence,* Oxford University Press (Oxford, England), 1994.

Roy Apps, *How to Handle Your Mum,* Hippo (London, England), 1994.

Jeremy Strong, *My Dad's Got an Alligator,* Viking (London, England), 1994.

Jacqueline Wilson, *The Bed and Breakfast Star,* Doubleday (London, England), 1994, published as *Elsa, Star of the Shelter,* A. Whitman (Morton Grove, IL), 1996.

Jacqueline Wilson, *Cliffhanger,* Doubleday (London, England), 1995.

Jacqueline Wilson, *The Dinosaur's Packed Lunch,* Doubleday (London, England), 1995.

(With Sue Heap) Jacqueline Wilson, *Double Act,* Doubleday (London, England), 1995.

Roy Apps, *How to Handle Your Gran,* Hippo (London, England), 1995.

Jill Bennett, compiler, *Playtime Poems,* Oxford University Press (Oxford, England), 1995.

Thomas Rockwell, *How to Eat Fried Worms,* Orchard (London, England), 1995.

Jeremy Strong, *The Indoor Pirates,* Dutton (London, England), 1995.

David Kitchen, *Never Play Leapfrog with a Unicorn,* Heinemann (London, England), 1995.

Gillian Cross, *The Crazy Shoe Shuffle,* Methuen Children's Books (London, England), 1995.

Jeremy Strong, *There's a Pharaoh in Our Bath!,* Dutton (London, England), 1995.

Jon Blake, *Danger Eyes,* Mammoth (London, England), 1995.

(With Sue Heap) Jacqueline Wilson, *Double Act,* Doubleday (London, England), 1995, Delacorte (New York, NY), 1998.

Roy Apps, *How to Handle Your Dad,* Hippo (London, England), 1996.

Jacqueline Wilson, *Bad Girls,* Doubleday (London, England), 1996, Delacorte (New York, NY), 2001.

Elizabeth Lindsay, *Hello Nellie and the Dragon,* Hippo (London, England), 1996.

Jeremy Strong, *The Hundred-Mile-an-Hour Dog,* Viking (London, England), 1996.

Thomas Rockwell, *How to Get Fabulously Rich,* Orchard (London, England), 1997.

Jacqueline Wilson, *Girls in Love,* Doubleday (London, England), 1997.

Jeremy Strong, *My Granny's Great Escape,* Viking (London, England), 1997.

Gina Willner-Pardo, *Spider Storch's Teacher Torture,* A. Whitman (Morton Grove, IL), 1997.

Gina Willner-Pardo, *Spider Storch's Carpool Catastrophe,* A. Whitman (Morton Grove, IL), 1997.

Emma Laybourn, *Robopop,* Yearling (London, England), 1997.

Gaby Goldsack, *Flower Power,* Hippo (London, England), 1997.

Jacqueline Wilson, *The Lottie Project,* Doubleday (London, England), 1997, Delacorte (New York, NY), 1999.

Jacqueline Wilson, *The Monster Story-Teller,* Doubleday (London, England), 1997.

Jeremy Strong, *Giant Jim and the Hurricane,* Viking (London, England), 1997.

Jeremy Strong, *The Indoor Pirates on Treasure Island,* Puffin (London, England), 1998.

Gillian Clements, *Calligraphy Frenzy,* Hippo (London, England), 1998.

Briane Morese, *Horse in the House,* Mammoth (London, England), 1998.

Anita Naik, *Is This Love,* Hodder (London, England), 1998.

Jill Bennett, compiler, *Seaside Poems,* Oxford University Press (New York, NY), 1998.

Jacqueline Wilson, *Girls under Pressure,* Doubleday (London, England), 1998.

Pat Moon, *Little Dad,* Mammoth (London, England), 1998.

Gina Willner-Pardo, *Spider Storch's Fumbled Field Trip,* A. Whitman (Morton Grove, IL), 1998.

Gina Willner-Pardo, *Spider Storch's Music Mess,* A. Whitman (Morton Grove, IL), 1998.

Tony Meeuwissen, *Remarkable Animals: 1000 Amazing Amalgamations,* Orchard (New York, NY), 1998.

(With Sue Heap) Jacqueline Wilson, *Buried Alive!,* Doubleday (London, England), 1998.

Roy Apps, *How to Handle Your Brother/Sister,* Hippo (London, England), 1998.

Geraldine Taylor and Gillian Harker, *Twinkle, Twinkle, Little Star,* Ladybird (London, England), 1998.

Jacqueline Wilson, reteller, *Rapunzel,* Scholastic (London, England), 1998.

Jill Bennett, compiler, *Christmas Poems,* Oxford University Press (Oxford, England, and New York, NY), 1999.

Jeremy Strong, *Dinosaur Pox,* Puffin (London, England), 1999.

Jacqueline Wilson, *The Illustrated Mum,* Doubleday (London, England), 1999.

Jacqueline Wilson, *Girls Out Late,* Doubleday (London, England), 1999.

Kaye Umansky, *Tickle My Nose and Other Action Rhymes,* Puffin (London, England), 1999.

Gina Willner-Pardo, *Spider Storch's Desperate Deal,* A. Whitman (Morton Grove, IL), 1999.

Chris d'Lacey, *Bubble and Float,* Hippo (London, England), 1999.

Roy Apps, *How to Handle Your Teacher,* Hippo (London, England), 1999.

Kes Gray, *Eat Your Peas,* Dorling Kindersley Publishing (New York, NY), 2000.

Kathy Tucker, *Do Knights Take Naps?,* A. Whitman (Morton Grove, IL), 2000.

Jacqueline Wilson, *The Dare Game,* Doubleday (London, England), 2000.

Roy Apps, *How to Handle Your Friends/Enemies,* Hippo (London, England), 2000.

Jeremy Strong, *I'm Telling You, They're Aliens!,* Puffin (London, England), 2000.

Jacqueline Wilson, *Vicky Angel,* Doubleday (London, England), 2000, Delacorte (New York, NY), 2001.

Irene Yates, *My First Picture Dictionary,* Collins (London, England), 2001.

Roy Apps, *How to Handle Your Cat/Dog,* Hippo (London, England), 2001.

Christine Mabileau and Irene Yates, *My First French Picture Dictionary,* Barron's (Hauppauge, NY), 2001.

Christine Mabileau and Irene Yates, *My First Spanish Picture Dictionary,* Barron's (Hauppauge, NY), 2001.

Gina Willner-Pardo, *Spider Storch, Rotten Runner,* A. Whitman (Morton Grove, IL), 2001.

Jacqueline Wilson, *The Cat Mummy,* Doubleday (London, England), 2001.

Jacqueline Wilson, *Sleepovers,* Doubleday (London, England), 2001.

Jacqueline Wilson, *Dustbin Baby,* Doubleday (London, England), 2001.

Jeremy Strong, *Krazy Kow Saves the World—Well, Almost,* Puffin (London, England), 2002.

Jeremy Strong, *The Monster Muggs,* Puffin (London, England), 2002.

Jeremy Strong, *The Shocking Adventures of Lightning Lucy,* Puffin (London, England), 2002.

Jacqueline Wilson, *The Worry Website,* Doubleday (London, England), 2002.

Kaye Umansky, *Wiggle My Toes,* Puffin (London, England), 2002.

Kes Gray, *Really, Really,* Bodley Head (London, England), 2002.

Jeremy Strong, *The Beak Speaks,* Puffin (London, England), 2003.

Giles Andreae, *Pants,* David Fickling Books (New York, NY), 2003.

Pippa Goodhart, *You Choose!,* Doubleday (London, England), 2003.

Julia Donaldson, *Conjurer Cow,* Puffin (London, England), 2003.

Thomas Rockwell, *How to Fight a Girl,* Orchard (New York, NY), 2003.

Kes Gray, *You Do!,* Bodley Head (London, England), 2003.

Jacqueline Wilson, *Lola Rose,* Doubleday (London, England), 2003.

Kes Gray, *Yuk!,* Bodley Head (London, England), 2004.

Julia Donaldson, *Wriggle and Roar!: Rhymes to Join in With,* Macmillan (London, England), 2004.

Sidelights

English author and illustrator Nick Sharratt is known for his child-appealing early-reader books. Sometimes his texts teach numbers, counting, or colors, but usually they are just plain fun for children who are learning to read, note critics. Sharratt generally illustrates his work in bold, bright colors to portray situations from the everyday to the adventurous. In *Look What I Found!,* for example, a little girl goes to the beach with her family and discovers fascinating objects along the shore, while in *Rocket Countdown,* readers learn about numbers while getting ready for a moon trip. Sharratt also uses humor in some of his books to keep young readers entertained. *Monday Run-Day* depicts funny scenes, such as dogs dressed in ties for Friday's tie day; and in *Snazzy Aunties,* a little boy's aunts wear or carry bizarre accessories.

My Mum and Dad Make Me Laugh, published in the United States as *My Mom and Dad Make Me Laugh,* is about a boy who has very odd parents. Father always wears clothes with stripes, while Mother always wears outfits with spots. Simon, however, prefers clothes that are gray. When the family goes on a safari, Father likes the animals that have stripes, such as the zebra, and Mother likes spotted creatures, including the leopards. Simon's favorite, though, is the elephant, and this explains why he always dresses in gray. *My Mom and Dad Make Me Laugh* drew praise from reviewers who enjoyed both Sharratt's narrative and illustrative techniques. *School Library Journal* contributor Mari-

anne Saccardi lauded the "pleasant, rhythmic quality" of the author's writing, as well as the "cartoon-style crayon drawings perfectly suit[ed to] the child narrator's tone." Carolyn Phelan, writing in *Booklist,* especially liked the illustrations, calling them "bold and sassy and full of spotty-stripy detail."

Graphic design also comes into play in books such as *Ketchup on Your Cornflakes?* Here, Sharratt uses a Dutch-door technique that lets children combine pictures in funny ways. Sharratt's text can be split up as well, so that equally inappropriate combinations can created: "Do you like ice cream in your bathtub?" or "Do you like toothpaste on your head?" "Useful as toy, game, and concept book, this seems likely to provoke endless giggles and riffs on the theme," declared Deborah Stevenson in the *Bulletin of the Center for Children's Books.* Sharratt uses the same Dutch-door technique in *A Cheese and Tomato Spider* to combine people, animals, and various kinds of food.

Another book sure to provoke giggles from the preschool set is *Pants,* a book that is one long jingle about underpants. And not just any underpants, but underpants that are "bigger, bolder and more ridiculous than any in real life," Julia Eccleshare declared in the *Guardian.* There are "giant frilly pig pants," "cheeky little monkey pants," even pants meant to be donned by camel humps. Sharratt's illustrations of Giles Andreae's text "reinforce the sense of fun with a series of gleeful, boldly outlined images in an electric palette," noted a *Publishers Weekly* reviewer.

In *Shark in the Park,* Sharratt once again combines "bright, cheerful, clean-lined illustrations and bouncy, repetitive text" to create an "enjoyable" easy reader, in the words of *Booklist* contributor Todd Morning. A little boy named Timothy has just received a new telescope, and now he is testing it out in the park. He keeps thinking that he sees a shark in the duck pond, and indeed, through a hole cut in the page, the reader can see what appears to be a shark's fin. But upon turning the page, the object in view is always shown to be something else: a cat's ear, a crow's wing, his father's black hair. The final spread reveals the truth—there really is a shark in the duck pond—but Timothy does not see it. Sharratt's carefully engineered illustrations combine with his text to make the point that one should beware of drawing hasty conclusions. "This crafty interactive picture book is one hundred percent bliss and very toothsome indeed," Lyn Gardner declared in the *Guardian.*

Sharratt has also become known to older audiences as the illustrator of Jacqueline Wilson's massively popular books for middle-graders and young adults. Wilson's stories tackle challenging topics, including death, mental illness, abandonment by one's parents, and the formation of blended families, although often with a light tone. Sharratt's cartoon-like illustrations are a good compliment for Wilson's style, reviewers have generally remarked. For example, Sharratt's drawings for *The Lottie Project* and *The Story of Tracy Beaker,* both of which are told partially through journals kept by their pre-teen protagonists, "match the book's informal tone and help lighten some of the more serious moments," as Kitty Flynn wrote in a *Horn Book* review of the first title, while a *Publishers Weekly* critic said of *The Story of Tracy Beaker,* "Sharratt's drawings help to keep the mood light."

Sharratt once told *SATA,* "I've been making pictures for as long as I can remember, and I was nine when I decided I was going to be an illustrator by profession. As a child, I always wanted the same things for birthdays and Christmas: a bumper pack of felt-tip pens and lots of drawing paper, and I liked nothing better than to spend all day in my room, drawing, eating sweets, and listening to the radio. Nothing's changed—except that nowadays I use other media besides felt tips. A complete workaholic, I find it very hard to have weekends off, and I invariably sneak ongoing projects into my suitcase when I'm supposed to be taking a holiday. That's what happens when you really love your work!"

Biographical and Critical Sources

BOOKS

Andreae, Giles, *Pants,* David Fickling Books (Oxford, England, and New York, NY), 2003.

Sharratt, Nick, *Ketchup on Your Cornflakes?: A Wacky Mix-and-Match Book,* Scholastic (London, England, and New York, NY), 1997.

PERIODICALS

Booklist, June 1, 1994, Carolyn Phelan, review of *My Mom and Dad Make Me Laugh,* p. 1845; September 1, 2002, Todd Morning, review of *Shark in the Park,* p. 137.

Bulletin of the Center for Children's Books, June, 1997, Deborah Stevenson, review of *Ketchup on Your Cornflakes?: A Wacky Mix-and-Match Book,* pp. 373-374.

Guardian (London, England), May 11, 1999, Philip Pullman, review of *The Illustrated Mum,* p. 4; October 31, 2000, Vivian French, review of *Eat Your Peas,* p. 59; December 11, 2001, Lindsey Fraser, review of *Remarkable Animals,* p. 49; March 12, 2002, Lindsey Fraser, review of *Secrets,* p. 63; May 29, 2002, Lyn Gardner, review of *Shark in the Park,* p. 11; November 16, 2002, Julia Eccleshare, review of *Pants,* p. 33; June 3, 2003, Lindsey Fraser, review of *Conjurer Cow,* p. 61; September 23, 2003, review of *The Beak Speaks,* p. 61; October 25, 2003, Julia Eccleshare, review of *You Choose,* p. 33.

Horn Book, November, 1999, Kitty Flynn, review of *The Lottie Project,* p. 746; September, 2001, review of *The Story of Tracy Beaker,* p. 598.

Independent (London, England), February 24, 2001, Nicholas Tucker, "The Fifty Best Books for Children," p. 4.

Kirkus Reviews, May 1, 1997, p. 727.

New York Times Book Review, July 19, 1998, review of *Seaside Poems,* p. 24.

Publishers Weekly, March 23, 1992, review of *I Look Like This* and *Look What I Found!,* p. 71; May 23, 1994, review of *My Mom and Dad Make Me Laugh,* p. 86; September 25, 1995, review of *Rocket Countdown,* p. 56; December 18, 1995, review of *Elsa, Star of the Shelter!,* p. 55; January 12, 1998, review of *Double Act,* p. 60; July 5, 1999, review of *Tickle My Nose and Other Action Rhymes,* p. 73; August 9, 1999, review of *Stack-a-Plane,* p. 355; November 29, 1999, review of *The Lottie Project,* p. 72; January 3, 2000, review of *The Time It Took Tom,* p. 74; January 8, 2001, review of *Bad Girls,* p. 68; July 23, 2001, review of *The Story of Tracy Beaker,* p. 77; August 13, 2001, review of *Vicky Angel,* p. 312; June 3, 2002, review of *Once Upon a Time,* pp. 89-90; April 21, 2003, review of *Vicky Angel,* p. 65; June 2, 2003, review of *Pants,* pp. 50-51.

School Library Journal, February, 1992, Andrew W. Hunter, review of *Machine Poems,* p. 81; June, 1992, Linda Wicher, review of *I Look Like This* and *Look What I Found,* pp. 102-103; November, 1992, Linda Wicher, review of *The Green Queen,* p. 78; December, 1992, Linda Wicher, review of *Monday Run-Day,* p. 91; August, 1994, Marianne Saccardi, review of *My Mom and Dad Make Me Laugh,* pp. 145-46; February, 1996, Jane Gardner Connor, review of *Elsa, Star of the Shelter!,* p. 104; November, 1997, Maura Bresnahan, review of *Spider Storch's Teacher Torture,* and Carrie A. Guarria, review of *Spider Storch's Carpool Catastrophe,* p. 103; March, 1998, Miriam Lang Budin, review of *Double Act,* p. 266; January, 1999, Judith Constantinides, review of *Seaside Poems,* p. 110; March, 1999, Elaine E. Knight, review of *Spider Storch's Fumbled Field Trip* and *Spider Storch's Music Mess,* p. 188; October, 1999, Maureen Wade, review of *Christmas Poems,* p. 65; January, 2000, Yapha Nussbaum Mason, review of *Spider Storch's Desperate Deal,* p. 114; March, 2000, Lisa Smith, review of *The Time It Took Tom,* p. 212; April, 2000, Ginny Gustin, review of *Do Knights Take Naps?,* p. 116; September, 2000, Lisa Dennis, review of *Eat Your Peas,* p. 198; March, 2001, Marilyn Ackerman, review of *Bad Girls,* p. 258; July, 2001, B. Allison Gray, review of *The Story of Tracy Beaker,* p. 116; October, 2001, Marlyn K. Roberts, review of *Vicky Angel,* p. 175; December, 2002, Kristin de Lacoste, review of *Shark in the Park,* p. 108.

Scotland on Sunday (Edinburgh, Scotland), June 3, 2001, review of *Eat Your Peas,* p. 15.

Sunday Times (London, England), October 29, 2000, Nicolette Jones, review of *Vicky Angel,* p. 46; August 11, 2002, Nicolette Jones, review of *Krazy Kow Saves the World—Well, Almost,* p. 47.

Times Educational Supplement, April 25, 2003, Geraldine Brenna, review of *Red Rockets and Rainbow Jelly,* p. 37.

ONLINE

Association of Illustrators Web Site, http://www.theaoi. com/ (February, 1999), interview with Sharratt.
British Broadcasting Company Web Site, http://www.bbc. co.uk/ (November 3, 2003), interview with Sharratt.*

*   *   *

STRASSER, Todd 1950-
(Morton Rhue)

Personal

Born May 5, 1950, in New York, NY; son of Chester S. (a manufacturer of dresses) and Sheila (a copy editor; maiden name, Reisner) Strasser; married Pamela Older (a businesswoman), July 2, 1981; children: Lia, Geoff. *Education:* Attended New York University; Beloit College, B.A., 1974. *Hobbies and other interests:* Fishing, skiing, tennis, surfing.

Addresses

Home—Westchester County, NY. *Office*—P.O. Box 859, Larchmont, NY 10538. *E-mail*—todd@toddstrasser.com.

Career

Freelance writer, 1975—. Beloit College, Beloit, WI, worked in public relations, 1973-74; *Times Herald Record,* Middletown, NY, reporter, 1974-76; Compton Advertising, New York, NY, copywriter, 1976-77; *Esquire,* New York, NY, researcher, 1977-78; Toggle, Inc. (fortune cookie company), New York, NY, owner, 1978-89. Speaker at teachers' and librarians' conferences, middle schools, and at junior and senior high schools. Lectures and conducts writing workshops for adults and teenagers.

Member

International Reading Association, Writers Guild of America, Authors Guild, Freedom to Read Foundation, PEN.

Awards, Honors

Best Books for Young Adults citations, American Library Association (ALA), 1981, for *Friends till the End: A Novel,* and 1982, for *Rock 'n' Roll Nights: A Novel;* New York Public Library's Books for the Teen Age citations, 1981, for *Angel Dust Blues,* 1982, for *The Wave* and *Friends till the End,* 1983, for *Rock 'n' Roll Nights,* and 1984, for *Workin' for Peanuts;* Notable Children's Trade Book in the Field of Social Studies, National Council for Social Studies/Children's Book Council, 1982, for *Friends till the End;* Young Reader Medal nomination, California Reading Association, 1983, for *Friends till the End;* Book Award, Federation of Children's Books (Great Britain), 1983, for *The Wave,*

Todd Strasser

and 1984, for *Turn It Up!;* Outstanding Book Award, Iowa Books for Young Adult Program, 1985, for *Turn It Up!;* Colorado Blue Spruce Award nomination, 1987, for *Angel Dust Blues;* Edgar Award nomination, Mystery Writers of America, 1998, for *The Accident;* Washington Irving Children's Choice Book Award, 1998, for *Abe Lincoln for Class President;* Volunteer State Book Award, 1998; New York State Charlotte Award, Rhode Island Teen Book Award, and Washington Irving Children's Choice Book Award, all 2002, all for *Give a Boy a Gun.*

Writings

Angel Dust Blues, Coward (New York, NY), 1979.
Friends till the End: A Novel, Delacorte (New York, NY), 1981.
Rock 'n' Roll Nights, Delacorte (New York, NY), 1982.
Workin' for Peanuts, Delacorte (New York, NY), 1983.
Turn It Up! (sequel to *Rock 'n' Roll Nights*), Delacorte (New York, NY), 1984.
The Complete Computer Popularity Program, Delacorte (New York, NY), 1984.
A Very Touchy Subject, Delacorte (New York, NY), 1985.

Wildlife (sequel to *Turn It Up!*), Delacorte (New York, NY), 1987.

The Mall from Outer Space, Scholastic (New York, NY), 1987.

The Family Man (novel for adults), St. Martin's (New York, NY), 1988.

The Accident (also see below), Delacorte (New York, NY), 1988.

(With Dennis Freeland) *Moving Target,* Fawcett (New York, NY), 1989.

Beyond the Reef, illustrations by Debbie Heller, Delacorte (New York, NY), 1989.

Over the Limit (teleplay based on Strasser's *The Accident*), *ABC Afterschool Special,* American Broadcasting Company (New York, NY), 1990.

The Diving Bell, illustrations by Debbie Heller, Scholastic (New York, NY), 1992.

Summer's End, Scholastic (New York, NY), 1993.

Summer's Promise, Scholastic (New York, NY), 1993.

Please Don't Be Mine, Julie Valentine, Scholastic (New York, NY), 1995.

How I Changed My Life, Simon and Schuster (New York, NY), 1995.

Abe Lincoln for Class President, Scholastic (New York, NY), 1996.

Howl-a-Ween, Scholastic (New York, NY), 1995.

Girl Gives Birth to Own Prom Date, Simon and Schuster (New York, NY), 1996.

Playing for Love, HarperCollins (New York, NY), 1996.

The Boys in the Band, HarperCollins (New York, NY), 1996.

Hey Dad, Get a Life!, Holiday House (New York, NY), 1996.

How I Spent My Last Night on Earth, Simon and Schuster (New York, NY), 1998.

Kidnap Kids, Putnam (New York, NY), 1998.

Kids' Book of Gross Facts and Feats, Watermill Press (Mahwah, NJ), 1998.

Close Call, Putnam (New York, NY), 1999.

Here Comes Heavenly, Pocket Books (New York, NY), 1999.

Dance Magic, Pocket Books (New York, NY), 1999.

Pastabilities, Pocket Books (New York, NY), 2000.

Spell Danger, Pocket Books (New York, NY), 2000.

Give a Boy a Gun, Simon and Schuster (New York, NY), 2000.

CON-Fidence, Holiday House (New York, NY), 2002.

Thief of Dreams, Putnam (New York, NY), 2003.

Can't Get There from Here, Simon and Schuster (New York, NY), 2004.

Also contributor to periodicals, including *New Yorker, Esquire, New York Times,* and *Village Voice.*

NOVELIZATIONS

(Under pseudonym Morton Rhue) *The Wave* (based on the television drama of the same title by Johnny Dawkins), Delacorte (New York, NY), 1981.

Ferris Bueller's Day Off, New American Library (New York, NY), 1986.

Cookie, New American Library (New York, NY), 1989.

Home Alone, Scholastic (New York, NY), 1991.

Home Alone 2: Lost in New York, Scholastic (New York, NY), 1991.

Honey, I Blew Up the Kids, Disney Press (New York, NY), 1992.

The Good Son, Pocket Books (New York, NY), 1993.

The Addams Family Values, Pocket Books (New York, NY), 1993.

The Beverly Hillbillies, HarperCollins (New York, NY), 1993.

Hocus Pocus, Disney Press (New York, NY), 1993.

The Rookie of the Year, Dell (New York, NY), 1993.

Super Mario Bros., Hyperion (New York, NY), 1993.

Disney's "The Villains" Collection, poems by Mark Rifkin, illustrated by Gil DiCicco, Disney Press (New York, NY), 1993.

The Three Musketeers, Disney Press (New York, NY), 1993.

Free Willy, Scholastic (New York, NY), 1993.

Disney's "It's Magic": Stories from the Films, with poems by Richard Duke, illustrated by Philippe Harchy, Disney Press (New York, NY), 1994.

Walt Disney's "Lady and the Tramp," illustrated by Franc Mateu, Disney Press (New York, NY), 1994.

Walt Disney's Peter Pan, illustrated by Jose Cardona and Fred Marvin, Disney Press (New York, NY), 1994.

Tall Tale: The Unbelievable Adventures of Pecos Bill, Disney Press (New York, NY), 1994.

Street Fighter, Newmarket Press (New York, NY), 1994.

Richie Rich, Scholastic (New York, NY), 1994.

Pagemaster, Scholastic (New York, NY), 1994.

The Miracle on 34th Street, Scholastic (New York, NY), 1994.

Ninjas Kick Back, Scholastic (New York, NY), 1994.

Little Panda, Scholastic (New York, NY), 1995.

Man of the House, Disney Press (New York, NY), 1995.

(With others) *Free Willy 2,* Scholastic (New York, NY), 1995.

Home Alone 3, Scholastic (New York, NY), 1997.

Star Wars Episode One, Journal, Anakin Skywalker, Scholastic (New York, NY), 1999.

"HELP! I'M TRAPPED" SERIES

Help! I'm Trapped in the First Day of School, Scholastic (New York, NY), 1994.

Help! I'm Trapped in My Teacher's Body, Scholastic (New York, NY), 1994.

Help! I'm Trapped in Obedience School, Scholastic (New York, NY), 1995.

Help! I'm Trapped in Santa's Body, Scholastic (New York, NY), 1997.

Help! I'm Trapped in My Sister's Body, Scholastic (New York, NY), 1997.

Help! I'm Trapped in My Gym Teacher's Body, Scholastic (New York, NY), 1997.

Help! I'm Trapped in the President's Body, Scholastic (New York, NY), 1997.

Help! I'm Trapped in Obedience School Again, Scholastic (New York, NY), 1997.

Help! I'm Trapped in the First Day of Summer Camp, Scholastic (New York, NY), 1998.

Help! I'm Trapped in an Alien's Body, Scholastic (New York, NY), 1998.

Help! I'm Trapped in a Movie Star's Body, Scholastic (New York, NY), 1999.

Help! I'm Trapped in the Principal's Body, Scholastic (New York, NY), 1999.

Help! I'm Trapped in My Lunch Lady's Body, Scholastic (New York, NY), 1999.

Help! I'm Trapped in the Camp Counselor's Body, Scholastic (New York, NY), 1999.

Help! I'm Trapped in a Professional Wrestler's Body, Scholastic (New York, NY), 2000.

Help! I'm Trapped in a Vampire's Body, Scholastic (New York, NY), 2000.

Help! I'm Trapped in a Supermodel's Body, Scholastic (New York, NY), 2001.

"WORDSWORTH" SERIES

Wordsworth and the Cold Cut Catastrophe, illustrated by Leif Peng, HarperCollins (New York, NY), 1995.

Wordsworth and the Kibble Kidnapping, HarperCollins (New York, NY), 1995.

Wordsworth and the Roast Beef Romance, HarperCollins (New York, NY), 1995.

Wordsworth and the Mail-Order Meatloaf Mess, HarperCollins (New York, NY), 1995.

Wordsworth and the Tasty Treat Trick, HarperCollins (New York, NY), 1995.

The Lip-Smacking Licorice Love Affair, HarperCollins (New York, NY), 1996.

"CAMP RUN-A-MUCK" SERIES

Greasy Grimy Gopher Guts, Scholastic (New York, NY), 1997.

Mutilated Monkey Meat, Scholastic (New York, NY), 1997.

Chopped-Up Birdy's Feet, Scholastic (New York, NY), 1997.

"AGAINST THE ODDS" SERIES

Shark Bite, Pocket Books (New York, NY), 1998.

Grizzly Attack, Pocket Books (New York, NY), 1998.

Buzzards' Feast, Pocket Books (New York, NY), 1999.

Gator Prey, Pocket Books (New York, NY), 1999.

"DON'T GET CAUGHT" SERIES

Don't Get Caught Driving the School Bus, Scholastic (New York, NY), 2000.

Don't Get Caught in the Girls' Locker Room, Scholastic (New York, NY), 2001.

Don't Get Caught Wearing the Lunch Lady's Hairnet, Scholastic (New York, NY), 2001.

Don't Get Caught in the Teachers' Lounge, Scholastic (New York, NY), 2002.

"IMPACT ZONE" SERIES

Close Out, Simon Pulse (New York, NY), 2004.

Cut Back, Simon Pulse (New York, NY), 2004.

Take Off, Simon Pulse (New York, NY), 2004.

Adaptations

Workin' for Peanuts was adapted for cable television as a Home Box Office "Family Showcase" presentation, 1985; *A Very Touchy Subject* was adapted for television as an "ABC Afterschool Special" titled *Can a Guy Say No?,* 1986; *Help! I'm Trapped in the First Day of School* was adapted for cable television by the Disney Channel, 1999; *Girl Gives Birth to Own Prom Date* was adapted as a major motion picture by Rob Thomas for Twentieth Century Fox, 1999.

Sidelights

Todd Strasser writes critically recognized realistic fiction for preteens and teenagers. In works ranging from *Friends till the End,* the story of a young man stricken with leukemia, to *Wildlife,* a study of the breakup of a successful rock group, Strasser blends humor and romance with timely subjects to address various concerns of teens, including drugs, sex, illness, popularity, and music. Lacing his work for younger readers with a vein of humor, Strasser has also tantalized even the most reluctant reader to open books with titles like *Hey Dad, Get a Life!; Help! I'm Trapped in My Gym Teacher's Body;* and *Greasy Grimy Gopher Guts.* In addition to his many original works of fiction, Strasser has also written novelizations of several popular motion pictures, including some from the Disney Studios. According to critics, his understanding of the feelings of children and adolescents has made his works popular with young people.

Angel Dust Blues appeared in 1979 and won Strasser critical acclaim. The story itself is about, as Strasser told Nina Piwoz in *Media and Methods,* "a group of fairly well-to-do, suburban teenagers who get into trouble with drugs." It was based on actual events Strasser had witnessed when he was growing up. Two years later, he published another young adult novel, again based on his own experiences. "My second book, *Friends till the End,* is about a healthy teenager who has a friend who becomes extremely ill with leukemia," he explained to Piwoz. "When I moved to New York, I had a roommate . . . an old friend of mine. Within a few weeks, he became very ill. I spent a year visiting him in the hospital, not knowing whether he was going to live or die."

Rock 'n' Roll Nights, Strasser's third novel under his own name, was a change of pace from the serious themes of his first two works. "It's about a teenage rock and roll band—something with which I had absolutely no direct experience," he told Piwoz. "However, I grew up in the 1960s when rock and roll was really our 'national anthem.' I relate much better to rock stars than to politicians. I always wanted to be in a rock band, as did just about everybody I knew." "I think the kind of music teens listen to may change, or what they wear may change," Strasser continued, "but dealing with being popular, friends or the opposite sex, or questions of morality and decency . . . [I don't think] those things really ever change. I hate to say this, but I think authors tell the same stories—just in today's language and in today's settings." Strasser continued the story of the band "Coming Attractions" in two sequels, *Turn It Up!* and *Wildlife.*

In his other works, Strasser continues to write hard-hitting, realistic stories about teenagers and their problems. For example, *The Accident,* which Strasser adapted for ABC-TV's *Afterschool Special* under the title "Over the Limit," deals with a drunken-driving incident in which three of four high-school swimming stars are killed. The surviving teen commits himself to understanding what actually happened the night of the accident, in a novel that, in the opinion of *Horn Book* reviewer Margaret A. Bush, "reads well and competently uses the troublesome occurrence of drunk driving and teenage death to provoke thought and discussion on multifaceted issues."

Strasser has also produced a large number of light-hearted books for middle-graders. *The Mall from Outer Space* is about aliens who have chosen, for mysterious reasons of their own, to construct shopping centers on Earth. *Hey Dad, Get a Life!* finds twelve-year-old Kelly and younger sister Sasha haunted by their deceased father. Ghostly Dad proves to be a great help around the house—he makes the girls' beds, tidies their room, does their homework, and even helps out on the soccer field. *Booklist* contributor Debbie Carton called the work a "light-hearted and occasionally poignant ghost story" that features "appealing, believable characters and a satisfying plot." Equally laudatory in *Bulletin of the Center for Children's Books,* Deborah Stevenson described *Hey, Dad, Get a Life!* as "touchingly yet surprisingly cheerful," calling it "a compassionate and accessible tale of a family's adjustment to loss."

Several novels reveal Strasser's more quirky, humorous side. *Girl Gives Birth to Own Prom Date* finds ardent environmentalist Nicole taking time off from saving the world to transform her grungy next-door neighbor Chase into the perfect prom date. Praising the novel's "goofy plot twists" and "effervescent dialogue," a *Kirkus Reviews* critic noted that Strasser's "high humor doesn't detract" from his "understated message about nonconformity and self-acceptance." The author's "Help! I'm Trapped" books position their young protagonists in everything from the unwieldy body of Santa Claus to the summer camp from hell. In *Help! I'm Trapped in Obedience School,* for example, Jake's dog Lance switches bodies with Jake's friend Andy, and while Andy excels at most things doggy—although he never quite acquires a taste for dog food—Jake spends his time in human

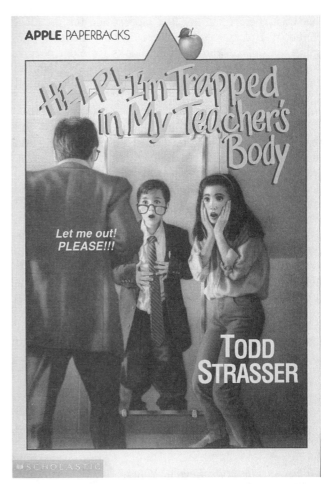

Fun-loving Jake finds he has switched bodies with the unpopular teacher Mr. Dirksen and both he and the teacher learn valuable lessons before they return to their usual roles.

form chasing squirrels and barking during school. Calling Strasser's tale "briskly paced," *Booklist* contributor Chris Sherman wrote that the "easy, breezy" story would appeal to reluctant readers. *School Library Journal* contributor Cheryl Cufari predicted that readers will relate to the "predicaments in which Strasser's energetic boys find themselves and enjoy this light, entertaining read."

Strasser once remarked, "Since I've written [many] books about teenagers, people often ask me how I know what today's teens are like. It's true that . . . years have passed since I qualified for that age group, so I suppose the question has some merit. I think the single most important thing I do to keep up with teens is accept invitations to speak at junior high and high schools all over the country. This year, for instance, I visited schools in Alaska, Iowa, Massachusetts, Pennsylvania, Ohio, and Colorado. Thus, I'm not only able to keep up with teens, but with teens from all over the country.

"Another question I'm often asked is why I concentrate solely on books for teens. Well, actually, I don't. . . . I guess I originally wrote a lot of books for teens because that was where I had my first success and felt the most confident. But as I grow older, I find my interests widening not only towards writing books for older people, but for younger ones as well. I'd like to think that the day will come when I will write books for people of all ages, from three to eighty-three.

"The other day, someone who didn't know me well said that because I was a writer I must be a 'free spirit' and lead a wonderful life. At first I wanted to tell him he was completely wrong, but then I thought about it and decided he was only half wrong. In a way, I am a free spirit, in that I am free to pick any idea or topic and write about it. That, indeed, is a wonderful freedom, and I am grateful to have it. Along with that freedom, however, comes an awful lot of hard work. Unless you are fortunate enough to be one of the handful of perpetual best-selling writers in this world, you really can not make a living writing a book every two or three years. My work is about as close to 'nine-to-five' as my schedule allows. Being a writer is great, but I can't say it's easy."

Biographical and Critical Sources

BOOKS

Children's Literature Review, Volume 11, Gale (Detroit, MI), 1986.

Nilsen, Alleen Pace, and Kenneth L. Donelson, *Literature for Today's Young Adults,* second edition, Scott, Foresman (Glenview, IL), 1985.

Roginski, Jim, *Behind the Covers: Interviews with Authors and Illustrators of Books for Children and Young Adults,* Libraries Unlimited (Littleton, CO), 1985.

St. James Guide to Young Adult Writers, 2nd edition, St. James Press (Detroit, MI), 1999.

PERIODICALS

Best Sellers, May, 1983, p. 75; June, 1984, p. 118.

Booklist, May 1, 1995, p. 1564; February 1, 1996, Chris Sherman, review of *Help! I'm Trapped in Obedience School,* p. 932; October 1, 1996, p. 344; February 15, 1997, Debbie Carton, review of *Hey Dad, Get a Life!,* p. 1024; October 1, 2000, Michael Cart, review of *Give a Boy a Gun,* p. 337; April 15, 2003, Ed Sullivan, review of *CON-fidence,* p. 1472.

Book Report, November, 1993, Annette Thorson, "Author Profile: Todd Strasser," p. 30.

Bulletin of the Center for Children's Books, February, 1980, p. 120; June, 1995, p. 361; March, 1997, Deborah Stevenson, review of *Hey Dad, Get a Life!,* p. 259; February, 1999, p. 219.

English Journal, September, 1982, p. 87; January, 1985; December, 1985; December, 1986; November, 1987, p. 93; March, 1988, p. 85.

Horn Book, April, 1980, p. 178; April, 1983, p. 175; May-June, 1985, p. 321; March-April, 1986, Todd Strasser, "Stalking the Teen," pp. 236-239; January-February, 1989, Margaret A. Bush, review of *The Accident,* p. 82; January, 1990, p. 90.

Journal of Adolescent and Adult Literacy, March, 2002, Devon Clancy Sanner, review of *Give a Boy a Gun,* p. 547.

Journal of Youth Services in Libraries, fall, 1988, pp. 64-70.

Kirkus Reviews, May 15, 1992, p. 676; August 1, 1996, review of *Girl Gives Birth to Own Prom Date,* p. 1158; September 1, 1998, p. 1293; December 1, 2002, review of *CON-fidence,* p. 1775; March 1, 2003, review of *Thief of Dreams,* p. 399.

Library Journal, January, 1988, p. 100.

Media and Methods, February, 1983, Nina Piwoz, "The Writers Are Writing: I Was a Teenage Boy—An Interview with Todd Strasser."

Publishers Weekly, November 27, 1981, p. 88; April 24, 1987, p. 73; December 4, 1987, p. 63; November 25, 2002, review of *CON-fidence,* p. 69; February 24, 2003, review of *Thief of Dreams,* p. 73.

School Library Journal, January, 1980, p. 81; March, 1982, p. 160; August, 1983, p. 80; August, 1984, p. 87; April, 1985, p. 100; February, 1988, p. 75; June-July, 1988, p. 59; September, 1989, p. 278; February, 1996, Cheryl Cufari, *Help! I'm Trapped in Obedience School,* p. 104; January 1, 2000, Shelle Rosenfeld, review of *Here Comes Heavenly,* p. 906; August, 2000, Jane Halsall, review of *Pastabilities,* p. 190; September, 2000, Vicki Reutter, review of *Give a Boy a Gun,* p. 237; March, 2003, Todd Morning, review of *Thief of Dreams,* p. 241.

Teacher Librarian, February, 2003, Teri S. Lesesne, "Surfing for Readers: An Interview with Todd Strasser," p. 48.

Variety, March 22, 1990, p. 14.

Voice of Youth Advocates, June, 1981, p. 32; December, 1982, p. 36; October, 1983, p. 209; June, 1984, p. 98; June, 1985, p. 136; December, 1986; December, 1988, p. 242; October, 1989, p. 217; October, 1995, p. 224; April, 1997, pp. 22, 33.

Writer's Digest, December, 1979.

ONLINE

Todd Strasser Home Page, http://www.toddstrasser.com/ (April 10, 2003).*

*   *   *

SUPEENE, Shelagh Lynne 1952-

Personal

Born June 1, 1952, in Clinton, Ontario, Canada; daughter of Harold and Margaret Supeene; married Tom Slee (a technical writer), May 2, 1987; children: Jamie, Simon. *Education:* McMaster University, B.A. (with

Shelagh Lynne Supeene

honors), 1979, studied Chinese language and philosophy at McMaster University, 1979-81.

Addresses

Agent—c/o Author Mail, Orca Book Publishers, 1030 North Park St., Victoria, British Columbia, Canada V8T 1C6. *E-mail*—slsupeene@sentex.net.

Career

Writer. Has also worked as teaching assistant in adult education center and dry cleaning clerk.

Member

Society of Children's Book Writers and Illustrators, Canadian Children's Book Centre, Writers' Union of Canada.

Awards, Honors

Nora Epstein Fiction Contest winner, 1970, for "The Pebble"; Ontario graduate scholarships, 1980 and 1981; Canada Council exploration grants, 1987 and 1988; selected by the Canadian Children's Book Centre for Our Choice, 2004, for "My Name is Mitch"; chosen as one of ten nominees for Silver Birch Award, 2005, for "My Name is Mitch.".

Writings

As for the Sky, Falling: A Critical Look at Psychiatry and Suffering (adult nonfiction), Second Story Press (Toronto, Ontario, Canada), 1991.
My Name Is Mitch, Orca Book Publishers (Victoria, British Columbia, Canada), 2003.

Contributor to *Toronto Star, Kitchener Record,* and other newspapers and newsletters.

Work in Progress

Like an Arrow, a young adult novel.

Sidelights

Shelagh Lynne Supeene began writing for youngsters when her own children were small. Prior to that time she had studied world religions, specializing in ancient Chinese philosophy and language. She has also researched mental illness and Myalgic Encephalomyelitis, better known as Chronic Fatigue Syndrome. Supeene's first published novel for young adults is *My Name Is Mitch,* a story about a nonconformist sixth-grader and his troubles at school and at home. Mitch is small for his age. He wears glasses and has trouble with bullies. How he handles these issues while trying to reconcile himself to his parents' breakup forms the crux of the novel. In *Resource Links,* Lisa Mowat suggested that *My Name Is Mitch* offers "topics teachers and students can really sink their teeth into." Sherie Posesorski in *Quill & Quire* praised the work for its "clear, engaging prose."

Because Supeene's first name is somewhat unusual, she sometimes goes as "Lynne Supeene." She lives in Canada with her family.

Biographical and Critical Sources

PERIODICALS

Quill & Quire, October, 2003, Sherie Posesorski, review of *My Name Is Mitch,* p. 43.
Resource Links, December 1, 2003, Lisa Mowat, review of *My Name Is Mitch.*

T-W

TAI, Sharon O.

Personal

Born in Jamaica. *Hobbies and other interests:* Dancing.

Addresses

Agent—c/o Author Mail, Bloomsbury Publishing, 38 Soho Square, London W1D 3HB, England.

Career

Dancer in Jamaica with Jayteens Dance Workshop and Movements Dance Company; writer.

Writings

Grandma, You're Dead!, Bloomsbury Publishing (London, England), 2001.

Sidelights

Sharon O. Tai is a native of Jamaica who has also lived in Brighton, England, Tokyo, and New York City. A year's stay in Japan convinced her to write books for children, and she loosely based *Grandma, You're Dead!* on her own childhood in Jamaica, where she grew up the middle child in a single-parent family of three. In *Grandma, You're Dead!,* young Deena is both terrified and fascinated when the ghost of her grandmother visits her and asks a very important favor. Tai's tale explores Jamaican spirit legends—on the island they call ghosts "duppies." In an interview on the *Bloomsbury Publishing* Web site, Tai said of her Jamaican setting: "I would love to see more Caribbean writers get published and their books available worldwide. The Caribbean has a rich culture and heritage to offer. It truly is a melting pot."

Before becoming a writer, Tai loved to dance. She performed with two troupes in Jamaica, Jayteens Dance Workshop and Movements Dance Company. She left the island in the 1980s. In her interview, she described herself as "a woman who gets the giggles at the oddest moments."

Biographical and Critical Sources

ONLINE

Bloomsbury Publishing, http://www.bloomsbury.com/childrens/ (June 2, 2004), "Sharon O. Tai."

* * *

UEGAKI, Chieri 1969-

Personal

Born February 21, 1969, in Quesnel, British Columbia, Canada; daughter of Takuo (a landscape architect) and Motoko (a homemaker) Uegaki; married Paul Douglas Mears (a builder), 1994. *Education:* University of British Columbia, B.F.A., 1990, also attended Simon Fraser University.

Addresses

Agent—c/o Author Mail, Kids Can Press, 29 Birch Ave., Toronto, Ontario, Canada M4V 1E2.

Career

Writer.

Writings

Suki's Kimono (picture book), illustrated by Stephane Jorisch, Kids Can Press (Toronto, Ontario, Canada), 2003.

Sidelights

Chieri Uegaki is a Canadian of Japanese heritage who was born and raised in British Columbia. Her picture book *Suki's Kimono* celebrates a nonconformist attitude

Young Suki loves the kimono given to her by her loving grandmother and the girl is determined to wear it on the first day of school no matter what her classmates might think. (From Suki's Kimono, *written by Chieri Uegaki and illustrated by Stephane Jorisch.)*

and gives spunky young girls of any ethnicity a heroine to emulate. On the first day of school, Suki insists on wearing her beautiful blue kimono to school, because her grandmother gave it to her on a happy day they spent together. Despite the dire warnings of her older sisters—who strive to be cool in the latest fashions—Suki skips to school in her kimono and wooden clogs. At first the sisters' predictions seem to ring true. Other children snicker and tease, and Suki gets plenty of stares. However, the teasing turns to admiration when Suki tells her new class about dancing with her grandmother at a festival. At the end of the day Suki's clothes get noticed, not her sisters'. "This charming book highlights the importance of being ourselves, reflecting what makes us distinctive," Kathryn McNaughton noted in *Resource Links.* "It also gives children the message that being true to what we value is worthwhile."

Uegaki, a 2000 finalist in the Writers' Union of Canada "Writing for Children" competition, garnered warm reviews for *Suki's Kimono.* A *Kirkus Reviews* critic called it "a wonderful story about being yourself, with the added bonus of teaching readers a little about Japanese culture." *School Library Journal* correspondent Sue Morgan deemed the work "an appealing story of courage and independence." A *Publishers Weekly* reviewer likewise found the tale "appealing," concluding: "Given the true-to-life character, readers may feel like applauding." To quote Linda Perkins in *Booklist,* Suki "is a lively, irrepressible girl, who gives new charm to a familiar story line."

Biographical and Critical Sources

PERIODICALS

Booklist, November 15, 2003, Linda Perkins, review of *Suki's Kimono,* p. 604.
Kirkus Reviews, October 1, 2003, review of *Suki's Kimono.*
New York Times Book Review, November 16, 2003, Marigny Dupuy, "The Dog Ate His Pants," p. 46.
Publishers Weekly, November 24, 2003, review of *Suki's Kimono,* p. 64.
Resource Links, October 1, 2003, Kathryn McNaughton, review of *Suki's Kimono.*
School Library Journal, December, 2003, Sue Morgan, review of *Suki's Kimono,* p. 129.

ONLINE

Vancouver International Writers & Readers Festival, http://www.writersfest.bc.ca/2003/ (June 4, 2004), "Chieri Uegaki."

*   *   *

WALLACE, Paula S.

Personal

Married; children: three. *Education:* Furman University, B.A.; Georgia State University, M.Ed., Ed.S.

Addresses

Office—Office of the President, Savannah College of Art and Design, 622 Drayton St., Savannah, GA 31401.

Career

Savannah College of Art and Design, Savannah, GA, co-founder, former academic dean and provost, presi-

Paula S. Wallace

dent, 2000—. Writer and book designer. Founder, Savannah Sidewalk Arts Festival and Savannah Film Festival.

Member

Georgia Film and Videotape Advisory Commission and Georgia Chamber of Commerce.

Awards, Honors

Named an "Outstanding Young Woman of America"; named employer of the year, Oglethorpe Business and Professional Women; James T. Deason Human Relations award; W. W. Law Legacy award; named to Savannah Business Hall of Fame.

Writings

The World of Birthdays, Gareth Stevens Publications (Milwaukee, WI), 2003.
The World of Food, Gareth Stevens Publications (Milwaukee, WI), 2003.
The World of Holidays, Gareth Stevens Publications (Milwaukee, WI), 2003.
The World of Sports, Gareth Stevens Publications (Milwaukee, WI), 2003.

Also author of *Remember This, Ricky and Rocky.*

Sidelights

Paula S. Wallace is president of the Savannah College of Art and Design, one of the nation's largest art and design colleges. Wallace helped to found the institution and served as an academic dean and provost prior to assuming the presidency in 2000. Additionally, Wallace has helped to extend the scope of artistic endeavors in Savannah, Georgia, by organizing art fairs, film festivals, and exhibits on the college's campus. Despite this daunting schedule, she also writes books for children, most notably the "World" series.

Each of Wallace's "World" series books uses the same ten countries: Australia, Brazil, Egypt, Germany, India, Japan, Mexico, Russia, South Africa, and the United States. She then examines each country on the topic at hand, from birthdays and food, through holidays and sports. The books all include craft and recipe ideas pertaining to each of the countries, and the sports book describes different games played in each nation. In a *School Library Journal* review of *The World of Birthdays,* Maryann H. Owen noted that the material Wallace makes available is "beautifully presented, concise, and useful." Also in *School Library Journal,* Andrew Medlar concluded that *The World of Sports* is that rare title indeed, "useful for art and gym teachers."

In **The World of Food,** *Paula S. Wallace describes culinary habits of people from various countries and includes a recipe from each land she discusses.*

Biographical and Critical Sources

PERIODICALS

School Library Journal, October 1, 2003, Maryann H. Owen, review of *The World of Food;* March, 2004, Andrew Medlar, review of *The World of Sports,* p. 69.

*   *   *

WILSON, Jacqueline 1945-

Personal

Born December 17, 1945, in Bath, England; daughter of Harry Albert (a civil servant) and Margaret (a local government officer; maiden name, Clibbens) Aitken; married William Millar Wilson (a police superintendent), August 28, 1965 (divorced); children: Emma Fiona. *Hobbies and other interests:* Browsing in bookshops, visiting art galleries, going to movies, swimming, line dancing.

Addresses

Home—1B Beaufort Rd., Kingston-on-Thames, Surrey KT1 2TH, England. *Agent*—David Higham Associates, 5-8 Lower John Street, Golden Square, London W1R 4HA, England.

Career

Journalist, freelance magazine writer, and author of books and radio plays. Employed by D. C. Thomsons, Dundee, Scotland, 1963-65.

Awards, Honors

Young Telegraph/Fully Booked Award, 1995, for *The Bed and Breakfast Star;* Smarties Prize and Sheffield Children's Book Award, both for *Double Act;* Whitbread shortlist, 1999, and *Guardian* Children's Fiction Award, 2000, both for *The Illustrated Mum;* Children's Book of the Year, British Book Awards, 1999; Order of the British Empire, 2002, for services to literacy in schools; W. H. Smith Book Award (children's genre), 2003, for *Girls in Tears.*

Writings

FICTION

Ricky's Birthday, illustrated by Margaret Belsky, Macmillan (London, England), 1973.

Nobody's Perfect, Oxford University Press (Oxford, England), 1982.

Waiting for the Sky to Fall, Oxford University Press (New York, NY), 1983.

The Other Side, Oxford University Press (Oxford, England), 1984.

The School Trip, illustrated by Sally Holmes, Hamilton (London, England), 1984.

The Killer Tadpole, illustrated by Rebecca Campbell-Grey, Hamilton (London, England), 1984.

How to Survive Summer Camp, illustrated by Bob Dewar, Oxford University Press (Oxford, England), 1985.

Amber, Oxford University Press (Oxford, England), 1986.

The Monster in the Cupboard, illustrated by Kate Rogers, Blackie (London, England), 1986.

Glubbslyme, illustrated by Jane Cope, Oxford University Press (Oxford, England), 1987.

The Power of the Shade, Oxford University Press (Oxford, England), 1987.

This Girl, Oxford University Press (Oxford, England), 1988.

The Party in the Lift, Blackie (London, England), 1989.

The Left-Outs, Blackie (London, England), 1989.

Falling Apart, Oxford University Press (Oxford, England), 1989.

Is There Anybody There? (includes *Spirit Raising* and *Crystal Gazing*), Armada (London, England), 1990.

Take a Good Look, Blackie (London, England), 1990.

The Dream Palace, Oxford University Press (Oxford, England), 1991.

The Story of Tracy Beaker, illustrated by Nick Sharratt, Doubleday (London, England), 1991, Delacorte (New York, NY), 2001.

The Werepuppy, illustrated by Janet Robertson, Blackie (London, England), 1991.

Video Rose, illustrated by Janet Robertson, Blackie (London, England), 1992.

The Suitcase Kid, illustrated by Nick Sharratt, Doubleday (London, England), 1992, illustrated by Ying-Hwa Hu, Delacorte (New York, NY), 1997.

Mark Spark, illustrated by Bethan Matthews, Hamilton (London, England), 1992.

Mark Spark in the Dark, illustrated by Bethan Matthews, Hamilton (London, England), 1993.

Deep Blue, Oxford University Press (Oxford, England), 1993.

The Mum-Minder, illustrated by Nick Sharratt, Doubleday (London, England), 1993.

The Werepuppy on Holiday, illustrated by Janet Robertson, Blackie (London, England), 1994.

The Bed and Breakfast Star, illustrated by Nick Sharratt, Doubleday (London, England), 1994, published as *Elsa, Star of the Shelter!,* Whitman (Morton Grove, IL), 1996.

Twin Trouble, illustrated by Philipe Dupasquier, Methuen (London, England), 1994.

The Dinosaur's Packed Lunch, illustrated by Nick Sharratt, Doubleday (London, England), 1995.

Cliffhanger, illustrated by Nick Sharratt, Doubleday (London, England), 1995.

Jimmy Jelly, illustrated by Lucy Keijser, Piccadilly (London, England), 1995.

Love from Katy, illustrated by Conny Jude, Ginn (Aylesbury, England), 1995.

Sophie's Secret Diary, illustrated by Natacha Ledwidge, Ginn (Aylesbury, England), 1995.

Double Act, illustrated by Nick Sharratt and Sue Heap, Doubleday (London, England), 1995, Delacorte (New York, NY), 1998.

Beauty and the Beast, illustrated by Peter Kavanagh, A & C Black (London, England), 1996.

Mr. Cool, illustrated by Stephen Lewis, Kingfisher (New York, NY), 1996.

Bad Girls, illustrated by Nick Sharratt, Doubleday (London, England), 1996, Delacorte (New York, NY), 2001.

Connie and the Water Babies, illustrated by Georgien Overwater, Methuen (London, England), 1996.

The Monster Story-Teller, illustrated by Nick Sharratt, Doubleday (London, England), 1997.

The Lottie Project, illustrated by Nick Sharratt, Doubleday (London, England), 1997, Delacorte (New York, NY), 1999.

The Wooden Horse, illustrated by Jan Nesbitt, Ginn (Aylesbury, England), 1998.

Rapunzel, illustrated by Nick Sharratt, Scholastic (London, England), 1998.

Buried Alive!, illustrated by Nick Sharratt, Doubleday (London, England), 1998.

Monster Eyeballs, Heinemann (London, England), 1999.

The Illustrated Mum, illustrated by Nick Sharratt, Doubleday (London, England), 1999.

Lizzy Zipmouth, Young Corgi (London, England), 2000.

Vicky Angel, Doubleday (London, England), 2000, Delacorte (New York, NY), 2001.

The Dare Game, illustrated by Nick Sharratt, Doubleday (London, England), 2000.

My Brother Bernadette, illustrated by David Roberts, Heinemann (London, England), 2001, Crabtree (New York, NY), 2003.

The Cat Mummy, illustrated by Nick Sharratt, Doubleday (London, England), 2001.

Dustbin Baby, illustrated by Nick Sharratt, Doubleday (London, England), 2001.

Sleepovers, illustrated by Nick Sharratt, Doubleday (London, England), 2001.

Secrets, illustrated by Nick Sharratt, Doubleday (London, England), 2002.

The Worry Web Site, illustrated by Nick Sharratt, Doubleday (London, England), 2002, Delacorte (New York, NY), 2003.

Lola Rose, illustrated by Nick Sharratt, Doubleday (London, England), 2003.

Midnight, illustrated by Nick Sharratt, Doubleday (London, England), 2003.

"GIRLS" SERIES

Girls in Love, illustrated by Nick Sharratt, Doubleday (London, England), 1997, Delacorte (New York, NY), 2002.

Girls under Pressure, illustrated by Nick Sharratt, Doubleday (London, England), 1998, Delacorte (New York, NY), 2002.

Girls out Late, illustrated by Nick Sharratt, Doubleday (London, England), 1999, Delacorte (New York, NY), 2002.

Girls in Tears, illustrated by Nick Sharratt, Doubleday (London, England), 2002, Delacorte (New York, NY), 2003.

"STEVIE DAY" SERIES

Supersleuth, Armada (London, England), 1987.
Lonelyhearts, Armada (London, England), 1987.
Rat Race, Armada (London, England), 1988.
Vampire, Armada (London, England), 1988.

"READ-ON" SERIES

Teddy Goes Swimming, Longman (Harlow, England), 1994.
Teddy at the Fair, Longman (Harlow, England), 1994.
Teddy in the Garden, Longman (Harlow, England), 1994.
Teddy Likes the Little One, Longman (Harlow, England), 1994.
Teddy Plays Hide and Seek, Longman (Harlow, England), 1994.
Come Back, Teddy!, Longman (Harlow, England), 1994.
Freddy's Teddy, Longman (Harlow, England), 1994.

SUSPENSE NOVELS; FOR ADULTS

Hide and Seek, Macmillan (London, England), 1972, Doubleday (Garden City, NY), 1973.

Truth or Dare, Macmillan (London, England), 1973, Doubleday (Garden City, NY), 1974.

Snap, Macmillan (London, England), 1974.

Let's Pretend, Macmillan (London, England), 1976.

Making Hate, Macmillan (London, England), 1977, St. Martin's Press (New York, NY), 1978.

OTHER

Author of radio plays *Are You Listening, It's Disgusting at Your Age,* and *Ask a Silly Question,* British Broadcasting Corporation (BBC; London, England), 1982-84;

and contributor to *Winter's Crimes,* edited by Virginia Whitaker, Macmillan (London, England), 1973. Wilson's books have been translated into twenty-three languages.

Adaptations

Double Act was adapted for stage; *The Story of Tracy Beaker* has been adapted as a miniseries by BBC1; three other titles have been adapted for television; *The Story of Tracy Beaker, The Bed and Breakfast Star,* and *The Dare Game* were all adapted for radio.

Sidelights

Jacqueline Wilson is considered one of England's best known writers for young readers. "Her books have sold two million copies, been translated into eleven languages, and she receives over 200 letters from readers a week (replying to them all)," wrote Anne Karpf in an introduction of Wilson in London's *Guardian.* In 2003, she ranked fourth in the Treasure Islands Favourite Children's Author poll, and the BBC's "The Big Read" poll ranked her novel *Double Act* tenth favorite out of one hundred—the only novel in the top ten written by a contemporary writer. Her books *Girls in Love, The Story of Tracy Beaker,* and *Vicky Angel* were also among the top one hundred. Sue Blackhall of *Evening Standard* proclaimed, "Jacqueline Wilson is the latest phenomenon in the world of storytelling."

Known for "the vitality of her writing style and the strong recognition factor in her characters," according to Mary Leland of *Irish Times,* Wilson's books feature "fierce funny girls who tell silly jokes and muck around and do wicked things," as Wilson herself described these heroines in *Books for Keeps.* Linda Newbery, reviewing Wilson's *The Dream Palace* in *School Librarian,* summarized the author's typical plot line as a story of "an ordinary young girl landing in a desperate situation and finding new resilience as a result." Many of the girls come from dysfunctional backgrounds, and all struggle with the reality of their world, trying to make the best of what they are given. Often told with humor as well as pain, Wilson's award-winning books include *Nobody's Perfect, The Other Side, The Story of Tracy Beaker, The Suitcase Kid, Bad Girls,* and *Double Act.* Though many of her early titles are available in the United States only as imports in British editions, she is increasingly gaining recognition on both sides of the Atlantic.

"I wrote my first novel when I was nine years old," Wilson once commented. Written in a school exercise book, this early work told the story of the Maggot family and their unruly offspring. An only child herself, Wilson happily gave the Maggots a slew of offspring. She had a richly imaginative childhood with fantasy friends, beasts lurking under the stairs, a love of magic, and a horror of joining in at school games. In an interview with *Scotsman,* she explained, "I knew all I ever wanted to do was write and wrote throughout my schooldays." She was, as she noted in *Books for Keeps,* "a sad, shy, weedy little kid." Such an upbringing also led to an early love for books. Wilson not only read voraciously, but also continued writing throughout her school years. Though she loved to read, her family did not own a lot of books. She told London *Sunday Times* reporter Louise Johncox, "There was a bookcase but we didn't have loads of books. Money was tight, but Mum always made sure I had a new book every birthday, Christmas, and summer holiday. . . . When I was ten, Mum asked if I could join the adult library because I'd run out of books to read."

Wilson responded to an advertisement looking for first a typist, then a writer, when she was seventeen years old. "By the time I was seventeen I was earning my own living by writing stories for teenage magazines," she once commented. "I was thrilled to see my stories in print (though the magazine editors cut out my finest descriptive passages and pared each character down to a sad stereotype), but it wasn't the sort of fiction I really wanted to write. I wasn't interested in the glossy fantasy world of the magazines. I wanted to write about young people and their problems, but I didn't want to pretend there were the easy solutions offered in the magazine stories."

Married at the age of nineteen to a police superintendent, Wilson turned her hand once again to the writing of novels, but now crime was her centerpiece. "I wrote five crime novels for adults," Wilson once commented, "but each one had a child as one of the major characters, and I knew I didn't really want to write about crime at all, I wanted to write about children." Her first juvenile novel was inspired by a newspaper account about adopted children trying to trace their biological parents, and in Wilson's mind this developed into the story of a young girl, Sandra, trying to track down her real father in *Nobody's Perfect.* Sandra's home life is a mess, and her stepfather is no substitute for the real thing, so one day Sandra sets out to find her real dad who, she knows, once wanted to be a writer just like she does now. Aided in her efforts by a younger teenage boy, Michael, whom she encounters in the British Museum, Sandra succeeds in finding her birth father, only to be disappointed. But she is not disappointed in her newfound friend. Zena Sutherland of the *Bulletin of the Center for Children's Books* noted that in this sensitively written story, "the characterization, plot, and pace all have impact," while the "treatment of relationships" is both "realistic and perceptive." A *Junior Bookshelf* commentator also praised this first juvenile novel, concluding that with the help of Michael, the book was "a good and worthwhile read which ends in a realistic but satisfying way." Lucinda Fox in *School Librarian* called *Nobody's Perfect* a "perceptive story which will appeal to teenagers identifying themselves with Sandra and some of her problems."

Apparent in Wilson's first title were several elements that would recur throughout her novels for young read-

ers: the female heroine; the outsider or quirky character; and the love of setting books partially or in whole in museums and galleries. Her next title, *The Other Side,* is the story of young Alison who thinks—as Wilson herself did as a girl—that if she stares at the ceiling hard enough, she will be able to levitate. In fact, Alison learns to fly around her bedroom and out of the window to navigate her neighborhood. Or is it all a dream induced by the difficulties Alison is having in her waking life with her parents' divorce and her mother's breakdown? "The book's called *The Other Side* because Alison learns the other side of her parents' situation, and she also has occult experiences on the 'Other Side,'" Wilson once explained. David Bennett, writing in *Books for Keeps,* noted that Wilson has shown "convincingly" how the collapse of family relationships "leaves only victims in its wake, no winners," and concluded that it was a "moving novel."

Another broken family is featured in *How to Survive Summer Camp,* when Stella is sent off to camp during her mother's honeymoon with her second husband. "I wrote [that book] to comfort all the shy subversive children who find the whole idea of summer camp sheer hell," Wilson once commented, and for her protagonist, Stella, the experience is far from delightful. She is afraid of water, the food at camp is terrible, and her favorite book is ruined—perhaps by jealous girls at the camp. A kindly camp counselor manages to save the day when he discovers Stella's love for storytelling by suggesting she start a camp magazine. Margery Fisher of *Growing Point* called the book a "pleasing and pointed look at a girl of ten or so in difficulties with her peers," while a *Junior Bookshelf* reviewer dubbed it a "shrewd and well observed story."

Wilson's love of books literally led her to her next teen novel. An inveterate reader—at last count she had well over 10,000 volumes scattered about her home—Wilson enjoys a favorite outing to a nearby village which has some twenty secondhand bookstores. Once, while visiting these shops, she also noticed the hippies who lived nearby, and the hippie children wandering about the town. She wondered what it would be like to have one of those children rebel against their unconventional life, and thus was born the eponymous heroine *Amber.* Amber has come to resent the freedom and unstructured nature of her life with her mother and longs for clean sheets and a steady home. Rescued for a time by a childhood friend, Amber finally must find her own way in the world. Dorothy Nimmo noted in *School Librarian* that the "stages in Amber's journey are small, true, and moving," and concluded that this was a story "to be enjoyed and admired." Bennett, writing in *Books for Keeps,* called *Amber* a "well-written, thought-provoking read for mid-teenagers."

Magic in various forms and guises comes to the fore in several of Wilson's titles, including *Glubbslyme, The Power of the Shade,* and *Is There Anybody There?,* which involve seances and time-travel. With *Glubb-*

slyme, witchcraft becomes a theme, in a book told from the perspective of a long-lived toad who is a witch's familiar. "I've tried to make him behave like a seventeenth-century character who is utterly appalled by the noisy new inventions of the modern world," Wilson once commented. In *The Power of the Shade,* May starts to believe she really *can* make magic when her friend Selina initiates her into witchcraft. May believes in these powers, even though Selina is probably only kidding, and subsequently spends hours in London's National Gallery staring at a painting of witches.

Typical problem novels from Wilson include *This Girl* and *The Dream Palace.* The former story is, according to *Books for Keeps* reviewer Adrian Jackson, a "brave exploration" of how a young girl copes with "opportunity and relationships." Coral is caught between her father's unemployment malaise and her mother's coquetry, and opts out of her home when she takes a position as a nanny. Her employers have created a Victorian fantasy in their home, yet the same old problems abide under the surface, and Coral turns to a young single mother, Deb, to help her make sense of the world. Dorothy Atkinson, writing in *School Librarian,* considered *This Girl* a "fine novel for teenagers" and "also an unusual one." In *The Dream Palace,* insecure Lolly thinks she does not measure up to her prettier friend, Lynn, and when Lynn goes on a fine vacation, Lolly is stuck taking a summer job at a nursing home. At her own home, things are not much better with her mother and stepfather, but when Lolly meets Greg, who is a member of a group of squatters, things start to change in her life. And when she finally leaves her home with Greg, she learns new truths about the world, as well. Linda Newbery noted in *School Librarian* that "teenage readers will be engrossed and challenged by this unputdownable, skillfully crafted book," a sentiment that was echoed by Stephanie Nettell in *Books for Keeps,* who wrote that Wilson's story "shocks, entertains, moves, and instructs," calling the book "teenage reading at its most skillful."

Though Wilson's books were received fairly well, it was not until 1991 with *The Story of Tracy Beaker* that Wilson finally hit her extreme level of popularity. Her novels had been around for quite awhile, but Tracy Beaker's story was the one that caught the media's eye. Wilson's first novel to be told in first person from a child's standpoint, *The Story of Tracy Beaker* was also the first of Wilson's books to be accompanied by the illustrations of Nick Sharratt. Tracy Beaker—"gutsy, stroppy and spirited," as Wilson once described her—is an aspiring ten-year-old writer who tells the story of the children's home where she resides. "Here is the ultimate in first-person journal writing . . . flip and funny," noted Maurice Saxby in a review for *Magpies.* Tracy's dream is to be taken in by a family that measures up to her demanding standards, though as Saxby observed, "underneath the brashness and bravado is a desperately unhappy, self-deluding, insecure personality." Angela Redfern, writing in *School Librarian,* concluded that a

Protagonist and narrator, energetic ten-year-old Tracy makes a connection with a writer who visits the group home where Tracy lives, harboring the hope that her delinquent mother or a foster parent will take her to live with them. (Cover illustration by Nick Sharratt.)

"real bonus is that the book genuinely celebrates the act of writing—and not by preaching." In *Horn Book,* a critic wrote that the author "does a commendable job of providing . . . a surprisingly well rounded picture of the seemingly callous but lonely young girl," while a critic for *Publishers Weekly* thought Tracy's "indomitable spirit and grit leaves little doubt that she will end up on top."

Humor is at the heart of some of Wilson's prize-winning novels, including *The Suitcase Kid* and *Double Act,* and it is comedy also that in part informs such popular works as *Elsa, Star of the Shelter!* and *Girls in Love.* Yet Wilson's humorous books are not frivolous—they deal with topics ranging from divorce and homelessness to bullying and developing a positive self-image. Wilson took on the difficult subject of divorce in *The Suitcase Kid,* another story told in diary form by a ten-year-old protagonist, detailing the tug-of-war Andrea is going through as she shuttles back and forth between mom and dad. Added to the brew are step-siblings and a new half-sister to make Andrea's life totally confusing.

Deborah Stevenson, writing in *Bulletin of the Center for Children's Books,* maintained that the book "taps into the righteous indignation of a child torn between two households, and it does so deftly," while Valerie Bierman in *Books for Your Children* observed that to "portray divorce with humour and sympathy takes great skill."

In *Double Act,* Wilson explores the trials and tribulations of being a twin in the story of ten-year-olds Ruby and Garnet. Identical physically, Garnet is shy and somewhat wimpy while her sister Ruby is brash and rude, and the duo take turns narrating this story in which they reluctantly move from the city to the country with their father and his new girlfriend—their mother being long dead. Ann Sohn-Rethel declared the book "another winner" in a review for *School Librarian,* while Stevenson, writing in *Bulletin of the Center for Children's Books,* felt the book would "intrigue youngsters who wonder what twinship would be like, and there are enough down and dirty double details here to satisfy them." Originally published as *The Bed and Breakfast Star, Elsa, Star of the Shelter!* deals with life in a children's shelter in a novel both "funny and brave," according to Roger Sutton in *Bulletin of the Center for Children's Books.* Humorously narrated by precocious, ten-year-old Elsa, the book "is a far cry from traditional middle-grade fiction," according to a *Publishers Weekly* reviewer who also felt the book was "eye-opening." *Booklist's* Lauren Peterson called *Elsa, Star of the Shelter!* a "bittersweet account of life in [a] . . . shelter," and concluded that though long, "the story is nicely paced and tender, and it provides loads of avenues to explore through discussion."

Taking up the situation of another young girl in *Bad Girls,* Wilson spins the tale of ten-year-old Mandy, the victim of incessant teasing by three girls at school, through her first-person narrative. She is hit by a bus, leaving her with a sprained arm, while fleeing from the girls, but they refuse to stop the bullying. Mandy must also deal with her over-protective mother. Her situation improves when Tanya, a foster child four years her senior, moves into the neighborhood. Through their relationship—despite getting into a bit of trouble with Tanya—"Mandy develops a strength and maturity that enables her to relate better to her mother and to brush off the barbs of the bullies," explained a *Publishers Weekly* reviewer, concluding, "Shaping convincing characters, dialogue and plot, Wilson proves that bad girls can make for a good story."

Adding a bit of historical fiction to her work, Wilson's *The Lottie Project* features Charlie, or Charlotte as her strict new teacher insists on calling her, and her changing life circumstances. Though eleven-year-old Charlie is content with her life, she is not able to prevent major changes: her single mother loses her steady job, must find multiple part-time work, and starts dating a man with a five-year-old son. In the midst of these events, Charlie develops a fictional journal of a girl living in Victorian times as part of a school project, and those entries intermix with Charlie's life to add another dimension to the story. A critic for *Kirkus Reviews* noted, "Funny, incisive, and true to life, this book introduces a heroine who is easy to root for—she's a terrific combination of feisty and fragile." Kitty Flynn, writing for *Horn Book,* concluded that "readers will empathize with many of the situations Charlie copes with and appreciate the message that, as in life, all loose ends may not be tied up at the end, but we can take what we've learned and carry on from there."

Delving deeper into social distress with *The Illustrated Mum,* Wilson speaks through the first-person account of Dolphin, the eleven-year-old daughter of unstable mother Marigold. It is eventually revealed that Marigold suffers from manic depression, but Dolphin and her older sister Star have developed numerous coping strategies. Inevitably, Marigold is hospitalized for treatment of her condition. Though a serious story, Valerie Coghlan wrote in *Books for Keeps* that "Wilson's style keeps a degree of the grimness at a distance, and the love which Marigold has for her daughters and they for her is evident throughout the story."

Wilson's "Girls" series is aimed at a slightly older audience and features three girls—Ellie, Magda, and Nadine—as they struggle with the teenage years, especially with body image and self-esteem. Narrated by Ellie, who is insecure about her weight when compared to her two willowy friends, *Girls in Love* tells of Ellie's attempt to use a male friend to play the part of her gorgeous boyfriend—and because he lives far away, she can describe him however she likes. When he comes to visit her, however, she begins to realize that judging him by his appearance may have made her miss out on a great friendship. In *Girls under Pressure,* Ellie struggles with her weight, opting to stop eating and flirting with bulimia. But when she meets a girl who actually suffers from an eating disorder, she realizes that the path she is treading is a dangerous one. Ellie gets into trouble by staying out with her friends and her artistic boyfriend in *Girls out Late; Girls in Tears* follows Ellie as she learns that the relationships she had assumed would be there forever might not be as sturdy as she had thought. "The way these best friends deal with these issues creates an amusing, entertaining tale with which teenagers will identify," wrote Ginny Harrell for *School Library Journal. School Librarian* critic Pat Williams noted that Wilson "finds the right mix of humour and hard-hitting content to deliver a message without lecturing or patronising" in *Girls under Pressure.* In a review of *Girls in Love,* a contributor to *Publishers Weekly* found "Ellie's first-person narration possesses a Bridget Jones-like energy and compulsiveness." In a review of the first three books in the series, *Kliatt* contributor Paula Rohrlick wrote, "Wilson deals with the road bumps of adolescence with insight and humor."

Vicky Angel, the story of best friends Jude and Vicky, takes a tragic twist when Vicky is hit by a car and killed.

In the midst of her grief, Jude revisits the site of the accident and finds, to her great surprise, Vicky's ghost. Vicky's continued presence is a comfort to her but at times interferes with the efforts of other people in Jude's life. Eventually, the friends must let go. "Wilson . . . poignantly addresses a tragic and traumatic experience," commented a *Publishers Weekly* reviewer. Ilene Cooper of *Booklist* noted, "Wilson's wonderful way with dialogue . . . makes this more incisive than depressing." A critic for *Kirkus Reviews* claimed the book worked well due to "its honest characters and dialogue, its unique coverage of grief, and its ability to unite readers with Jude's healing process."

It is not a traumatic death but a traumatic birth that plagues April, the heroine of Wilson's *Dustbin Baby*. Born on April 1st, April was discarded in an alley behind a restaurant, to be found later and raised by a caring, if not entirely understanding, foster mother. After an argument with her foster mother about April's inherent right to own a cell phone, April wanders off to learn more about her past, trying to come to terms with the mother who rejected her the moment she was born. "This is a book that will resonate with many teenage girls and encourage them to give their mums, or caring guardians, a hug this Christmas, even if there's no Nokia under the tree," wrote Helen Brown in *Daily Telegraph*.

Secrets is one of Wilson's few books to feature a girl from an economically well-off family. India, an only child whose parents do not pay her much attention (except to help her mind her weight), deals with her frustrations about life by keeping a diary, just like her hero, Anne Frank. India becomes friends with Treasure, a girl from the poor side of town who also keeps a diary; when Treasure's life begins to fall apart, India hides her friend in her attic to protect her. But though Treasure's family has its issues, they truly love her—a feeling India misses from her own parents. "Wilson's chatty style is effortless to read," praised Julia Eccleshare in *Guardian*. Lisa Allardice of *Daily Telegraph* wrote that Wilson "is not just an astute chronicler of contemporary childhood, but an imaginative storyteller."

Six short stories by Wilson and one short story by one of her fans, the winner of an online contest sponsored by Wilson, make up the content of *The Worry Web Site*. Each story features a narrator who posts his or her troubles on a Web site, and each of the stories are linked together by shared characters. In sponsoring the contest, Wilson received more than 15,000 entries, which led a *Kirkus Reviews* critic to comment that *The Worry Web Site* "shows plenty of potential for turning young readers into young writers."

Wilson, who visits schools in England regularly, tries to stay in touch with her young readers and their problems, anxieties, and sense of humor. Her appearance is not necessarily what her readers expect; according to Daphne Lockyer of London *Times*, "She dresses only in black from head to toe, and wears a large ring on each of her fingers. Her hair is that of a spiky grey elf; her boots are those of a pixie." Wilson has told reporters that when in her "full jewelry," she sets off metal detectors in airports. But her eccentric dress does not detract from the realism of her books. As she noted in *Books for Keeps*, "I might write about girls but I want to be read by girls *and* boys." To that end, her female protagonists are not "girly girls so the boys don't feel funny reading about them." As she once commented, her inspiration over the years has not really changed: the desire to tell a story, to create a pretend life and universe. "When I was young, I used to keep quiet about my imaginary games to my friends because I knew they'd think I was crazy—some of them seemed to think that anyway—but now that I'm grown up and a writer, I can play pretend games all the time so long as I write them down on paper and turn them into novels."

Biographical and Critical Sources

BOOKS

St. James Guide to Children's Writers, 5th edition, St. James Press (Detroit, MI), 1999.

Ninth-grader Ellie is hellbent on getting a boyfriend even if it means lying, a recourse that brings trouble and humorous bedlam. (Cover illustration by Brad Martin.)

PERIODICALS

Booklist, January 1, 1996, Lauren Peterson, review of *Elsa, Star of the Shelter!,* p. 836; October 15, 1997, Kay Weisman, review of *The Suitcase Kid,* p. 407; January 1, 1998, Ilene Cooper, review of *Double Act,* p. 799; October 1, 1999, Ilene Cooper, review of *The Lottie Project,* p. 360; June 1, 2001, Ilene Cooper, review of *The Story of Tracy Beaker,* p. 1884; November 15, 2001, Ilene Cooper, review of *Vicky Angel,* p. 575; May 15, 2002, Gillian Engberg, review of *Girls in Love,* p. 1592; January 1, 2004, Gillian Engberg, review of *The Worry Web Site,* p. 864.

Books for Keeps, March, 1987, David Bennett, review of *The Other Side,* p. 13; September, 1988, David Bennett, review of *Amber,* p. 12; November, 1990, Adrian Jackson, review of *This Girl,* p. 12; May, 1991, p. 14; January, 1992, Stephanie Nettell, review of *The Dream Palace,* p. 24; March, 1995, p. 12; March, 1996, p. 24; September, 1996, p. 13; September, 1999, Valerie Coghlan, review of *The Illustrated Mum,* p. 28.

Books for Your Children, spring, 1993, Valerie Bierman, review of *The Suitcase Kid,* p. 23.

Bulletin of the Center for Children's Books, April, 1984, Zena Sutherland, review of *Nobody's Perfect,* p. 158; July-August, 1986, p. 219; February, 1996, Roger Sutton, review of *Elsa, Star of the Shelter!,* p. 209; July-August, 1997, Deborah Stevenson, review of *The Suitcase Kid,* pp. 416-417; February, 1998, Deborah Stevenson, review of *Double Act,* p. 224; December, 1999, Deborah Stevenson, review of *The Lottie Project,* p. 154.

Carousel, summer, 1998, p. 31.

Daily Telegraph (London, England), December 1, 2001, Helen Brown, "Of Hormones, Hair, and Handsets," review of *Dustbin Baby;* March 30, 2002, Lisa Allardice, "Modern Girls Keep It Real," review of *Secrets.*

Evening Standard (London, England), January 4, 2002, Sue Blackhall, "Another Success Story Thanks to Children's Books," p. 19.

Growing Point, March, 1985, pp. 4390-4391; March, 1986, Margery Fisher, review of *How to Survive Summer Camp,* p. 4596; March, 1988, pp. 4935-4937; July, 1989, pp. 5188-5190; November, 1989, pp. 5241-5243.

Guardian (London, England), November 6, 1999, Anne Karpf, article about Jacqueline Wilson, p. 11; March 25, 2000, Julia Eccleshare, "In Dol's House," p. 9; March 28, 2001, Dina Rabinovich, "The Original Jackie," p. 9; June 22, 2002, Julia Eccleshare, "Treasure in the Attic," review of *Secrets,* p. 32; March 1, 2003, Julia Eccleshare, "Family Fortunes," p. 33; March 26, 2003, Maggie Brown, "Drama Queen," p. 14; February 13, 2004, John Ezard, "Granny Spice Becomes Queen of Libraries," p. 12.

Horn Book, November, 1999, Kitty Flynn, review of *The Lottie Project,* p. 746; September, 2001, review of *The Story of Tracy Beaker,* p. 598.

Independent (London, England), October 20, 2001, Hilary Macaskill, interview with Jacqueline Wilson, p. 10.

Irish Times (Dublin, Ireland), May 1, 2003, review of the stage version of *Double Act,* p. 31.

Junior Bookshelf, August, 1982, review of *Nobody's Perfect,* p. 156; April, 1986, review of *How to Survive Summer Camp,* p. 83; February, 1992, pp. 24-25; December, 1992, pp. 248-249; February, 1994, pp. 37-38; April, 1994, p. 76; August, 1996, p. 152.

Kirkus Reviews, August 1, 1997, p. 1230; January 1, 1998, p. 63; October, 1999, review of *The Lottie Project,* p. 1585; September 1, 2001, review of *Vicky Angel,* p. 1304; November 1, 2001, review of *Girls in Love,* p. 1556; September 15, 2003, review of *The Worry Web Site,* p. 1185.

Kliatt, September, 2002, Paula Rohrlick, review of *Girls in Love, Girls under Pressure,* and *Girls in Tears,* p. 14; July, 2003, Paula Rohrlick, review of *Girls under Pressure* and *Girls out Late,* p. 28.

Magpies, November, 1991, Maurice Saxby, review of *The Story of Tracy Beaker,* pp. 29-30; March, 1993, pp. 29-30.

Observer (London, England), March 2, 2003, Kate Kellaway, "Dear Ms. Comfort," p. 19.

Publishers Weekly, December 18, 1995, review of *Elsa, Star of the Shelter!,* p. 55; January 12, 1998, review of *Double Act,* p. 60; November 29, 1999, review of *The Lottie Project,* p. 72; January 8, 2001, review of *Bad Girls,* p. 68; July 23, 2001, review of *The Story of Tracy Beaker,* p. 77; August 13, 2001, review of *Vicky Angel,* p. 312; December 3, 2001, review of *Girls in Love,* p. 61; July 1, 2002, "The British Invasion," p. 26; April 21, 2003, review of *Vicky Angel,* p. 65; April 28, 2003, review of *Girls under Pressure,* p. 73; June 9, 2003, "And Now, Back to Our Story," p. 54; July 7, 2003, review of *Girls out Late,* p. 74; December 1, 2003, review of *The Worry Web Site,* p. 56.

School Librarian, September, 1982, Lucinda Fox, review of *Nobody's Perfect,* p. 256; September, 1986, Dorothy Nimmo, review of *Amber,* p. 276; February, 1989, Dorothy Atkinson, review of *This Girl,* p. 32; May, 1991, Angela Redfern, review of *The Story of Tracy Beaker,* p. 62; May, 1992, Linda Newbery, review of *The Dream Palace,* p. 74; May, 1994, pp. 63, 74-75; August, 1995, Ann Sohn-Rethel, review of *Double Act,* p. 111; November, 1997, p. 216; spring, 1999, Pat Williams, review of *Girls under Pressure,* p. 49.

School Library Journal, February, 1996, Jane Gardner Connor, review of *Elsa, Star of the Shelter!,* p. 104; September, 1997, Kathy East, review of *The Suitcase Kid,* p. 227; March, 1998, Miriam Lang Budin, review of *Double Act,* p. 226; June, 2000, Ginny Harrell, review of *Girls under Pressure,* p. 86; March, 2001, Marilyn Ackerman, review of *Bad Girls,* p. 258; July, 2001, B. Allison Gray, review of *The Story of Tracy Beaker,* p. 116; October, 2001, Marlyn K. Roberts, review of *Vicky Angel,* p. 175; January, 2002, Susan Riley, review of *Girls in Love,* p. 141; December, 2002, Susan Riley, review of *Girls under Pressure,* p. 151; July, 2003, Michele Shaw, review of *Girls in Tears,* p. 135; December, 2003, Rebecca Sheridan, review of *The Worry Web Site,* p. 162.

Scotsman (Edinburgh, Scotland), November 30, 2002, "Bibliofile," p. 7; December 4, 2002, Leila Farrah, "My School Days," interview with Wilson, p. 14.

Sunday Times (London, England), March 3, 2002, Nick Rennison, review of *Secrets,* p. 44; November 2, 2003, Louise Johncox, interview with Jacqueline Wilson, p. 3.

Time International, March 12, 2001, "Watch out, Harry Potter: Childhood Can Be Hard and Parents Weird, but Jacqueline Wilson's Best-Sellers Don't Need Fantasy," p. 57.

Times (London, England), February 23, 2002, interview with Jacqueline Wilson, p. 3; February 24, 2002, Catherine O'Brien, "Nice Smile," p. 8; March 29, 2003, Daphne Lockyer, "Are You Sitting Uncomfortably?," p. 26.

Western Mail (Cardiff, Wales), March 30, 2002, "Children's Drama to Be Filmed in Wales," p. 14; May 28, 2003, "Tracy Beaker Creator Wows Young at Hay," p. 2.

ONLINE

Kids at Random House, http://www.randomhouse.co.uk/childrens/ (February 1, 2004), profile of Jacqueline Wilson.

Young Writer, http://www.mystworld.com/youngwriter/ (February 14, 2002), "Issue 15: Jacqueline Wilson."*

*　　*　　*

WINTERS, Katherine 1936-
(Kay Winters)

Personal

Born October 5, 1936, in Trenton, NJ; daughter of Robert (an aerospace engineer) and Luella (a homemaker) Lanning; married Earl D. Winters (a consultant), August 27, 1960; children: Linda. *Education:* Beaver College (now Arcadia University), B.S.; attended Boston University; Wheelock College, M.S.; attended Lehigh University. *Politics:* Democrat. *Religion:* Protestant. *Hobbies and other interests:* Reading, biking, walking, gardening, traveling.

Addresses

Home and office—Box 339, Richlandtown, PA 18955. *E-mail*—KayWin@aol.com.

Career

Children's book author, reviewer, and consultant. Massachusetts Public Schools, Newton, MA, elementary education teacher, 1960-63; Palisades School District, Kintnersville, PA, elementary education teacher and supervisor, 1968-92. American International Schools, education consultant, 1970-80.

Member

International Reading Association, Society of Children's Book Writers and Illustrators, Authors Guild.

Katherine Winters

Awards, Honors

Pick of the List selection, American Booksellers Association, 1997, and Best Books of the Year citation, Bank Street College of Education, both for *Wolf Watch;* Best One Hundred Books of the Year selection, International Reading Association, for *Tiger Trail;* Best Books of the Year citation, Bank Street College of Education, Best Book citation, Chicago Public Library, Junior Library Guild selection, Chapman Award for Best Classroom Read-Alouds, Planet Esme, and C-SPAN 2 *Book TV* selection, all 2003, for *Abraham Lincoln: The Boy Who Loved Books;* Best Book citation, Chicago Public Library, 2003, for *Voices of Ancient Egypt.*

Writings

FOR CHILDREN; AS KAY WINTERS

Did You See What I Saw?: Poems about School, illustrated by Martha Weston, Viking (New York, NY), 1996.

(Reteller) *Talk! Talk! Talk! A Haitian Fable,* illustrated by JoAnn Kitchel, Celebration Press (Glenview, IL), 1996.

The Teeny Tiny Ghost, illustrated by Lynn Munsinger, HarperCollins (New York, NY), 1997.

Wolf Watch, illustrated by Laura Regan, Simon & Schuster (New York, NY), 1997.

Where Are the Bears?, illustrated by Brian Lies, Bantam Doubleday Dell (New York, NY), 1998.

How Will the Easter Bunny Know?, illustrated by Martha Weston, Yearling (New York, NY), 1999.

Whooo's Haunting the Teeny Tiny Ghost?, illustrated by Lynn Munsinger, HarperCollins (New York, NY), 1999.

Tiger Trail, illustrated by Laura Regan, Simon & Schuster (New York, NY), 2000.

But Mom, Everybody Else Does, illustrated by Doug Cushman, Dutton Children's Books (New York, NY), 2002.

Abraham Lincoln: The Boy Who Loved Books, illustrated by Nancy Carpenter, Simon & Schuster (New York, NY), 2003.

Voices of Ancient Egypt, illustrated by Barry Moser, National Geographic Society (Washington, DC), 2003.

My Teacher for President, illustrated by Denise Brunkus, Dutton Children's Books (New York, NY), 2004.

The Teeny Tiny Ghost and the Monster, illustrated by Lynn Munsinger, HarperCollins (New York, NY), 2004.

OTHER; AS KAY WINTERS

(With Marta Felber) *The Teacher's Copebook: How to End the Year Better Than You Started,* Fearon, 1980.

Winters has also written reading textbooks for Scott Foresman and Houghton Mifflin.

Sidelights

Katherine Winters once told *SATA:* "From the time I was seven years old, I was a writer. I kept diaries, journals, wrote for the school and camp newspapers, and the college magazine. When I graduated from Beaver College (now Arcadia University) with a bachelor of science degree in elementary education and a minor in English, I took additional writing courses at Boston University. I submitted poems, essays, articles, and stories to educational journals and textbooks. Now and then they were published. But making a living by writing books did not seem like a viable possibility at that time. My husband and I were just out of graduate school, and we had a big educational debt to pay to Massachusetts Institute of Technology (MIT), as well as a new baby.

"For the next twenty-nine years, I worked in public schools as a teacher, a reading specialist, an educational consultant, and a college instructor. And I loved it. At every conference I attended, I always went to hear the authors instead of the latest theory on the wonder of phonics. I continued to send in manuscripts now and then, but teaching was very consuming. There was little time for writing. In 1980, I coauthored a book for teachers with Marta Felber, *The Teachers Copebook: How to End the Year Better Than You Started.* In order to finish that project, I had to get up every morning at 4 a.m., sneak downstairs to my frosty office, and garbed in a fur robe, woolen gloves, and fleece-lined boots, would type until it was time to teach.

"In 1992, my school board offered early retirement. My resignation was on the superintendent's desk the next day. This was my chance! I was taking it. I started to write full time the day after I retired. I imagined that the Palisades School District was paying me to stay home and write. And write I did. I wrote every day. I went to The New School in New York and took classes in writing for children with instructors Margaret Gable and Deborah Brodie. I attended conferences and met editors. I went to New York to the Children's Book Council and read all of the picture books from the years 1991 and 1992 that they had on their shelves.

"Gradually, the rejection forms from publishers changed into personal letters. Finally, in 1994, I got a phone call from an editor at HarperCollins. They were interested in *The Teeny Tiny Ghost.* From there, my writing career began to take off. Publishers were soon interested in *Wolf Watch* and *Did You See What I Saw?: Poems about School.* In the meantime, I was also writing reading textbooks. Soon, *Where Are the Bears?* and *How Will the Easter Bunny Know?* were going to press, and I was writing *Whooo's Haunting the Teeny Tiny Ghost?,* a sequel to *The Teeny Tiny Ghost,* and *Tiger Trail,* the companion to *Wolf Watch.* I was researching *Abraham Lincoln* and delving into *Voices of Ancient Egypt.*"

In *The Teeny Tiny Ghost,* Winters addresses the importance of mastering one's fears. In this take on a well-

A small ghost battles his own fears in his attempts to learn to be scary at haunting school in Kay Winter's touching picture book. (From The Teeny Tiny Ghost, *illustrated by Lynn Munsinger.)*

known tale, a diminutive specter is afraid of his own boos and howls. On Halloween night, a rap on the door sends shivers through him and his teeny tiny kittens. But summoning up all his courage, he swears to protect his feline companions and opens the door to his ghostly pals who have come to take him trick-or-treating. Janice M. Del Negro, writing in *Bulletin of the Center for Children's Books,* said, "tucked into this humorously written and illustrated tale is the kernel of stoutheartedness that makes young children love the hero." "This tale of banishing fear has just the right blend of wit and supernatural suspense," commented a reviewer in *Publishers Weekly.*

The Teeny Tiny Ghost returns in *Whooo's Haunting the Teeny Tiny Ghost?* Coming home from his teeny tiny school one day, the pint-sized phantom finds some invisible creature "stomp, stomp, stomping" around his teeny tiny house. The Teeny Tiny Ghost and his two teeny tiny cats are scared, but once again, the small spirit finds the courage to save the day. He confronts the creature and discovers that it is just his cousin, Brad, whose homework assignment was to practice haunting. The tale "convey[s] a feeling of spookiness without being overtly scary," Lauren Peterson noted in *Booklist,* which makes the book good "for younger, more sensitive children." Describing the work as "an all out charmer," a *Publishers Weekly* critic called *Whooo's Haunting the Teeny Tiny Ghost?* "the treat of the Halloween season."

Drawing on her twenty-seven years of teaching elementary school, Winters wrote a book of poems devoted to life in the classroom. The day-to-day goings on in a typical schoolroom are highlighted in *Did You See What I Saw?: Poems about School.* Everything, from the pleasure evoked by a new box of crayons to snow days and passing notes in class, is explored in lighthearted verse. Poems such as "Lots of Spots," about the travails of chicken pox, and "Groundhog Day" paint amusing pictures of school life. "The rhythms and sounds and wordplay . . . are part of the fun," Hazel Rochman suggested in *Booklist.*

In the award-winning *Wolf Watch,* Winters uses poetic quatrains to tell the story of four wolf pups from birth until their first foray out of the den. The habits of a wolf pack are introduced, from howling to hunting and fending for their young. Danger is present in the form of a golden eagle who awaits the chance to prey upon one of the defenseless pups. *School Library Journal* contributor Susan Scheps called *Wolf Watch* "a treasure of a book," and noted that "there is a lot of information to be gleaned from this sparsely written visual masterpiece." A critic for *Kirkus Reviews,* meanwhile, hailed *Wolf Watch* as "a splendid complement to titles with a more fact-based approach to wolf life."

Another educational title is *Abraham Lincoln: The Boy Who Loved Books,* which uses "strong, economical language," in the words of a *Kirkus Reviews* contributor,

Winters's juvenile biography of the sixteenth President pays particular tribute to his fondness for reading while he was young. (From Abraham Lincoln: The Boy Who Loved Books, *illustrated by Nancy Carpenter.)*

to tell the story of America's sixteenth president. Written in free verse, the book strings together several episodes and vignettes from the president's life to explain how a poor frontier boy's love of books and learning led him to the White House. Winters has "an eye for details of particular interest to a young audience," noted a *Publishers Weekly* reviewer, and *Booklist*'s Kay Weisman thought that *Abraham Lincoln*'s "simple language" and "engaging narrative" make the book "a good choice for reading aloud."

In a statement posted at her Web site, Winters explained how she came to write Lincoln's story: "I was drawn to exploring the life of Abe Lincoln because I wondered how someone could be born in extreme poverty, lose his mother at age nine, have less than a year of education, few role models, yet overcome these obstacles to become a beloved President whose words we remember today. I was delighted to discover that books made the difference." This respect for literacy came through in Winters's text: a reviewer for *Kirkus Reviews* called *Abraham Lincoln* "a moving tribute to the power of books and words."

Winters's book *Voices of Ancient Egypt* uses "evocative words and an arresting design to bring a long-gone civilization to life," Ilene Cooper explained in *Booklist.* Winters profiles a variety of prototypical Egyptians,

During the Old Kingdom in Egypt, various workers and artisans explain their jobs in Winters's historical book. (From Voices of Ancient Egypt, *illustrated by Barry Moser.*)

from the scribes and pyramid-builders to the often overlooked weavers, bird-catchers, clothes-washers, and other laborers. Each person is given a two-page spread, on which he or she explains his or her duties in free-verse poems written in the first person. This book is "a lovely browsing title," thought *School Library Journal*'s Eve Ortega, in addition to "contain[ing] valuable information for students."

How Will the Easter Bunny Know? was inspired by a real-life incident. Winters told Jodi Duckett of the *Morning Call* that her husband's friend had been asked by his young nephew, "Uncle John, if I come to your house for Easter, how will the Easter bunny know?" Using that question and its worry as her starting point, Winters tells the story of a six-year-old boy who figures out a variety of ways to inform the Easter bunny that he is staying at his grandmother's house. He draws a map to grandmother's apartment, even carefully including a picture of her green door, leaves a letter to the Easter bunny, and makes signs to guide him. "The child has to solve the problem by himself; that's an unwritten rule in children's books," Winters explained to Duckett. Carolyn Phelan in *Booklist* called *How Will the Easter Bunny Know?* the "likable story of a child-size dilemma."

In *But Mom, Everybody Else Does!* a young girl tries to "convince her mother that her acts and desires are not only legitimate but also universal," as a *Kirkus Reviews* contributor wrote. All children have messy rooms, they all failed the test at school, they all get bigger allowances, and so on. The girl tells her mother that no one walks to school, everyone sleeps with the dog, nobody has to practice, and everybody can paint better than she can. Cushman's illustrations stretch these "statements to the point of absurdity," Kathy Piehl noted in *School Library Journal,* for example showing pupils riding to school on everything from dinosaurs to spaceships when the girl complains about having to walk to school. *Booklist* reviewer Hazel Rochman believed that "this farce reinforces every kid's frustration about bossy grown-ups."

About her books for children, Winters told *SATA,* "*Voices* is being used all over the country as a readers' theater, as well as resource material for the study of ancient Egypt. *My Teacher for President* is spawning writing contests as second and third graders write three sentences about why a teacher they know should be president! Told in a humorous way, but describing real election issues—environment, peace, jobs, tolerance—children get a chance to examine candidate platforms and realize how many positive qualities their own teachers possess."

Winters once explained to *SATA,* "I write because that's how I know what I think. When I see what I say, ideas that were fuzzy come clear to me. And sometimes I am surprised at what I find out about myself.

"I write because I love to read and I want to give others that pleasure. Some of my happiest moments are when I am curled up by the fire in our old stone farmhouse in Bucks County. My husband and I seldom watch television. On summer evenings, we read in the gazebo, which looks out on our ten acres of meadows and woods. The hummingbird stops by for a sip from our feeder. Butterflies light on the cosmos. We have wild turkeys, deer, and pheasants who visit. I hope that children will become more aware of small wonders from my books.

"I write because I love to learn. Writers have the chance to play many parts, hear many voices, and dream many dreams. One of the exciting fringe benefits of being a writer is the ability to pursue what you care about. I am interested in so many things, nature, people, history, humor. Writing gives me a powerful motivation for learning. I loved finding out about wolves, presenting their warm family life, and dispelling the 'big bad wolf' myth in *Wolf Watch*. It's important to examine how to face fears and cope, as I explored in *The Teeny Tiny Ghost,* or how to observe and share experiences and memories, as in *Did You See What I Saw?: Poems about School.* I liked putting myself in the place of a six year old, as if I was going to Grandma's house for Easter and had no way of letting the Easter Bunny know of my whereabouts in *How Will the Easter Bunny Know?* Or imagining twin bear cubs, Sassy and Lum, in *Where Are the Bears?*, figuring out which activities they would copy as they met campers for the very first time. As I worked on the book about Abraham Lincoln, I lost myself in the wilderness, suffered on his hundred-mile trek to Indiana, and sympathized with Abe as he searched for books and learned to use words to lift himself out of grinding poverty. In *Tiger Trail,* I love putting myself in the place of the mother tigress and feeling her fear, her concern, and her triumph as she taught her cubs survival skills. When I was writing my book on ancient Egypt, the pharaohs seemed to come alive and walk right off the pages in their royal sandals. I hope that as youngsters meet the characters in my stories, they will realize that whatever their own circumstances may be, they can choose—to be brave, to forge ahead, to take positive risks, to be kind, to overcome severe obstacles, to appreciate the moment.

"My work habits are similar to those I used when I was teaching. I work every day. I am always on the watch for a story, even when we are on vacation riding elephants in Thailand or sailing on Lake Nockamixon. I have been very influenced by writers who use poetic prose, such as Karen Hesse, Jane Yolen, and Byrd Baylor. I love poetry by Aileen Fisher. I think Patricia Reilly Giff gets into the heads of her characters in a way I admire. And even though I frequently try to use other genres, poetic prose seems to speak up the most often. I am more interested in character development than plot. The story comes from the characters, and they frequently have a mind of their own. Still, writing

the book is only the beginning. I also visit schools, attend book signings, speak at colleges, conferences, and bookstores.

"My advice for aspiring writers is to work, revise, and persist. Treat writing like a job. Make contacts. Go to conferences. Read current children's books. Join a writer's group. I am lucky to have a husband who is an excellent editor. Don't send your manuscript right off when you finish it. Let it breathe. Look at it again. And be grateful that you have chosen a career that makes every day matter. Whatever is going on in your life today will fit somewhere, sometime, in a story."

Biographical and Critical Sources

BOOKS

Winters, Katherine, *Whooo's Haunting the Teeny Tiny Ghost?*, illustrated by Lynn Munsinger, HarperCollins (New York, NY), 1999.

PERIODICALS

Booklist, August, 1996, Hazel Rochman, review of *Did You See What I Saw?: Poems about School,* p. 1903; September 1, 1997, Lauren Peterson, review of *The Teeny Tiny Ghost,* p. 141; November 1, 1997, Julie Corsaro, review of *Wolf Watch,* p. 485; March 15, 1999, Carolyn Phelan, review of *How Will the Easter Bunny Know?,* p. 1339; September 1, 1999, Lauren Peterson, review of *Whooo's Haunting the Teeny Tiny Ghost?,* p. 151; October 15, 2000, Lauren Peterson, review of *Tiger Trail,* p. 448; December 15, 2002, Hazel Rochman, review of *But Mom, Everybody Else Does,* p. 770; January 1, 2003, Kay Weisman, review of *Abraham Lincoln: The Boy Who Loved Books,* p. 901; September 15, 2003, Ilene Cooper, review of *Voices of Ancient Egypt,* p. 239.
Bulletin of the Center for Children's Books, November, 1997, Janice M. Del Negro, review of *The Teeny Tiny Ghost,* p. 107.
Kirkus Reviews, October 1, 1997, review of *Wolf Watch,* p. 1539; August 15, 2002, review of *But Mom, Everybody Else Does,* p. 1239; November 15, 2002, review of *Abraham Lincoln,* p. 1703.
Morning Call, March 26, 1999, Jodi Duckett, article, *Kay Winters Shares a Great Story Idea Family Fun,* p. D. 07.
New York Times Book Review, November 16, 1997, J. D. Biersdorfer, review of *Wolf Watch,* p. 58.
Publishers Weekly, October 6, 1997, review of *The Teeny Tiny Ghost,* p. 48; October 27, 1997, review of *Wolf Watch,* p. 75; September 27, 1999, review of *Whooo's Haunting the Teeny Tiny Ghost?,* p. 47; November 25, 2002, review of *Abraham Lincoln,* p. 67.
School Library Journal, October, 1996, Marilyn Taniguchi, review of *Did You See What I Saw?,* p. 119; November, 1997, Meg Stackpole, review of *The Teeny*

In a lyrical picture book that teaches young readers about the habits of tigers, a mother tiger cares for and instructs her two newborn cubs. (From Tiger Trail, *written by Winters and illustrated by Laura Regan.)*

Tiny Ghost, pp. 103-104, and Susan Scheps, review of *Wolf Watch,* p. 104; April, 1999, Gale W. Sherman, review of *How Will the Easter Bunny Know?,* p. 110; September, 1999, Martha Link, review of *Whooo's Haunting the Teeny Tiny Ghost?,* p. 210; September, 2002, Kathy Piehl, review of *But Mom, Everybody Else Does,* p. 208; November 25, 2002, review of *Abraham Lincoln,* p. 67; September, 2003, Eve Ortega, review of *Voices of Ancient Egypt,* p. 239.

ONLINE

Katherine Winters Web Site, www.kaywinters.com/ (January 14, 2004).

*   *   *

WINTERS, Kay
See WINTERS, Katherine

Y-Z

YUMOTO, Kazumi 1959-

Personal
Born 1959, in Tokyo, Japan. *Education:* Tokyo University of Music, degree in composition.

Addresses
Agent—Japan Foregin Rights Centre, 2-27-18 Nakaochiai 2-chome, Shinjuku-ku, Tokyo 161-0032, Japan.

Career
Writer.

Awards, Honors
Batchelder award and *Boston Globe-Horn Book* award for fiction, both 1997, both for *The Friends.*

Writings

The Friends, translated from the Japanese by Cathy Hirano, Farrar, Straus & Giroux (New York, NY), 1996.

The Spring Tone, translated from the Japanese by Cathy Hirano, Farrar, Straus & Giroux (New York, NY), 1999.

The Letters, translated from the Japanese by Cathy Hirano, Farrar, Straus & Giroux (New York, NY), 2002.

Adaptations
The Friends, The Spring Tone, and *The Letters* have all been recorded as audio books.

Sidelights
Kazumi Yumoto' novels speak to the universal nature of human feelings while also capturing elements of Japanese urban culture. Translated for an English-speaking audience by Cathy Hirano, Yumoto's award-winning works show children and teenagers wrestling with the big issues of life and death, not from idle curiosity but with deep engagement and commitment. Yumoto's first novel, *The Friends,* won the prestigious *Boston Globe-*

In a small Japanese town, three boys, extremely curious about death, spy on an old man who gradually befriends them and together they learn about life as well as its end. (Cover illustration by Kazuhiko Sano.)

Horn Book award for fiction, and it announced the themes that would pervade her work: confrontation with death, the power of inter-generational friendships, and the understanding of the arc of life that comes with maturity. "Children in Japan have difficulty appreciating life's worth because they are unable to conceive of the limitless possibilities that each life offers," the author said in her acceptance speech for the *Boston Globe-Horn Book* award. "And that is why fiction is so important in this day and age," she added. "Fiction nurtures the imagination and gives the reader a creative vision of the diversity of life's possibilities. This is fiction's greatest power."

The Friends tells the story of Yamashita, Kawabe, and Kiyama, three twelve-year-old boys who are fascinated by death. None of them has ever seen a dead person, and they wonder aloud about the moment at which life ends, whether there is an afterlife, and whether ghosts exist. In search of answers, they begin to spy on an elderly man who looks as if he's nearing death. The man soon discovers their efforts and elicits their help with his household chores. In the process of helping him with gardening and laundry, the three boys come to understand the man's humanity, and a friendship is forged that profoundly affects the youngsters when the man finally does die. From a morbid fascination with death, the boys learn to see it as part of a full life's process in which the memories of loved ones enrich others' lives.

It is never easy to translate from Japanese to English, and Yumoto has publicly expressed her gratitude to Hirano, who managed to convert the childish slang of Japanese youngsters into something to which an American audience could relate. According to a *Publishers Weekly* reviewer, *The Friends* is "an eloquent initiation story that first touches and then pierces the heart." Hazel Rochman in *Booklist* felt that readers would be moved by "the terror of death, the bond across generations, and the struggle of those whom society labels losers." In *Horn Book,* Nancy Vasilakis declared that the boys' unusual curiosity about dying "is artfully transformed into a celebration of life and friendship."

The finality of death is juxtaposed with the everchanging emotions of adolescence in *The Spring Tone.* Told from the point of view of Tomomi Kiriki, *The Spring Tone* addresses guilt, anxiety, and the difficulties of growing up in a strife-filled household. After her grandmother dies, Tomomi worries that she *wished* death upon the old woman. Tomomi is plagued with nightmares in which she turns into a monster. Her mother is obsessed with a boundary dispute, and her brother disappears to run the city by himself. Only when Tomomi accompanies her brother to his secret place—a junkyard—does she discover a kindly eccentric who feeds stray cats and helps her to sort out the jarring changes in her life. Given the freedom to express herself, Tomomi finds comfort from her grandfather, whose own life has held its share of monsters. A *Horn Book* reviewer found *The Spring Tone* a "sensitive coming-

Tomomi is about to enter junior high school and she battles with problems at home as well as her own anxieties and the mystifying physical changes in her body in Yumoto's emotive novel about an urban family in Japan.

of-age novel" in which all the characters "are fully realized and sympathetically drawn." In *Publishers Weekly,* a critic also cited the novel as a "sensitively wrought story," adding that the author "offers remarkably wise and deeply personal insight into the pains of growing up." *Booklist* correspondent Susan Dove Lempke praised the book for its "fascinating glimpse into Japanese urban living" and its "compassionate look at the difficulties . . . in family life."

A grieving child grows into a healthy young adult in *The Letters,* Yumoto's third novel. Chiaki Hoshino attends the funeral of a woman who had helped her, years ago, to reconcile herself to her father's untimely death. The woman, Mrs. Yanagi, had promised that when she died, she would deliver letters Chiaki wrote to Chiaki's father in the afterlife. The many letters Chiaki wrote and gave to Mrs. Yanagi helped heal the grief, and friendship with Mrs. Yanagi broadened Chiaki's view of humankind. All of the warm feelings Chiaki holds for

A Japanese woman reminisces about the time shortly following the death of her father when she writes a series of letters to him that allow her to grieve, move beyond, and embrace life again. (Cover illustration by Kim McGillivray.)

her friend come to fruition at the funeral, where Chiaki discovers that many others had written letters to their loved ones for Mrs. Chiaki to deliver as well. This story "effectively portrays nature's healing gifts," to quote Jennifer M. Brabander in *Horn Book*. Brabander added that *The Letters* is "a reflective, affecting novel about life and death." In a starred review, a *Publishers Weekly* critic noted that the novel "once again addresses the subject of death with extraordinary grace and dignity. . . . The author offers a consolatory message for those left behind."

In her *Boston Globe-Horn Book* award acceptance speech, published in *Horn Book*, Yumoto said that one memorable incident in her childhood shaped her decision to become a writer. A lonely child who hated school, she found a fledgling sparrow that had fallen from its nest and nurtured it until it became tame. The sparrow became attached to Yumoto, and so its death

was particularly difficult for the young child to bear. She took to her bed and wept. Her mother, hearing the grief, consoled her with conversation and affection, reminding her that all things must die and that God controls the time of death. Gradually the youngster felt soothed and stopped crying. "Whenever I think of the power of words, I recall that night and cannot help but be grateful to my mother," the author recalled. "Were it not for this incident, I might not have become a writer."

Biographical and Critical Sources

PERIODICALS

Booklist, October 15, 1996, Hazel Rochman, review of *The Friends,* p. 425; December 15, 1997, Jeanette Larson, review of *The Friends,* p. 711; May 15, 1999, Susan Dover Lempke, review of *The Spring Tone,* p. 1689; October 15, 2001, Lolly Gepson, review of *The Spring Tone,* p. 428.

Horn Book, November-December, 1996, Nancy Vasilakis, review of *The Friends,* p. 741; November-December, 1997, Kristi Beavin, review of *The Friends,* p. 701; January 1, 1998, Kazumi Yumoto, "'The Friends': *Boston Globe-Horn Book* Acceptance Transcript"; January 1, 1999, Cathy Hirano, "Eight Ways to Say You: The Challenges of Translation"; May, 1999, review of *The Spring Tone,* p. 341; September-October, 2002, Jennifer M. Brabander, review of *The Letters,* p. 585.

New York Times Book Review, July 18, 1999, Deborah Hautzig, review of *The Spring Tone,* p. 25.

Publishers Weekly, October 14, 1996, review of *The Friends,* p. 84; February 8, 1999, review of *The Spring Tone,* p. 215; April 15, 2002, review of *The Letters,* p. 65.

School Library Journal, December, 1996, Carol A. Edwards, review of *The Friends,* p. 124; May, 1999, Francisca Goldsmith, review of *The Spring Tone,* p. 133; June, 2000, Barbara Wysocki, review of *The Spring Tone,* p. 86.

*   *   *

ZACHARIAS, Gary L. 1946-

Personal

Born April 30, 1946, in San Diego, CA; son of Ronald (a postal clerk) and Evea (a secretary; maiden name, Horton) Zacharias; married Sharon (a homemaker), June 16, 1967; children: Jared, Jordan. *Ethnicity:* "Caucasian." *Education:* San Diego State University, M.A. (English; with distinction), 1985. *Hobbies and other interests:* Sports, biking, reading, family activities.

Addresses

Office—Department of English, Palomar College, 1140 West Mission Rd., San Marcos, CA 92069. *E-mail*—zachs@cox.net.

Career

West Coast director of a foreign-student study program, 1981-87; Palomar College, San Marcos, CA, instructor in English, 1990—.

Writings

(Editor, with Jared Zacharias) *The Bill of Rights,* Greenhaven Press (San Diego, CA), 2003.
(Editor) *Events That Changed the World, 1900-1920,* Greenhaven Press (San Diego, CA), 2004.

Contributor to reference books. Contributor of articles and reviews to periodicals.

Sidelights

Gary L. Zacharias told *SATA:* "I teach writing for a living. But I write because of my love for the written word. It is a pleasure to see a blank page transformed by my words into something others may learn from." Zacharias's reference books on the twentieth century and the Bill of Rights are aimed at students who are doing research and preliminary studies of the subjects at hand. In her *Booklist* review of *Events That Changed the World, 1900-1920,* Stephanie Zvirin stated that "there's plenty to intrigue history students, who will relish seeing disparate pieces of history slide smoothly together." *School Library Journal* contributor Dana McDougald said that *The Bill of Rights* "brings the historical background to life."

Biographical and Critical Sources

PERIODICALS

Booklist, April 1, 2004, Stephanie Zvirin, review of *Events That Changed the World, 1900-1920,* p. 1371.
School Library Journal, January, 2004, Dana McDougald, review of *The Bill of Rights,* p. 162.

ONLINE

Palomar College, http://www.palomar.edu/english/ Zacharias/ (June 8, 2004), "Gary Zacharias: Biographical Information."

*   *   *

ZEMAN, Ludmila 1947-

Personal

Born April 23, 1947, in Gottwaldov, Czechoslovakia (now Zlín, Czech Republic); immigrated to Canada, 1984; became Canadian citizen, 1988; daughter of Karel

Ludmila Zeman

Zeman (a filmmaker); married Eugene Spaleny (an animator and director); children: two daughters. *Education:* Attended art school in Czechoslovakia, and Palacky University.

Addresses

Home—Montreal, Quebec, Canada. *Agent*—c/o Author Mail, Tundra Books of Northern New York, P.O. Box 1030, Plattsburgh, NY 12901.

Career

Filmmaker, illustrator, animator, and writer. Built puppets and painted backgrounds for Karel Zeman's films, including *Mr. Prokouk the Acrobat;* sold first animated short film to Czech TV at age nineteen; created films for *Sesame Street* and the National Film Board of Canada. Emily Carr College of Art, Vancouver, British Columbia, Canada, instructor.

Awards, Honors

Certificate of Merit, Art Directors Club, and Pick of the List selection, American Booksellers Association, both 1992, and Black-Eyed Susan Picture Book selection, State of Maryland, 1995-96, all for *Gilgamesh the King; Gilgamesh the King* and *The Revenge of Ishtar* were both selected for the Illustrators Exhibition at the Bologna Children's Book Fair, 1994; Governor General's Award for Illustration, Canada Council, 1995, for *The Last Quest of Gilgamesh.*

Writings

(And director and animator; with husband, Eugene Spaleny) *Lord of the Sky* (film; also known as *Le maître du ciel*), National Film Board of Canada (Montreal, Quebec, Canada), 1991.

(Self-illustrated) *The First Red Maple Leaf,* Tundra Books (Plattsburgh, NY), 1997.

Also illustrator of the Czech book *Linda, the Gardener's Cat.* Zeman's works are also available in French, Portuguese, and Japanese.

"GILGAMESH" TRILOGY; RETELLER; SELF-ILLUSTRATED

Gilgamesh the King, Tundra Books (Plattsburgh, NY), 1992.
The Revenge of Ishtar, Tundra Books (Plattsburgh, NY), 1993.
The Last Quest of Gilgamesh, Tundra Books (Plattsburgh, NY), 1995.

RETELLER; SELF-ILLUSTRATED

Sinbad: From the Tales of the Thousand and One Nights, Tundra Books (Plattsburgh, NY), 1999.
Sinbad in the Land of Giants, Tundra Books (Plattsburgh, NY), 2001.
Sinbad's Secret, Tundra Books (Plattsburgh, NY), 2003.

Work in Progress

A feature film based on her "Gilgamesh" trilogy.

Sidelights

Czech-born Canadian author Ludmila Zeman has lived in the world of professional storytellers since she was a child. Her father, Karel Zeman, was a well-known creator of films for children in Czechoslovakia. During school vacations, Zeman spent most of her time at her father's studio, where she helped to create puppets and paint backgrounds. When she was nineteen, Zeman tried her hand at building the puppets for and animating her own short film. The resulting creation was sold to Czech television. Zeman also illustrated a popular Czech children's book, *Linda, the Gardener's Cat,* before an offer to teach at the Emily Carr School of Art in Vancouver, British Columbia, Canada, led her to leave her native country. Since arriving in Canada, Zeman and her husband have continued to make films, and Zeman has become the author of several self-illustrated books in English.

Zeman drew on the folklore of the Middle East for two trilogies of picture books. The first, a retelling of the ancient Mesopotamian legend of Gilgamesh, won her the prestigious Governor General's Award for Illustration. The second trilogy retells the legends of Sinbad's adventures, which were originally recounted in *The Thousand and One Nights.* Throughout these books, Zeman draws on the art as well as the stories of the Middle East. The "lavish" illustrations are "framed with designs reminiscent of Persian carpets," Ann Ketcheson observed in a *Resource Links* review of *Sinbad's Secret.* Margaret A. Chang, writing in *School Library Journal*

Drawing upon **The Thousand and One Nights** *for stories about Sindbad, Zeman has created a trilogy of self-illustrated picture books ending with* **Sindbad's Secret,** *in which the famous sailor has several adventures, rescues a slave girl who becomes his wife, and discovers life's greatest secret.*

about the same work, found the book's "richly colored illustrations, detailed, coherent, and carefully composed, . . . reminiscent of Persian miniatures." Zeman's texts for the "Sinbad" trilogy were also praised. The original stories from *The Thousand and One Nights* are full of adventure, and Zeman's writing reflects this: it is "exciting, fast moving and lyrical," Isobel Lang wrote of *Sinbad in the Land of Giants* in *Resource Links.* Yet, as Ketcheson observed, "Zeman retains the somewhat formal speech expected in a classic story."

Biographical and Critical Sources

PERIODICALS

Booklist, November 15, 1992, Nancy McCray, review of *Lord of the Sky,* p. 615; August, 2001, Hazel Rochman, review of *Sinbad in the Land of Giants,* p. 2126.
Books in Canada, July, 2001, review of *Sinbad in the Land of Giants,* p. 33.
Canadian Children's Literature, spring, 2001, review of *Sinbad: From the Tales of the Thousand and One Nights,* pp. 169-171.
Canadian Literature, autumn, 1995, Gernot R. Wieland, review of *The Revenge of Ishtar,* pp. 146-147.

Canadian Materials, January, 1993, review of *Gilgamesh the King,* pp. 20-21.

Maclean's, November 22, 1999, Patricia Chisholm, Patricia Hluchy, and Barbara Wickens, review of *Sinbad,* p. 98.

Publishers Weekly, January 3, 2000, review of *Sinbad,* p. 75; February 24, 2003, review of *Sinbad's Secret,* p. 74.

Quill and Quire, September, 1993, review of *The Revenge of Ishtar,* p. 67; June, 1997, review of *The First Red Maple Leaf,* pp. 63-64; February, 1999, review of *Sinbad,* p. 45; June, 2001, review of *Sinbad in the Land of Giants,* p. 51.

Resource Links, August, 1997, review of *The First Red Maple Leaf,* p. 255; February, 2000, review of *Sinbad,* p. 6; October, 2001, Isobel Lang, review of *Sinbad in the Land of Giants,* p. 7; April, 2003, Ann Ketcheson, review of *Sinbad's Secret,* pp. 50-51.

School Library Journal, June, 1993, Nancy Palmer, review of *Gilgamesh the King,* p. 124; January, 2000, Grace Oliff, review of *Sinbad,* p. 127; August, 2001, Ann Welton, review of *Sinbad in the Land of Giants,* p. 174; March, 2003, Margaret A. Chang, review of *Sinbad's Secret,* p. 225.

ONLINE

Canadian Children's Book Centre, http://www.bookcentre. ca/ (April 20, 2004), "Ludmila Zeman."

Tundra Books Web Site, http://www.tundrabooks.com/ (January 14, 2004), interview with Zeman.

Writers Union of Canada Web Site, http://www.writers union.ca/ (January 14, 2004), "Ludmila Zeman."*

Illustrations Index

(In the following index, the number of the *volume* in which an illustrator's work appears is given *before* the colon, and the *page number* on which it appears is given *after* the colon. For example, a drawing by Adams, Adrienne appears in Volume 2 on page 6, another drawing by her appears in Volume 3 on page 80, another drawing in Volume 8 on page 1, and so on and so on. . . .)

YABC

Index references to *YABC* refer to listings appearing in the two-volume *Yesterday's Authors of Books for Children,* also published by The Gale Group. *YABC* covers prominent authors and illustrators who died prior to 1960.

Author Index

The following index gives the number of the volume in which an author's biographical sketch, Autobiography Feature, Brief Entry, or Obituary appears.

This index includes references to all entries in the following series, which are also published by The Gale Group.

YABC—*Yesterday's Authors of Books for Children: Facts and Pictures about Authors and Illustrators of Books for Young People from Early Times to 1960*
CLR—*Children's Literature Review: Excerpts from Reviews, Criticism, and Commentary on Books for Children*
SAAS—*Something about the Author Autobiography Series*